A Guide for Developing Interdisciplinary Thematic Units

Third Edition

Patricia L. Roberts

Richard D. Kellough

California State University, Sacramento

PEARSON

Merrill
Prentice Hall

Upper Saddle River, New Jersey
Columbus, Ohio

Library of Congress Cataloging-in-Publication Data

Roberts, Patricia
    A guide for developing interdisciplinary thematic units / Patrica L. Roberts, Richard D. Kellough.—3rd ed.
        p. cm.
    Includes bibliographical references and index.
    ISBN 0-13-098605-4
        1. Interdisciplinary approach in education—United States. 2. Lesson planning—United States. I. Kellough, Richard D. (Richard Dean) II. Title.

LB1570 .R55 2004
375'.001—dc21

2002037968

Vice President and Executive Publisher: Jeffery W. Johnston
Executive Editor: Debra A. Stollenwerk
Editorial Assistant: Mary Morrill
Production Editor: Kris Robinson
Production Coordination: Amy Gehl, Carlisle Publishers Services
Photo Coordinator: Sandy Schaefer
Design Coordinator: Diane C. Lorenzo
Cover Designer: Chris Webster
Cover art: Corbis
Production Manager: Pamela D. Bennett
Director of Marketing: Ann Castel Davis
Marketing Manager: Darcy Betts Prybella
Marketing Coordinator: Tyra Poole

This book was set in Palatino by Carlisle Communications, Ltd. It was printed and bound by Banta Book Group. The cover was printed by Phoenix Color Corp.

Photo Credits: KS Studios/Merrill, p. 1; Barbara Schwartz/Merrill, p. 39; Anne Vega/Merrill, pp. 72, 141; Scott Cunningham/Merrill, pp. 65, 93, 135; Tom Watson/Merrill, p. 119.

Pearson Education Ltd.
Pearson Education Singapore Pte. Ltd.
Pearson Education Canada, Ltd.
Pearson Education—Japan

Pearson Education Australia Pty. Limited
Pearson Education North Asia Ltd.
Pearson Educación de Mexico, S.A. de C.V.
Pearson Education Malaysia Pte. Ltd.

10 9 8 7 6 5 4 3 2 1
ISBN 0-13-098605-4

PREFACE

In the future, perhaps no single task will be more important than that of the challenge of improving our approaches as educators to facilitate student learning. Focusing on one element of this task, we are becoming increasingly aware of the role of an interdisciplinary thematic unit for quality learning. In keeping with this awareness, the purpose of this guide is to provide a practical approach for (1) university and college students who are preparing to become competent school teachers and (2) credentialed teachers who are interested in developing interdisciplinary thematic units. The focus is on one concise approach; therefore, this guide should serve as a supplement to what you learn (or have learned) in a general methods course.

In addition, this guide is suitable for administrators as well as those who work with students in school libraries, youth groups, or home schooling situations. For any interested educator, the content and interactive exercises are intended to provide guidance for developing interdisciplinary thematic units.

OUR BELIEFS

We believe the interdisciplinary thematic unit (ITU) is an instructional strategy that will help define a new expression of our professionalism. Certainly, developing and presenting an ITU in the classroom can be challenging to the teacher—this approach often tests one's dedication and ingenuity. The ITU as an expression of our professionalism reflects the view that such a unit can provide the most meaningful way to prepare students for the everyday requirements of the 21st century. This includes living life on a worldwide information superhighway and moving in a fast cyber-lane.

In these initial years of the 21st century, we believe that

- Life on the information superhighway will encompass students' interpretation of their own learning through both assigned studies and self-selected independent inquiries.
- Integrated instructional experiences will equalize educational opportunities for all students.
- Emphasis will be increased on students determining meaning from the interrelationships found in the content areas of various fields of study.
- Education will consist mainly of inquiry-oriented processes that require students to ask questions and to develop their thinking skills through various approaches to research and the use of diverse resources.
- Action-oriented students will focus on pertinent questions and issues (concepts, generalizations, principles, theories) with not only local, regional, and state significance but also global importance.

We are confident that the interdisciplinary thematic approach can be useful in classrooms, although only if questioning is given the same priority that Albert Einstein gave it when he reflected in writing on his own learning (see Chapter 4).

If we are to improve our educational approaches significantly in the years ahead, then all of us must join in making that effort. Strong action will be necessary at all educational levels. Presenting interdisciplinary thematic units in the classroom can be part of that action. Further, private citizens and volunteer groups must join in partnerships to support the effort, including businesses and industries; labor and farm organizations; and scientific, health, and educational institutions. Quantitatively, every part of our society has a responsibility. Qualitatively, it is important that the improvement of our educational approaches be seen as a national and international concern.

HOW THIS GUIDE IS ORGANIZED

This step-by-step guide, with many examples, strives to be user-friendly and educationally helpful. It is one of the few books available to successfully integrate interdisciplinary content, technology, diversity, and classroom management. It is intended for a teacher interested in offering, assessing, and evaluating an integrated curriculum through the inclusion of interdisciplinary thematic units of instruction. Its focus is designed for pre-credentialed teacher preparation at the college and university level, for inservice seminars and workshops at the district level, and for independent use by credentialed teachers. In the organization of the guide's five chapters, you will find helpful guidelines for initiating an ITU, interactive exercises for developing objectives and learning activities, highly informative materials on assessment, and sample units and planning masters useful for making transparencies for the overhead projector to aid in discussions, introduction of material, and reviews.

As a pre- or post-credentialed teacher, the following features will be of interest to you. This guide

- Discusses curriculum standards in strong integrated coverage through the chapters. Standards with websites are introduced in Chapter 1, the discussion on standards is continued in Chapter 2, and the topic of preparing instructional objectives in Chapter 3 includes links to curriculum standards. There is more discussion of standards within the context of assessment in Chapter 4, and standards, along with goals and objectives, are also included in the three sample ITUs in Chapter 5.
- Has perforated pages to provide you with easy removal of self-check exercises and other material.
- Has key terms in bold in text to reflect glossary entries.
- Presents advantages and limitations on ITUs and has examples of objectives.
- Provides examples of various ways an ITU can be created and evaluated, because teaching and learning styles vary.
- Provides examples of performance assessment, including scoring guides.
- Has flexible lesson plan concepts and step-by-step easy-to-follow instructions for developing an ITU.
- Has a format for sample lesson plans and for evaluating lesson plans that helps assess how well a thematic unit is written.

- Integrates interdisciplinary content, technology, diversity, and class management in ITU planning and features unique margin notes that emphasize this integration with a code of **D** (diversity), **T** (technology), and **M** (management).
- Has an evaluation tool at the end of the book.
- Has planning masters in the Appendix for making transparencies for the overhead projector. For example, a teacher-student interaction planning master allows teachers to identify which areas of student behavior they need to be more aware of as the lesson/unit progresses.
- Has a glossary and indexes of children's literature, names, and subject headings to give further reference material/sources.

Each chapter also has

- Meaningful, interactive exercises.
- An end-of-chapter feature titled *Facts on Praxis and Other Teacher Tests* that contains information about ways this guide may be helpful when studying for professional educational tests.
- A feature titled *If a Colleague, Community Member, or Parent Asks You About . . .* at the end of each chapter that offers questions for discussion to increase your understanding of selected subject matter.
- Features titled *Chapter Notes* and *For Further Reading* at the end of each chapter.
- Useful checklists, scoring guides, and self-check exercises.
- Motivational statements through Albert Einstein's words that provide insight into this inquiring scientist's thoughts. The brief statements are found at the beginning of each chapter and are recorded in his personal documents in *The Importance of Albert Einstein* (Lucent Books, 1994) by Clarice Swisher.

Chapter 1 gives you an explanation of the integrated curriculum and its potential advantages and limitations. It explains the concept of the interdisciplinary thematic unit and the foundation theories that support its development and implementation. You will get an overview of the development of themes, recommendations related to curriculum standards, and the scope and sequence of an ITU in Chapter 2. In Chapter 3 you are provided with guidelines and interactive exercises to help you in developing objectives. The assessment component of student learning is addressed in Chapter 4. After instruction in Chapter 5 on the development of your lessons and types of learning activities for the ITU, you are asked to complete the development of your own ITU. In addition, Chapter 5 has three complete (or nearly complete—due to limited space in this book) sample ITUs for your review.

NEW TO THIS EDITION

Chapters 1 through 5 were rewritten for this edition. The main reason for the changes was the request by nearly every reviewer for more content about curriculum standards, scoring guides, and the ITU approach and its relationship to professional educational tests—in a text that could not increase in the number of pages.

This third edition differs from the previous one in the following ways:

- *Focus on standards.* As mentioned previously, standards with websites are introduced in Chapter 1, a review of the history of standards and further discussion of standards is continued in Chapter 2, and standards are connected to preparing instructional objectives in Chapter 3. Additionally, selected standards are discussed in the context of assessment in Chapter 4 and linked to the ITUs with selected examples in Chapter 5.
- *New features.* One new feature titled *If a Colleague, Community Member, or Parent Asks You About...* contains questions and/or activities for group discussions, oral responses, and individual inquiries; it appears at the end of each chapter. New sidebars contain updated content related to tests for teacher licensing; the sidebars are titled *Facts on Praxis and Other Teacher Tests* and are found at the ends of the chapters.
- *Websites.* Recent addresses of Internet websites for curriculum standards and professional organizations are included.
- *Updates.* Updates of further reading selections are found at the end of every chapter. Updated assessment material in Chapter 4 includes more on scoring guides, portfolios, and assessment items.
- *Expansion.* Information about and examples of the role of student input in ITUs are expanded, along with ITUs, as vignettes in highlighted boxes at the beginning of each chapter.
- *Reflection and selection.* Further, revised interactive exercises were designed to help an educator assess and reflect continually on his or her progress in understanding this approach to developing an interdisciplinary thematic unit. Because it is unlikely that all exercises would be appropriate for a particular teaching situation, class members, peers, and the instructor can select the exercises to be done.

In summary, *A Guide for Developing Interdisciplinary Thematic Units,* Third Edition, is intended as a beginning point for caring educators who find themselves challenged by students who face a world with many complex concerns. These students are in need of problem-solving skills that may best be developed through the most meaningful kinds of learning—such as can be offered through the use of ITUs in an integrated curriculum. Although even the most dedicated and responsible educators cannot determine the future of the students in their charge, they can become positive role models as professionals who offer and support interdisciplinary teaching and learning. Furthermore, teachers can enhance their curricula by accepting the students' input and placing carefully planned activities into units that will guide the students toward developing the problem-solving skills and knowledge needed not only in today's changing times but also in the years ahead.

ANCILLARIES

The following related ancillaries are available to the instructors who adopt this text. To request information about any of the following, contact your Prentice Hall representative or visit the Merrill/Prentice Hall website at *http://www.prenhall.com*. If you are unable to contact your local representative, please call faculty services at 1-800-526-0485 for information.

- A companion website for information about ITUs in Chapter 6 of a related text, *A Resource Guide for Elementary School Teaching: Planning for Competence,* Fifth Edition by R. D. Kellough and P. L. Roberts, is available. Please visit the website at *http://www.prenhall.com/kellough*.

When we checked the web addresses mentioned in this text, they were correct. However, in recent months, some websites may have found their top level domains suddenly connected to advertisements for unsavory sites that are unrelated to education, if any owners failed to renew claims to the names. We have found this particularly disconcerting in the past and in this text have included mainly the sites of professional organizations in the hope that the addresses will remain educational ones and furnish you with information related to your teaching.

ACKNOWLEDGMENTS

Many teachers have encouraged and helped us by giving us suggestions during the development of the third edition. For the features that are good, give them the credit. For those that are not so good, admonish us. We want to express our warmest appreciation to the teachers who provided us with samples of materials they have developed and whose names are acknowledged in the guide. We also want to thank the students who have used our text for their reviews—the reviews have given us additional insight in writing this latest edition. Here are some of their comments:

- . . . text has helped me to better understand the process of building an ITU . . . serves as a step-by-step guide for novice teachers and as a resource for experienced educators.
- . . . text was an excellent resource for developing my first interdisciplinary thematic unit. I would highly recommend this text for both new teachers and teachers who are developing their first ITU.
- . . . perfect text to use if you are creating or learning about an Interdisciplinary Thematic Unit. This text is user-friendly, helpful and full of worthy examples. I can't say enough about this text and the help it has provided me while creating an ITU.
- I would highly recommend this text because of its detail and examples. This text will help you create a professional ITU that will wow your faculty members and/or professor.

We also want to thank the following colleagues who served as reviewers for their thoughtful and positive comments from the classrooms that turned into suggestions for improvements. We hope that they will agree the improvements are well reflected in this edition. They are John Michael Bodi, Bridgewater State College; Susan Dauer, Western Oregon University; Thomas Erb, University of Kansas; Sherry McCarthy, William Woods University; and Gary L. Willhite, Southern Illinois University Carbondale.

We continue to respond to the other reviewers and users of this guide and also have made changes as a result of their comments. We are very grateful to those who have provided their contributions. They are JoAnne Buggey, University of Minnesota; Swen H. Digranes, Northwestern State University; Maureen Gillette, College of St. Rose; Bob Hoffman, San Diego State University; Barbara Kacer, Western Kentucky University; Betty J. Krenske, Concordia University; Cynthia G. Kruger, University of Massachusetts-Dartmouth; Cynthia E. Ledbetter, University of Texas at Dallas; Linda Levstik, University of Kentucky; Connie H. Nobles, Southeastern Louisiana University; and Veana Ostertag, Nova Southeastern University.

Additionally, we want to express our sincere appreciation to our friends at Merrill/Prentice Hall, especially to Debbie Stollenwerk, our editor, who encouraged us to write this guide and who provided intelligent technical suggestions and unfaltering support throughout its development.

We are indeed appreciative to our families and the other people who have interacted with us as we developed this guide. Writing this guide was a time-consuming process and they understood our motivation and educational belief that teaching is the *most* rewarding profession. For that understanding, we dedicate this edition to them.

P.L.R.
R.D.K.

ABOUT THE AUTHORS

Patricia L. Roberts, Emeritus Professor of Education, received her Ed.D. at the University of the Pacific and joined the faculty of the School of Education at California State University, Sacramento, where she taught courses in children's literature, reading, and language arts, and served as coordinator of a Teacher Education Center in Elementary Education and Chair of the Department of Teacher Education. In addition, Dr. Roberts is the author of many teacher resource books and texts, writes for journals, and is a member of the National Council of Research on the Teaching of English and other professional groups. Her current research centers on teaching curriculum content with children's literature and family values found in fiction for children. Dr. Roberts, a biographee in *Who's Who in America* (2003), is the recipient of the Distinguished Alumnus of the Year Award from the University of the Pacific and the California State University's Award for Merit for Teaching. The Award of Merit is given for a superior teaching record and outstanding service to the institution and to the community. Additional recongitions include listings in *International Who's Who of Intellectuals, Two Thousand Notable American Women, The World Who's Who of Women, The Directory of Distinguished Americans, International Directory of Distinguished Leadership,* and *International Who's Who of Contemporary Achievement.*

Richard D. Kellough, Emeritus Professor of Education, received his Ed.D at Oregon State University and is currently among the faculty of the School of Education at California State University, Sacramento, where he has given over thirty years of service. Dr. Kellough is the author or co-author of dozens of textbooks, including *A Resource Guide for Teaching K-12, Teaching Young Adolescents: A Guide to Methods and Resources,* and *Secondary School Teaching: A Guide to Methods and Resources* (the latter two with N. Kellough), as well as numerous journal articles. A member of several prominent organizations, Dr. Kellough has been elected to the Phi Sigma Society, the Botanical Society of America, and the American Bryological Society, and was the recipient of an Outstanding Biology Teacher Recognition Award from the National Biology Teachers Association, State of California. His many recognitions include being named a National Science Foundation Research Fellow at the University of California, Davis, as well as listings in *The International Authors and Writers Who's Who, Leaders in Eco Education, Men of Achievement* (Volume 1), *Dictionary of International Biography,* and *Leaders in Education.*

BRIEF CONTENTS

CONTENTS

CHAPTER 4   Assessing Student Learning   93

CHAPTER 5   Completing Your ITU: Finalizing Activities, Lessons, and Units   135

NOTE: Every effort has been made to provide accurate and current Internet information in this book. However, the Internet and information posted on it are constantly changing, so it is inevitable that some of the Internet addresses listed in this textbook will change.

CHAPTER 1

Introduction to an Interdisciplinary Thematic Unit

*One cannot help but be in awe when one contemplates the
mysteries of eternity, of life, of the marvelous structure of reality.*

—Albert Einstein

INTERDISCIPLINARY THEMATIC UNIT EXAMPLE FOR HIGH SCHOOL STUDENTS: CIVILIZATIONS—*HEART OF A JAGUAR* AND MAYA CULTURE

Einstein's remarks about contemplating the marvelous structure of reality are as relevant today as they were when he posed them. In contemplating today's reality of education, you'll find there is an increasing interest in the structure of curriculum standards and state exams seeking validation for the question of effective teaching and, as part of this, educators are encouraged to consider the effectiveness of teaching an integrated curriculum through an interdisciplinary thematic unit. Once a theme is determined in this approach, instruction is planned around a sequence of activities that focus on that theme; an increasing number of teachers have incorporated this approach into their classrooms. As an example, two high school teachers in Illinois asked students to contemplate the reality of people's lives from the past through the themes of culture, emersion, and civilization as a way to introduce a study of people. To begin a study about the Maya, these teachers introduced a video about the people—*Maya: Lords of the Jungle* (PBS Home Video A1660). The teachers also included the concept of cultural emersion with an announced *emergency alert.* This alert declared that the students would become time travelers to Mexico in a week's time back to the year 1200 A.D. The students would arrive in the Yucatan region during the last years of the ancient Maya and would face some threatening situations, such as droughts and invasions. The students would have exactly one week to prepare, so they could survive the experience. In other words, they would have one week to learn anything they think would help them survive in this civilization, which would be different from their own. The students' preparation activities were related to several disciplines:

- *Geography.* Pictures of the environment from various sources found by the students were placed in the classroom. The students were asked to label the pictures and write explanations of what was shown.
- *History.* With the teacher, the students brainstormed related topics and got acquainted with resources for inquiry available in class and in the library. They searched for entries in the bibliography of M. Talbert's *Heart of a Jaguar* and referred to a Maya dictionary found in the back of the book.

- *Literature and language.* The students read *Heart of a Jaguar,* the story of a Maya boy Balam who struggles to achieve manhood. During a drought, he participates in the fasts, prayers, and rituals that must be done to appease the gods and bring rain to his village in the Yucatan peninsula near Chich'én Itz'a. In addition, the students listened to the poem "Journey of the Nightly Jaguar" written by B. Albert and illustrated by R. Roth (New York: Atheneum, 1996). The students selected Maya names to be their own during the study and practiced Maya pronunciations such as *hahah* (rain) and *yax* (forest leaves). They located and read paragraphs rich in sensory language and transformed the paragraphs into forms of poetry. They also located, read, and shared aloud Maya stories related to folkloric beliefs. Related to this, three Aztec legends in English/Spanish text are currently available: *The Turtle's Shell* and *The People's Corn* (Mexican Fine Arts Center Museum, 1852 W. 19th Street, Chicago, IL, 60608) and *People of Corn: A Maya Story* (New York: Little, Brown, 1995), a story that tells how people were originally created from corn.
- *Social studies.* In addition to their independent inquiry to learn anything they think would help them survive in the Maya civilization, the students divided into research teams. Individuals on each team were assigned a topic and then reported back to their whole team. The students researched the past to study crops, diet, food preparation, local animals, hunting techniques, family structure, social structure, and government structure. As part of today's reality, they also connected the past to the present by discovering ways that ancient Maya practices and beliefs and modern Spanish influences blend together in the lives of today's young people. Additionally, they met in groups to discuss their understandings of the Maya culture, similarities and differences of values in the ancient Maya culture and today's culture, evidence of violence in a culture, the issue of becoming desensitized to violence, and ways to see one's actions through the window of a culture different from one's own (Ham & Ham, 1997).

CHAPTER INTRODUCTION

In this chapter, you are introduced to an overview of an **interdisciplinary thematic unit** (ITU) for *Heart of a Jaguar* that shows the power a unit draws from various disciplines. Two high school teachers initiated the unit so that the students developed an awareness and appreciation for the topic and then got involved in various activities that connected what was being learned with their own lives. Later in this chapter, you will be provided with an introduction to developing an interdisciplinary thematic unit and will acquire information about the levels of curriculum integration. You'll become aware of a foundation for using an ITU; read a brief review of the history of curriculum integration, related theory, **learning styles,** and modalities; and become aware of recent applications in the classroom. You'll find questions for discussion titled *If a Colleague, Community Member, or Parent Asks You About . . .* and, at the end of the chapter, suggestions for further reading. To further reflect upon this content, you will be able to turn your attention to the exercises at the end of this chapter. Exercise 1.1 allows you to brainstorm ideas related to an ITU, Exercise 1.2 helps you discover informational sources about ITUs, and Exercise 1.3 asks you to interview a teacher about using ITUs.

KNOWLEDGE AND MEANINGFUL LEARNING

It has become quite clear to many teachers that to be the most effective in helping students develop meaningful understandings (and hence support their motivation to learn), much of the learning in each discipline can be made more effective and longer lasting when that learning is integrated with the whole curriculum and made meaningful to the lives of the students. This approach appears more successful than simply teaching unrelated and separate disciplines at the same time each day. **Meaningful learning** then is defined as learning that results when the learner makes connections between a new experience, prior knowledge, and experiences that were stored in his or her long-term memory.

If learning is defined only as being the accumulation of small parts of information, we can say we already know how small parts are learned and how to teach this accumulation. The accumulation of tiny pieces of information, however, is at the lowest end of a spectrum of types of learning and leads to what is sometimes referred to as **procedural knowledge.** In contrast, learning that is most meaningful and longest lasting and that includes higher levels of thinking is referred to as **conceptual knowledge.** To

support the development of conceptual knowledge, research results indicate using (1) a curriculum in which disciplines are integrated, and (2) instructional techniques that involve the learners in social interactive learning such as problem-based and **project-centered learning, cooperative learning, peer tutoring,** and **cross-age teaching.**

STYLES OF LEARNING AND IMPLICATIONS FOR INTERDISCIPLINARY THEMATIC INSTRUCTION

Teachers who are most effective adapt their teaching styles and methods to their students and use approaches that interest the students (and are neither too easy nor too difficult), that match the students' learning styles and learning capacities, and that are relevant to the students' lives. This adaptation process is further complicated because each student is different from every other one. All do not have the same interests, abilities, backgrounds, or learning styles or capacities. As a matter of fact, not only do students differ from one another, but each student can change to some extent from one day to the next. What appeals to a young person today may not have the same appeal tomorrow. Therefore, you need to consider the nature of both young people in general and each student in particular. Since you probably have already experienced a recent course in the psychology of learning, what follows is only a brief synopsis of knowledge about learning.

Learning Modalities

Learning modality refers to the sensory portal, or input channel, by which a student prefers to receive sensory reception (modality preference) or the actual way a student learns best (modality adeptness). Some K–12 students prefer learning by seeing, a **visual modality;** others prefer learning through instruction from others (through talk), an **auditory modality;** while many others prefer learning by doing and being physically involved, the **kinesthetic modality,** and by touching objects, the **tactile modality.** Note that a student's modality preference is not always that student's modality strength. While primary modality strength can be determined by observing students, the strength can fluctuate and can change as the result of experience and intellectual maturity. As one might suspect, modality integration (i.e., engaging more of the sensory input channels, using several modalities at once, or alternating them) has been found to contribute to better **achievement** in student learning.

Regardless of the grade level and subject(s) you intend to teach, an effective approach to consider is to use strategies that integrate the modalities. When well designed, interdisciplinary thematic instruction and project-based learning incorporate modality integration. In conclusion, when teaching any group of students of mixed learning abilities, modality strengths, language proficiency, and cultural backgrounds, integrating learning modalities is a must for the most successful teaching.

Learning Styles

Related to learning modality is **learning style,** which can be defined as independent forms of knowing and processing information. While some students may be comfortable beginning to learn a new idea in the abstract (e.g., visual or verbal symbolization), most need to begin with the concrete (e.g., learning by actually doing). Some students prosper while working in groups while others prefer working alone. Some are quick in their studies, whereas others are slow, methodical, cautious, and meticulous. Some can sustain attention on a single topic for a long time, becoming more absorbed in their study as time passes. Others are slower starters and more casual in their pursuits but are capable of shifting with ease from subject to subject. Some can study in the midst of music, noise, or movement, whereas others need quiet, solitude, and a desk or table. The point is this: people vary not only in their skills and preferences in the way knowledge is received, but also in how they mentally process information once it has been received. This latter process is a person's style of learning.

Classifications of Learning Styles

It is important to note that learning style is *not* an indicator of intelligence, but rather an indicator of how a person learns. Although there are probably as many types of learning styles as there are individuals, David Kolb describes two major differences in how people learn: (1) how they perceive situations and (2) how they process information.[1] Relying on the concepts of perceiving and processing and some of the work by Carl Jung on psychological types,[2] McCarthy has described four major learning styles. The styles, beginning with an analytic learner style, are presented in the following paragraphs.[3]

The **analytic learner** perceives information abstractly and processes it reflectively. The analytic learner prefers sequential thinking, needs details, and values what experts have to offer. Analytic learners do well in traditional classrooms.

The **common sense learner** perceives information abstractly and processes it actively. Common sense learners are pragmatic and enjoy **hands-on learning.** They sometimes find school frustrating unless they can see immediate use to what is being learned. In the traditional classroom, the common sense learner is likely at risk of not completing school or of dropping out.

The **dynamic learner** perceives information concretely and processes it actively. Dynamic learners also prefer hands-on learning and are excited by anything new. They are risk takers and are frustrated by learning if they see it as being tedious and sequential. In a traditional classroom, the dynamic learner could likely be an at-risk student.

The **imaginative learner** perceives information concretely and processes it reflectively. Imaginative learners learn well by listening and sharing with others and by integrating the ideas of others with their own experiences. They often have difficulty adjusting to traditional teaching, which depends less on classroom interactions and students' sharing and connecting of their prior experiences. In a traditional classroom, the imaginative learner is likely to be an at-risk student.

Learning Capacities: The Theory of Multiple Intelligences

In contrast to the concept of learning styles just mentioned, Gardner introduced what he calls learning capacities exhibited by individuals in differing ways.[4] Originally—and sometimes still—referred to as **multiple intelligences,** or ways of knowing, the capacities thus far identified are

- **Bodily/kinesthetic.** Ability to use the body skillfully and to handle objects in a skillful manner; efficient, proficient
- **Existentialist.** Ability to understand and pursue the ultimate philosophical questions, meanings, and mysteries of life
- **Interpersonal.** Ability to understand people and relationships
- **Intrapersonal.** Ability to assess one's emotional life as a means to understand oneself and others
- **Logical/mathematical.** Ability to handle chains of reasoning and recognize patterns and orders
- **Musical/rhythmic.** Sensitivity to pitch, melody, rhythm, and tone
- **Naturalist.** Ability to draw on materials and features of the natural environment to solve problems or fashion products
- **Verbal/linguistic.** Sensitivity to the meaning and order of words

From this information about learning styles and learning capacities, consider at least two facts:

1. *Intelligence is not a fixed or static reality but can be learned, taught, and developed.* As the teacher, you can help promote a positive role model that supports the idea that intelligence is a set of characteristics that, through a feeling of "I can" and with proper coaching, can be developed. When students understand that intelligence is incremental—something that is developed over time—they tend to be more motivated to work at learning than when they believe intelligence is a fixed entity.[5]

2. *Not all students learn and respond to learning situations in the same way.* A student may learn differently according to the situation or according to the student's ethnicity, cultural background, or socioeconomic status.[6] A teacher who uses only one style of teaching for all students or who teaches to only one or a few styles of learning day after day is short-changing those students who learn better another way.

Interdisciplinary thematic instruction is absolutely compatible with the best we know about how people vary not only in their skills and preferences in the way knowledge is received, but also in how they mentally process information once it has been received—in short, it is consistent with the best we know about how children learn.

INTEGRATED CURRICULUM AND RELATED TERMS

When learning about integrated curriculum, you might be confused by the plethora of terms that are used, such as *integrated studies, integrated curriculum, interdisciplinary curriculum, interdisciplinary thematic instruction, holistic education, multidisciplinary teaching,* and *thematic instruction.* In essence, regardless of which of these terms is being used, the reference is to the same teaching strategy—plans for teaching by relating disciplines.

Curriculum and Instruction

Originally derived from a Latin term referring to a race course for the Roman chariots, the term *curriculum* still has no widely accepted definition. As used for this guide, curriculum is that which is planned and encouraged for teaching and learning. This includes both school and nonschool environments, overt (formal) and hidden (informal) curriculums,[7] and broad and narrow notions of content—its development, acquisition, and consequences. Related to this, **instruction** is the planned arrangement of experiences to help a learner develop understanding and to achieve a desirable change in be-

havior. Because it is not always easy to determine where *curriculum* ends and *instruction* begins, in regard to integrated curriculum, there is basically no difference. The terms *integrated curriculum* and *integrated instruction* both refer to expected learning experiences.

Integrated Curriculum Defined

The term **integrated curriculum,** or any of its synonyms mentioned previously, refers to a way of teaching and a way of planning and organizing the instructional program so the discrete disciplines of subject matter are interrelated in a design that (1) matches the developmental needs of the learners[8] and (2) helps connect the students' learning in ways that are meaningful to their current and past experiences. In that respect, integrated curriculum is the antithesis of traditional, disparate, subject-matter-oriented teaching and curriculum designations.

Integrated Curricula Past and Present

One reason for the various terminology related to integrated curriculum is that throughout most of the history of education in this country, educators' efforts to integrate student learning have provided numerous labels. Without completely reviewing that history prior to today's times, the most recent popularity stems from the late 1950s, initiated by some of the **discovery**-oriented, student-center projects supported by the National Science Foundation. These projects include *Elementary School Science* (ESS), a hands-on, integrated science program for grades K–6; *Man: A Course of Study* (MACOS), a hands-on, anthropology-based program for fifth grades; and *Environmental Studies* (name later changed to ESSENCE), an interdisciplinary program for use at all grades, K–12, regardless of subject matter orientation.

Today's interest in curriculum integration is also generated from several inextricably connected sources: (1) the success at curriculum integration that has been enjoyed by middle-level schools since the beginning of the **middle school** movement in the 1960s;[9] (2) the literature-based whole-language movement in reading and language arts that began in the 1980s;[10] (3) the diversity of children in the regular classroom coupled with growing acceptance of the philosophy that a certain percentage of school dropouts is not a viable assumption;[11] (4) the needs of the workplace, the advancement of technology, and a concomitant trend of integrating vocational education with academic education in **secondary schools;**[12] (5) the challenges students will face in the 21st century, the application of information technologies to K–12 education in the United States, the recent recommendations of the President's Committee of Advisors on Science and Technology (PCAST) to strengthen the use of technology in America's schools;[13] and (6) the recent research in cognitive science and neuroscience demonstrating the necessity of helping learners establish bridges between school and life, knowing and doing, and content and context, with a parallel rekindled interest in constructivism (e.g., that learning encompasses the construction/reshaping of mental **schemata** and that mental processes mediate learning) as opposed to a strictly behaviorist philosophical approach to teaching and learning.[14]

Multilevel Instruction

Since students in your classroom have their own independent ways of knowing and learning, they also may be at different stages (and substages) of cognitive development. It is important to know how each student best learns and where each student is developmentally, that is, to individualize both the content and the methods of learning. In doing so, it is helpful to use **multilevel instruction** (or **multitasking**). Multilevel instruction happens when different students or groups of students are working at different tasks or doing **multitext reading** to accomplish either the same or different objectives. An example is the classroom scenario shown in Figure 1.1.

When integrating student learning as shown in Figure 1.1, multitasking is an important and useful, perhaps even necessary, strategy. Project-centered teaching, often a valuable instructional component of interdisciplinary thematic instruction, is a method that easily allows and provides multilevel instruction. Multilevel teaching occurs when several levels of teaching and learning are going on simultane-

ously; individual students and small groups do different activities at the same time to accomplish the same or different objectives. While some students may be working independently of the teacher, others may be receiving **direct instruction** from the teacher, perhaps in a traditional mode to obtain procedural knowledge.[15]

CURRICULUM INTEGRATION: SUMMARY OF PURPOSES

The major purposes of curriculum integration can be summarized in the following way:

1. **Learner assistance.** To assist students in following their interests through individualized and personalized instruction
2. **Learner facilitation.** To facilitate and make things less difficult for students as they learn together to become independent problem solvers
3. **Learner involvement.** To involve students in direct, purposeful, and meaningful learning; to provide opportunities for students to learn what they need and to support their motivation to learn rather than have them learn only what a particular curriculum dictates
4. **Learner understanding.** To promote students' understanding that learning is interrelated, that knowledge across disciplines is inextricably interconnected, and that the process of learning, as in life, is whole and connected rather than a series of specific and unrelated pieces of knowledge, subjects, topics, and disparate skills; also, to introduce curriculum in a comprehensive manner and not teach separate subjects each day

FIGURE 1.1 Using the Theory of Learning Capacities (Multiple Intelligences) and Multilevel Instruction: A Classroom Scenario

During 1 week of a 6-week thematic unit on weather in a seventh-grade classroom, students concentrated on learning about the water cycle. For this study of the water cycle, the teacher divided the class into groups of three to five students. The groups worked simultaneously on six projects to learn about the water cycle. One group of students designed, conducted, and repeated an experiment to discover the number of drops of water that can be held on one side of a worn penny. Working in part with the first group, a second group designed and prepared graphs to illustrate the results of the experiments of the first group. A third group created and composed the words and music of a rap song about the water cycle. The fourth group incorporated their combined interests in mathematics and art to design a project, collect the necessary materials, and create a colorful and interactive bulletin board about the water cycle. A fifth group read about the water cycle in materials the students researched from the Internet. Finally, a sixth group created a drama about the water cycle. On Friday, the groups shared their projects with the whole class.

INTEGRATED CURRICULUM: A SPECTRUM OF DESIGN

To facilitate the students' content learning along with their experiences, a teacher's efforts will fall at various places on a spectrum or continuum, from the least integrated instruction (Level I) to the most integrated (Level V), as illustrated in Figure 1.2.[16] To distinguish the levels, we use the factors of student input and decision making and the blending of disciplines. The diagram in Figure 1.2 should not be thought of as going from worst-case scenario (far left) to best-case scenario (far right), although some people may interpret it as such. In reality, there are various interpretations to a **spectrum** of design of curriculum integration, and on the basis of many factors each teacher must make an individualized decision about its use. Figure 1.2 is meant solely to show how efforts to integrate fall on a continuum of sophistication and complexity.

Level I

Level I is the traditional organization of curriculum and classroom instruction, during which teachers plan and arrange the subject-specific scope and sequence in the format of topic outlines. If there is an attempt to help students connect their learning and their experiences, then it is up to individual classroom teachers to do it. A student who moves during the school day from classroom to classroom, teacher to teacher, subject to subject, from one topic to another is likely learning at a Level I instructional environment. A topic in science, for example, might be *earthquakes.* A related topic in social studies might be "the social consequences of earthquakes and other natural disasters." These two topics may or may not be studied by a student at the same time. Such a traditional approach can be common in certain classrooms where the children receive subject-specific instructions at precise times during the school day (e.g., if it is Tuesday at 8:00 a.m., it must be math). But even then, this type could be called a Level I approach to curriculum integration when what the children are doing in math is related in a way they understand with one or more additional disciplines, such as social studies or science. For example, consider children in kindergarten through second grade who are reading or listening to the story *Francis, The Earthquake Dog* written by J. R. Enderle and S. G. Tessler and illustrated by B. Scudder (Chronicle Books, 1996). This story (literature) is about a young boy and a dog based on fact (history) that reflects some of the disastrous consequences of an earthquake (social studies) and can lead to a study of causes of tremors (science). Set in San Francisco in 1906, the story tells of young Edward who saves a stray terrier from being hit by a vegetable cart and takes him to his father, a chef at the St. Francis Hotel. The earthquake begins that evening and even while he and his father look for shelter in the tent city at Golden Gate Park, Edward worries about the dog. When the two return to the hotel, they hear barking from under the ruins and discover the lost canine. After the story, the children relate their reading to a discussion about whether the solution of a tent city used for the homeless in 1906 would be a solution that would work today and about what assistance, if any, is provided for animals during earthquakes and other natural disasters. They get involved in a project to learn what to do during an earthquake in their area and report ways to be prepared to survive for several days without government and agency help after a major quake.[17] The children also suggest several questions to answer through individual and group study: (1) What food, clothing, and first-aid materials could be made available for their families? (2) What preparations could be made for animal companions? and (3) What resource personnel could be contacted for information about earthquake preparedness programs sponsored by city, country, and state agencies in the area?

Level II

If the same students are learning English/language arts, social studies/history, mathematics, or science using a thematic approach rather than a topic outline, they are learning at Level II. Even if various disciplines are still taught at specific times of the school day (e.g., math at 8:00 a.m., reading at 9:00 a.m., and so on), many teachers can base much or all of the learning day (or several days) around a central

FIGURE 1.2   Continuum of Curriculum Integration: A Spectrum of Design

Level I	Level II	Level III	Level IV	Level V
Least integrated	Material blended from various disciplines	Material kept in separate disciplines	Few distinct discipline boundaries	Most integrated No discipline boundaries

theme. When doing so, they are teaching at Level II integration. Note that at Level II integration at the intermediate and secondary grade levels, themes for one discipline (e.g., social studies or history) are not necessarily planned and coordinated to correspond to integrate with themes of another (e.g., mathematics) or planned to be taught simultaneously.

Level III

When the same cohort of students is learning two or more core subjects (English/language arts, social studies/history, or mathematics and science) around a common theme such as *survival* from one or more teachers, they are learning at Level III integration. At this level teachers agree on a common theme, then they deal with it *separately* in their subject areas, usually at the same time in the school year. Therefore, the content that the student is learning from one teacher in one class is related to and coordinated with the content that the student is learning from another teacher in another class or several other classes. Some authors may refer to Levels II or III as coordinated or parallel curriculum.[18] At Level III, students may have some input into the decision making involved in selecting and planning themes and content.

Level IV

When teachers and students clearly collaborate on a common theme and its procedural and conceptual content and when discipline boundaries begin to disappear as teachers teach about a common theme—either solo as a self-contained classroom or as an interdisciplinary teaching team—Level IV integration is achieved. As one example, at Indian Trail Junior High School (Addison, IL), working with the same cohort of students, a team of teachers from English, mathematics, physical education, science, and social studies implemented a 5-day unit about truth and justice titled *Inspector Red Ribbon*. The truth-and-justice unit began with a video showing a prom night automobile accident. Students had 5 days to review the evidence, investigate further, recommend an indictment, and present their conclusions at a mock press conference. During those 5 days the students worked on the case in each of their classes.[19] For another example, sophomores at the Illinois Mathematics and Science Academy engaged in long-term thematic studies concerning the critical decisions that have driven American development while seniors at the academy investigated dilemmas resulting from modern advances in science and technology.[20]

Level V

A Level V integrated thematic approach is evident when teachers and their students have collaborated on a common theme and its content. Discipline boundaries are truly blurred during instruction, and teachers of several grade levels and various subjects teach toward student understanding of aspects of a common theme.[21]

Topic versus Theme. The difference between a topic and a theme is not always clear. For the purposes of this guide, a theme is the point, the message, or the main idea that underlines a study. A theme is the word, phrase, or sentence that is the educational glue that can integrate separate bits of information to help a student develop a meaningful framework of knowledge in an ITU study. A **theme** can be one word that represents an important concept (e.g., *survival*), or it can be a phrase or short sentence (people can survive in various environments) or a question (How do people's actions help them survive in various environments?). It can also be a **problem-centered inquiry** (What can people do to help themselves survive in an unfamiliar environment?). A **topic,** however, is the subject of a selected, often brief, discourse (e.g., *earthquakes*). Every topic—even the topic of earthquakes—that is considered for teaching in an ITU can be reconsidered to become a theme with the question, "What is it about this topic that leads to concepts that could become a theme?" Thus, the topic of earthquakes could lead to the one-word theme *survival* or to a theme stated in a sentence such as "People adapt and enhance their ability to survive after nature's earthquakes and other disasters." Many topics can be included in an ITU that is organized around a theme. In the previous sentence, "People adapt. . . . ," students can identify the topics of people, ability, earthquakes, disasters, and so on. Also in the previous sentence, words that represent the concepts of adapting and surviving can lead a teacher and the students to themes of adaptation, perhaps courage, and survival. Sometimes, the theme of a study becomes clearer to students when the theme is expressed as an overall guiding question, "What adaptation/survival action happens in our society after natural disasters?" Discussing the question can lead the students to other words that represent certain concepts that can become more themes—*courage, adaptation, survival.* Beginning at Level II and up, the students may have some input into the decision making involved in planning themes, topics, and content from various disciplines.

Some educators say that the integrated curriculum of the 21st century will be based on broad, unchanging, and unifying concepts, that is, on conceptual themes.[22] If so, it would be a recycling of an approach from the 1960s, such as that professed by Jerome Bruner and implemented in some of the National Foundation-sponsored curriculum projects in that era.[23] In fact, action already has begun in that direction; for example, the National **Standards** for English/Language Arts from the National Council of Teachers of English and the International Reading Association draw upon concepts such as *culture* and *diversity.* The National Standards for Science Education for grades K–12 are centered around unifying conceptual and procedural schemes, too, such as *systems, order and organization,* and *form and function.*[24] National standards are discussed further in this chapter in Figure 1.4—Fostering Human Relations Through an ITU Approach, and in other chapters when initiating a unit, assessing, and reviewing sample units are considered.

Advantages and Limitations of an Integrated Curriculum

Many researchers and educators emphasize that using the interdisciplinary thematic unit is a highly effective, meaningful, and authentic educational approach, but like any other instructional approach it may well have limitations.[25]

Advantages. Some advantages from the point of view of research and implementation include the following:

1. Advocates emphasize that traditional curriculum has been largely a fragmented set of subjects as teachers present them, and as knowledge of the learning processes increases, integrative curriculum makes sense and is being employed more often. As one example, teachers at Gladstone High School (Portland, OR) integrate English and science to create a "philosophy of care" for students to help them better understand both disciplines. As another example, teachers at Hudson's Bay High School (Vancouver, WA) created a school-within-a-school to integrate the learning of English, mathematics, and science. Additionally, teachers at Willamette Primary School (West Linn, OR) use inquiry through project-centered investigations as the basis for integrated curriculum.[26]

2. Supporters applaud the educational variety that is central to an integrated curriculum and that is developmentally appropriate for the learning of children and adolescents—no two days are ever the same and the curriculum changes depending on the active students. As part of this variety,

students become responsible for their own learning, share their ideas in authentic communication processes, expand respect for peers through interaction, see relationships among ideas/concepts through inquiry related to a theme, and see connections to in-school and out-of-school topics.

3. Advocates say that students increase their level of concentration, are motivated, and become active participants in their learning, not simply passive learners. All levels of abilities can be acknowledged. The curriculum is planned carefully but remains flexible and somewhat open ended. Supporters emphasize that interdisciplinary thematic instruction enables teachers to serve a large and diverse number of students and to use students' classroom research to determine changes in approach that will enhance learning. It also empowers students with responsibility for their own learning.[27]

4. Some supporters mention that teachers will be able to pass on the success of their research to others more quickly. In this approach, the teacher is the facilitator of learning.

5. Some advocates emphasize that the teacher can easily elicit the students' ideas as the primary focus of the study and can lead students into their own explorations as the teacher stays within the curriculum mandates of the school, district, and state. Students can learn effectively as they see relationships among ideas, vocabulary, facts, and concepts. ITUs allow students to investigate topics in depth and cross disciplines to explore an issue.

6. Other supporters seem to agree that teachers and students can best meet their varied needs in different environments through ITUs. Indeed, it is argued that the more diverse the students, the more integrated the curriculum should be. An ITU includes self-selected reading resources and is not dictatorial (as some scripted reading programs are) and supports self-selection in acquiring resources and studying (in contrast to some reading programs that negate self-selection). An ITU includes students' needs, interests, and preferences (in contrast to some reading programs that ignore students' interests but force them into books that are in a particular reading zone that is determined by a publisher). For more information about contributions of ITUs, see Figure 1.3, ITUs: What Research and Scholarly Opinion Tell Us.

7. Other advocates mention that the use of an integrated curriculum can attract support and needed resources from the school and the

FIGURE 1.3   ITUs: What Research and Scholarly Opinion Tell Us

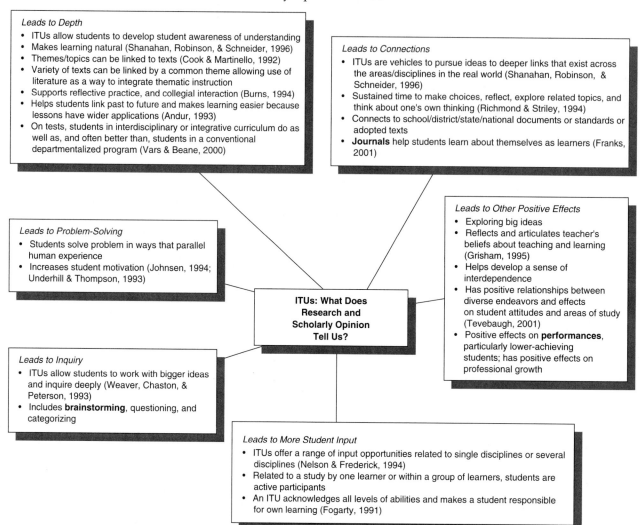

Leads to Depth
- ITUs allow students to develop student awareness of understanding
- Makes learning natural (Shanahan, Robinson, & Schneider, 1996)
- Themes/topics can be linked to texts (Cook & Martinello, 1992)
- Variety of texts can be linked by a common theme allowing use of literature as a way to integrate thematic instruction
- Supports reflective practice, and collegial interaction (Burns, 1994)
- Helps students link past to future and makes learning easier because lessons have wider applications (Andur, 1993)
- On tests, students in interdisciplinary or integrative curriculum do as well as, and often better than, students in a conventional departmentalized program (Vars & Beane, 2000)

Leads to Connections
- ITUs are vehicles to pursue ideas to deeper links that exist across the areas/disciplines in the real world (Shanahan, Robinson, & Schneider, 1996)
- Sustained time to make choices, reflect, explore related topics, and think about one's own thinking (Richmond & Striley, 1994)
- Connects to school/district/state/national documents or standards or adopted texts
- **Journals** help students learn about themselves as learners (Franks, 2001)

Leads to Problem-Solving
- Students solve problem in ways that parallel human experience
- Increases student motivation (Johnsen, 1994; Underhill & Thompson, 1993)

Leads to Other Positive Effects
- Exploring big ideas
- Reflects and articulates teacher's beliefs about teaching and learning (Grisham, 1995)
- Helps develop a sense of interdependence
- Has positive relationships between diverse endeavors and effects on student attitudes and areas of study (Tevebaugh, 2001)
- Positive effects on **performances**, particularly lower-achieving students; has positive effects on professional growth

ITUs: What Does Research and Scholarly Opinion Tell Us?

Leads to Inquiry
- ITUs allow students to work with bigger ideas and inquire deeply (Weaver, Chaston, & Peterson, 1993)
- Includes **brainstorming**, questioning, and categorizing

Leads to More Student Input
- ITUs offer a range of input opportunities related to single disciplines or several disciplines (Nelson & Frederick, 1994)
- Related to a study by one learner or within a group of learners, students are active participants
- An ITU acknowledges all levels of abilities and makes a student responsible for own learning (Fogarty, 1991)

district, and from outside the district. For example, the New York State New Compact for Learning *requires* schools to do interdisciplinary community-based instruction.[28]

8. Supporters indicate that a sense of community develops among students as they work together on projects and in groups, and take part in continuous **assessment** related to their learning. Interdisciplinary instruction reflects the real world better than single-discipline-based instruction, which is unnecessarily fragmented, and translates into greater student interest and higher academic achievement. Also, interdisciplinary instruction enhances professional satisfaction and creates collegiality. Teachers work together to do integrative work and plan interdisciplinary instruction, thus supporting positive networking in their profession.

As an educator interested in ITUs, you may want to add your own supportive points (or limitations) to the ones made by educators and to the statements in Figure 1.3. All advocate the use of an interdisciplinary thematic unit as an approach to teaching and learning.[29]

Limitations.   Following are some limitations that educators have considered:

1. Not all educators believe there is adequate time or an adequate group of resources to plan and implement an ITU. One problem that often arises in developing an ITU is finding common planning time for members of an **interdisciplinary teaching team,** in addition to teachers' individual preparation periods.

2. Some critics are uncomfortable with the idea that there is no precise manual of instructions to

follow that could provide the themes, connections, metaphors, stories, and other materials to help integrate the learning.[30]

3. Not all educators believe that an ITU approach is effective in the classroom with all students. According to an analysis published in an ERIC document, "findings on the effectiveness of integrative education are inconclusive."[31] Similarly, another problem could arise when a predeveloped ITU is used in which the students have no, or only limited, opportunity to participate. Such a unit might affect the learning of only a few students in a positive way and be a waste of valuable instructional time for others.

4. Other critics believe that an ITU does not fully contribute to research, because the population in any one classroom or cohort may not be representative; therefore, the benefits seemingly accrued would not be transferable to other groups of students.

5. Not all educators believe that an ITU is easy to implement (and, indeed, they are correct, but nobody ever said that good teaching was easy). With additional student involvement, movement, and noise, successful classroom management and control may become difficult.[32] An ITU might be difficult to plan and implement because of restraints on resources and time generated from the home, the community, the classroom, the school, and the district. For example, there is no agreed-upon structure, scope and sequence, content, or time regulation for study across the disciplines through the grade levels. Also, there are still many classes with no access to the Internet in their rooms. When schools acquire that access, computer use may be limited to only a few students at a time, unless, of course, the classroom has equipment such as a light pad to project the computer screen onto a larger screen. Finally, working with the Internet can be very time consuming.

6. Still other critics believe that the ITU approach may not be accepted by a majority of students, parents, and teachers. For example, an ITU would require much teacher preparation time and an interest by all in its implementation. Additionally, a teacher should understand the theory and philosophy behind such an instructional approach to implement the interdisciplinary aspect effectively.

7. Not all educators believe that teachers know where the students are in terms of knowledge and skills and that some teachers lack the imagination to predict how students at different grade levels could benefit through an ITU. Also, interdisciplinary teaching tests teachers' knowledge and asks them to get into topics beyond their expertise.

8. Some think that the students who are empowered with more direction for their own learning will not challenge their own assumptions to gain accurate procedural and conceptual knowledge. As a consequence, those students will retain inaccurate knowledge and be limited in their skills.

ROLE OF THEORETICAL ORIGINS OF INSTRUCTIONAL STYLES AND THEIR RELATION TO CONSTRUCTIVISM AND INTEGRATED CURRICULUM

In a broad sense, **behaviorism** is a theory that equates learning with predicted changes in observable behavior. **Constructivism** is a theory that holds that learning involves the construction or reshaping of mental **schemata** (a learner's intellectual organizations of environment) and that mental processes mediate learning. Whereas behaviorists are concerned with behaviors that are overt, constructivists are interested in both overt and **covert behavior.**[33] Perhaps the following will help clarify how learning theory affects changes to curriculum and instruction.

Instructional styles are deeply rooted in certain theoretical assumptions about learners and their development. Although it is beyond the scope of this text to explore those assumptions in depth, three major theoretical positions with research findings suggest different ways of working with children, each based on certain philosophical and psychological assumptions. These theoretical positions are educational underpinnings for teaching and are as follows:

- **Romanticism-maturationism.** Linked to the theoretical positions of romanticism-maturationism is the assumption that the learner's mind is neutral-passive to good-active, and that the main focus in teaching should be the addition of new ideas to a subconscious storage of old ideas. Key persons include Jean J. Rousseau and Sigmund Freud; key instructional strategies include classic lecturing with rote memorization.
- **Behaviorism.** Tied to the theoretical position of behaviorism is the assumption that the learner's mind is neutral-passive with innate reflexes and needs, and the main focus in teaching should be on the successive, systematic changes in the learner's environment to increase the possibilities

of desired behavior responses. Key persons include John Locke, B. F. Skinner, A. H. Thorndike, Robert Gagne, and John Watson. Key instructional strategies include practice reinforcement as in workbook drill activities and programmed instruction.

- **Cognitive-experimentalism.** Related to the theoretical position of cognitive-experimentalism (including constructivism) is the assumption that the learner is a neutral-interactive, purposive individual in simultaneous interaction with physical and biological environments. The main focus in teaching should be on facilitating the learner's gain and construction of new perceptions that lead to desired behavioral changes and ultimately to a more fully functioning individual. Key persons are John Dewey, Lev Vygotsky, Jerome Bruner, Jean Piaget, John Dewey, and Arthur W. Combs. Key strategies are facilitating and eclectic ones.

With a diversity of students, an effective teacher should have a strong emphasis toward cognitive-experimentalism-constructivism because of this theory's focus on divergence in learning and on the importance given to learning as a change in perceptions. Learning as a change in perceptions utilizes, at appropriate times, the best of strategies and knowledgeable instructor behaviors, regardless of whether individually they can be classified within any style dichotomy such as "direct or indirect," "formal or informal," or "traditional or progressive."

An integrated curriculum approach may not necessarily be the best approach for every school or for all learning for every student, nor is it necessarily the manner by which every teacher should or must always plan and teach. As evidenced by practice, the truth of this statement becomes apparent.

ROLE OF THE TEACHER IN AN INTEGRATED CURRICULUM

When initiating an integrated curriculum, you will want to provide a warm, friendly, and accepting environment in which the students can freely engage in learning activities that are developmentally appropriate—that relate to their interests, needs, and abilities. It may well be that the diversity of the student cohort will dictate the level of integration of the curriculum.

In this integration, a single theme can be the organizational focus of both the literacy/language arts activities and the various content areas (disciplines such as history, mathematics, and science). To do this, you can provide ways for students to study a topic in depth and help them identify a concept (related to the topic) that can become a theme for the study (conceptual knowledge) and to develop a variety of skills (procedural knowledge) in the process. Accordingly, you will want to have an assortment of classroom learning materials available for the students to touch, manipulate, explore, and use in experiments. You can take advantage of all the school-based learning related to the activities. Through it all, you can act as a catalyst who stimulates the learning of the students as they explore issues that are meaningful to their lives. Here are some examples related to the sample ITUs you'll find in Chapter 5:

- If students are studying ancient Greece (and the theme of civilization), consider "How does a community of that time compare with their own neighborhood community of today?" (See sample ITU titled *Early Civilizations: Dawn of a New Age in Ancient Greece.*)
- If students are studying early newcomers to the colonies in America (and the theme of migration), consider "How were newcomers of that time treated compared with newcomers today?" (See sample ITU titled *Migrations: Early Newcomers in North America.*)
- If students are studying spring weather during the seasons (and the theme of changes), consider "How does a current day/week/month/season and its changes compare with a past day/week/month/season?" or "What issues related to seasonal changes (spring flooding, summer burning of rice fields) and the students' lives can be explored?" (See sample ITU titled *Changes: Spring as a Time of Growth, Beauty, and Transformation.*)

Diversity and Multiculturalism

Most teachers realize that today's students comprise a great diversity of individuals, with a full range of cultural, ethnic, and economic heritage and first languages. They realize that America's people are multi-everything—multilingual (our features of language), multiethnic and multicultural (our features of customs, religions, traditions, histories)—and that the students in their classrooms represent the changing demographics of our pluralistic nation. With this diversity, every teacher should want to improve the quality of human relations in the classroom to foster an appreciation in students for the multiethnic composition of our society at large and our communities in general. Every teacher should want to help students become aware of who they are as unique individuals and who they are as Americans—for they all have had an American experience to relate to others. Thus, an interdisciplinary thematic unit can be a useful vehicle for improving the quality of human relations in the classroom, especially when it includes projects designed to provide a multicultural perspective. Such projects can help students understand the idea of *e pluribus unum* (out of many, one), enriching their sense of the tremendous variety of American experiences and what being an American means to each individual American.

Several projects are shown in Figure 1.4 that focus on human relations, diversity, and multiculturalism. Ironically, to show the *wholeness* of many interdisciplinary possibilities, the different areas in the figure had to be divided into parts for the purposes of discussion instead of being melded together in the figure. To support the projects and connect them to curriculum standards, selected language arts standards are recorded on the page. Of course, you can add standards from other content areas.

Effective Teacher Defined

Researchers emphasize the qualities of effective teachers—especially those who work with culturally diverse students.[34] Being effective is defined as (1) having teaching behaviors (knowledge, skills, feelings, and emotions) that engage the students in learning that produces rates of academic learning as high as (or higher than) the rates reported in previous research on effective teaching and (2) being seen as effective in delivery of instruction and organization by other teachers and school personnel, as well as by students and parents.[35]

Effective Teacher Qualities

Effective teachers of culturally and linguistically diverse students are those who

- Believe that classroom practices that tend to validate the cultural and linguistic heritage of students are important ways of fostering self-esteem in students (feelings and emotions)
- Believe that multicultural awareness enriches the lives of all students (e.g., learning about a particular culture not only benefits the students of that culture but also helps develop a sensitivity to another culture in other students) (feelings and emotions)
- Communicate clearly when giving directions and presenting new information (skills)

- Demonstrate the ability to communicate rationales for instructional techniques and participate in staff development through courses, seminars, and workshops (knowledge)
- Demonstrate specific instructional skills (e.g., organize instruction so it is meaningful to students), incorporate hands-on (that is, doing it) and minds-on (that is, thinking about what is being done) learning, use patterned books for reading, plan lessons around individual skills, encourage collaborative and cooperative interactions among students, and use a thematic curriculum in consultation with the students (skills)
- Engage students in instruction by pacing instruction appropriately, by involving the students in the lessons through collaborative and cooperative learning, by monitoring the progress of each student and by providing prompt feedback (skills)
- Mediate instruction for limited-English-proficient (LEP) students by alternately using the students' native language and English for instruction, thus providing clarity (skills)
- Seek help from others and provide help when asked; describe themselves as collaborative, confident, creative, energetic, and resourceful; and often spend their own money to get the material needed for meaningful learning activities (disposition)
- Specify expected outcomes and demonstrate high expectations (although not necessarily identical expectations) for all students (attitude and skills)

Various teacher interactions, a number of which are shown in Figure 1.5, can be suitably integrated into an interdisciplinary thematic unit. (Planning Master 1.1 in the Appendix will be helpful in preparing an overhead transparency for a group discussion.) What other interactions for the classroom teacher would you add to the diagram? What examples would you place under the headings?

Class Management in an Atmosphere of Active Inquiry

When children are actively learning, they are exactly that—active, and when children are active, they can be noisy, even boisterous. Certainly they are noisier than when they are in the traditional classroom where all students are seated with their chairs facing the front of the room and the teacher spends much of the time doing direct, teacher-centered instruction. When actively learning via a student-centered, project-oriented ITU, however, the movements and noise made by students are more likely to be educational and productive. When a student's movement

FIGURE 1.4   Fostering Human Relations through an ITU Approach: Activity Web and Connections to English/Language Arts/Reading Standards (National Council of Teachers of English (NCTE) and International Reading Association) (IRA). See http://www.ncte.org

Visual and Performing Arts

How can we show what we know about the multiculturalism in America through the expressive arts (art, dance, music, sculpture)?
- Learn about the art work, dances, folk songs, musical instruments, and stories of various ethnic groups represented by students in the class.
- Construct group displays to show the contributions of various ethnic groups in American culture.
- Create puppets and other ways to act out many folk tales, legends, and favorite stories from the students' ethnic culture.

Standards:
- *Students develop skills in spoken and written language for the purpose of enjoyment, persuasion, exchanging information, and learning about a particular interest.*
- *They develop competence in English and understanding of content across the curriculum.*

Anthropology

How can our experience(s) in America help us understand the way other people live? How can they hinder understanding?
- Conduct family history projects to discover students' own ethnic backgrounds.

Standards:
- *Students read for personal fulfillment.*
- *They build an understanding of themselves and of cultures of the United States and the world.*

Diversity/Multiculturalism: Fostering Human Relations through ITU Approach

Geography

How has geography influenced multiculturalism?
- Have students locate ancestors' country on world map.
- Conduct group discussions of settlements of newcomer groups in America and write about the discussions.
- Invite community members to present information about social roles, geographic regions, diversity in dialects.

Standards:
- *Students adjust spoken and written language vocabulary to communicate effectively with audiences and for different purposes.*

History

How has diversity changed over time in America?
- Study regional history to discover which ethnic groups first settled there and in what ways their influence is shown currently.
- Invite community members from different ethnic groups to class to talk about how their families first settled in the area.
- Visit museums that display artifacts/ information about ethnic groups of the community/region/state.

Standards:
- *Students develop respect for diversity in language use, patterns, and dialects across cultures, ethnic groups, geographic regions, and social roles.*

or noise is not necessary or enhancing to the learning activity, then—just as when using any other type of instructional strategy—you must implement your usual **class management** plan (perhaps a peer conflict resolution meeting) or remind the students of procedures and, if necessary, apply the established consequences of not following those procedures.

To successfully implement an ITU may require a shift in your concept of classroom management and control, and perhaps even that of the school administrator. Integrated studies require students to take more responsibility for their own learning and for their own conduct. Much less class time is spent in teacher-centered, worksheet-oriented,

Economics

What work in the economy is done by people we know?
- Using different writing approaches, make a class book about people in an ethnic group who have made contributions in the community.
- Invite community members to the classroom to tell about their achievements and the special procedures they follow in their work; then have students write about the visit in different ways (e.g., to persuade someone to consider the same type of work as a career choice, to tell of the visit in a narrative manner, to explain the message, or to focus on the procedure of the visit).

Standards:
- *Students develop skills in using different writing elements, (e.g., narrative writing, procedural writing, persuasive writing, explanatory writing) to communicate with different audiences for a variety of purposes.*
- *They apply knowledge of sentence structure, language conventions of spelling, capitalization, punctuation, media techniques, figurative language, and genre to create and critique.*

Mathematics

How can we express what we know about diversity/multiculturalism through mathematics?
- Detect and graph a pattern of the dominance of ethnic groups with names in region's telephone directory.
- Compare data with that found in a directory of another area in the state (available at large library).

Standards:
- *Students use a variety of resources such as databases, computer networks, libraries, or videos to gather and synthesize information and to create and communicate knowledge.*

Political Science

How have people organized themselves to provide information about government and politics?
- Collect news articles about the position/organization of an ethnic group in a conflict situation.
- Read related fiction/nonfiction.

Standards:
- *Students will read a range of literature in many genres to build an understanding of human experience.*
- *They will read a variety of texts—fiction, nonfiction, classic, and contemporary works—to acquire new information to respond to the needs and demands of society and the workplace.*

Science

How have scientists from diverse heritages contributed to our way of life?
- Ask students to research inventors from diverse groups.
- Invite scientists from various groups to class to discuss their inquiries and accomplishments.

Standards:
- *Students conduct research on issues and interests by generating ideas and questions and by posing problems.*
- *They can gather, evaluate, and synthesize data from a variety of sources such as print/nonprint texts, artifacts, and people, and can communicate their discoveries in ways that suit their purpose and audience.*

Sociology

In what ways can we participate in the community to resolve a real problem related to diversity?
- Research contemporary groups with ethnic memberships and groups' goals to resolve problems they see, and read related texts from many sources.
- Invite members of ethnic groups to class to talk about cultural roots, language, customs, and real problems related to diversity.
- Take trips to businesses, city council, county supervisor meetings, and state legislature when meetings focus on concerns of ethnic groups.
- Organize "Stop the Violence" or "Stop the Hate Crimes" forums.
- Elicit suggestions about ways to foster better human relations in the classroom, implement them, and hold ongoing class meetings and discussions.
- Display a calendar of holidays for the school year that are observed by students in the class and read a variety of texts related to the observances.

Standards:
- *Students will demonstrate that they can comprehend, evaluate, and appreciate texts. To do this, they can discuss their prior experience, their interactions with others, their knowledge of word meanings, their word identification strategies, and their understanding of sound-letter correspondence, sentence structure, context, and graphics.*
- *They can demonstrate that they can be reflective, creative, and critical in their responses.*

and textbook instruction. Thus, for teachers who have difficulty sharing authority with their students, an approach that incorporates active inquiry means confronting in new ways what has traditionally been referred to as control and discipline. An emphasis on student initiative and responsibility produces a much greater frequency of those teachable moments that mean so much to both students and adults. Because ITUs usually take on a life of their own, students also assume responsibility for their own academic lives more willingly. They enjoy having the trust and independence to be more responsible for themselves and their learning.[36]

FIGURE 1.5   Teacher Interactions in Visual Web

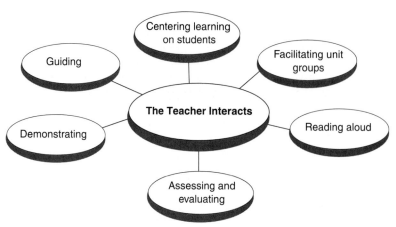

ROLE OF THE STUDENTS AND INPUT IN AN INTEGRATED CURRICULUM

In an integrated curriculum, the emphasis could be on the cooperation, responsibility, and initiative that students demonstrate both in the activities and throughout the learning process. You'll see several examples in Figure 1.6. This emphasis should be central to the students' involvement in and responsibility for their learning. For example, in various learning activities, students will be expected to work with others in partnerships and small groups. Membership and roles within groups will vary, depending both on the activity and on each student's interest. As part of that interest, an individual student can reserve a particular topic of study. The student then searches for answers to questions that he/she has asked in consultation with the teacher. The student's search may include moving around the classroom, asking questions, consulting others, and referring to a variety of data sources.

What additional examples of student input would you place under the grade levels in Figure 1.6? Various student interactions, a number of which are mentioned in Planning Masters 1.2, 1.3, and 1.4 in the Appendix, also can be integrated into an interdisciplinary thematic unit. What other student interactions would you add to the Planning Masters in the Appendix?

ROLE OF THE SCHOOL FOR OPTIMAL CURRICULUM INTEGRATION

For years, teachers in elementary schools have, to some extent, used integrated instruction, especially those teaching in self-contained classrooms for all or most of the school day. Most teachers of middle and secondary schools, until recently, have not had the advantage of meeting their students for long blocks of time. As many teachers have discovered, the traditional scheduling of instructional periods of 45 to 60 minutes each (a common schedule for the upper grades) is not conducive to the most effective implementation of interdisciplinary thematic instruction. The current effort to restructure schools to deliver quality learning to all students has included a major interest in nontraditional scheduling.

Sometimes, however, it may appear that more energy is devoted to organizational change (how the curriculum is delivered) than to school curriculum (what is taught). Note that the two are inseparable. School organization has a direct effect on what students learn, evident in the fact that educators spend much valuable time trying to restructure their schools to achieve the most productive delivery of the curriculum—both the planned (**formal**) and the hidden (**informal**, not always known) curricula. Although constant change can be unsettling and even distracting to a classroom teacher, many researchers conclude that rather than reaching some organizational plateau, exemplary schools are those that establish and maintain a climate of constant modification; they are in a continual process of inquiry, reflection, and change.[37]

Organizational Change for Optimal Curriculum Integration

Organizational changes are referred to as **school restructuring,** a term that has a variety of connotations, including not only curriculum integration but also nontraditional scheduling, site-based management, collaborative decision making, school choice, personalized learning, and collegian staffing. School

FIGURE 1.6 Classroom Examples: Range of Student Input

- *First Grade:* Students as young as first grade, age 6-7, have participated in ITUs by selecting a focus/theme and then establishing guiding questions to answer. Also, in a primary-age group, visually impaired children have participated in an integrated curriculum about incubation with hatching chicken eggs—a motivating real-life event for them (Swenson, 1991). In other ITUs, students have used a graphic representation of a wheel with a theme written in the center (hub) and discipline headings written on radii (spokes) to explore a theme from the point of view of different areas. They have identified activities based on their interests and observed a teacher modeling thinking aloud; they have engaged in discussion about types of questions they can choose (Nelson & Frederick, 1994). *Characteristics:* Tend to ask questions and become aware that symbols have meanings and that there is a process to figuring out the symbols. They are interested in beginning reading, writing, and vocabulary; they act out stories and do concrete problems.

- *Second Grade:* Students at this grade level, age 7-8, have had input in ITUs in several ways related to such themes as communities, change, power, and interactions (Martinello & Cook, 1992). They tend to be curious about their chosen theme and are able to display a longer attention span, thereby staying on tasks or on the project for a longer period of time than those age 6-7. *Characteristics:* Can be speedy in some responses; are interested in conclusions and logical endings; are aware of their community and the world; and have an increasing sense of money, property, possessions, ownership, and time.

- *Third Grade:* Students age 8-9 have participated in ITUs through learning centers in the classroom. For example, in a study of Changes: Chromatography, third graders developed a question map about what they wanted to know. They then worked at a learning center on related activities (i.e., to test the colors of water-soluble ink markers and make predictions about the separations of their colors). They recorded their predictions and wrote results on data sheets, and they observed capillary actions of water moving up paper strips and recorded their observations. Other learning activities related to art (creating a class mural), ecology (study of camouflage and history of people/animals who used camouflage), language arts (writing a mystery about unusual spots of color on clothing), science (making different colored filters for cardboard eyeglass frames through which to observe items and predict color changes). *Characteristics:* Enjoy exploring familiar and unfamiliar places and time periods; like reading their favorite stories are humorous ones, fairy tales, and adventures; are conscious of their work and that of others; like playing games, sending/receiving correspondence, bartering, swapping, and having collections; express themselves orally and in writing often with humor, and sometimes, poetically.

- *Fourth-Fifth Grade:* Students age 9-10 have participated in ITUs with different themes, including explorations (Pappas, Kiefer, & Levstik, 1990) and freedom (Hickman & Bishop,1993), that are developed over a longer period—perhaps 4 or 5 weeks. They can think critically, reason, judge, apply experiences, and persuade others. They think about their own thinking, use skills to solve real-life problems, and prefer active learning over a passive approach. They can use primary source materials, study themes through a variety of texts that include autobiographies, biographies, historical fiction, and poetry. *Characteristics:* Do research, write in journals, and use a variety of writing approaches; engage in problem solving, role-playing, math activities, science experiments, and art experiences.

- *Sixth-Eighth Grade:* Students age 12-14 have participated in such ITUs as the theme of changes in clouds and weather (Franks, 2001), entomology (Tevebaugh, 2001), and adaptation (Cook & Martinello, 1994) and can engage in a longer study period—sometimes 6 or 7 weeks. They can reason, judge, apply their experiences, persuade others, and think critically. They like interaction with peers, active learning, and activities outside of school. *Characteristics:* Can design, conduct, and repeat experiments; prepare graphs; compose poems, music, and drama, and create interactive bulletin boards; can work in groups and share information with others.

- *Ninth Grade and Up:* Students age 15 and older are independent critical thinkers and have participated in ITUs such as one centered on the theme of changes in genetic disorders and biotechnology (Greenberg & Haynie, 2001) and the theme of civilizations (Ham & Ham, 1997). They reason, judge, and apply their experiences, and can persuade others. They realize what they know and do not know and learn what is useful to them. They like interaction with peers and activities outside of school and often participate in ITUs that are introduced with a text (i.e., a selected novel, video, or visual images). *Characteristics:* Can brainstorm related topics to a theme introduced by the teacher; can respond to hypothetical situations (even life-threatening ones) and can research, study, and prepare for the "hypothetical;" can work in research teams in which individuals are assigned topics related to a theme and then report back to the team or group; can relate ways that the past blends together in the lives of people living today.

restructuring has been defined as "activities that change fundamental assumptions, practices, and relationships, both within the organization and between the organization and the outside world, in ways leading to improved learning outcomes."[38] No matter how school restructuring is defined, educators agree on the following point: the design and functions of schools should reflect the needs of the young people of the 21st century, rather than the needs of the 19th century.

The redesigning of schools into "houses," each with an interdisciplinary team of teachers plus additional support personnel, represents a movement that is becoming increasingly common across the country. This movement is from what has been referred to as a "system of schooling" rooted in the "Industrial Age" toward a design more in touch with the emerging demands of the new millennium, or the "Information Age."[39] With this redesign, the intention is that schools will address more fully the needs and capabilities and uniqueness of each student.

Block Scheduling

To allow for more instructional flexibility, and to accommodate mutual planning time for teachers, increasingly more schools are using some form of block scheduling in which blocks of time ranging from 70 to 140 or more minutes replace the traditional structure of 45- to 60-minute classes for at least part of the day. Even small schools with enrollment of less than 400 students[40] are meeting pressures to expand curriculum options through integrated curriculum and block scheduling. The possible variations are nearly limitless.

Advantages and Limitations of Block Scheduling.

Consistently reported in the research about schools using **block scheduling,** where students and teachers work together in longer but fewer classes at a time, are (1) greater satisfaction among teachers and administrators and (2) improvement in both behavior and learning of students. It seems that students do more writing as they pursue an issue in greater depth, enjoy classes more, feel more challenged, and gain deeper understandings. In addition, learning time is optimized when between-class time is reduced, instruction is coordinated, scheduling is flexible, and teaching colleagues collaborate on instruction. With teachers teaching fewer students in fewer courses, instruction can be significantly greater, with more students taking advanced courses; the student-teacher interaction can be more productive; and the school has fewer discipline problems. Because planning periods are longer, teachers have time to plan and interact with par-

ents. Further, teachers get to know the students better and, therefore, are able to respond to a students' needs with greater care.[41] In evaluations of schools using block scheduling, it was found that more course credits were completed, students had equal or better mastery and retention of materials, and there was an impressive reduction in suspensions and dropout rates.[42]

Nontraditional school schedules also have problems. Some that might arise are (1) content coverage in a course may be less than what was formerly covered, (2) community relations problems might occur when students are out of school or off campus at nontraditional times—perhaps on the dates when state tests are given to students, and (3) a mismatch may result between content actually covered and that expected by state-mandated tests. However, one teacher noted that she had *always* divided the instruction among specific skills to be learned related to the ITU/school curriculum document/state tests/national curriculum standards and time for the students to follow their inquiries in an ITU and use a variety of resources such as databases, computer networks, libraries, or videos. In addition, she mentioned that she planned a dual schedule for several weeks prior to a state-mandated test. On Monday, Tuesday, and Wednesday, she scheduled highly focused lessons related to the topic/theme of the interdisciplinary thematic unit the students were studying. These teacher-initiated lessons centered on specific skills around the theme, such as knowledge of word meanings, word identification strategies, sound-letter correspondence, and sentence structure. Other lessons highlighted different approaches to writing—for enjoyment, persuasion, exchanging information, and outlining procedures. Still other lessons focused on other skills. On Thursday and Friday, the students followed their interests in inquiries but were expected to use the skills they had learned in the highly focused lessons. Even when one considers the time-consuming problem of dual scheduling and all of the problems mentioned earlier, little doubt remains that longer blocks of instructional time with students is a positive factor that contributes to their meaningful learning and, correspondingly, supports the use of interdisciplinary thematic instruction.

ROLE OF CURRICULUM STANDARDS

In 1994, the United States Congress passed *Goals 2000: Educate America Act* amended in 1996 with an Appropriations Act that encouraged states to set standards. This action also reflected the interest of national professional organizations related to various disciplines. These organizations had been defining standards before Congress acted (See Figure 1.7 for an overview of the support for curriculum standards by the professional groups.)

The current **standards** represent the professional determination by specialists to identify essential basics as a core of subject knowledge that all students should acquire. These standards are academic teaching guidelines to encourage curriculum development to promote higher student achievement. The developers of state and local curriculum can decide the extent to which the standards are used—indeed, some state boards of education are establishing lists of accommodations for students with disabilities and limited English learners and others. As an example related to special education students, some boards are considering that the accommodations for a high school student's exit exam must be stated in a student's individual educational plan (IEP). If they are not on the district/state's list of accommodations, then approval for the accommodation must be granted through a district process (more in Chapter 2).

ROLE OF MODERN TECHNOLOGY AND COMMUNITY RESOURCES IN AN INTEGRATED CURRICULUM

Students cannot use what is unavailable to them. Thus, interdisciplinary thematic instruction can consume many hours of precious preinstructional time to ensure that materials, equipment, and other resources for the students' learning will be available to them. As one teacher exclaimed after her first year of using ITUs, "I've never worked so hard in my life; I never enjoyed teaching so much."

Buildings, community members, geographic features, historic sites, monuments, and other places in the students' local area make up one of the richest instructional laboratories that can be imagined. To take advantage of this accumulated wealth of resources, and to build school-community partnerships, you should start a computer file of community resources. For instance, you can include files about the skills of the students' parents and other family members, noting which ones could be resources for the study occurring in your classroom. Also, you might include files on various resource people who could speak to the class and add headings on free and inexpensive materials, on places for trips, and on what other communities of teachers, students, and adult helpers have done. (See Chapter 2 for more information about the community as a resource.)

Vehicles for Obtaining and Sharing Ideas and Information

The Arctic Yearbook Project: Example 1. What began as a study of plankton from the school's own pond in Hamburg, Germany, turned into a study of what was going on in the Elbe River, the North Sea, and then the Northern Atlantic Ocean. For secondary-level students of English as a foreign language, an international, cross-curriculum project known as Arctic Yearbook was the catalyst for teachers of biology, English, German, history, and math to work with a common cohort of students as they studied the development of plankton. The goal was to enlarge the students' perspective gradually from the school pond to the Northern Atlantic Ocean. The project involved communicating with the Bremerhaven-based Alfred Wegener Institute, which was conducting research near Greenland, and then establishing telecommunications with the Institute's research vessel, *Polarstern*. During this study, the students developed their understandings in biology, history, language, and math.[43]

The Neshonoc Project: Example 2. What began as an isolated, single-grade, telemunications-dependent project for sixth graders at West Salem Middle School (Wisconsin) eventually developed into a longer-term, cross-grade interdisciplinary program of students and adults working together to design and develop a local nature preserve.[44] Sixth graders began their study by interacting with explorer Will Steger as he led the international Arctic Project's first training expedition. Electronic on-line messages via the Internet allowed students to receive and send messages to Steger and his team in real time. Students researched the physical environment and the wildlife, read stories and novels about survival, kept their own imaginary journals, got information about the impact of industrialized society on the Arctic, and conversed with students from around the world. But something very important was missing—a connection between the students' immediate environment and the far-away Arctic.

To connect this, the team of sixth-grade teachers brainstormed ideas to develop an interdisciplinary approach to the study of a nearby geographical feature—the local 700-acre Lake Neshonoc, an impoundment of the LaCrosse River, a tributary of the Mississippi River. Special activities, including an all-day "winter survival" adventure, gave students a sense of what real explorers experience. Students learned about hypothermia, winter trekking by cross-country skiing, and building their own snow caves.

West Salem Middle School's focus became the lake. Although many students had enjoyed its

FIGURE 1.7   Curriculum Standards by Areas of Content with Internet Sites/Addresses

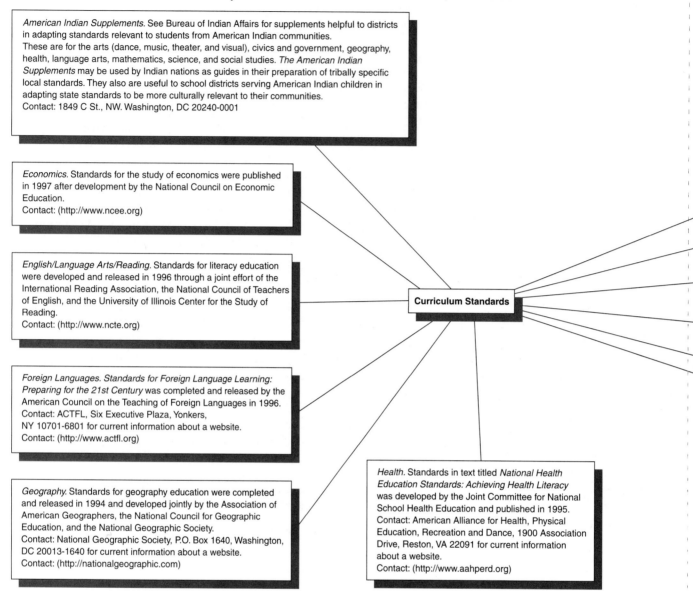

American Indian Supplements. See Bureau of Indian Affairs for supplements helpful to districts in adapting standards relevant to students from American Indian communities.
These are for the arts (dance, music, theater, and visual), civics and government, geography, health, language arts, mathematics, science, and social studies. *The American Indian Supplements* may be used by Indian nations as guides in their preparation of tribally specific local standards. They also are useful to school districts serving American Indian children in adapting state standards to be more culturally relevant to their communities.
Contact: 1849 C St., NW. Washington, DC 20240-0001

Economics. Standards for the study of economics were published in 1997 after development by the National Council on Economic Education.
Contact: (http://www.ncee.org)

English/Language Arts/Reading. Standards for literacy education were developed and released in 1996 through a joint effort of the International Reading Association, the National Council of Teachers of English, and the University of Illinois Center for the Study of Reading.
Contact: (http://www.ncte.org)

Foreign Languages. Standards for *Foreign Language Learning: Preparing for the 21st Century* was completed and released by the American Council on the Teaching of Foreign Languages in 1996.
Contact: ACTFL, Six Executive Plaza, Yonkers, NY 10701-6801 for current information about a website.
Contact: (http://www.actfl.org)

Geography. Standards for geography education were completed and released in 1994 and developed jointly by the Association of American Geographers, the National Council for Geographic Education, and the National Geographic Society.
Contact: National Geographic Society, P.O. Box 1640, Washington, DC 20013-1640 for current information about a website.
Contact: (http://nationalgeographic.com)

Curriculum Standards

Health. Standards in text titled *National Health Education Standards: Achieving Health Literacy* was developed by the Joint Committee for National School Health Education and published in 1995.
Contact: American Alliance for Health, Physical Education, Recreation and Dance, 1900 Association Drive, Reston, VA 22091 for current information about a website.
Contact: (http://www.aahperd.org)

recreational opportunities, they had never formally studied it. The Neshonoc Partners—a committee of environmentalists, community leaders, parents, students, and teachers—was established to assist in setting goals, brainstorming ideas, and developing the program for a year's study. Students showed immediate interest in becoming involved and active in the project. A second committee involving parents, students, and the teacher met during lunchtime on a weekly basis to allow for more intensive discussions about the lake and the overall project.

For several weeks, students learned about the ecosystem of Lake Neshonoc through field experiences led by local environmentalists and community leaders. Guest speakers told their stories about life on the lake and their observations about the lake's health. Student sketchbooks provided a place to document and write about personal observations concerning the shoreline (narrative writing), water testing (procedural writing), animal and plant life (descriptive writing and sketching), and the value of the lake (persuasive writing). From these sketchbooks, student creations were compiled to create books to share electronically with students who had similar interests in Missouri, Nevada, South Carolina, and Washington, DC, as well as Canada and Russia. The opportunity to share findings about their local watershed sparked discussions about

Mathematics. Revised standards were released in a text titled *Curriculum and Evaluation Standards for School Mathematics* in 2000 by the National Council of Teachers of Mathematics.
Contact: (http://www.nctm.org)

Physical Education. Published standards were released in a text titled *Moving Into the Future: National Standards for Physical Education* in 1995 by the National Association of Sport and Physical Education.
Contact: (http://www.aahperd.org)

Science. In 1995, with input from the American Association for the Advancement of Science and the National Science Teachers Association, the National Research Council's National Committee on Science Education Standards and Assessment published the standards for science education.
Contact: (http://www.nap.edu/readingroom/books/intronses/)

Social Studies/Government/Civics/History. All published in 1994, standards for civics and government were developed by the National Center for Social Studies and the Center for Civic Education while standards for history were completed by the National Center for History in the Schools.
Contact: (http://www.ncss.org)

Technology. With input from teachers, technology coordinators, public officials, and others, and with the support of initial funding from the National Science Foundation and the National Aeronautics and Space Administration, the National Educational Technology Standards (NETS) in collaboration with the International Technology Education Association, were released in 2000 with updates in 2001.
Contact: (http://www.iteawww.org) or http://www.iste.org (click on NETS)

Visual and Performing Arts. National standards for arts education were completed and released in 1994 and prepared jointly by the American Alliance for Theater and Education, the National Art Education Association, the National Dance Association, and the Music Educators National Conference.
Contact: Visual Arts (http://www.naes-reston.org)
Music (http://www.menc.org)
Theater (http://www.byu.edu/tma/arts-ed)

how students can make a difference in their own communities. Comparative studies gave students a chance to consider how other watersheds were impacted by humans and nature.

West Salem students also worked with the local county parks and recreation department to assist in developing a sign marking the new county park where a nature sanctuary would reside. The students brainstormed ideas and then constructed a redwood sign with the help of a local technical education teacher. Today, the sign is a symbol of the partnership that was established between the students and the community. It remains a concrete reminder that together everyone worked for the com-

mon good of the community and the environment. Students celebrated the study of the lake with a closure. Steger, along with community leaders, parents, school board members, and staff, commended the students for what is sure to be the start of a long and enduring relationship—a partnership created out of common respect and appreciation for the value of the ecosystem.

As shown in the previous examples, teachers who want to make their classrooms more student-centered, collaborative, interdisciplinary, and interactive increasingly are turning to telecommunications networks. These webs of connected computers allow teachers and students from around the world to communicate with each other directly and gain access to quantities of information previously unimaginable. Students using networks learn and develop new inquiry and analytical skills in a stimulating environment and perhaps gain an increased appreciation of their roles as world citizens. A sample lesson plan illustrating student use of the Internet is shown in Chapter 5 and suggestions related to technology are found in the margins of the units in the same chapter.

BEGINNING AN INTERDISCIPLINARY THEMATIC UNIT

When considering an interdisciplinary thematic unit, you will want to plan parts of the unit in advance during the proactive (early planning) phase of your decision making; however, the unit will develop as the students' study evolves—as their interests become known and their input is included. To review more decision making and thought processing as phases of instruction, focus your attention on the following section.

Decision-Making and Thought-Processing Phases of Instruction: Collaborative Decision Making

You probably have heard that during any single school day, a classroom teacher makes hundreds, perhaps thousands, of decisions. It has been said that a teacher makes about 3,000 nontrivial decisions every day.[45] Some of those decisions will have been made prior to meeting the students for instruction, others will be made during instruction—by the teacher and also collaboratively with the students— and still others are made later as the teacher reflects on the instruction for that day.

Realizing that different decisions are made at different times, a teacher will note that instruction can be divided into four **decision-making** and thought-processing phases: (1) the early planning or proactive phase, (2) the teaching or interactive phase, (3) the analyzing and evaluating or reflective phase, and (4) the application or projective phase.[46] The proactive phase consists of all those intellectual functions and decisions you will make prior to actual instruction. The interactive phase includes all the decisions made during the immediacy and spontaneity of teaching and learning. Decisions made during this phase are likely to be more intuitive and routine than those made during the early planning phase. The reflective phase is the time you will take to reflect on, analyze, and judge the decisions and behaviors that occurred

during the interactive phase as a result of this reflection. Decisions are made—individually or collaboratively with your students—to use what was learned in subsequent instructional actions. At this point, you are in the projective phase, abstracting your reflection and projecting your analysis into subsequent instructional activities. When teaching an integrated curriculum, you will want to involve your students in all phases of decision making and thought processing.

Essential Steps in Developing an ITU

The essential steps in developing an ITU, which are discussed in more detail in later chapters, include the following:

1. **Select a theme.** Choose a general theme (school, district, state documents will be helpful); finalization of the theme title and its topics will be done in collaboration with your students (perhaps a class meeting) and any members of your teaching team. If your teaching team is collaborating for the first time in curriculum integration, you should probably think small; that is, not try to accomplish too much.
2. **Write an overview.** Write the unit overview (summary); related goals; if appropriate, major concepts to be addressed; and instructional objectives to the fullest extent possible. Some of these will change, and new ones can be added as the unit develops during implementation.
3. **Identify instructional resources.** Anticipate and locate instructional resources that might be needed, including technological and community resources. Student input will be needed for this as the unit develops.
4. **Organize the subject matter.** Select and organize the subject matter, including writing some questions, and then develop potential experiences and activities (e.g., constructing, discussing, drawing, evaluating, experimenting, inquiring, listening, observing, organizing, performing drama roles, problem solving, sharing, and taking field trips). These experiences and activities will develop further after starting the unit as you build upon the students' curiosity about the theme.[47]
5. **Arrange classroom environment.** Plan and arrange the classroom environment with materials that will interest and stimulate the students to want to know more about the theme. The classroom is your place of work and the students' place of learning. Involve your students in this atmosphere. Ways to involve students initially include the following: making available an artifact, a book, a display, or a computer simulation;

or taking a field trip, having a problem to solve, providing a learning center, discussing students' questions, role-playing, or scheduling a visit from a resource person in the community.

6. **Plan ITU closure, culminating activity, or finale.** If appropriate for the group, plan a finale to close the unit in collaboration with the students, and engage them in summarizing what they have learned with other students or with their parents or other community members. The finale can include both written and oral presentations with visuals done by the students. Written reports by the students can be punched up in different creative ways with encouragement by the teacher. There is more information about culminating activities in Chapter 5, but here are a few suggestions:

- use the alphabet as the form of the final report with "A is for . . . " and "B is for . . . " and so on through Z
- use book quotes and display them on charts with illustrations about the theme
- create a catalog related to the theme
- give choralspeak reports by letting peer groups ask predetermined questions in a chorus and having students respond to the questions
- prepare a chart with two columns and two headings (1) The Author Says This . . . and (2) I Say That. . . . Display the chart so students can refer to it to review what an author has said about the theme and to show what the students have learned and written in their own words

- participate in debate, read brief scripts with dialogue, or read aloud free verse or poems written in concrete shapes (shapes that look like objects—i.e. trees, houses, flowers) on the theme
- report with time lines, a student-made book, or through an activity of "Twenty Questions" in which the group asks questions about the content of the theme studied by the students

7. **Assess.** Plan assessment procedures that include
   (1) diagnostic assessment (preassessment) at the start of the unit to discover what students already know or think they know about some of its content
   (2) formative assessment, which is an ongoing daily assessment to determine how students are doing
   (3) summative assessment to discover what, in fact, was learned from the unit.

As an example of formative assessment, some teachers record each assigned essay, homework, quiz, test, project, and class participation with equal weight on a scoring guide to give each student the chance to participate in equity in grading. As an example of this, each unit of study can close with a culminating project. Each project can include a scoring guide sheet with criterion related to what was to be learned from the unit and possible points listed. The teacher and students can agree to assign a value for each criterion before the final project begins. The scoring guide allows the student to self-assess and talk about the determined score with the teacher, who then can agree or disagree before recording a final grade.

FACTS ON PRAXIS AND OTHER TEACHER TESTS

Most state departments of education now require prospective teachers to take a content-area exam or a curriculum, instruction, and assessment exam before they are licensed to enter the classroom. In some cases, they must participate in an in-classroom supervised assessment *after* they enter the classroom. Tests for teacher credentialing for teaching in various states, such as the CBEST (Basic Educational Skills Test) in California, are published by the Educational Testing Services or other agencies/companies. These credentialing tests are used by certain states, colleges, and universities and are developed by advisory groups made up of teachers, teacher ed-

ucators, administrators, and representatives from professional organizations. Based on current research, the committees determine the test content and are responsible for all questions and exercises on the tests. While some states have their own tests of basic skills, other states use similar tests. For example, one group of similar tests currently required in over 30 states is the Praxis Series. This series, as in other credentialing tests, covers tasks and skills such as interdisciplinary instruction and is required of beginning teachers.

To assist teachers interested in tasks and skills related to teaching with ITUs—and please note that some states now require schools to include interdisciplinary community-based instruction—this guide is a resource to develop an ITU and reflects one approach for developing an ITU. It reviews the knowledge/planning skills needed to initiate, develop, and teach an ITU from theory to practice. To support this professional interest and others related to teacher tests, all chapters in this guide offer selected exercises to assist those interested in interdisciplinary instruction and topics related to curriculum and instruction. For example, interested educators are asked

- To get involved with group work and peer feedback (Exercise 1.1); to become aware of ITU content (Exercise 1.2); and to respond to interview-stimuli and write a brief response (Exercise 1.3)
- To collaboratively work with partners (Exercise 2.1); to select ITU resources (Exercise 2.2); to identify an ITU scope and sequence plan (Exercise 2.3)
- To recognize verbs that are acceptable for writing ITU objectives (Exercise 3.1); to rec-

ognize objectives that are measurable (Exercise 3.3); to self-check one's recognition of cognitive, affective, and psychomotor objectives (Exercise 3.4); to prepare selected ITU objectives (Exercise 3.5)

- To prepare ITU assessment items (Exercise 4.1); to engage in self-reflection; to write an essay related to the value of teaching with an ITU and develop a scoring guide for the essay (Exercise 4.2)
- To connect questions and activities for an ITU (Exercise 5.2) and to write a specific teaching plan that combines writing objectives, selecting resources, and planning learning activities (Exercise 5.3); to plan culminating/final activities (Exercise 5.4); to analyze a lesson that failed (Exercise 5.5); to prepare lesson plans for peer feedback (Exercise 5.6); to evaluate ITU plans (Exercise 5.7); and finally, to reflect and self-evaluate the extent of one's success in developing an ITU (Exercise 5.8)

SUMMARY

As you studied this chapter, bits and pieces of new information about the advantages and limitations of an ITU, curriculum integration, related theory, and classroom examples were stored in your short-term memory where the new information can be rehearsed until it is ready to be stored in your long-term memory. If the new information is not rehearsed, it will be essentially meaningless and may fade from your short-term memory. If it is rehearsed and made meaningful through connections with other stored knowledge (which is one of the purposes of the chapter exercises and the feature with questions and activities in *If a Colleague, Community Member, or Parent Asks You About. . . .*), then this new knowledge is transferred to and stored in

your long-term memory. This is done either by adding to existing schemata or by forming new schemata. The format in this resource is designed to facilitate your rehearsal of new information and build new understandings or rebuild previous ones about integrated curriculum through interdisciplinary thematic teaching. Further, this chapter gave you a foundation for using an ITU, a review of the history of curriculum integration, and information about related theory and classroom applications. As mentioned earlier, chapter notes, questions for discussion, and suggestions for further reading are provided at the end of the chapter. To further reflect on the content in this chapter, turn your attention to Exercises 1.1 through 1.3 that follow.

IF A COLLEAGUE, COMMUNITY MEMBER, OR PARENT ASKS YOU ABOUT. . . .

1. **Class management.** If a colleague asked you to identify three or four class management problems commonly experienced by teachers at a

specific grade level, what would you say? In what ways do you believe teaching an integrated curriculum using ITUs would cause an increase or decrease in the types and frequencies of common management problems experienced by teachers of that grade level? Share your response with others in your class.

2. **Integrated curriculum.** If a colleague asks you for some guidelines for teaching integrated curriculum, what would you suggest? Ask your peers about classroom observations and experiences they have had that are related to the use of integrated instruction and ITUs and have them share their observations with you in small group or whole group discussions. Take notes on the discussion and with the group members suggest some guidelines for teaching with ITUs that you infer from those notes.

3. **ITU development.** If a parent asks you how you developed an ITU in your classroom, what would be your response? To get more background information about this, offer any questions you have about teaching with ITUs to peer volunteers to develop a question map on the board, an overhead transparency, a chart, or a large sheet of butcher paper. Copy the final question map and use one of the questions to start your own individual inquiry about ITUs. Report what you find to others in a group meeting.

4. **ITU purposes.** If a parent asked you what the purposes for teaching an ITU were, what would you respond? To prepare for such a question, review the text section on the summary of purposes for curriculum integration. With which ones do you agree? Disagree? Are there other purposes you would add? Explain your answer.

5. **Thematic instruction.** Some critics are concerned that interdisciplinary thematic instruction takes too much time—time that should be directly devoted to preparing students for learning that is more likely to be measured by the mandatory standardized tests that are given in the spring. If a parent or colleague or community member expresses this concern to you, how would you respond? How would you communicate to that person that interdisciplinary thematic instruction is worth (or not worth) the instructional time?

NOTES

EXERCISE 1.1

Brainstorming Ideas Related to an ITU

Instructions.   With others in a small group, brainstorm ideas related to an interdisciplinary thematic unit and offer suggestions. Your purpose is to develop a list of topics related to a theme or topic of your choice. Remember, there are no right or wrong ideas—all are accepted. Consider the suggestions in the following schematic web to keep the brainstorming alive if the ideas should lag.

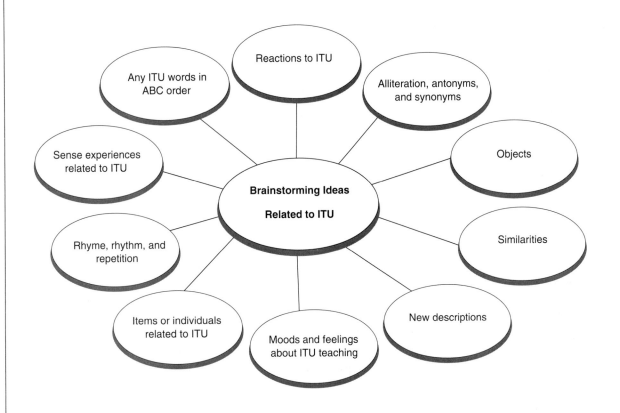

Involve two volunteers from the group to record your group's ideas on a chart or on a transparency that can be shown to others in the class. You can organize the ideas in the web or in another format if you wish. Follow these steps in completing the exercise:

1. Suggest ways to categorize ideas about developing an ITU and then suggest a theme and headings for the categories in the web included in this exercise.

2. Individually, locate one professional article about an ITU and read it; perhaps select one mentioned in the chapter notes or for further reading in this chapter. Take notes.

3. Return to your small group and add any information to the web that you gained from the article.

4. Meet back with the whole group and report on your small group's ideas about the ITU. Note the similarities and the differences in the schemata among the groups. If needed, use the space that follows for your notes about the whole group discussion.

EXERCISE 1.2

Discovering Informational Sources about ITUs

Instructions. You have an important responsibility to be knowledgeable about an integrated curriculum before you develop an ITU for your students. What informational sources stand out as useful in your mind? Your educational purpose for this exercise is to record what will help you in developing an ITU around a theme you have selected. Share what you have found with others in your class. One of your sources might be just the source that someone else needs to develop and implement a unit. To begin your search, you may want to select from the *For Further Reading* section in Chapter 1 or do searches on the Internet. Look for material that will help you develop and implement a thematic unit of your choice.

1. Source: _____

_____

_____

Reason selected: _____

_____

_____

2. Source: _____

_____

_____

Reason selected: _____

_____

_____

3. Source: _____

_____

_____

Reason selected: _____

_____

_____

4. Source: _____

_____

_____

Reason selected: _____

_____

_____

5. Source: _____

_____

_____

Reason selected: _____

_____

_____

6. Source: _____

_____

_____

Reason selected: _____

_____

_____

7. Source: _____

_____

_____

Reason selected: _____

_____

_____

8. Source: _____

_____

_____

Reason selected: _____

_____

_____

EXERCISE 1.3

Interviewing a Teacher about Interdisciplinary Thematic Units

Instructions. For this exercise, interview one or more elementary, middle, or high school teachers. Perhaps you will want to interview one who is new to the education profession and then interview one who has been teaching for 5 years or more. As an option, you may want to interview a person who is teaching in elementary school and one who is teaching either at a middle school or a high school. For this exercise, you may make copies of this form. Use the questions to guide the interview and then report back to the whole group.

1. How long have you been an employed teacher?

2. In what ways have you used (or do you use) ITUs?

3. If you have used ITUs, was it individually or as a member of a team? Explain.

4. Why are you using (or not using) ITUs?

5. What training about ITUs did you have?

_____

_____

_____

6. What initial advice in terms of preparing an ITU can you offer me?

_____

_____

_____

7. In what ways do you use community resources? Technology?

_____

_____

_____

8. In what ways do you attend to the importance of diversity and multiculturalism in your classroom?

_____

_____

_____

9. What do you like most about teaching with an ITU? What do you like least?

_____

_____

_____

10. What other specific advice do you have for those of us who are developing and preparing to implement an ITU?

_____

_____

_____

11. What do you do each day that is related to teaching integrated curriculum or an ITU?

_____

_____

_____

12. What is the biggest problem you face when teaching an ITU?

_____

_____

_____

13. What is your biggest satisfaction about teaching an integrated curriculum or an ITU?

_____

_____

_____

14. What would you like to tell other teachers about the real day-to-day world of teaching an ITU?

_____

_____

_____

15. What would help you most to do your job better when teaching an ITU?

_____

_____

_____

NOTES

CHAPTER NOTES

1. D. A. Kolb, *Experimental Learning: Experience as the Source of Learning and Development* (Upper Saddle River, NJ: Prentice Hall, 1984).

2. C. G. Jung, *Psychological Types* (New York: Harcourt Brace, 1923).

3. See B. McCarthy, "A Tale of Four Learners: 4MAT's Learning styles," *Educational Leadership, 54*(6), 47–51 (March 1997).

4. For Gardner's distinction between "learning style" and "intelligences," see H. Gardner, "Multiple Intelligences: Myths and Messages," *International Schools Journal, 15*(2), 8–22 (April 1996) and the many articles in the "Teaching for Multiple Intelligences" theme issue of *Educational Leadership, 55*(1) (September 1997).

5. See, for example, R. J. Marzano, "20th Century Advances in Instruction," in R. A. Brandt (ed.), *Education in a New Era*, Chapter 4, p. 26 (Alexandria, VA: ASCD Yearbook, Association for Supervision and Curriculum Development, 2001).

6. See P. Guild, "The Culture/Learning Style Connection," *Educational Leadership 51*(8), 16–21 (May 1994).

7. The hidden curriculum is defined as the accepted or implied values and attitudes and the unwritten rules of behavior students must learn to participate and to be able to succeed in school. See K. Ryan, "Mining the Values in the Curriculum," *Educational Leadership, 51*(3) (November 1994).

8. A Learning Style Inventory (LSI) was given to students, grades 3–5, to define their learning styles related to environmental, sociological, emotional, and physical conditions. Results indicate that the low-achieving group preferred a more formal learning environment that included chairs and desks, learning with a peer, and studying new materials in the afternoon rather than the morning—while high achievers preferred learning alone and informal classroom design. Middle group achievers did not show a significant preference for a particular learning style. See E. Collinson, "A Survey of Elementary Students' Learning Style Preferences and Academic Success," *Contemporary Education 71*(4), 42–48 (Fall 2000); Also see Chap. 2 "Meeting the Challenge: Recognizing and Supporting Student Differences" in *A Resource Guide for Elementary School Teaching: Planning for Competence*, 5th Edition by Richard D. Kellough and Patricia L. Roberts (Upper Saddle River, NJ: Merrill/Prentice Hall, 2002); Chap. 1 in *Secondary School Teaching: Planning for Competence, A Guide to Methods and Resources*, 6th Edition by Richard D. Kellough and Noreen G. Kellough (Upper Saddle River, NJ: Merrill/Prentice Hall, 1999); Chap. 2 in *Middle School Teaching: A Guide to Methods and Resources*, 6th Edition by Richard D. Kellough and Noreen G. Kellough (Upper Saddle River, NJ: Merrill/Prentice Hall, 1999).

9. See, for example, C. K. McEwin et al., *America's Middle Schools: Practices and Progress: A 25 Year Perspective* (Columbus, OH: National Middle School Association, 1996).

10. During the past 50 years, various movements and approaches have been used to try to find the most successful approach to teaching English and the language arts. These movements have been called whole language, integrated language arts, communication arts and skills, literature based, and so forth. Whatever the cognomen, certain common elements and goals prevail: student choice in materials to be read; student reading and writing across the curriculum; time for independent and sustained silent reading in the classroom; use of integrated language arts skills across the curriculum; use of nonprint materials; use of trade books rather than textbooks and basal readers.

11. See W. Malloy, "Essential Schools and Inclusion: A Responsible Partnership," *Educational Forum, 60*(3), 228–236 (Spring 1996).

12. See W. Schwartz, *Preparing Middle School Students for a Career* (New York: ERIC Clearinghouse on Urban Education, 1996); Southern Regional Education Board, 1995, *Outstanding Practices: High Schools That Work* (Atlanta, GA: author, 1995); and B. A. Lankard, *Restructuring and Vocational Education: Trends and Issues Alerts* (Columbus, OH: ERIC Clearinghouse on Adult, Career, and Vocational Education, 1996).

13. In *Report to the President on the Use of Technology to Strengthen K–12 Education in the United States* by David E. Shaw, Chair, Panel on Educational Technology (Washington, DC: President's Committee of Advisors on Science and Technology, 1997). The Panel concluded that systematic research on educational technology will prove necessary to ensure the efficacy and cost-effectiveness of technology use in K–12 schools in the United States.

14. See G. Solomon, "Of Mind and Media," *Phi Delta Kappan, 78*(5), 375–380 (January 1997) and J. Abbott, "To Be Intelligent," and C. R. Pool, "Maximizing Learning: A Conversation with Renate Numeerla Caine," *Educational Leadership, 54*(6), 6–10 and 11–15 (respectively) (March, 1997).

15. See, for example, P. W. Airasian and M. E. Walsh, "Constructivist Cautions," *Phi Delta Kappan, 78*(6), 444–449 (February 1997).

16. The section titled "The Spectrum of Integrated Curriculum" was developed by Richard D. Kellough and appears in a similar form in several Prentice Hall texts. See those by Kellough and Roberts in the readings listed at the end of this chapter.

17. Patricia L. Roberts, *Literature-Based History Activities for Children, Grades 1–3* (Needham Heights, MA: Allyn & Bacon, 1998), p. 154.

18. National Research Council, *National Science Education Standards* (Washington, DC: National Academy Press, 1996), p. 104. Also see B. Tucker et al., "Integrating Middle School Curriculum: A Two-Tiered Development Model," *Research in Middle Level Education Quarterly, 19*(1), 43–58 (Fall 1995).

19. K. Rasmussen, "Using Real-Life Problems to Make Real-World Connections," *ASCD Curriculum Update*, pp. 4–5 (Summer, 1997).

20. See W. J. Stepien et al., "Problem-Based Learning for Traditional and Interdisciplinary Classrooms," *Journal for the Education of the Gifted, 16*(4), 338–357 (Summer 1994); and W. Stepien and S. Gallagher, "Problem-Based Learning: As Authentic As It Gets," *Educational Leadership, 50*(7), 25–28 (April 1993).

21. For detailed accounts of teaching at this level, see C. Stevenson and J. F. Carr (eds.), *Integrated Studies in the Middle Grades* (New York: Teachers College Press, 1993).

22. See, for example, E. M. Lolli, "Creating a Concept-Based Curriculum," *Principal, 76*(1), 26–27 (September 1996); and H. L. Erickson, *Stirring the Head, Heart, and Soul: Redefining Curriculum and Instruction* (Thousand Oaks, CA: Corwin Press, 1995).

23. J. S. Bruner, *Process of Education* (Cambridge, MA: University Press, 1960).

24. National Research Council, *National Science Education Standards* (Washington, DC: National Academy Press, 1996) p. 104. Also see B. Tucker et al., "Integrating Middle School Curriculum: A Two-Tiered Development Model," *Research in Middle Level Education Quarterly, 19*(1), 43–58 (Fall, 1995).

25. J. Coate and N. White, "History/English Core," *Social Studies Review, 34*(3), 12–115 (Spring 1996) discusses pluses and minuses of using an integrated curriculum; See also L. Doig and J. Sargent, "Light, Camera, Action," in the same issue for a description of an integrated curriculum with history/language arts.

26. J. Barunger and S. Hart-Landsberg, *Crossing Boundaries: Explorations in Integrative Curriculum* (Portland, OR: Northwest Regional Educational Laboratory, 1994).

27. J. M. Low and W. Shironaka, "Letting Go—Allowing First Graders to Become Autonomous Learners," *Young Children, 51*(1), 21–115 (November, 1995); see also R. Novick, *Developmentally Appropriate and Culturally Responsible Education: Theory in Practice* (Portland, OR: Northwest Regional Educational Laboratory, 1996).

28. P. Impson et al., "Interdisciplinary Education—You Bet It Works!" *NASSP Bulletin, 79*(569), 32–37 (March 1995).

29. A. Hall, "Using Social Studies as a Basis for Interdisciplinary Teaching, *State of Reading, 2*(1), 23–28 (Spring 1995); see also T. Shanahan et al., (eds.), "Avoiding Some of the Pitfalls of Thematic Units (Integrating Curriculum)," *Reading Teacher, 49*(8), 718–719 (May 1995).

30. C. B. Decorse, "Current Conversations, Teachers and the Integrated Curriculum: An Intergenerational View," *Action in Teacher Education, 18*(1), 85–92 (Spring 1994); see also D. L. Kain, "Recipes or Dialogue? A Middle School Team Conceptualizes 'Curricular Integration'," *Journal of Curriculum and Supervision, 11*(2), 163–187 (Winter 1996).

31. D. Walker, *Integrative Education, ERIC Digest*, Number 101 (Eugene, OR: ERIC Clearinghouse on Educational Management, 1996); see also B. Borwood, "Energy and Knowledge: The Story of Integrated Curriculum Packages," *Pathways: The Ontario Journal of Outdoor Education, 7*(4), 14–18 (January 1995).

32. C. White, "Making Classroom Management Approaches in Teacher Education Relevant," *Teacher Education and Practice, 11*(1), 15–21 (Spring/Summer 1995).

33. See J. G. Brooks and M. G. Brooks, *In Search of Understanding: The Case for Constructivist Classrooms* (Arlington, VA: Association for Supervision and Curriculum Development, 1993).

34. See C. Dwyer, *Language, Culture, and Writing* (Berkeley, CA: Center for the Study of Writing, University of California, 1991); and See A. M. Villegas, *Culturally Responsible Pedagogy for the 1990s and Beyond* (Princeton, NJ: Educational Testing Service, 1991).

35. See C. Danielson, *Enhancing Professional Practice: A Framework for Teaching* (Alexandria, VA: Association for Supervision and Curriculum Development, 1996).

36. Many resources are available to help the teacher who wants to establish a cooperative, responsive classroom environment. See, for example, Chapter 11 of P. R. Burden, *Classroom Management and Discipline: Methods to Facilitate Cooperation and Instruction* (New York: Longman, 1995); and Chapter 20 of M. Hunter, *Enhancing Teaching* (New York: Macmillan College Pub. Co., 1994).

37. See the final chapter of S. N. Clark and D. C. Clark, *Restructuring the Middle Level School: Implications for School Leaders*, Middle Schools and Early Adolescents Series (Albany, NY: State University of New York Press, 1994); and also S. Parks and S. Hirsh, *A New Vision for Staff Development* (Alexandria, VA: Association for Supervision and Curriculum Development, 1997), p. 46.

38. D. T. Conley, "Restructuring: In Search of Definition," *Principal, 72*(3), 12 (January, 1993).

39. See also J. Villars, *Restructuring through School Design*, Fastback 322 (Bloomington, IN: Phi Delta Kappa Educational Foundation, 1991), p. 41.

40. C. Roelike, *Curriculum Adequacy and Quality in High Schools Enrolling Fewer than 400 Pupils* (Charleston, WV: ERIC Clearinghouse on Rural Education and Small Schools, 1996).

41. S. Willis, "Are Longer Classes Better?" *ASCD Curriculum Update, 35*(3), 3 (March 1993).

42. See also J. M. Carroll, "Organizing Time to Support Learning," *The School Administrator, 51*(3), 26–28, 30–33 (March 1994).

43. J. A. Levin and C. Thurston, "Research Summary: Electronic Networks," *Educational Leadership, 54*(3), 46–50 (November 1996) and other articles in that theme issue titled "Networking."

44. J. Wee, "The Neshonoc Project: Profiles in Partnership," *World School for Adventure Learning Bulletin* (Fall 1993) pp. 2–3. Adapted and used by permission. See also M. R. Davenport et al., "Negotiating Curriculum (Integrating Curriculum)," *Reading Teacher, 49*(1), 60–62 (September 1995).

45. See C. Danielson, *Enhancing Professional Practice: A Framework for Teaching* (Alexandria, VA: Association for Supervision and Curriculum Development, 1996).

46. A. L. Costa, *The School as a Home for the Mind*, (Palatine, IL: Skylight Publishing, 1991), pp. 97–106.

47. M. R. Davenport et al., "Negotiating Curriculum (Integrating Curriculum)," *Reading Teacher, 49*(1), 60–62 (September 1955).

FOR FURTHER READING

Akerson, V. L. (2001, April). Teaching science when your principal says, 'teach language arts'. *Science and Children, 38*(7), 42–47.

Andur, D. (1993, May). Arts and cultural context: A curriculum integrating discipline-based art education with other humanities subjects at the secondary level. *Art Education, 46*(3), 12–19.

Barton, R. C., & Smith, L. A. (2000, September). Themes or motifs? Aiming for coherence through interdisciplinary outlines. *Reading Teacher, 54*(1), 54–63.

Burns, R. C. (1994). *Interdisciplinary teamed instruction: Development and pilot test.* Arlington, VA: Educational Research Service. (ED384456 243 pp.)

Campbell, L., & Campbell, B. (1999). *Multiple intelligences and student achievement: Success stories from six schools.* Alexandria, VA: Association for Supervision and Curriculum Development.

Carr, J. F., & Harris, D. E. (2001). *Succeeding with standards: Linking curriculum, assessment and action planning.* Alexandria, VA: Association of Supervision and Curriculum Development.

Childers-Burpo, D. M. (2002, Spring). Mirrors and microscopes: The promise of national board certification in the era of accountability. *Contemporary Education, 72*(1), 14–17.

Clark, J. H., & Agne, R. M. (1997). *Interdisciplinary high school teaching: Strategies for integrated learning.* Boston: Allyn & Bacon.

Cook, G. E., & Martinello, M. L. (1992, January). Topics and themes in interdisciplinary curriculum. *Middle School Journal, 1*, 40–43.

Fogarty, R. (1991, October). Ten ways to integrate curriculum. *Educational Leadership, 10*, 107–111.

Fogarty, R. (1991). *How to integrate the curricula.* Palatine, IL: Skylight Publishing Co.

Franks, L. (2001, March). Charcoal clouds and weather writing: Inviting science to a middle school language arts classroom. *Language Arts, 78*(4), 319–324.

Greenberg, D., & Haynie, W. J., III (2001, March). Genetic disorders: An integrated curriculum project. *Technology Teacher, 60*(6), 10–13.

Grisham, D. L. (1995). *Integrating the curriculum: The case of an award-winning elementary school.* Arlington, VA: Educational Research Service. (ED385502, 48 pp.)

Ham, J. E., & Ham, S. (1997, Summer). Maya emersion: An integrated cultural unit based on *heart of a jaguar* by Marc Talbert. *SIGNAL Journal, 21*(3), 15–16.

Hargreaves, A., & Moore, S. (2000, Winter). Curriculum integration and classroom relevance: A study of teachers' practice. *Journal of Curriculum and Supervision, 15*(2), 89–112.

Hickman, J., & Bishop, R. S. (1993, Winter). African-Americans: Journey to freedom. *The Web, 17*(2), 19.

Jacobs, H. H., ed. (1989). *Interdisciplinary curriculum: Design and implementation.* Alexandria, VA: Association for Supervision and Curriculum Development.

Johnsen, S. (1994, May/June). Figuring out interdisciplinary curriculum. *Gifted Child Today Journal, 17*(3), 37–39.

Lawton, M. (2000, July/August). The "brain-based" ballyhoo. *Harvard Education Letter, 15*(4), 5–7.

Martinello, M. L., & Cook, G. E. (1992, February). Interweaving the threads of learning: Interdisciplinary curriculum and teaching. *Curriculum Report, 21*(3), 68–73.

Miles, N., & Schuster, H. (2000). *Teaching American diplomacy: Using primary sources. The expansion of NATO.* Denver, CO: Center for Teaching International Relations, University of Denver.

Morgan, R. R., Ponticell, J. A., & Gordon, E. E. (2000). *Rethinking creativity.* Fastback 458. Bloomington, IN: Phi Delta Kappa Educational Foundation.

Nelson, J. R., & Frederick, L. (1994, February). Can children design curriculum? *Educational Leadership, 2*, 71–73.

Nowicki, J. J., & Meehan, K. F. (1997). *Interdisciplinary strategies for English and social studies classrooms: Toward collaborative middle and secondary teaching.* Boston: Allyn & Bacon.

Pappas, C., Kiefer, B. Z., & Levstik, L. S. (1990). *An integrated language perspective in the elementary school: Theory into action.* Columbus: Longman.

Piaget, J. (1970). *Science of education and the psychology of the child.* New York: Orion.

Post, T. R., et al. (1997). *Interdisciplinary approaches to curriculum: Themes for teaching.* Upper Saddle River, NJ: Merrill/Prentice Hall.

Richmond, G., & Striley, J. (1994, October). An integrated approach. *The Science Teacher,* 42–45.

Ross, E. P. (1994). *Using children's literature across the curriculum.* Fastback 374 Bloomington, IN: Phi Delta Kappa Educational Foundation.

Scully, P., Howell, J., & Corbey-Scullern, L. (2000, May). From a bean cake to a classroom kingdom: An idea becomes five weeks of learning. *Young Children, 55*(3), 28–35.

Shanahan, T., Robinson, R., & Schneider, M. (1996, May). Integrating curriculum: Avoiding some of the pitfalls of thematic units. *The Reading Teacher, 48*(8), 718–719.

Shaw, D. G., & Sunal, D. W. (1996, March/April). Interdisciplinary social studies and science lessons with a native American theme. *Social Studies, 87*(2), 72–88.

Silver, H. F., Strong, R.W., & Perini, M. J. (2000). *So each may learn: Integrating learning styles and multiple intelligences.* Alexandria, VA: Association for Supervision and Curriculum Development.

Swenson, A. M. (1991, Spring). Eggs and chicks: An integrated curriculum for children with disabilities. *Teaching Exceptional Children, 24*(2), 102–104.

Tevebaugh, T. (2001, March). Welcome to our web: Integrating subjects through entomology. *Language Arts, 78*(4), 343–347.

Thompson, S. (2001, January). The authentic standards movement and its evil twin. *Phi Delta Kappan, 82*(5), 358–362.

Tomlinson, C. A. (1999). Learning environments that support differentiated instruction. Chapter 4 in *The differentiated classroom.* Alexandria, VA: Association for Supervision and Curriculum Development.

Underhill, R. G., & Thompson, P. (1993, September/October). In curriculum, as in life, the whole is more than the sum of the parts. *Social Studies and the Young Learner, 6*(1), 14–16, 27.

Vars, G. F., & Beane, J. A. (2000). *Integrative curriculum in a standards-based world.* Champaign, IL: ED441618,

ERIC Clearinghouse on Elementary and Early Childhood Education.

Weaver, C., Chaston, J., & Peterson, S. (1993). *Theme exploration: A voyage of discovery.* Portsmouth, NH: Heinemann.

Wineburg, S., & Grossman, P. (eds.). (2000). *Interdisciplinary curriculum: Challenges to implementation.* New York: Teachers College Press.

Wolfe, P. (1999). *Brain matters.* Alexandria, VA: Association for Supervision and Curriculum Development.

CHAPTER 2

Initiating an Interdisciplinary Thematic Unit

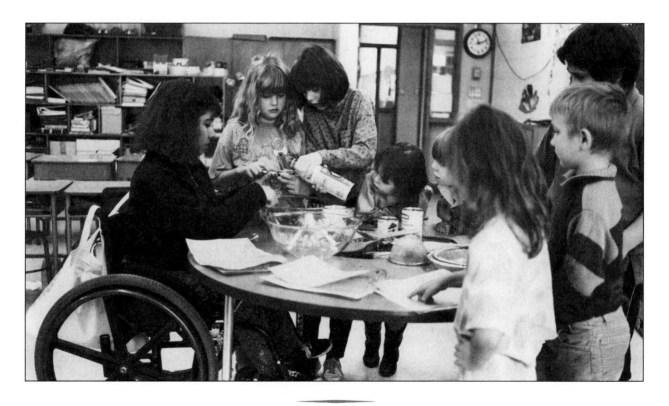

Curiosity of inquiry, aside from stimulation, stands mainly in need of freedom.

—Albert Einstein

INTERDISCIPLINARY THEMATIC UNIT EXAMPLE FOR INTERMEDIATE GRADE STUDENTS: EXPLORATIONS

The curiosity of fourth- and fifth-grade students was stimulated when their team teachers began a unit about explorations with a broad overview of ways exploration occurs. The theme of explorations was selected as a launch into an interdisciplinary 20-day study to give students inquiry situations as well as classroom freedom to consider explorations in the arts, history, language, science, and time. In this far-ranging ITU, the theme material was adjusted to meet local requirements as part of regional studies in the fourth grade and as part of a national history study in the fifth grade. The unit also met state requirements for reading and language arts with language activities integral to the whole curriculum. Some classes were shortened when art, music, physical education, and library periods were scheduled. In the unit, the students participated in creative and factual activities related to the theme and several disciplines:

- *English/Language Arts.* To begin, the students explored other people's lives by reading biography, autobiography, poetry, and historical fiction, and then by writing a fictionalized biography and role-playing.
  - Through reflective inquiry, they were asked to study the concept of exploration intensively and use primary source materials.
  - Later, the students discussed word origins, made dictionaries of word origins, collected regional expressions, learned sign language, and created metaphors and similes.
  - They wrote journals about journeys they had taken or wished they had taken.

- They role-played a discussion at an early explorer's settlement about ways to interact with the native people nearby. They reversed their roles and explored the native people's perspective.
- *Expressive arts.* The students made a time line of the history of selected musical instruments (problem solving), listened to the recordings of styles of music developed over time, explored different art mediums, and suggested dance steps to reflect the theme of exploration.
- *History.* The students created a second time line around the classroom to show noteworthy explorations and collected information for a comparison chart to show positive and negative effects of explorations.
- *Science.* The students explored the concept of time by displaying ways that time can be measured, and by researching still another time line of important discoveries/explorations in medicine in the last 200 years. They also invited an astronomer to class for a question-and-answer period about explorations and discoveries in time and space.
- *Social science.* The students researched the different forms of government that various explorers took to the worlds they explored. They discussed the topics of good government and freedom. As part of the study of the concepts of government and freedom, they visited work sites realizing that the people there had the freedom to choose their contemporary careers under their government. They also conducted an inventory of needed skills for the careers.

CHAPTER INTRODUCTION

In this chapter you will be provided with an overview of ways to initiate an ITU, including selecting a theme to study and planning the scope and sequence of a unit. You will see how guiding questions can isolate concept words and then use the concept words to write generalizations that represent knowledge related to the thematic study. Further, there is an overview of the history of curriculum standards, selected national and state standards, mandated testing of students, types of learning experiences, and the value of using the community as a rich learning resource. As mentioned in the previous chapter, suggestions in this resource text are guidelines, not universals and absolutes for developing an ITU. There are as many successful variations on these guidelines as there are successful implementations of ITUs.

SELECTING A THEME FOR AN INTERDISCIPLINARY THEMATIC UNIT

You will recall, as defined in Chapter 1, a theme title is or should be more than simply a topic—it is the essence (point), the communication (message), or the idea (concept, precept, pattern, design) that underlines a study. When working within an integrated curriculum, students might study a theme on an ongoing basis—perhaps a long-term thematic study as exemplified by the vignette at the opening of this chapter or by the examples from the West Salem Middle School and the Illinois Mathematics and Science Academy that were mentioned in Chapter 1.

Developing a Rationale for a Theme

Sometimes themes are selected by the teacher or by a teaching team before meeting the students for the first time. Other times, the themes are selected by the teachers in collaboration with students. As we will be emphasizing, even when the theme is preselected with guidance from the teacher, students still should be given major responsibility for deciding the final theme title, topics, and corresponding learning activities. Integrated thematic instruction works best when students have ownership in the study, when they have been empowered with major decision-making responsibility. See Figures 2.1 and 2.2 for examples of selected theme words and sentences.

FIGURE 2.1   Sample Theme Words

adaptation	crusades	inventions
administrations	cultures	issues
adventures	declarations	journeys
adversaries	democracies	justice
aeronautics	demonstrations	liberty
agreements	departures	lodgings
ambitions	deprivations	machines
arbitrations	depths	migrations
aristocracies	determinations	minority rights
beginnings	dictators	modern society
blockades	dignity	nationalism
bonanzas	dilemmas	nations
boundaries	diplomacy	navigations
boycotts	disasters	needs
bravery	discoveries	neighborhoods
breakthroughs	diversity	nonviolence
buildings	dynasties	oppressions
business	emancipations	ordeals
calamities	emigrations	patterns
campaigns	encounters	pollution
caring	environments	power
cause/effect	exploitations	prejudice
celebrations	explorations	relationships
changes	extinctions	relativity
citizenship	families	resources
civilization	fighters	revolutions
colonization	freedoms	searches
communications	governments	segregation
conflict with climate	hardships	self-awareness
conflict with self/others	heritages	settlements
conservation	heroes	social groups
constitutions	hibernations	survival
contributions	independence	traditions
controversies	individuality	others by students
cooperation	inspirations	
courage	interactions	

FIGURE 2.2 Sample Theme Sentences

People are affected by war in different ways.

People are interdependent.

People are sensitive to nature.

People can be courageous and inspiring.

People can be independent and resourceful.

People can overcome handicaps.

People can see change(s) as beneficial.

People can see that cultures can clash.

People can see that laws and rules affect families.

People can see that motives and drives affect their environment.

People have conflicts within themselves, with others, and with the environment.

People remember their loved ones and preserve their memory.

People search for freedom.

A theme also can provide an emotional dimension to the unit that goes beyond the information related to the study of a topic. For instance, the theme might be a phrase—*the acceptance of one's self or others, overcoming fear,* or *overcoming prejudice.* The theme might be a word—*justice, integrity,* or *ethics.* It can also be an inspiration or an understanding of human emotions, perhaps an understanding that gives students respect for life that includes the lives of animals, plants, and humans.

When suggested by students, themes often relate to such ideas as *families are important, fears can be overcome, friendship is important, prejudice is harmful,* and *self-understanding can be developed.* Other themes might focus on ideas such as the benefits of accepting others, of cooperation, of giving and receiving support from others, of having a moral code to guide one's actions, of valuing education, and of establishing a positive relationship with an adult—a significant and caring other.

Developing Criteria for Theme Selection

The basis for theme selection should satisfy two criteria: The theme should (1) fit within the expected scope and sequence of mandated content, and (2) should be of interest to the students. Regarding the first criterion, many teachers have told us that when they and their students started an interdisciplinary study, they did so without truly knowing where the study would go or what the

learning outcomes finally would be—and they were somewhat frightened by that fact (we learned this ourselves when we were classroom teachers). When the unit was completed, however, their students had learned everything (or nearly everything) that the teachers would have expected them to learn had the teachers used a more traditional content-centered approach. And, it was more fun!

The second criterion is easy to satisfy when the students are truly empowered with decision-making responsibility for what and how they learn. So, once a theme is selected (one that satisfies the first criterion), its final title, subtopics, and corresponding procedural activities should be finalized in collaboration with the students.

In some schools, a general theme is selected and identified for each grade, one that can be considered from the perspective of the past, the present, and the future and one that reflects the school's educational goals (see Figure 2.3). A common example is the theme of *awareness of self/individual* for kindergarten and first grade. A few sample themes that have been commonly used for various grades are change, communities, families, environments, heritage, freedom, systems and interactions, and transportation.

REVIEWING CURRICULUM STANDARDS
History and Status

Curriculum standards define what students should know (content) and be able to do (process and performance). At the national level, curriculum standards did not exist until some were developed and released for mathematics education by the National Council for Teachers of Mathematics in 1989 (revised in 2000). Shortly after the release of the mathematics standards, support for national goals in education was endorsed by the National Governors Association. The National Council on Education Standards and Testing recommended that in addition to standards for mathematics, standards for subject matter content in K–12 education should be developed for the arts, civics/social studies, English/language arts/reading, geography, history, and science. The U. S. Department of Education provided initial funding for the development of these national standards. As mentioned in Chapter 1, the United States Congress passed the *Goals 2000: Educate America Act* (1994), and then amended it (1996) with an Appropriations Act that encouraged states to set curriculum standards. Long before, however, as was done for mathematics, national organizations devoted to various disciplines were already defining standards. Please refer to Figure 1.7 in Chapter 1,

FIGURE 2.3   Sample Grade Level Themes from History and Social Studies

Kindergarten: Individuals are interdependent: Awareness of Self in a Social Setting

1st Grade: Group members are interdependent: The Individual in Primary Social Groups (Understanding School and Family Life)

2nd Grade: People can see that basic needs affect their environment: Meeting Basic Needs in Nearby Social Groups (Neighborhood)

3rd Grade: People can see that motives and drives affect their environment: Sharing Earth's Resources with Others (Community)

4th Grade: People have conflicts in themselves, with others, and with the environment: Understanding Human Life in Varied Environments (Region)

5th Grade: People, weak and strong, can help each other: Understanding People of the Americas (The United States and its Close Neighbors)

6th Grade: People can see that cultures can clash: Understanding People and Cultures (Eastern Hemisphere)

7th Grade: People can see change(s) as beneficial: Understanding a Changing World (Global View)

8th Grade: People can see that laws and rules affect families: Building a Strong and Free Nation (The United States)

9th Grade: People can see that laws and rules affect families: Understanding Systems that Make a Democracy Work (Law, Justice, and Economics)

10th Grade: People can see that cultures can clash: Understanding Origins of Major Cultures (World History)

11th Grade: People can see change(s) as beneficial: The Maturing of America (History of the United States)

12th Grade: People can see change(s) as beneficial: Selections often made from (1) Issues and Problems of Modern Society and (2) Social Sciences

where we first introduced curriculum standards, to see the graphic that depicts selected curriculum standards by content area and discipline-specific Internet listings. See Figure 2.4 for general Internet resources on standards.

Recommendations for Curriculum Standards

Curriculum standards represent the best thinking by expert panels including teachers from the field about the essential elements of a basis of subject knowledge that all K–12 students should acquire. These standards serve not as national mandates but rather as voluntary guidelines to encourage curriculum development to promote higher student achievement; state and local curriculum developers decide the extent to which the standards are used. Related to this, a summary of recommendations for mathematics instruction is shown in Figure 2.5. The essence of many of these recommendations—a thematic hands-on, inquiry-oriented, performance-based approach to learning less but

learning better—can be found in the standards that were subsequently developed for other disciplines (see recommendations for English/language arts in Figure 2.6, and recommendations for science instruction in Figure 2.7).

State Curriculum Standards

Strongly influenced by the standards from national professional groups, nearly all states have completed and are implementing some of their own standards for the various disciplines. Here are some examples:

- **Massachusetts.** Standards are found in several Curriculum Frameworks that include Arts, English/Language Arts, Health, Mathematics, Science and Technology, Social Studies, and World Languages.
- **Montana.** Content and Performance Standards are found in documents for the Arts, Library Media, Literature, Health Enhancement, Mathematics, Media Literacy, Reading, Science, Social Studies, Speaking and Listening, Technology,

FIGURE 2.4   Resources for Curriculum Standards and Frameworks*

General and multiple disciplines
- (http://www.mcrel.org) general, multiple disciplines
- (http://www.enc.org/reform/fworks/index.htm), for math and science, both national and state

Standards state by state, discipline by discipline with information about proficiency testing
- (http://www.statestandards.com)

National Standards
National Council for Accreditation of Teacher Education (NCATE) (http://www.ncate.org)

American Association of Colleges for Teacher Education (AACTE) (http://www.aacte.org/eric/news3.html)

The International Society for Technology in Education (ISTE) (http://www.iste.org/standards/index.html)

The Association for Educational Communications and Technology (AECT) (http://www.aect.org)

The National Council of Teachers of Mathematics (http://www/nctm.org) or (http://www.math.umass.edu)

*All resources operable when checked by authors in spring 2003.

FIGURE 2.5   Mathematics Instruction and Summary of Recommendations

Increased emphasis on
- Active involvement of students in constructing and applying mathematical ideas
- Assessment of learning as an integral part of instruction
- Effective questioning techniques that promote student interaction
- Establishment and application of the interrelatedness of mathematical topics
- Student communication of mathematical ideas orally and in writing
- Systematic maintenance of student learnings and embedding review in the content of new topics and problem situations
- Use of variety of instructional formats such as individual explorations, peer instruction, and small groups

Decreased emphasis on
- Extended periods of individual seatwork practicing routine tasks
- Instruction by teacher exposition
- Paper-and-pencil manipulative skill work
- Relegation of testing to an adjunct role with the sole purpose of assigning grades
- Rote memorization of facts and procedures
- Teacher and text as exclusive sources of knowledge

FIGURE 2.6 English/Language Arts Instruction and Summary of Recommendations

Increased emphasis on
- Adjusting spoken/written language to communicate effectively with different audiences and for different purposes
- Communicating on issues/interests from a variety of sources
- Reading a range of literature/texts to acquire new information to respond to needs of society, to read for personal fulfillment, and to build an understanding of themselves and others
- Respecting diversity in language use, patterns and dialects across cultures, ethnic groups, geographic regions, and social roles
- Using a variety of resources such as computer networks, databases, libraries, or videos to gather and synthesize information and to create and communicate knowledge
- Using strategies to comprehend texts that include word identification strategies, sound-letter correspondence, sentence structure, word meanings, content, and graphics; develop competence in English and understanding a content across curriculum

Decreased emphasis on
- Single-discipline learning
- Traditionally distinct content areas
- Teacher always at the center of classroom interaction
- Unclear goals of teaching (i.e., goals that lack meaning)

FIGURE 2.7 Science Instruction and Summary of Recommendations

Increased emphasis on
- Continuously assessing student understanding
- Focusing on student use of scientific knowledge, ideas, and inquiry processes
- Guiding students in active and extended scientific inquiry
- Selecting and adapting curriculum
- Sharing responsibility for learning with students
- Supporting a classroom community with cooperation, shared responsibility, and respect
- Working with other teachers to enhance the science program

Decreased emphasis on
- Asking for recitation of acquired knowledge
- Focusing on student acquisition of information
- Maintaining responsibility and authority
- Presenting scientific knowledge through lecture, text, and demonstration
- Rigidly following curriculum
- Supporting competition
- Treating all students alike and responding to the group as a whole
- Testing students for factual information at the end of the unit or chapter
- Working alone

World Language, Work Place Competencies, and Writing.

- **North Carolina.** The Standard Course of Study presents curriculum in Arts Education, Computer/Technology Skills, English/Language Arts, Healthful Living, Mathematics, Science, Second-Language Studies, Social Studies, and Work-Force Development (which includes many sections on Planning, Agricultural Education, Business Education, Career Development, Family and Consumer Sciences, Health Occupations, Marketing Education, Technical Education, and Trade and Industrial Education).

- **Texas.** Standards are reflected on the Texas Essential Knowledge and Skills (TEKS) tests, which became effective in 1998 and are included in many areas: (1) the foundations areas of English/Language Arts and Reading, Mathematics, Science, Social Studies, Spanish Language Arts, and English as a Second Language; (2) the enrichment areas of Languages Other Than English, Fine Arts, Health, Physical Education; and (3) Technology Applications (which includes Agricultural Science and Technology, Business Education, Career Orientation, Health Science Technologies, Home Economics Education, Technology Education/Industrial Technology Education, Marketing Education, and Trade and Industrial Education).

Both national and state standards, accessible on the Internet (see listing in Figure 2.4), provide guidance to the developers of the standardized tests that are used in what today is called high-stakes testing. High-stakes testing refers to the tests being used at various grade levels to determine student achievement, promotion, and rewards to schools and even to individual teachers and students. In about half of the 50 states, some tests may be a requirement for graduation from high school.

STANDARDS AND HIGH-STAKES TESTING: WHEN ALL STUDENTS ARE EXPECTED TO DO WELL ON A MANDATED ASSESSMENT, THEN ALL SHOULD BE GIVEN EQUAL OPPORTUNITY TO PREPARE FOR IT

The adoption of tougher K–12 learning standards throughout the United States coupled with an emphasis on increased high-stakes testing to assess how schools and teachers are helping their students meet those standards has provoked considerable debate, actions, and reactions among educators, parents and guardians, politicians, and the business

world. Some argue that this renewed emphasis on testing means too much teaching to the test at the expense of more meaningful learning, and that it ignores the leverage that home, community, and larger societal influences have over the education of children and young people today. Sosniak and other educators[1] have indicated that we need to find ways to identify what others in the business world are doing to promote education, because schools cannot do all the work alone. Nevertheless, here is what some teachers do:

- Responding to the call for increased accountability, teachers in some schools put aside the regular curriculum for several weeks before the testing date and concentrate on the direct preparation of their students for the test.

- Preparing for the tests, some teachers address the regular curriculum 2 days a week and prepare for tests 3 days a week during a pretest period.

- Still other teachers use selected materials that are available to help prepare students for state-mandated tests, such as the TAAS Texas Assessment of Academic Skills Master Student Practice Books and standards-based material. Other helpful resources are TestSmart Digital Lessons on CD based on IRA and NCTE standards (both are from ECS Learning Systems, Inc., P.O. Box 791439, San Antonio, TX 78279-1439). The TAAS Practice Books address the objectives for given subject areas, represent instructional targets, focus on content, familiarize students with the test question format, and contain authentic reading passages. The CD digital lessons relate to areas of reading/language arts standards such as genres, language expressions, mechanics, listening, reading operations, speaking, spelling, study skills, and writing. Using such materials, teachers are well aware of the possibility (although certainly not an all-inclusive situation) that state and federal funding may be withheld from schools and/or jobs may be on the line for teachers and administrators when students do not score well.

Although the interest in student practice for pretesting has been rekindled in recent years, this often-called "drill and kill" approach is certainly not new. When comparing standardized testing of today with that of the past half century, it is probably reasonable to conclude that

- The purpose of state-wide standardized testing remains unchanged; it is to determine how well students are learning, at least to the extent determined by the particular test instrument.

- The test design is accomplished today with much greater precision and accuracy.

- The focus of today's testing is taking precious time away from the most creative aspects of teaching and learning.
- The manner in which test results are being used today and the long-term results of that use may have ramifications considerably more serious than at any time before.

You may be interested in knowing that students with access to computers can practice and prepare for the state-mandated standardized tests online. In schools with the required computer technology and with the appropriate number of computers to provide access time to individual students, selected software programs can help students prepare for the tests. Two such programs are *eduTest* (http://www.eduTest.com) and *Homeroom. com* (http://www.homeroom.com). Proponents of such online preparation argue that a major advantage is the immediate scoring of practice testing with feedback about each student's areas of weakness, thereby providing the teacher with information necessary for immediate remediation. If their arguments are accurate, then it would seem that students of such technology-rich schools would clearly be at an advantage over students in schools where this technology is not available. It would follow that district and government agencies that mandate the standards and specific assessment practices should provide avenues and tools to assure equity and success for all students toward reaching the expected learning outcomes within the designated learning time.

Your national professional associations are also sources for up-to-date information about this issue and others. For Internet addresses, see Figure 2.8, National Professional Associations for Teachers.

SELECTING A THEME: A BEGINNING PROCESS

The process of selecting a theme differs somewhat depending on the extent to which you are working independently or as a member of a team.

When Working Independently

If you are working solo, you might want to first list all the possible themes and topics that you can find in existing documents that were discussed in the preceding section. As you make the list, note any of the themes and topics that might be relevant to your goals. Then decide on a theme that can be correlated with each subject area without violating the educational plans for which you are responsible during the academic year. Sometimes, you may have to select a large amount of content from two or more units that you have planned previously; at other times, you may want to integrate a small amount of content from a previous unit. If a theme for the ITU under consideration is not yet apparent, now is the time to select one, using the topic(s) you (perhaps with your students) have checked in your list. Critique your selected theme by examining it for various characteristics using the questions in Figure 2.9. See Planning Master 2.1 for use later in collaboration with your students (if appropriate for your grade level) as you refine and finalize the theme title.

When Working as a Team Member

Often a team of two or more teachers collaborate in teaching an ITU. When working on particular units, teaching teams sometimes invite temporary members such as specialty teachers and experts from the community. In the primary grades, teams of teachers

FIGURE 2.8 National Professional Associations for Teachers

AAE:	Association of American Educators, 26012 Marguerite Parkway #333, Mission Viejo, CA 92692 (http://www.aaeteachers.org/info.html#board)
AFT:	American Federation of Teachers, AFL-CIO, 555 New Jersey Avenue, NW, Washington, DC 20001 (http://www.aft.org)
NAPE:	National Association of Professional Educators, Suite 300, 900 17th Street, Washington, DC 20006 (http://www.teacherspet.com/napeindx.html)
NEA:	National Education Association, 1201 16th Street, NW, Washington, DC 20036-3290 (http://www.nea.org)

FIGURE 2.9   Critiquing a Theme

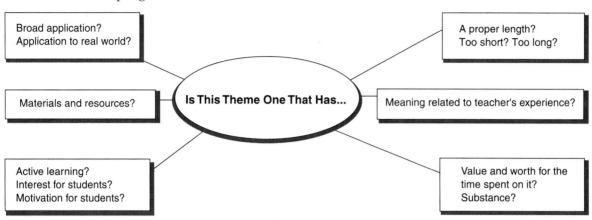

may collaborate on a grade-level unit, or teams from more than one grade level might collaborate on a sequence of related units for several or all grades at a school. At middle-level schools and high schools, interdisciplinary teaching teams will consist of teachers from two or more disciplines.

First Step: Decide How Team Will Work Together

The first step is for the team members to discuss how unit development will proceed as a collaborative endeavor. All team members—and guest members, if desired—are encouraged to participate as equally as possible. Usually a team leader is selected for the school term or for the development of this particular unit. If team members do not have a common planning time during the daily school schedule, they will need to decide how frequently and when they will meet. Ideally, during development and implementation of an ITU, interdisciplinary teams share a minimum of 6 hours of common planning time each week.

Second Step: Decide on Student Learning Expectations

The second step is for the team to arrive at a consensus about what the students should achieve from the interdisciplinary unit of study, in terms of both conceptual and procedural knowledge. To set goals, the team will probably discuss some of the subject-specific frameworks, goals, objectives, curriculum guides, textbooks, supplemental materials, and units that are already in existence. The discussion among team members should focus on what each member will contribute to the development and implementation of the unit and to the accomplishment of the

unit's educational goals. Taking this step will help clarify the scope and sequence of the unit, so that all members of the team will have an understanding of what can and cannot be done. Be realistic—talk about limitations and constraints you see in this undertaking. Taking time to play the part of educational "troubleshooters" will enable the team to identify various stumbling blocks before potential problems impede the progress of the unit. This will make implementation of the ITU go more smoothly. For instance, early in ITU development members may want to clarify the purpose of working together (i.e., professional development, reflective practice, collegial interaction, student motivation), write a mission statement for the team, and make suggestions for turning that statement into a working plan.

Third Step: Decide on Materials and Brainstorm Ideas

An ITU pulls materials from across the curriculum; therefore, the team will need to review information that each team member presents from his or her subject area. Together, members should list possible topics that can be found in existing curriculum documents. Meanwhile, new ideas will emerge as brainstorming is inevitable. Remember that dialogue and compromise are essential—a give-and-take is needed in these discussions because some themes and topics will correlate with certain subject areas better than with other areas. Also keep in mind that for team teachers, the goal is to find a theme or topic that works for everyone. All team members will want a theme that relates well with each subject area and that will not disturb (too much) the educational plans that individual team teachers already have in place for the academic year (please see Figures 2.1, Sample Theme Words, and 2.2, Sample Theme Sentences, earlier in the chapter).

In some cases, the team might have to select content from units that one or more teachers have planned previously. In other cases, the team may have to merge some content from previous units. At this point, if a theme for the ITU has not yet become apparent, the time has come to derive a theme from the topic(s) that team members have put forward.

Evolving Themes

Although the unit may evolve from parts of previously implemented units of instruction, the most effective ITUs are often those that are the most current. This means that ever-changing global, national, and local topics provide an educational smorgasbord from which to choose. Teaching teams must constantly be aware of the changes in the world, the society, and the interests of students to update old plans and develop new and exciting ones.

Communicating with Other Teams

One teaching team's units should not conflict with another's at the same or another grade level. If a school has two or more second-grade teams, for example, the teams may want to develop units on different themes and share their products.

Furthermore, a middle school team may want to share its units with high school teams and perhaps with affiliated elementary schools. The lines of communication within, between, and among teams and schools are critical to the success of integrated curriculum and interdisciplinary thematic instruction.

Once selected, a theme should be critiqued by examining it for various characteristics, as we mentioned earlier. A review of the questions in Figure 2.9 might be of help in this critique. Now, to develop additional insight into the process of selecting a theme for an ITU, do Exercises 2.1 and 2.2 at the end of this chapter.

GIVING THE ITU A NAME

Giving the unit a name should be done in collaboration with your students. Before selecting a theme title, discuss with the students ways the unit will be meaningful to the members of the class and the school, and how it will be integrated to real-life experiences. Emphasize that the major part of the unit's value will come from its interdisciplinary approach. Decide with the students how a final title will be selected—perhaps by brainstorming possibilities and then voting on them. The agreed-upon title should be one that makes academic sense and that has meaning to the students.

DEVELOPING A SCOPE AND SEQUENCE FOR CONTENT AND INSTRUCTION

Once the theme has been selected and named, develop a schedule for the unit to assign dates to certain topics and identify activities in a logical sequence. This sequence could incorporate any or a combination of the following arrangements.

Focusing on One Content Area

Sometimes, when selecting a theme, you may find that it is specifically related to one discipline, such as history. Consider the following examples related to this discipline:

- Civilization, cultural diffusion/colonization, and innovation (e.g., the evolution of major civilizations over time)
- Human interaction with the environment (e.g., people's choices throughout history made available by geography)
- Conflict and cooperation (e.g., historical causes of conflicts and war, and approaches to peace)
- Comparative history of major development (e.g., revolutionary, reactionary, and reform periods across time and place)
- Social and political interactions (e.g., historical changes in class, ethnic, gender, and racial relations and patterns)

Although one discipline (e.g., history/social studies) may be the primary focus in the unit's sequence of activities, a multitude of other areas may be included in the activities as well. Consider, for example, an ITU whose theme is colonization—with a beginning focus on children and their families in America's colonies. The students can begin their study into the concept of colonization with a teacher's broad overview of ways colonization occurs. The theme of colonization can be a way to give students inquiry situations as well as classroom freedom to consider colonization related to the arts, history, language, science, and time, and thus make this as far-ranging a unit as they wish. The sequence of activities might include several related to history/social studies such as the colonists' connections to the rest of the world, their activities in their daily lives, their economic status, and their beliefs and manners. Each of the activities, or study areas, could comprise a certain time period, and students would learn within a historical context as they explored related art of the period, biographies of famous people, drama, music, and literature, as well as how the politics of the time affected children and their families.

Focusing on Two Content Areas

Consider that both history/social studies and English/language arts play equally important roles in the unit's sequence of activities. This was the approach in a large high school in Brooklyn where the same students shared a social studies-English teaching team. Each team coordinated its 8-week ITU, guided by themes of *human environment interaction* and *tradition and change,* during a common preparatory period. The students' learning was focused on exploring ways that people/cultures interacted with their environment, kept their cultures through traditions, and made changes based on needs/circumstances. Examples include the following:

- **English.** Readings in English class included Richard Connell's "The Most Dangerous Game" (the short story about a famous hunter who finds himself being hunted on a Caribbean island) and articles on animal cruelty.
- **Expressive arts.** The students went to the Chamber Theater in New York City to see an adaptation of Connell's story and discussed the similarities and differences between the short story version and the play. They were asked to explain why the changes were made and the extent to which they worked effectively. A related journal assignment asked them to read an article about hunting and trapping and then react to it from a personal point of view or from the point of view of someone/something else.
- **Social studies.** In social studies, students identified geographical features of selected areas of the Caribbean, researched the rain forest and its surrounding degrading environment, studied loss of animal species, and shared their findings in collaborative groups. They discussed the choices made by Connell's hunter that were affected by his knowledge of the geographic area he was in. In a decision-making exercise, they worked independently and in groups to identify and justify the three most important objects they would take along as resources to find their way out of a jungle/rainforest.
- **Geography.** A culminating activity was a simulation called "How Can We Get to Rio?" In triads, they used maps and charted a course from New York City to Rio de Janeiro by land or sea with each group given a different travel time during the year. Once they identified routes, the groups were told that they had crashed in a specific location and had to find a way out of their predicament. A final follow-up discussion focused on ways their choices were based on the environment and climate, and on topographical and vegetation maps. The discussion also led to more research to identify the precise island referred to in Connell's story and to justify their selection.[2]

Focusing on Three (or More) Content Areas

When three or more disciplines such as history/social studies, English/language arts, and science play equally important roles, the goal is to integrate the areas just as they are integrated into our lives. For a unit whose theme is colonization, you can engage the students not only in the activities mentioned in the previous two arrangements but in others you would like to incorporate. You might assist the students in locating the colony of Jamestown on a map. You might ask them to research climatic conditions at that time and the wildlife that was prevalent in that region. Then considering their findings, you might ask them where they would locate the colony if they were the first settlers. Perhaps you would like to design a problem-solving inquiry similar to the one illustrated in Figure 2.10, Inquiry and Problem Solving: Locating a Colony.

If working solo, you may find it valuable to give a copy of the sequence of your activities/learning experiences to a teaching colleague. If working as a member of a team, then you and the members of the team will need to exchange ideas related to the learning experiences. Ask for a colleague's suggestions about the experiences and the sequence you have identified. If most of the remarks are positive, you will know that the sequence you planned appears workable from another's point of view. If difficulties arise, you may want to consider modifications in the learning experiences themselves or in the sequence in which they are offered.

Developing Focus Questions

Following the selection of a theme title, in collaboration with members of your teaching team and your students, you can develop focus questions to guide the study. Consider the following examples:

- How did early African Americans begin their journey to freedom?
- How did early Pilgrims complete their journey to freedom?
- What happened during those journeys?
- What are the reasons people celebrate freedom and liberty? How do they celebrate?

FIGURE 2.10   Inquiry and Problem Solving: Locating a Colony

Presenting the Problem. In groups of three or four, the students receive the following information:

Background. You (your group is considered as one person) are 1 of 120 passengers on the ship *The Prince William.* You left England 12 weeks ago. You have experienced many hardships, including a stormy passage, limited rations, sickness, cold and damp weather, and hot foul air below deck. Ten of your fellow immigrants to the New World including three children have died and were buried at sea. You are now anchored someplace off the coast of the New World; your captain believes it to be somewhere north of the Virginia Grants. Seas are so rough and food so scarce that you and your fellow passengers have decided to settle here. A landing party has returned with a map they made of the area. As one of the elders, you must decide at once where the settlement is to be located. The tradespeople want to settle along the river, which is deep, even though this seems to be the season of low water levels. Within 10 months, you and others expect deep water ships from England with more colonists and merchants. Those within your group who are farmers say they must have fertile, workable land. The officer in charge of the landing party reported seeing a group of armed natives that fled when approached. He thinks the settlement must be located so that it can be defended from the natives and from the sea.

Presenting the Directions.

Step One. You (your group) are to select a site on the attached map that you feel is best suited for a colony. Your site must satisfy the different factions aboard the ship. Several possible sites are already marked on the map (letters A–G). You may select one of these locations or use them as reference points to show the location of your colony. When your group has selected its site, list and explain the reasons for your choice. When each group has arrived at its tentative decision, these decisions will be shared with the whole class.

Step Two. After each group has made its presentation and argument, a class debate is held about where the colony should be located.

Notes to teacher: For the debate, we suggest you have a large map drawn on the writing board or on an overhead transparency, where each group's mark can be made for all to see and discuss. After each group has presented its argument for its location and against the others, we suggest that you mark on the large map, the two, three, or more possible locations (assuming that, as a class, there is no single favorite location). Then take a straw vote of the students, allowing each to vote on his or her own, independently rather than as members of a group. At this time, you can end the activity by saying that if the majority of students favor one location, then that is the solution to the problem—the colony is located at the site that the majority of class members indicate. No sooner will that statement be made by you than someone will ask, "Are we correct?" or "What is the right answer?" They will ask such questions because, as students in school, they are used to solving problems that have right answers (Level I inquiry teaching). In real-world problems, however, there are no "right" answers, although some answers may seem better than others. It is the process of problem solving that is important. You want your students to develop confidence in their ability to solve problems and to understand the tentativeness of "answers" to real-life problems.

(Source: J. Devine and D. Devine, by permission.) Adapted from unpublished material.

Planning and Selecting Learning Experiences for the Unit

When planning and selecting learning experiences/activities for meaningful understanding, it is important to select ones that are as direct as possible. You will want students involved in hands-on experiences to encourage the full use of their learning modalities—auditory, visual, tactile, and kinesthetic—which often results in the most effective and longest lasting learning. Figure 2.11, The Learning Experiences Ladder, illustrates types of learning experiences, ranging from the most concrete (direct) at the bottom of the ladder, where students are likely to be using all their sensory input channels and their

FIGURE 2.11 The Learning Experiences Ladder

Source: Earlier versions of this concept were Charles F. Hoban, Sr. et al., *Visualizing the Curriculum* (New York: Dryden, 1937), p. 39; Jerome S. Bruner, *Toward a Theory of Instruction* (Cambridge: Harvard University Press, 1966), p. 49; Edgar Dale, *Audiovisual Methods in Teaching* (New York: Holt, Rinehart & Winston, 1969), p. 108; and Eugene C. Kim and Richard D. Kellough, *A Resource Guide for Secondary School Teaching,* 2nd Edition. (Upper Saddle River, NJ: Merrill/Prentice Hall, 1978), p. 136.

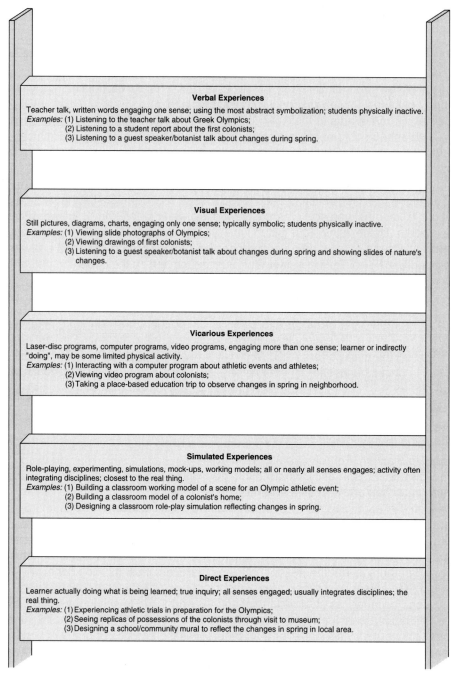

Verbal Experiences
Teacher talk, written words engaging one sense; using the most abstract symbolization; students physically inactive.
Examples: (1) Listening to the teacher talk about Greek Olympics;
(2) Listening to a student report about the first colonists;
(3) Listening to a guest speaker/botanist talk about changes during spring.

Visual Experiences
Still pictures, diagrams, charts, engaging only one sense; typically symbolic; students physically inactive.
Examples: (1) Viewing slide photographs of Olympics;
(2) Viewing drawings of first colonists;
(3) Listening to a guest speaker/botanist talk about changes during spring and showing slides of nature's changes.

Vicarious Experiences
Laser-disc programs, computer programs, video programs, engaging more than one sense; learner or indirectly "doing", may be some limited physical activity.
Examples: (1) Interacting with a computer program about athletic events and athletes;
(2) Viewing video program about colonists;
(3) Taking a place-based education trip to observe changes in spring in neighborhood.

Simulated Experiences
Role-playing, experimenting, simulations, mock-ups, working models; all or nearly all senses engages; activity often integrating disciplines; closest to the real thing.
Examples: (1) Building a classroom working model of a scene for an Olympic athletic event;
(2) Building a classroom model of a colonist's home;
(3) Designing a classroom role-play simulation reflecting changes in spring.

Direct Experiences
Learner actually doing what is being learned; true inquiry; all senses engaged; usually integrates disciplines; the real thing.
Examples: (1) Experiencing athletic trials in preparation for the Olympics;
(2) Seeing replicas of possessions of the colonists through visit to museum;
(3) Designing a school/community mural to reflect the changes in spring in local area.

learning is integrated, to the most abstract (least direct) at the top of the ladder, where learners are using only one or two sensory input channels.

Planning the Details

Team members work together to schedule dates, coordinate topics, avoid duplication, and identify activities in a logical sequence. With the school calendar in mind, a time line or schedule for the ITU is agreed upon. Establish and write important dates on the calendar, including deadlines for having certain material prepared, and the beginning and closing dates of the unit study. Indicate dates that will be important to the students, such as when reports are due and when the culminating learning experience will be held.

This time line, called Time Line A, should contain a record of all dates when any assigned work for the development of the ITU must be done by a team member. The team can then turn its attention to a second time line, Time Line B, which should contain all dates important to both the students and the teachers. For example, Time Line B can indicate when the ITU begins (and in which period), various due dates during the unit, and when the ITU ends.

Now explore the scope and sequence of an ITU by doing Exercise 2.3, "Making Early Decisions: More about Scope and Sequence," found at the end of the chapter.

USING THE COMMUNITY AS A RICH RESOURCE

Many people in your community will be willing to serve as resources for people-based learning, and there are many places that you and the students can visit for place-based education (see Figure 2.12 for options later in this section). You will want to identify and select persons and places that will contribute to the students' understanding of the theme-related topics.

Incorporating Student Choices

A class meeting is beneficial in focusing the students' attention on decisions to be made about the use of community resources, especially available people and places. Figure 2.13 shows a visual web that can be used as a discussion focus with the students and that is suitable for an overhead transparency (see also Planning Master 2.2). With this web as a guide for a discussion, students can write their own headings, questions, responses, and re-

sponsibilities on a blank transparency for the overhead projector as they make choices and plan to use resources in their community.

Incorporating People-Based Learning

As witnessed by the West Salem Middle School experience (in Chapter 1), people from the community can make a significant contribution to a thematic unit of instruction. West Salem's experience pointed out that when invited with care, a community resource person can be asked to spend time with the students for an instructional purpose related to the unit. A discussion with the students and a survey of parents/guardians of the students and the yellow pages in the telephone directory can provide a wealth of information about the people who could serve as resources for people-based learning.

Incorporating Place-Based Learning

When you plan a class excursion to a place off the school campus, make sure the trip coincides with the ITU and anticipate any problems that might arise during the outing. For all trips, you will want to have a clear purpose, keeping the safety of the students foremost in mind and creating good public relations between the students and the citizens in the community. Possible locations for off-campus

FIGURE 2.12 Resources for Place-Based and People-Based Learning in the Community

airport	doctor's office	newspaper plant
apiary	farm/factory	observatory
aquarium	fire department	Olympic trials
archeological site	fish hatchery	park/nature area
art gallery	flea market	poetry reading
assembly plant	foreign embassy	police station
bakery	forest/preserve	post office
bird/wildlife sanctuary	freeway maintenance	recycling center
book publisher	gas company	retail store
botanical gardens	geological site	sanitation department
broadcasting station	hospital	sawmill
building razed	highway construction	shopping mall
canal lock	highway patrol site	shoreline
cemetery	historical sites	theater
chemical plant	legislature	town meeting
city council	levee/reservoir	universities
computer plant	library and archive	utility company
courthouse	mass transit site	warehouse
dairy	mine	water plant
dam and flood plain	museum	weather bureau
dock and harbor	Native American site	wetlands

FIGURE 2.13   Planning Place-Based Learning: A Field Trip

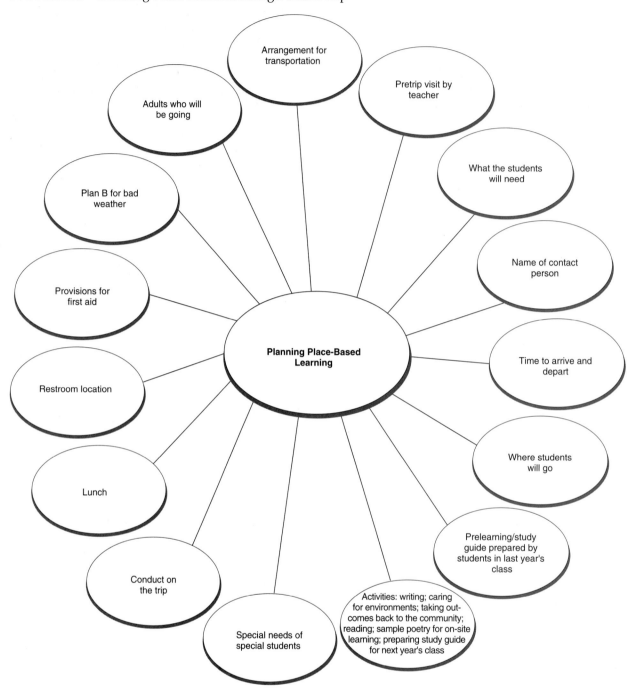

excursions for place-based learning/field trips and resource persons for people-based education are shown in Figure 2.12, Resources for Place-Based and People-Based Learning in the Community.

Off-campus excursions are often vital components to successful interdisciplinary thematic instruction. Preparing for and implementing a successful field trip requires three important stages of planning—before, during, and after. This in-

cludes making critical decisions; Figure 2.13 will help you and the students consider some of those decisions.

After Place-Based Learning

All sorts of follow-up learning experiences can be planned as an educational wrap-up to this valuable, firsthand experience. For instance, the students can

FACTS ON PRAXIS AND OTHER TEACHER TESTS

Currently, many teacher candidates are interested in teacher education tests, especially the Praxis Series Tests, as a part of the teacher credentialing process. As mentioned in Chapter 1, these tests reflect current educational research and important tasks and skills required of teachers. Some tests include classroom-related performance assessments that focus on writing essays, oral response tasks, listening tasks, portfolio reviews, interview/video stimuli, and in-class observations. Related to that focus, this text reflects knowledge and planning skills that are needed for teaching performance and in-class observations and reflect one way to initiate, develop, and teach an ITU. To support this professional interest, all chapters in this guide offer selected exercises to assist teachers interested in interdisciplinary instruction.

divide into bulletin board committees to plan and prepare an attractive display to summarize the trip. Additionally, the students can write about their own experiences in their journals or as papers. Small groups can give oral reports to the class about what they did and learned. Their reports can then serve as springboards for further class discussion. The group can prepare study brochures or field guides to be given to the students in next year's class. Finally, for future planning, all who were involved should contribute to an assessment of the experience.

SHARING MATERIALS BEFORE AND DURING UNIT IMPLEMENTATION

Whether you include place-based education in your ITU or not, you may find it of value to give a copy of your unit to a colleague for comments and suggestions about the unit, including any suggestions about print and nonprint materials and other resources. If you are working independently on the ITU, you realize that your unit cannot function without materials, and so you must plan for the resources that are needed—including media equipment, references, reading materials, and community resources. If most of your colleague's remarks are positive, you will know that the unit you planned appears workable from another's point of view. If there are difficulties, you may want to consider more modifications in the ITU.

When working as a team, it is useful for each member to provide other team members with two copies of his/her draft unit. Each member then reviews the draft copies of other members, particularly examining a member's attention to the organization of the materials—media equipment and materials, reference books, reading sources, resource people, and other community resources. Each member then returns a copy with comments and suggestions to the other members, keeping the other copy to plan complementary lessons. Depending on the remarks and feedback from other team members, a member can have confidence in his or her plan or make modifications as needed.

SUMMARY

In this chapter, you read about ways to initiate units—including focusing on the approach the teachers selected in the chapter-opening vignette. Specifically, the roles of the teacher and students were considered further. Generally, you had an overview of selecting a theme to study and planning the scope and sequence of a unit. You were given examples of using guiding questions to isolate concept words and then using the concept words to write generalizations that represent knowledge related to the theme. You also read about learning experiences, the importance and value of using technology, and the community as resources. In one chapter exercise, you were asked to select a theme for a unit, formulate questions to guide the study, and select resources related to those questions. In another exercise, you collected information related to the scope and sequence of a unit in the classroom of your choice. This information built on the previous chapter—you'll recall that you were introduced to the purposes of integrating the curriculum, the levels of curriculum integration, theories that support curriculum integration, and some applications. In addition, you were introduced to what educators consider to be advantages and limitations of engaging the students of today's diverse and multicultural classrooms in learning experiences by way of curriculum integration and interdisciplinary thematic instruction. For more information about some successful ventures in teaching with ITUs, see *For Further Reading* at the end of the chapter.

IF A COLLEAGUE, COMMUNITY MEMBER, OR PARENT ASKS YOU ABOUT. . .

1. **Impact of standards.** If a colleague asked you to share any evidence you have that indicates that the national or state curriculum standards for the various content areas have made an impact on curriculum documents, what would you say? What standards do you know about that are being produced by teachers from schools in your local geographical area? How would you explain standards-based education to someone?

2. **Organizing instruction.** If a parent asked you to explain the value of organizing instruction into units, how would you respond? For a specific grade level, identify and describe criteria for selecting a theme for a unit of study. Related to this, mention some activities that could be used in the introductory phase of a unit.

3. **Presenting content.** If a colleague asked you to name additional resources you have found to enhance a teacher's implementation of the students' achievement cycle that includes a standards-based curriculum, performance objectives/tasks, assessment, and authentic learning, what resource would you suggest? You might consider *Smart Start II: Why Standards Matter* (New York: Fulcrum Resources, 2001) by Patte Barth and Ruth Mitchell. The authors encourage educators to tell everyone what students should know and be able to do, and then test what students know and can do. Then, educators are encouraged to make decisions about ways to ensure that students can do what is required by the standards. Also consider *Performance Assessment and Standards-Based Curricula: The Achievement Cycle* and *Performance Standards and Authentic Learning* (1998 and 1999, respectively, Eye of Education Publishing, 6 Depot Way West, Larchmont, NY 10538) by Allan A. Glatthorn and others.

4. **Using standards and testing.** If a colleague asked you if one set of standards was sufficient for a classroom, how would you respond? Note that with today's emphasis on curriculum standards and high-stakes proficiency testing, the challenge is to design standards and tests that are not so high that many students cannot reach them, nor so low that they become meaningless and risk boring students who learn more quickly. The reality is, for example, that on any middle school campus there are students doing algebra and geometry and students the same age who cannot do simple multiplication. The question can be restated in this way: for your area of the curriculum, is one set of standards sufficient or should there be multiple standards (such as a set of minimal standards and another set that will challenge the most capable)? Share your thoughts about this with your classmates.

5. **Using community resources.** If another teacher asked you about the value and use of community resources to your students' background knowledge and frame of reference for learning, how would you respond? Related to this, what useful ideas for community involvement in an ITU do you have to suggest to others in your group?

EXERCISE 2.1

Beginning an ITU: An Exercise in Collaboration

Instructions. The purpose of this exercise is to collaboratively work with a partner or partners to gain insight into selecting a theme for an ITU. First divide your class into partnerships representing elementary, middle, or high school interests and then have two or more partnerships work together. Each group is to decide the grade level for which their ITU will be suitable.

1. If appropriate, simulate a cooperative group structure, assigning the following roles to members in each group of partnerships. (If this is not desired, move on to Step 2.)

   Facilitator. The person responsible for seeing that every member gets the assistance that he or she needs.

   Checker. The person responsible for seeing that every member finishes his or her work for the day.

   Reporter. The person responsible for discussing what the group members learned during the final debriefing session held each day after group work.

2. The task is to select a theme for study just as the students in your classroom could self-select their lines of inquiry. Theme:

   What sources will you consult *before* you finally select a theme?

		Yes	No
a.	Curriculum standards for particular subjects	_____	_____
b.	State curriculum frameworks	_____	_____
c.	Local curriculum guides and documents	_____	_____
d.	Student texts and teacher's guide for texts	_____	_____
e.	Students' interests and questions	_____	_____
f.	Resources on the Internet	_____	_____
g.	Professional literature	_____	_____
h.	Other	_____	_____

3. Working individually, brainstorm as many word and phrase associations about the theme as possible. Write your theme in the center of the space provided and group your associations around the theme (i.e., construct a visual web). Then share your ideas with others in your group.

4. Join a small group or the total group and contribute the word and phrase associations from Step 3 to the common sharing of ideas. Have a volunteer write everyone's ideas in the form of a visual web, and then replicate the web in the space provided. Take notes on any discussion about it. Keep the web for reference as you continue your study of ITUs.

5. Ask any questions you have related to any of the words and phrases on the web. Assist the group members as they classify all members' questions into categories. Draw lines to connect any related categories and then label the categories with headings of your choice (thereby making the visual web a graphic of the theme). Sketch the categories and their labels in the space provided that follows or use another sheet of paper.

EXERCISE 2.2

Beginning an ITU: Investigating Specific Questions and Identifying Selected Resources

Instructions. The purpose of this exercise is to develop your skills in investigating specific questions and in selecting resources related to an ITU. For this exercise, use the theme and questions your group developed in Exercise 2.1.

1. *Questions.* From Exercise 2.1, select three (or more) questions about the group's theme that you would like to investigate.

   a.

   b.

   c.

   d.

2. *Disciplines.* Now focus on the interdisciplinary aspect of the unit by writing questions about the theme from the perspective of people from various disciplines. You might begin with the disciplines that are closely related to your theme. Ask yourself, "What would an anthropologist want to know about this theme? An artist? A biologist? A historian? A mathematician? A sociologist?" Writing these questions will help you determine how many subject areas you will incorporate in your thematic unit—a great many or just a few? Consult with others in your class if necessary.

   For each of the disciplines, review the following examples relating to an ITU you will examine in Chapter 5 called Migrations: Newcomers in North America. Use the examples to spur your own thinking about writing questions.

   Anthropologist: How have anthropologists (people who study how the people of a certain time and place act and what they believe in) helped us learn about the topic? How can we discover a relationship about the people's behavior and their beliefs?

   Artist: How can we show what we know about the topic through dance, literature, music, painting, sculpture? What contributions did artists (people with special skills and talents) make in the lives of early newcomers in North America?

   Historian: What contributions did history make in the lives of early people, explorers, and settlers? How have historians (people who study or write about past events) helped us learn about the topic? How has the acceptance or rejection of the idea of colonies changed through time?

   Mathematician: In what ways did early explorers and settlers use mathematics? In what way can we express what we know about the topic through mathematics? How have mathematicians (people who study numbers, quantities, shapes, measurement, and relationships of things to one another) helped us learn about this topic?

   Sociologist: What groups in society operate to bring us information about the topic? How have sociologists (people who study the way society works) contributed to the topic?

   Other:

3. *Concepts and big ideas.*   Reread your questions and underline words that represent concepts to be learned. What generalizations (big ideas) can be written related to this thematic study?

4. *Generalizations.*   Select one or more generalizations from Step 3. Then look at the student textbooks, teacher's manuals, and curriculum guidelines for your grade to see if your generalizations can be taught through the topic identified in any of these resources. What did you discover?

5. *Resources.*   For each question that you selected for further study (Step 1), identify the resources you could/would consult to investigate the question further. The resources can range from using the community as a laboratory to reading printed material. Make a list of the resources.

EXERCISE 2.3

Making Early Decisions: More about Scope and Sequence

Instructions. The purpose of this exercise is to begin identifying the scope and sequence plan of your interdisciplinary thematic unit. In your ITU plan, you want to incorporate the major concepts and generalizations that are in the curriculum guide for your grade level, plus the ones you identified in Exercise 2.2. You also need to make various decisions about grouping, unit length, unit structure, and disciplines to be included.

1. *Individual work and group work.* You might plan to have all types of groups in your thematic unit. For example, you could begin each elementary day or period with a theme and then have students work with partners or in small groups. As an alternative, you could invite students to participate in a whole-group study of the theme and ask students to request— and thus *reserve*—one area of related study for their individual inquiries. Write your decisions about individual work and group work:

2. *Length of study.* Your theme study can be of varying lengths. You may develop an ITU for a 2-week grading period or a 6-week grading period. You may plan four separate thematic units during the entire year, or you may plan for a different length of time of your choice. Write your decisions about the length of study:

3. *Concentrated structure and/or expanded structure.* You may decide on an expanded structure in which the students have common experiences in whole-group situations, and then select separate areas of study to explore as individual inquiries or small-group inquiries. Conversely, you could decide on a concentrated structure in which the students learn mainly in whole-group situations with some partnership and small-group work. In the concentrated structure, the students realize the ITU has a beginning and an end. Write your decisions about structure:

4. *Disciplines to include.* You may decide to include many subject areas or only a few. Write your decisions about disciplines:

CHAPTER NOTES

1. L. Sosniak, "The 9% Challenge: Education in School and Society," Teachers College Record (Online only, 2001, (http://www.tcrecord.org) ID Number: 10756, Date Accessed: 5/7/01).

2. G. O. Martin-Kniep, D. M. Feige, and L. C. Soodak, "Curriculum Integration: An Expanded View of an Abused Idea," *Journal of Curriculum and Supervision* 10(3), 227–249 (Spring 1995).

FOR FURTHER READING

Carr, J. F., & Harris, D. E. (2001). *Succeeding with standards: Linking curriculum, assessment, and action planning.* Alexandria, VA: Association of Supervision and Curriculum Development.

Danielson, C. (1996). *Enhancing professional practice: A framework for teaching.* Alexandria, VA: Association for Supervision and Curriculum Development.

Dever, M. T., & Jared, E. J. (1996, March). Remember to include arts and crafts in your integrated curriculum. *Young Children, 51*(3), 69–73.

Hargreaves, A., & Moore, S. (2000, Winter). Curriculum integration and classroom relevance: A study of teachers' practice. *Journal of Curriculum and Supervision, 15*(2), 89–112.

International Society for Technology in Education. (2000). *National educational technology standards for students: Connecting curriculum and technology.* Eugene, OR: Author.

Martens, M., & Anderson, M. (2000). *Teaching American diplomacy using primary sources. The establishment of Israel.* Denver, CO: Center for Teaching International Relations, University of Denver.

Mayer, R. H. (1999, May/June). Use the story of Anne Hutchinson to teach historical thinking. *Social Studies, 90*(3), 105–109.

Miles, M., & Schuster, H. (2000). *Teaching American diplomacy using primary sources. The expansion of NATO.* Denver, CO: Center for Teaching International Relations, University of Denver.

Post, T. R., et al. (1997). *Interdisciplinary approaches to curriculum: Themes for teaching.* Upper Saddle River, NJ: Merrill/Prentice Hall.

Shaw, D. G., & Dybdahl, C. S. (1996). *Integrating science and language arts: A sourcebook for K–6 teachers.* Boston: Allyn & Bacon.

Shoemaker, B. J. E. (1989). *Integrative education: A curriculum for the twenty-first century.* Eugene, OR: Oregon School Study Council.

Sunal, C. S., & Sunal, D. W. (1996, March/April). Interdisciplinary social studies and science lessons with a Native American theme. *Social Studies, 87*(2), 72–88.

Thompson, S. (2001, January). The authentic standards movement and its evil twin. *Phi Delta Kappan, 82*(5), 358–362.

Wineburg, S., & Grossman, P. (Eds.). (2000). *Interdisciplinary curriculum: Challenges to implementation.* New York: Teachers College Press.

NOTES

CHAPTER 3

Developing Objectives

I can still remember—or at least believe I can remember—that this experience (seeing a compass needle always turn north) made a deep and lasting impression on me.

—Albert Einstein

INTERDISCIPLINARY THEMATIC UNIT EXAMPLE FOR PRIMARY GRADE STUDENTS: THEME, CHANGES, TOPIC, CHROMATOGRAPHY

Just as the experience of seeing a compass needle turn north made an impression on Einstein, a third-grade teacher anticipated that the experience of separating mixtures into various colored layers (chromatography) to emphasize the theme of changes would make an impression on the students. In this situation, the ITU about changes included a number of multidisciplinary activities related to chromatography. To initiate the unit, the teacher captured the students' attention with the development of a question map, a useful way to initiate an ITU. The students' questions lead to the initial activity in which the students tested the colors of water-soluble ink markers and made predictions about the separations of their colors. To begin, they tested the ink of a green marker (blue and yellow), the ink of an orange marker (red and yellow), the ink of a purple marker (red and blue), and the ink of other markers selected by the students. They recorded their predictions and results on data sheets with headings similar to the following:

Ink I Used   What I Predicted   What I Observed
1. green
2. orange
3. purple
4. other

To test the colors of the inks, the students used long strips of paper towels. They folded the top of each strip so that it hung from the rim of a plastic drinking glass and so the bottom of each strip almost touched the inside bottom of the glass. When the strips were folded to the correct length, the students marked a band of color about 2 inches up from the bottom of each strip. After placing a marked strip in a glass, students added about an inch of water, 0.5 inch or more below the color band and enough to cover about 0.25 inch of the bottom of the paper strip. The students then observed what happened as the water moved up the strip (by capillary action) and into, through, and above the colored band, and recorded the results of their observations on their data sheets.

Following are additional examples of how the teacher and the students connected the beginning activity to other disciplines:

• *Art.* Students put colors of ink markers on coffee filters and repeated the initial experiment by using the filters. They then cut different shapes from the filters to mount on a class chart to demonstrate what colors the different inks separated into during their experiments. Additional shapes of insects and animals that used camouflage in their environments, verified by individual student research, also were cut from the filters and glued to a class mural paper. Drawings around the shapes were added by the students to camouflage the creatures and to show the effectiveness or lack of effectiveness that some of the colors might have in protecting living things from danger. *Links to standards:* listen and participate for personal fulfillment and to build an understanding of the use of the arts.

• *Ecology.* Students in dyads, small groups, and individually participated in further study about rain forest habitats and the camouflage used by living creatures there. *Links to standards:* constructing and applying science ideas; using variety of instructional formats like pairs, triads, small groups; communicating science ideas with others.

• *History.* Some students researched individuals in history who had in some way or another been protected by camouflage. One example was the "mossbackers" of Civil War days—the people who hid in the southern swamps to avoid conscription. *Links to standards:* constructing and applying ideas related to history/social sciences studies; communicating ideas from history/social sciences with others.

• *Language arts.* The students were presented with a fictional situation in which spots of a foreign material were found on a piece of clothing; then the students created a mystery/detective story about it. *Links to standards:* apply knowledge of language, spelling, capitalization, punctuation, figurative language, and media techniques to create/critique writing.

• *Science.* The teacher planned further instruction by using a learning center and journal writing with a sequence of activities that focused on the theme. Additional experiments were available at the learning center and the students recorded their observations and discussed what they wrote: *Experiment #1*: Students placed celery in food dye to observe the movement of molecules and note capillary action; *Experiment #2*: Students used litmus paper to determine if a substance was acidic or basic; *Experiment #3*: Students learned the technique of marbleizing paper to observe actions; *Experiment #4*: Students placed drops of primary colors of food dye in a clear glass bowl of water on the overhead projector stage and wrote their predictions; then they mixed the drops and observed the primary colors turn into secondary ones; they first mixed blue and yellow, then red and yellow, then red and blue; *Experiment #5*: Students observed items through red, yellow, and blue cellophane lenses in eyeglasses they constructed from heavy artpaper frames. They made predictions about what would happen to the color of the items when seen through the different cellophane lenses. They tested their predictions and recorded their results on a journal page with the following headings:

Colored Item I Selected	What I Predicted	What I Observed
1.	1.	1.
2.	2.	2.
3.	3.	3.

Links to standards: to focus on student use of knowledge; give opportunity for discussion/debate; assess student understanding; allow work with others; lead students to inquiry; provide for discussion and debate; focus on student understanding and use of scientific knowledge.[1]

• *Literature.* Literature was introduced that was related to the ITU. For current classes, here are some choices: *Wart Hogs Paint: A Messy Color Book* by Pamela Edwards (New York: Hyperion, 2001) could be presented so the students could see how the fictional wart hog-artists use three primary colors to create green, orange, and purple to paint a colorful rainbow on a blank white kitchen wall in their house. A second title, *My World of Color* (Hyperion, 2002) by M. W. Brown, could be displayed to introduce children to different colors. *Links to standards:* read a range of literature and texts—fiction, nonfiction, classic, contemporary—to build understanding of the experiences of others and to acquire new information.

CHAPTER INTRODUCTION

In this chapter, you will further define aims, goals, and objectives; prepare performance (outcome-based) objectives; and focus further on selecting resources for an ITU. You will become familiar with standards-based education, performance outcomes, the domains of learning, and the value of character education, and will consider the developmental needs of students you teach. You will be encouraged to observe for meaningful learning and to use logs, journals, and portfolios for assessment. If appropriate, you can participate with others to develop a question map to initiate a unit and then use the questions to identify concept words for the unit. Also, you will learn to recognize verbs that are acceptable for writing overt objectives and to recognize objectives that are measurable. You will be asked to identify criterion-referenced objectives and to assess objectives among the three domains. For more complete information on learning activities that match your objectives and are suitable for ITUs, turn to Chapter 5.

CLARIFYING AIMS, GOALS, AND OBJECTIVES

Once you have identified your theme and some of its related topics and subtopics, you need to identify specific performance expectations—what students will be expected to do as a result of learning experiences of the ITU. These performance expectations are stated as specific instructional objectives, known also as performance, behavioral, or terminal objectives. (The term *terminal* is sometimes used to distinguish between instructional objectives that are intermediate and those that are final, or "terminal," to an area of learning.) Instructional objectives are statements describing what the student will be able to do upon completion of the instructional experience.

As a teacher, you frequently will encounter the compound structure that reads "goals and objectives," as you likely found in the curriculum documents that you reviewed for Chapter 2. This is a distinction that needs to be understood. To distinguish the difference between goals and objectives, first consider your intent. To do this, consider that goals are ideals that you intend to reach, that is, ideals that you would like to accomplish. Goals may be stated as teacher goals, as student goals, or collaboratively as team goals. Ideally, in all three the goal is the same. If, for example, the goal is to improve students' reading skills, it could be stated as follows: "To help students develop their reading skills" (teacher or course goal) or "To improve my reading skills" (student goal).

Educational goals are general statements of intent and are prepared during the first phase of decision making and ITU planning (see Chapter 1). (Note: although some writers use the phrase "general goals and objectives," it is incorrect usage.) Goals are general; objectives are specific. Goals are useful when planned cooperatively with students and/or when shared with students as advance mental organizers to establish a mindset about what is to be studied. The students then know what to expect and will begin to prepare mentally to learn it. From the goals, objectives are prepared. Objectives are *not* intentions. They are the actual behaviors that students are expected to display. In short, objectives are what students do.

The most general educational objectives are often called aims; the objectives of schools, curricula, and courses are called **goals;** the objectives of units and lessons are called **instructional objectives. Aims** are more general than goals, goals are more general then objectives. Instructional objectives are quite specific. Aims, goals, and objectives represent the targets, from general to specific statements of learning expectations, to which curriculum is designed and instruction is aimed.

RELATING INSTRUCTIONAL OBJECTIVES TO ALIGNED CURRICULUM AND AUTHENTIC ASSESSMENT

As implied in the preceding section, goals guide the instructional methods; objectives drive student performance. Assessment of student achievement in learning should be an assessment of that perfor-

mance. When the assessment procedure does match the instructional objectives, the assessment is referred to as aligned or **authentic** (discussed further in Chapter 4). When objectives, instruction, and assessment match the stated goals we have what is referred to as an aligned curriculum.

Goals are general statements, usually not even complete sentences and often beginning with the infinitive "to," that identify what the teacher intends the students to learn. Objectives, stated in performance terms, are specific actions and should be written as complete sentences that include the verb "will" *to indicate what each student is expected to be able to do as a result of the instructional experience.* The last part of the previous sentence is emphasized because one of the most common errors made by beginning teachers when writing instructional objectives for their unit and lesson plans is to state what they, the teachers, intend to do rather than what the anticipated student performance is.

Although instructional goals may not always be quantifiable (that is, really measurable), instructional objectives should be measurable. Furthermore, those objectives become the essence of what is measured for in instruments designed to assess student learning; they are the learning targets. Consider the examples shown in Figure 3.1.

CLARIFYING GOAL INDICATORS AND STANDARDS-BASED EDUCATION

One purpose of writing objectives in performance terms is to be able to assess with precision whether the instruction has resulted in the desired behavior. In many schools the educational goals are established as learning targets, competencies that the students are expected to achieve and that are derived from the district and state curriculum standards. These learning targets are then divided into performance objectives, sometimes referred to as goal indicators. Instruction is designed to teach toward those objectives. When the students perform the competencies called for by these objectives, their education is considered successful. This is known variously as **criterion-referenced,** competency-based, performance-based, results-driven, or outcome-based education. When the objectives are aligned with specific curriculum standards, as they usually are (or should be), then it can also be referred to as standards-based education. Expecting students to achieve one set of competencies before moving on to the next set is called **mastery learning.** The success of the student achievement, teacher performance, and school may each be assessed according to these criteria.

FIGURE 3.1   Example of Goals, Objectives, and Links to Standards

---

Goals

1. To acquire knowledge about the geologic history of the Earth.

2. To develop an appreciation for music.

3. To develop enjoyment for reading.

Objectives

1. On an Earth's geologic time line map, the student will identify the time that the dinosaurs were the dominant creatures on Earth.

2. The students will identify 10 different musical instruments by listening to a tape recording of the Boston Pops Symphony Orchestra and identify which instrument is being played at specific times as determined by the teacher.

3. Within a 2-month period, the student will read two books, three short stories, and five newspaper articles at home and will maintain a daily written journal log of these activities.

Links of Standards

1. Science: focus on student use of knowledge, opportunity for discussion/debate, assess student understanding, work with others.

2. Arts: listen and participate for personal fulfillment and to build an understanding of the arts in the world's cultures.

3. English/Language Arts: read a range of literature and texts (fiction, nonfiction, classic, contemporary) to build understanding of the human experience and to acquire new information about needs/demands of society and cultures of the world.

CONSIDERING OVERT AND COVERT PERFORMANCE OUTCOMES

Assessment of student learning is not difficult to accomplish when the desired performance outcome is overt behavior—that is, when it can be observed directly. Each of the sample objectives shown in Figure 3.1 is an example of an objective that is overt. Assessment is more difficult when the desired behavior is covert, that is, when it is not directly observable. Although certainly no less important, behaviors that call for "appreciation," "discovery," or "understanding," for example, are not directly observable because they occur within a person and so are covert behaviors. Since covert behavior cannot be observed directly, the only way to tell whether the objective has been achieved is to observe behavior that may be indicative of that achievement. The objective, then, is written in overt language, and evaluators can only assume or trust that the observed behavior is, in fact, reasonably close to being indicative of the expected learning outcome.

CONSIDERING PERFORMANCE OUTCOMES—ASSESSMENT COMPATIBILITY

When assessing the extent to which an objective has been achieved—that learning has occurred—the assessment device must be consistent with the desired learning outcome. Otherwise, the assessment is not aligned: it is invalid. When the measuring device and the learning objective are compatible, we say that the assessment is authentic. For example, a person's competency to teach specific skills in mathematics to seventh graders is best (i.e., with highest reliability) measured by directly observing that person *doing* that very thing—teaching specific skills in mathematics to seventh graders. Using a standardized paper-and-pencil test to determine a person's ability to teach specific math skills to seventh grade students is *not* authentic assessment. As another example, a person's competency to teach a particular phonics lesson to first graders is best (i.e., with highest reliability) measured by directly observing that person *doing* that very thing—teaching a particular phonics lesson to first graders. Using a standardized paper-and-pencil test of multiple-choice items to determine a person's ability to teach a phonics lesson to first-grade students is *not* authentic assessment. In either instance, you might note that the particular multiple-choice item assessment device might indeed be valid (the degree to which it measures that which it is intended to measure)—but it is not **authentic.**

CONSIDERING BALANCE OF BEHAVIORISM AND CONSTRUCTIVISM

While behaviorists **(behaviorism)** assume a definition of learning that deals only with changes in overt behavior, constructivists **(constructivism** or cognitism) hold that learning entails the building, construction, or reshaping of mental schemata and that mental processes mediate learning and so are concerned with both overt and covert behaviors.[2] Does this mean that you must be one or the other, a behaviorist or a constructivist? Probably not. For now, as you read this guide about developing ITUs, an initial point is that when writing instructional objectives, you should write most (or all) of your basic expectations (minimal competency anticipations, educational desires, lesson benefits) in overt terms. The next section has more on this topic to assist you. A second point is that you'll realize that you cannot be expected to foresee *all* learning that occurs nor be able to translate all that is learned into performance terms—most certainly not before it occurs.

TEACHING TOWARD MULTIPLE OBJECTIVES, UNDERSTANDINGS, AND APPRECIATIONS; THE REALITY OF CLASSROOM INSTRUCTION

Any effort to write *all* learning objectives in performance terms can result, in effect, in a neglect of the individual learner for whom it is supposed to be concerned. Why? Such an approach does not allow for diversity among learners. Learning that is most meaningful to the individual student is not so neatly written or easily predicted or isolated for every lesson. Rather than teaching one objective at a time, much of the time you are encouraged to direct your teaching toward the simultaneous learning of multiple objectives, understandings, and appreciations. Even though you may be interested in the approach of the students' simultaneous learning of many ob-

jectives, it is suggested that when you assess for learning, you assess one objective at a time so your focus is direct and clear about what is being learned.

Learning That Is Not Immediately Observable

Unlike behaviorists, constructivists do not limit the definition of learning to observable behavior; nor should you. As a teacher, your responsibility is to provide learning experiences that will result in the creation of new schemata as well as the modification of existing schemata.

To be effective, the challenge is to use performance-based criteria but to simultaneously use a teaching style that encourages the development of intrinsic sources of student motivation and that allows, provides, and encourages coincidental learning—learning that goes beyond what might be considered predictable, immediately measurable, and representative of minimal expectations.

It has become quite clear to many teachers that to be most effective in helping students to develop meaningful understandings, learning can be integrated within the whole curriculum. This means that the learning related to each discipline is made more effective, longer lasting, and more meaningful to the lives of the students in an approach such as an interdisciplinary thematic unit.

For higher levels of thinking and for learning that is most meaningful and longest lasting, the results of research support using (a) a curriculum where disciplines are integrated and (b) instructional techniques that involve the learners in social interactive learning, such as project-centered learning, cooperative learning, peer tutoring, and cross-age teaching—all techniques that can be incorporated into an ITU.

Integrated Curriculum in a Standards-Based Environment

It is still too early to collect a large amount of reliable data on how students in integrated curriculum programs fare on mandatory statewide standardized proficiency tests. However, it should be reassuring to today's classroom teacher to know that from their analysis of recent data, researchers Vars and Beane conclude that "almost without exception, students in any type of interdisciplinary or integrative curriculum do as well as, and often better than, students in a conventional departmentalized program. These results hold whether the combined curriculum is taught by one teacher in a self-contained or block-time class or by an interdisciplinary team."[3]

PREPARING INSTRUCTIONAL OBJECTIVES

When preparing instructional objectives, you must ask yourself, "How is the student to demonstrate that the objective has been reached?" or "What student performance will indicate that the objective has been achieved?" The objective must include an action that demonstrates whether the objective has been achieved. Inherited from behaviorism, this portion of the objective is sometimes called the terminal behavior or the anticipated measurable performance.

Writing Objectives: Key Components

When written in behavioral terms, an instructional objective has four key components: audience, behavior, conditions, and degree of expected performance. To help you understand and remember, you can refer to these as the ABCDs of writing performance objectives.

In the ABCDs of writing objectives, the letter **A** stands for the audience—the student for whom the objective is intended. To address this aspect, sometimes teachers begin their objectives with the phrase, *The student will be able to,* or, to personalize the objective, *You will be able to.* (Note: to conserve space, in examples that follow we eliminate *be able to* and write simply *The student will.* For greater brevity, writers of objectives sometimes use the abbreviation TSWBAT for *The student will be able to*).

The letter **B** is for the expected behavior and should be written with verbs that are measurable, that is, with action verbs to allow direct observation when an objective has been reached. As discussed, some verbs are vague, ambiguous, and not clearly measurable. When writing objectives, you should avoid verbs that are not clearly measurable—verbs that are covert such as *appreciate, comprehend,* and *understand* (see Figure 3.2).

In contrast to the verbs to avoid in Figure 3.2, return to the three examples of objectives given in Figure 3.1. You'll see that in objectives 1 and 2, the behaviors are action-oriented and the verbs are overt—"will identify." For objective 3, the verbs/behaviors

are "will read and maintain." To assess and further understand how to select verbs for objectives, complete Exercise 3.1.

The letter **C** is for the third ingredient of objectives, conditions, and includes the setting in which the behavior will be demonstrated by the students and observed by the teacher. For the three sample objectives in Figure 3.1, the conditions are "on a map," "by listening to a tape recording of the Boston Pops Symphony Orchestra," "specified times as determined by the teacher," and " at home within a 2-month period."

Lastly, the letter **D** stands for two components, that is, the degree or level of expected performance and the design of an objective that a teacher declares to be a link to school district, state, or national standards. The degree or level of expected performance and determined link to standards are not always included in objectives written by teachers. For example, when mastery learning is expected (often achievement of 85 percent to 100 percent), the level of expected performance is usually omitted (because it is understood). In teaching for mastery learning, the performance-level expectation is 100 percent. In reality, however, the performance level will most likely be between 85 percent and 95 percent, particularly when working with a cohort of students rather than with an individual student. The 5 percent to 15 percent difference allows for human error, as can occur when using written and oral communication. Additionally, the design of a particular objective that is determined to be a link to standards is not always indicated by teachers—especially in educational situations where the standards that are accepted/adopted by the district or state are understood to be an ongoing educational basis for teaching and thus connected to all objectives focused on in the classroom. Now do Exercise 3.2 to reinforce your comprehension and recognition of the components of a performance objective.

Performance level is used to assess student achievement and sometimes to evaluate the effectiveness of the instruction. When given, student grades might be based on performance levels, and evaluation of teacher effectiveness might be based on the level of student performance. Now do Exercise 3.3 to try your skill at recognizing objectives that are measurable.

FIGURE 3.2 Verbs to Avoid When Writing Overt Objectives

appreciate	familiarize	learn
believe	grasp	like
comprehend	indicate	realize
enjoy	know	understand

REVIEWING DOMAINS OF LEARNING AND THE DEVELOPMENTAL NEEDS OF STUDENTS

Educators attempt to design learning experiences to meet the five areas of developmental needs of the total child: intellectual, physical, emotional/psychological, social, and moral/ethical.

Classifying Instructional Objectives

When planning instructional objectives, it is useful to consider the three domains of learning objectives: **cognitive domain**—involves mental operations from the lowest level of simple recall of information to complex, high-level evaluative processes; **affective domain**—involves attitudes, feelings, and values, and ranges from the lower level of acquisition to the highest level of internalization and action; and **psychomotor domain**—ranges from the simple manipulation of materials to the communication of ideas and, finally, to the highest level of creative performance and includes gross/fine motor control. Whereas the intellectual needs are primarily within the cognitive domain and the physical needs are within the psychomotor domain, the other three areas of developmental needs (emotional/psychological, social, and moral/ethical) are mostly within the affective domain.

Too frequently, teachers focus on the cognitive domain while assuming that the psychomotor and affective domains will take care of themselves. Some experts argue that teachers should do just the opposite: that when the affective domain is considered directly, the psychomotor and cognitive domains naturally develop. In our opinion (we have no strong research basis for this opinion), the use of integrated thematic instruction not only allows but encourages this situation to happen; as the affective domain is considered, the psychomotor and cognitive domains develop.

As we shall emphasize later in this chapter, the preceding information is not to imply the imposition of an inflexible learning hierarchy. It is intended to indicate that there are levels of learning, but recent research about learning indicates that students can be engaged in higher-order thinking about a topic right from the start, as opposed to being guided from the lowest to the highest levels of operation within each domain.[4] That is the reason so many teachers today structure their thematic units around key ideas and central questions designed to encourage student inquiry and self-directed learning. It is the basis for curriculum integration, problem-based learning, and project-oriented teaching. Regardless of the name given to the method of helping students to interlink and correlate ideas across content areas, the intent is to facilitate the union of their experiences with knowledge. Learning is complex and not so neatly compartmentalized as this text may seem to imply.

The three domains are discussed next to guide your understanding of each of the five areas of need. Notice the illustrated verbs within each hierarchy. These verbs will help you fashion objectives when developing your ITUs and lessons. Be aware, however, that considerable overlap occurs among the levels at which some action verbs may be appropriately used. For example, the verb *identifies* is appropriate in each of the following objectives at different levels within the cognitive domain:

- Knowledge level: The student will identify the correct definition of the term *osmosis.*
- Comprehension level: The student will identify examples of the principle of osmosis.
- Application level: The student will identify the osmotic effect when a cell is immersed into a hypotonic solution.
- Analysis level: The student will identify the osmotic effect on pressure when the cell is placed in a hypotonic solution.

Cognitive Domain

In a widely accepted taxonomy of objectives, Bloom and his associates arranged cognitive objectives into classifications according to the complexity of the skills and abilities they embodied.[5] The result was a ladder ranging from the simplest to the most complex intellectual processes. (Theoretically within each domain, prerequisite to a student's ability to function at one particular level of the hierarchy is the ability to function at the preceding level or levels.) In other words, when a student is functioning at the third level of the cognitive domain, that student is automatically also functioning at the first and second levels. Rather than an orderly progression from simple to complex mental operations as illustrated by Bloom's taxonomy, other researchers prefer an organization of cognitive abilities that ranges from simple information storage and retrieval, through a higher level of discrimination and concept attainment, to the highest cognitive ability to recognize and solve problems.[6]

Working independently, the teacher takes the time to review content and skills-teaching.

The six major categories (or levels) in Bloom's taxonomy of cognitive objectives are (1) knowledge—recognizing and recalling information, (2) comprehension—understanding the meaning of information, (3) application—using information, (4) analysis—dissecting information into its component parts to comprehend their relationships, (5) synthesis—putting components together to generate new ideas, and (6) evaluation—judging the worth of an idea, notion, theory, thesis, proposition, information, or opinion. In this taxonomy, the top four categories or levels—application, analysis, synthesis, and evaluation—represent what are called higher-order thinking skills, as are the higher categories of the affective and psychomotor domains.[7] Although space does not allow elaboration here, Bloom's taxonomy includes various subcategories within each of these six major categories. For reasons implied in the previous section, it is our opinion that it is less important that an objective be absolutely classified than it is to be cognizant of hierarchies of thinking and doing and to understand the importance of attending to student intellectual behavior from lower to higher levels of operation in all three domains. Discussion of each of Bloom's six categories follows.

Knowledge. The basic element in Bloom's taxonomy concerns the acquisition of knowledge—the ability to recognize and recall information. Although this is the lowest of the six categories, the information to be learned may not itself be of a low level. In fact, it may be of an extremely high level. Bloom includes here knowledge of principles, generalizations, theories, structures, and methodologies, and knowledge of facts and ways of dealing with facts. Action verbs appropriate for this category include *choose, complete, define, describe, identify, indicate, list, locate, match, name, outline, recall, recognize, select,* and *state.* Following are two example objectives at the knowledge level. Note especially the verb component in italics used in each example.

- From memory, the student *will recall* the letters in the English alphabet that are vowels.
- The student *will name* the positions of players on a soccer team. (Note: for additional sample objectives at various levels within each of the three domains, see the sample lesson plan in Chapter 5, Figure 5.5).

The remaining five categories of Bloom's taxonomy of the cognitive domain deal with the use of knowledge. They encompass the educational objectives aimed at developing cognitive skills and abilities including comprehension, application, analysis, synthesis, and evaluation of knowledge.

Comprehension. Comprehension includes the ability to translate, explain, or interpret knowledge and to extrapolate from it to address new situations. Action verbs appropriate for this category include *change, classify, convert,* and the other related verbs listed in Figure 3.3. Following are examples of objectives in this category:

- From a sentence, the student *will recognize* the letters that are vowels in the English alphabet.
- The student *will recognize* the positions of players on a soccer team.

Application. Once learners understand information, they should be able to apply it. Action verbs in this category of operation include *compute, demonstrate, develop,* and others seen in Figure 3.3. Following are examples of objectives in this category:

- The student *will use* in a sentence a word that contains at least two vowels.
- The student *will relate* how the positions of players on a soccer team depend upon each other.

Analysis. This category includes objectives that require learners to use the skills of examining something to distinguish its parts, components, or elements separately or consider the relationship of each to the whole. Action verbs suitable for this category include *analyze, break down, categorize,* and the other related terms in Figure 3.3. Following are examples of objectives in this category.

- From a list of words, the student will differentiate between words that contain single vowel sounds and those that do not.
- Using a writing board, the student will illustrate the different positions of players on a soccer team.

Synthesis. This category of synthesis—combining parts of elements to form a whole or combining simple concepts into complex conceptions—includes objectives that involve such skills as designing a plan, proposing a set of operations, or deriving a series of abstract relationships. Action verbs appropriate for synthesis include *arrange, categorize, compile,* and others listed in Figure 3.3. Following are examples of objectives in this category:

- The student *will rearrange* a list of words into several lists (synthesize whole lists) according to the vowel sounds contained in each.
- Using the writing board, the student *will illustrate* an offensive plan (synthesize whole plan) that uses the different positions of players on a soccer team.

Evaluation. The highest category of Bloom's cognitive taxonomy, evaluation, includes offering opinions and making value judgments. Action verbs

FIGURE 3.3   Examples of Verbs for Bloom's Categories

1. Knowledge Verbs					
choose	complete	define	describe	identify	indicate
list	locate	match	name	outline	recall

2. Comprehension Verbs					
change	classify	convert	defend	estimate	expand
explain	generalize	infer	interpret	paraphrase	predict

3. Application Verbs					
apply	calculate	demonstrate	develop	discover	modify
operate	participate	perform	plan	predict	relate

4. Analysis Verbs					
analyze	break down	categorize	compare	contrast	debate
deduce	diagram	differentiate	identify	illustrate	outline

5. Synthesis Verbs					
arrange	categorize	combine	compile	constitute	create
design	develop	devise	document	explain	formulate
generate	modify	organize	originate	plan	produce
rearrange	reconstruct	revise	rewrite	summarize	synthesize

6. Evaluation Verbs					
appraise	argue	assess	compare	conclude	consider
contrast	criticize	decide	evaluate	explain	interpret
judge	justify	rank	rate	relate	standardize

appropriate for this category include *appraise, argue, assess,* and the other related verbs listed in Figure 3.3. Following are examples of objectives in this category.

- The student *will listen to and evaluate* other students' identification of vowels from words in sentences written on the board.
- The student *will interpret* the reasons for an opposing team's offensive use of the different positions of players on a soccer team.

Affective Domain

Bloom, along with Krathwohl and Masia, developed a useful taxonomy of the affective domain.[8] Following are the major levels or categories from least internalized to most internalized. (1) *receiving*—being aware of the affective stimulus and beginning to have favorable feelings toward it; (2) *responding*—taking an interest in the stimulus and viewing it favorably; (3) *valuing*—showing a tentative belief in the value of the affective stimulus and becoming committed to it; (4) *organizing*—placing values into a system of dominant and supporting values; and

(5) *internalizing*—demonstrating behavior and consistent beliefs that have become a way of life. Although one category considerably overlaps another within the affective domain, these categories give a basis by which to judge the quality of objectives and the nature of learning within these areas. A discussion of each of the five categories follows.

Receiving.   At the receiving level, which is the least internalized, the learner exhibits willingness to give attention to particular phenomena or stimuli, and the teacher is able to arouse, sustain, and direct that attention. Action verbs appropriate for this category include *ask, choose, differentiate,* and others found in Figure 3.4. Examples of objectives at this level are

- The student *will describe* another person's position on biological evolution.
- The student *will identify* examples of sensitivity shown to others related to their concerns.

Responding.   At the responding level, learners respond to the stimulus they have received. They may do so because of some external pressure, because

FIGURE 3.4 Examples of Verbs for the Affective Domain

---

1. Receiving Verbs

ask	choose	describe	differentiate	distinguish	hold
identify	locate	name	point to	recall	recognize

2. Responding Verbs

answer	applaud	approve	assist	command	comply
discuss	greet	help	label	perform	play
practice	read	recite	report	select	tell

3. Valuing Verbs

argue	complete	describe	explain	follow	form
initiate	invite	join	justify	propose	protest
read	report	select	share	study	support

4. Organizing Verbs

adhere	alter	arrange	balance	combine	compare
defend	identify	integrate	modify	order	organize

5. Internalizing Verbs

act	complete	display	influence	listen	perform
practice	propose	qualify	question	revise	serve

---

they find the stimulus interesting, or because responding gives them satisfaction. Action verbs appropriate for this category include *answer, applaud, approve,* and other related verbs shown in Figure 3.4. Following are examples of objectives at this level:

- The student *will discuss* the messages of others and restate in his/her own words what they have said.
- The student *will cooperate* with others during group activities.

Valuing.   Objectives at the valuing level deal with the learner's beliefs, attitudes, and appreciations. The simplest objectives concern the acceptance of beliefs and values; the higher ones involve learning to prefer certain values and finally becoming committed to them. Action verbs appropriate for this level include *argue, assist, complete,* and others found in Figure 3.4. Following are examples of objectives in this category:

- The student *supports* a position of her/his choice on a selected issue.
- The student *argues* a position of his/her choice on a selected issue.

Organizing.   The next level in the affective domain concerns the building of a personal value system. Here, the learner is conceptualizing and arranging values into a system that recognizes their relative importance. Action verbs appropriate for this level include *adhere, arrange, balance,* and other related verbs found in Figure 3.4. Following are examples of objectives in this category:

- The student *integrates* her/his values into a personal work ethic.
- The student *defends* some important selected values of a particular subculture.

Internalizing.   The last and highest category within the affective domain, internalizing, is the level at which the learner's behaviors have become consistent with his or her beliefs. Action verbs appropriate for this level include *act, complete, display,* and others in Figure 3.4. Following are examples of objectives in this category:

- The student *practices* accurate verbal and nonverbal communication.
- The student *performs* independently.

Behaviors and Beliefs.   As an example of students performing independently and practicing verbal communication in the category of internalizing that blends well with teaching an ITU, a teacher can introduce the strategy of "Classroom Mailbox: Attitudes, Feelings, and Values Feedback" to the students in the classroom. There are several steps in this activity:

1. **Initiate classroom mailbox.** To begin the activity for third-grade students and older, the teacher places a classroom mailbox (large cardboard box or file folder) in a convenient place and when a student complains about another or praises another for a kind or good action, the teacher suggests that the student write about the other student and place the praise/complaint in the classroom mailbox.

2. **Initiate guidelines.** The teacher reminds the students that the writing must follow formal letter writing guidelines (e.g., guidelines the teacher has displayed in the room on a chart and reviewed with the class on the first day the teacher introduced the mailbox activity) and must be in legible handwriting. Guidelines for formal letter writing for the mailbox can include the following *who, what, when, where,* and *how* elements: (1) *who* was involved; (2) *what* happened, *when* it happened, and *where* it happened; and (3) *how* the writer suggests the student be recognized in a positive way for this good behavior; *how* this complaint/incident can be avoided during the school year; or *how* the writer suggests that the teacher/principal handle the complaint and/or similar ones in the future?

3. **Initiate follow-up.** The teacher should plan to follow-up on the written letters at the end of the day or on a following day—perhaps a discussion to go over the elements of who, what, when, where, and how as well as ways to suggest a positive reaction for someone's good behavior or a resolution for a complaint situation. (Note that the written letters will often identify a student's attitudes, feelings, and values.)

4. **Initiate communication.** Note that for students who receive more than three complaints, a teacher may need to communicate what is going on with a child's guardian/parents and the complaint notes, written in formal letter writing style from his/her peers, are often quite powerful in telling whose classroom rights were being supported or violated. The letters also provide a documented file for the principal, counselor, and teacher and can be made available to document and consider the various students' point of view when mediating a situation.[9]

Psychomotor Domain

Whereas identification and classification within the cognitive and affective domains are generally agreed upon, less agreement exists on the classification within the psychomotor domain. Originally, the goal of this domain was simply to develop and categorize proficiency in skills, particularly those dealing with gross and fine muscle control. The classification of the domain presented here follows this lead, but includes at its highest level the most creative and inventive behaviors, thus coordinating skills and knowledge from all three domains. Consequently, the objectives are in a hierarchy ranging from simple gross locomotor control (such as turning on a computer) to the most creative and complex control requiring originality and fine locomotor control (such as designing a software program). Harrow offers the following taxonomy of the psychomotor domain: (1) moving, (2) manipulating, (3) communicating, and (4) creating.[10] A discussion of the four categories follows.

Moving. The moving level involves gross motor coordination. Selected action verbs appropriate for this level include *adjust, carry, clean, grasp, jump, locate, obtain,* and *walk.* Sample objectives for this category are

- The student *will carry* the microscope to the desk correctly.
- The student *will grasp* the putter correctly.

Manipulating. The manipulating level refers to fine motor coordination. Selected action verbs suitable for this level include *assemble, build, calibrate, connect, play, thread,* and *turn.* Sample objectives for this category include the following:

- The student *will play* the C-scale on the piano.
- The student *will turn* the fine adjustment until the microscope is in focus.

Communicating. The communicating level involves the sending and receiving actions related to ideas and feelings. Selected action verbs appropriate for this level are *analyze, ask, describe, draw, explain,* and *write.* Sample objectives for this category are

- The student *will describe* her/his feelings about a particular issue such as the cloning of humans.
- The student *will draw* what she/he observes on a slide through the microscope.

Creating. The highest level of this domain (and all domains) is creating—for creating represents the student's coordination of thinking, behaving, and learning in all three domains. Selected action verbs for this level include *create, design,* and *invent.* Sample objectives for this category include the following:

- The student *will create, choreograph,* and *perform* a dance pattern.
- The student *will invent and build* a kite pattern.

Now do Exercise 3.4, Assessing Recognition of Cognitive, Affective, and Psychomotor Objectives: Self-Check to review your skill in identifying performance objectives according to which domain each belongs. If needed, turn to Planning Masters 3.1, 3.2, and 3.3 for more objectives to classify in small groups or with the whole group. Then do Exercise 3.5, Preparing My Objectives for an ITU, to practice writing your own objectives for your ITU.

CONSIDERING THE DOMAINS AND CHARACTER EDUCATION

Related especially to the affective domain, although not exclusive of the cognitive and psychomotor domains, is an interest in the development of students' values, especially those of honesty, kindness, respect, and responsibility. This interest is sometimes called *character education* (see discussion and listing of resources in Chapter 2). Related to this, Wynne and Ryan state that "transmitting character, academics, and discipline— essentially "traditional" moral values—to pupils is a vital educational responsibility."[11] If one agrees with that interpretation, then the teaching of moral values is the transmission of character, academics, and discipline and clearly implies learning that transcends the three domains of learning presented in this chapter. Stimulated by a perceived need to reduce student antisocial behaviors (such as drug abuse and violence) and to produce more respectful and responsible citizens with a primary focus on the affective domain, some schools are developing curricula in character education and instruction in conflict resolution. The ultimate goal of those efforts is to develop values in students that lead to emotional intelligence, responsible citizenship, and moral action.

USING THE TAXONOMIES OF THE DOMAINS

Theoretically, the taxonomies are constructed so that students achieve each lower level before they move to the higher levels. Because categories and behaviors overlap, however, this theory does not always hold in practice. "Thoughts and feelings are inextricably interconnected—we 'think' with our feelings and 'feel' with our thoughts."[12]

The taxonomies are important because they emphasize the various levels that instruction can reach. For student learning to be worthwhile, you must formulate and teach objectives from both the higher levels and the lower levels of the taxonomies. By teaching with these objectives, you can move student thinking and behaving from the lowest to the highest levels of thinking and behavior. In the end, it is perhaps the highest level of the psychomotor domain—that of creating—to which we aspire.

In using the taxonomies, remember that the point is to formulate the best objectives for the job to be done. In schools that use results-driven education or outcomes-based education models, those models describe levels of mastery standards (scoring guides/rubrics) for each outcome. The taxonomies provide the mechanism for ensuring that you do not spend a disproportionate amount of time on facts and other low-level learning that is relatively trivial. They can also be of tremendous help when teachers are expected to correlate learning activities to one or more of the school or district's outcome standards (see Figure 3.5).

Preparing objectives is essential to the preparation of good items for the assessment of student learning. Clearly communicating your performance expectations to students—and then specifically assessing student learning against those expectations—makes the teaching most efficient and effective and makes the assessment of the learning closer to being authentic. However, you will not always write performance objectives for everything taught or always be able to measure accurately what students have learned. Learning that is meaningful to students is not as easily compartmentalized as the taxonomies of educational objectives would imply.

OBSERVING FOR CONNECTED LEARNING: JOURNALS, LOGS, AND PORTFOLIOS

As discussed earlier, in regard to learning that is most important and most meaningful to students, the domains are inextricably interconnected. Consequently, when assessing for student learning, both during instruction (formative assessment) and at the conclusion of the instruction (summative assessment), you must look for these connections.

Ways of looking for connected learning include (1) maintaining a teacher's (or teaching team's) log with daily or nearly daily entries about the progress of each student and (2) asking the students to maintain individual learning portfolios that document their thinking, work, and learning experiences. Dated and chronologically organized items that

FIGURE 3.5   Selected School District Expected Learning Outcome Standards

Results-driven education helps produce people who are effective communicators and lifelong learners, who have high self-esteem, and who demonstrate that they are

Community contributors who

- have an appreciation of diversity
- have an awareness of individual, civic, national, and international responsibilities
- have an understanding of basic health issues

Problem solvers who

- are able to set personal and career goals
- are able to solve problems in their academic and personal lives
- are innovative thinkers
- can use knowledge, not simply display it
- demonstrate higher-level analytical thinking skills when they evaluate or make decisions

Quality producers who

- are able to use their knowledge to create intelligent, artistic products that reflect originality
- can communicate effectively in a variety of situations (aesthetic/artistic, oral, nonverbal)
- have high standards

Self-directed learners who

- are independent workers
- can read, comprehend, and interact with text
- have self-respect, with an accurate view of themselves and their abilities

Workers who

- are able to work independently and collaboratively
- have an appreciation of different cultures
- have their own values and moral conduct
- show respect for others and their point of view

students can place in their working/ongoing portfolios include the following:

awards
brainstorming records
class objectives
contributions to
    class/team
learning contracts
mnemonics
notes/communication
photos of bulletin
    board contributions
records of debate
    contributions

records of demonstrations
records of peer coaching
records of reading
records of service
sketches of charts, posters,
    displays, and models
    made by the students
tests, grade records, peer
    evaluations
work accomplished

Depending on the age and maturity level of the students, another way of documenting connected learning is to have them keep a response journal in

which they reflect and respond to their learning, using the five categories shown in Figure 3.6.[13] The topics of portfolios and student journals are discussed further in Chapter 4.

REFINING GOALS AND OBJECTIVES: ANOTHER SHARING OF MATERIALS

As a *raison d'etre* (overview) for your ITU, you should write its educational goals, especially those linked to pertinent school, district, and state documents, to give yourself an overview and help you identify the topic of the unit and what the students are to learn as recommended/mandated/suggested by the documents. An overview of the unit can be extended to indicate what you hope the students

FIGURE 3.6 Categories of Ways Students Connect Learning Through Journals and Logs

Category 1. *"I never knew that."*
Knowledge. In this category, student responses are primary to factual information, to their new knowledge, and to the bits and pieces of raw information often expected to be memorized regardless of its value to students. However, because this knowledge is fragmented and merely scratches the surface of all meaningful learning, it must not be the end of all student learning. Learning that is truly meaningful goes beyond the "I never knew that" category, and students should be encouraged to expand upon the bits and pieces, connect them to something previously known when possible, and write about how the facts make sense related to what they are learning as individuals.

Category 2. *"I never thought of that."*
Perception. In this category, student responses are connected to an additional way of perceiving. Their responses may include some elements of "not knowing" but can also reveal higher-level thinking as a result of their reflection on that knowledge.

Category 3. *"I never felt that."*
Feelings. In this category, student responses are connected to the affective response, eliciting a more emotional statement than a cognitive one. Learning that is truly meaningful is much more than intellectual understanding—it is connected to a "felt" meaning.[14]

Category 4. *"I never appreciated that."*
Appreciation. Responses in this category connect to a sense of recognition that one's own life can be enriched by what others have created or done or that something already known can be valued from an additional perspective.

Category 5. *"I never realized that."*
Realization. In this category, student responses are connected to an awareness of overall patterns and dynamic ways in which behavior is holistic. Through their responses, they establish meaningful and potentially useful connections among knowledge they have, values, and purposes.

FACTS ABOUT PRAXIS AND OTHER TEACHER TESTS

Related to a teacher credentialing test that you are interested in—CBEST, Praxis, or others—find out if there is more than one exam so you can study appropriately. You'll no doubt discover that you will be responsible mainly for knowledge about curriculum and instruction; for content related to your skills in teaching reading, writing, and mathematics; for the content of any other subjects you will be teaching; and perhaps for your classroom performance including assessment. To that end, this guide is a useful resource for supporting an interested teacher's classroom performance regarding the curriculum, instruction, and assessment of the development and teaching of an ITU. You'll recall that first this resource guide introduced an interested teacher to an ITU (Chapter 1) and then showed ways to initiate the unit (Chapter 2). Next, the teacher reviewed ways to develop objectives (Chapter 3). In upcoming chapters, the teacher will make an initial selection of learning activities and then consider assessment of student learning (Chapter 4). Finally, the teacher gets to the stage of the final selection of learning activities, and then, to the action of completing lessons and the final unit (Chapter 5).

will learn—your teacher goals. You can include what understandings the students will develop, what skills will be fostered, and what attitudes and appreciations will be addressed during the unit.

After writing the *raison d'être*, take the time to complete your goals and rewrite/polish your objectives for the ITU that you want to initiate. If you are working as a member of a teaching team, each team member should give every other team member a copy of goals and objectives written independently. Then each member can refine the ITU from that member's point of view as she/he reads and reviews the objectives and goals of the other team members. This process should help the team avoid any confusion in the students' minds when the unit is presented. It also should help eliminate any unnecessary overlap of process or content.

SUMMARY

In developing your ITU, you'll recall that you will want to write an overview to give you the scope and sequence of the thematic study as mentioned in Chapter 2. Chapter 3 was developed specifically to assist you in preparing objectives (and recognizing suitable verbs) to design a unit for an integrated curriculum in standards-based education. You realized the need to recognize the components of a well-written objective and the value of planning objectives related to specific learning activities (more about this in Chapter 5) that will be the core of the unit. In this chapter, you were asked to recognize the differences among cognitive, affective, and psychomotor objectives, and to review the taxonomies of these domains of learning and how they relate to the developmental needs of students. Also, with a question map like the one presented in the ITU on the first page of this chapter, you have a model to help you use any questions generated by a selected theme as foci to start a unit. If appropriate for your grade level, you, too, can initiate a unit with a similar question map and then, with student input, locate resources that might be useful in exploring those questions. Information from such resources can be recorded by the students in various ways—in charts, graphs, notes in learning logs, portfolios, and others. In Chapter 4, you'll consider an assessment component for interdisciplinary thematic instruction. There is more information about selecting learning activities and the final culminating activity for an ITU in Chapter 5 along with examples of other ITUs.

IF A COLLEAGUE, COMMUNITY MEMBER, OR PARENT ASKS YOU ABOUT . . .

1. **Educational practice.** If a colleague asks for an example of educational practice that seems to conflict with exemplary practice/theory, what would you point out? In a small group, present to others your explanation of one educational practice that seems contradictory to exemplary practice or theory as presented in this guide.

2. **Other ITUs.** If a colleague asks you where to find other examples of ITUs, what would you suggest? Explore research articles, professional journals, and the Internet to find additional examples of ITUs. Look especially for examples of initiating, ongoing, and culminating activities of learning activities as preparation for your own ITU. Share what you find with your peers.

3. **Recalling K–12 schooling.** If a colleague asks you to recall a memorable time from your own schooling, what would you talk about? What do you really remember? Most likely you remember projects—your presentations, the lengthy research you did, and your extra effort doing art work to accompany your presentation. Maybe you remember a compliment by a teacher or a pat on the back by your peers. Most likely, you do not remember the massive amount of factual content that was covered. Discuss this memorable time and your feelings about it with your classmates.

4. **Student cooperation.** If a colleague asked you how you responded to students who failed to cooperate, what would you say? Participate in a discussion of examples of student cooperation put forth by group members. Despite your best intentions, is it possible that there will be some students who fail to cooperate and do not construct meaning in what they do? In what ways might this be determined in the classroom? How might it be remedied?

5. **Teaching/Learning approaches.** If a parent asks you to name some of the teaching approaches you use in your ITU, how would you respond? In small groups, discuss the complex and challenging tasks of collaborative learning, cooperative learning, negotiated curriculum, risk-taking, group-initiated learning, and visuals as several teaching and learning processes that can be part of an ITU in the classroom. Each member of the group can be responsible for presenting information about one of the approaches. Discuss the uses of each approach and, if time allows, any abuses you know about from personal experience.

EXERCISE 3.1

Recognizing Verbs That Are Acceptable for Overt Objectives: Self-Check Exercise

Instructions.   The purpose of this exercise is to check your recognition of verbs that are suitable for use in overt objectives. From the following list of verbs, circle those that should not be used in overt objectives—those that describe covert behaviors that are directly observable and measurable. Check your answers against the answer key that follows. Discuss any problem that you have with this exercise with your classmates and instructor.

1. apply	11. design	21. know
2. appreciate	12. diagram	22. learn
3. believe	13. enjoy	23. name
4. combine	14. explain	24. outline
5. comprehend	15. familiarize	25. predict
6. compute	16. grasp	26. realize
7. create	17. identify	27. select
8. define	18. illustrate	28. solve
9. demonstrate	19. indicate	29. state
10. describe	20. infer	30. understand

Answer key

The following verbs should be circled: 2, 3, 5, 13, 15, 16, 19, 21, 22, 26, 30. If you missed more than a couple, then you need to review the preceding sections and discuss your errors with your classmates and instructor.

EXERCISE 3.2

Recognizing the Parts of Criterion-Referenced Objectives

Instructions. The purpose of this exercise is to practice your skill in recognizing the four components of a behavioral objective that establishes criteria—standards and preset guidelines for student behaviors. In the following two objectives, identify the parts of each by underlining the *audience* once, the *behavior* twice, the *conditions* three times, and the *performance level* (the degree or standard of performance) four times.

Check your answers against the answer key that follows and discuss with your classmates and instructor any problem that you have.

1. Given a metropolitan transit bus schedule, at the end of the lesson the students will be able to read the schedule well enough to determine at what time buses are scheduled to leave randomly selected locations, with at least 90 percent accuracy.
2. Given five rectangular figures, you will correctly compute the area in square centimeters of at least four figures, by measuring the length and width with a ruler and computing the product using an appropriate calculation method.

Answer key

	objective 1	*objective 2*
audience	The student	You
(underlined once)		
behavior	will be able to read the schedule	will compute
(underlined twice)		
conditions	given a metropolitan transit bus schedule	given five rectangular figures
(underlined three times)		
performance level (degree)	well enough to determine (and) with at least 90 percent accuracy	correctly compute the area in square centimeters of at least four figures
(underlined four times)		

NOTES

EXERCISE 3.3

Recognizing Objectives That Are Measurable

Instructions. The purpose of this exercise is to assess your ability to recognize objectives that are measurable. Place an X before each of the following that is an overt, student-centered learning objective—an objective that is clearly measurable. Although the term's audience, conditions, or performance levels may be absent, ask yourself, "As stated, is this a student-centered and measurable objective?" If so, place an X in the blank. A self-checking answer key follows. After checking your answers, discuss any problems you have with the exercise with your classmates and instructor.

_____ 1. To develop an appreciation for literature

_____ 2. To identify the celestial bodies that are known planets

_____ 3. To provide meaningful experiences for the students

_____ 4. To recognize antonym pairs

_____ 5. To boot up a selected program on the computer

_____ 6. To analyze and compare patterns of data or specific quartile maps

_____ 7. To develop skills in inquiry

_____ 8. To identify which of the four causes is most relevant to the major events leading up to America's Civil War

_____ 9. To use maps and graphs to identify the major areas of world petroleum production and consumption

_____ 10. To know the causes for the diminishing atmospheric ozone concentration

Answer key

You should have marked items 2, 4, 5, 6, 8, and 9.

Items 1, 3, 7, and 10 are inadequate because of their ambiguity. Item 3 is not even a student learning objective—it is a teacher goal. The phrases *to develop* and *to know* can have too many interpretations. Although the conditions are not given, items 2, 4, 5, 6, 8, and 9 are clearly measurable. The teacher would have no difficulty determining when a learner has reached those objectives.

NOTES

EXERCISE 3.4

Assessing Recognition of Cognitive, Affective, and Psychomotor Objectives: Self-Check

Instructions. The purpose of this exercise is to recognize objectives and classify them as being in the cognitive, affective, or psychomotor domain. In the blank space, write the appropriate letter according to the domain: (C) cognitive, (P) psychomotor, or (A) affective. Check your responses at the end of this exercise.

_____ 1. The student will jump rope until he or she can jump it 10 subsequent times without missing.

_____ 2. The student can identify and spell the capitals of all 50 states.

_____ 3. The student can summarize the origin of the Peace Corps in the United States.

_____ 4. The student will demonstrate an interest in using the microscope by volunteering to work with it during free time.

_____ 5. The student will volunteer to help keep the classroom tidy.

_____ 6. The student will be able to identify respective poets after reading and discussing several poems.

_____ 7. The student will translate a Spanish poem into English.

_____ 8. The student will accurately predict the results of combining genes from the available gene pool.

_____ 9. The student will voluntarily read additional material about ancient Greek civilization.

_____10. The student will practice the ring toss until achieving a minimum of 7 in 10 attempts.

How did you do with this exercise? If you scored 100 percent, then go on to Exercise 3.5. If you missed any, talk them over with your classmates.

Answer key
    (C) 2, 3, 6, 7, 8
    (P) 1, 10
    (A) 4, 5, 9

EXERCISE 3.5

Preparing My Objectives for an ITU

Instructions.   The purpose of this exercise is to give you an opportunity to write your own instructional objectives. To begin, select a grade level and content topic you will likely teach. Write nine specific instructional objectives for the topic, and include both performance and conditions.

_____

(grade level)

_____

(content topic)

Cognitive knowledge

Cognitive comprehension

Cognitive application

Cognitive analysis

Cognitive synthesis

Cognitive evaluation

Psychomotor

Affective (low level)

Affective (high level)

When you have completed this exercise, exchange papers with a member of your group. Discuss the objectives that were written and make any changes that are needed.

CHAPTER NOTES

1. This unit by K. Traiger is discussed in *California Catalyst* (1993), San Jose Unified School District, San Jose, CA.

2. See, for example, the many articles in "The Constructivist Classroom," theme issue of *Educational Leadership, 57*(3), November 1999.

3. G. F. Vars and J. A. Beane. *Integrative Curriculum in a Standards-Based World* (Champaign, IL: ED441618, ERIC Clearinghouse on Elementary and Early Childhood Education, 2000).

4. T. L. Good and J. E. Brophy, *Looking in Classrooms* (New York: Longman, 1997) p. 399.

5. B. S. Bloom (ed.), *Taxonomy of Educational Objectives, Book I, Cognitive Domain* (White Plains, NY: Longman, 1984).

6. See R. M. Gagné, L. J. Briggs, and W.W. Wager, *Principles of Instructional Design* (4th ed.) (New York: Holt, Rinehart and Winston, 1994).

7. Compare Bloom's higher-order thinking skills with R. H. Ennis's "A Taxonomy of Critical Thinking Dispositions and Abilities," in J. B. Barron and R. J. Sternberg (eds.), *Teaching Thinking Skills: Theory and Practice* (New York: W. H. Freeman, 1987) and with Marzano's "complex thinking strategies" in R. J. Marzano, *A Different Kind of Classroom: Teaching with Dimensions of Learning* (Alexandria, VA: Association of Supervision and Curriculum Development, 1992).

8. D. R. Kratwohl, B. S. Bloom, and B. B. Masia, *Taxonomy of the Psychomotor Domain* (New York: David McKay, 1964).

9. C. A. Perks, "Write 'Em Up!" *Teaching K–8*, pp. 74–75 (September 1996).

10. A. J. Harrow, *Taxonomy of the Psychomotor Domain* (New York: Longman, 1997). A similar taxonomy for the psychomotor domain is that of E. J. Simpson, *The Classification of Educational Objectives in the Psychomotor Domain: Volume 3* (Washington, DC: Gryphon House, 1972).

11. E. A. Wynne and K. Ryan, *Reclaiming Our Schools: Teaching Character, Academics, and Discipline,* (2nd ed.), (Upper Saddle River, NJ: Prentice Hall, 1997), p. 1.

12. G. Caine and R. N. Caine, "The Critical Need for a Mental Model of Meaningful Learning," *California Catalyst*, p. 19 (Fall 1992).

13. Adapted from S. Fersh, *Integrating the Trans-National/Cultural Dimension* (Bloomington, IN: Fastback 36, Phi Delta Kappa Educational Foundation, 1993), pp. 23–24.

14. G. Caine and R. N. Caine, p. 19.

FOR FURTHER READING

Barton, K. C., & Smith, L. A. (2000, September). Themes or motifs? Aiming for coherence through interdisciplinary outlines. *The Reading Teacher, 54*(1), 54–63.

Churma, M. (1999). *A guide to integrating technology standards into the curriculum.* Upper Saddle River, NJ: Merrill/Prentice Hall.

Cornett, C. E. (1999). *The arts as meaning makers: Integrating literature and the arts throughout the curriculum.* Upper Saddle River, NJ: Merrill/Prentice Hall.

Crane, B. E. (2000). *Teaching with the Internet: Strategies and models for K–12 curricula.* New York: Neal-Schuman.

Davidson, D. M., Miller, K. W., & Metheny, D. L. (1999). *Integrating science and mathematics in the elementary curriculum.* Fastback 444. Bloomington, IN: Phi Delta Kappa Educational Foundation.

Decker, K. A. (2001). Meeting state standards through integration. *Science and Children, 36*(6), 28–32, 69.

Duffy-Hester, A. M. (1999). Teaching struggling readers in elementary classrooms: A review of classroom reading programs and principles of instruction. *The Reading Teacher, 52*(5), 480–495.

Kellough, R. D. (1997). *A resource guide for teaching K–12* (4th ed.). Upper Saddle River, NJ: Merrill/Prentice Hall.

Kellough, R. D., & Kellough, N. G. (1999). *Secondary school teaching: A guide to methods and resources* (2nd ed.). Upper Saddle River, NJ: Merrill/Prentice Hall.

Kellough, R. D., & Roberts, P. L. (1998). *A resource guide for elementary school teaching: Planning for competence* (5th ed.). Upper Saddle River, NJ: Merrill/Prentice Hall.

Lambert, L. T. (2000). The new physical education. *Educational Leadership, 57*(6), 34–38.

Lerner, L. S. (1998). *State science standards: An appraisal of science standards in 36 states.* Washington, DC: Thomas B. Fordham Foundation.

Novick, R. (1996). *Developmentally appropriate and culturally responsive education: Theory in practice.* Portland, OR: Northwest Regional Educational Laboratory.

Nuthall, G. (1999). The way students learn: Acquiring knowledge from an integrated science and social studies unit. *Elementary School Journal, 99*(4), 303–341.

Ohanian, S. (1999). *One size fits few: The folly of educational standards.* Portsmouth, NH: Heinemann.

Ohanian, S. (2000). Goals 2000: What's in a name? *Phi Delta Kappan, 81*(5), 344–355.

O'Neill, J. (2000). SMART goals, SMART schools. *Educational Leadership, 57*(5), 46–50.

Piazza, C. L. (1999). *Multiple forms of literacy: Teaching literacy and the arts.* Upper Saddle River, NJ: Merrill/Prentice Hall.

Roberts, P. L. (1997). *Literature-based history activities for children, grades 1–3.* Boston: Allyn & Bacon.

Roberts, P. L. (1997). *Literature-based history activities for children, grades 4–8*. Boston: Allyn & Bacon.

Roberts, P. L. (1998). *Language arts and environmental awareness: 100+ integrated books and activities for children*. New Haven, CT: Linnet Professional Publications.

Robin, D. (2000). *Teaching elementary language arts: A balanced approach* (6th ed.). Needham Heights, MA: Allyn & Bacon.

Saxe, D. W. (1998). *State history standards: An appraisal of history standards in 37 states and the District of Columbia*. Washington, DC: Thomas B. Fordham Foundation.

Schmoker, M., & Marzano, R. J. (1999). Realizing the promise of standards-based education. *Educational Leadership, 56*(6), 17–21.

Stirling, D. (2000). *Character education connections for school, home, and community: A guide for integrating character education*. Bloomington, IN: Phi Delta Kappa International.

Tomlinson, C. A. (1999). *The differentiated classroom*, Chapter 5. Alexandria, VA: Association for Supervision and Curriculum Development.

Victor, E., & Kellough, R. D. (2000). *Science for the elementary and middle school* (9th ed.). Upper Saddle River, NJ: Merrill/Prentice Hall.

CHAPTER 4

Assessing Student Learning

The important thing is not to stop questioning.

—Albert Einstein

During a given day or time period, you and the students can look at a problem/theme or topic/subject of study from the point of view of many separate disciplines, and as Einstein recommended in his words that opened this chapter, you and the students can do the "important thing"... "not to stop questioning." If appropriate, return to Chapter 1, Figure 1.4, to see ways to use roles to introduce students to various disciplines and related questions. Such an interdisciplinary approach related to a problem or concern has been adopted not only by educators but by other professionals because this approach encompasses meaningful **learning** and real-life problem-solving. As an example, consider the fact-finding and decision-making method of public officials in Colorado when confronted with the task of making decisions about projects proposed for watersheds in their state. While gathering information, the officials contacted Dave Rosgen, a state hydrologist. Rosgen accompanied the officials to selected sites to demonstrate specific ways in which he helped control erosion and rehabilitated damaged streams. At one site— Wolf Creek—the officials put on high waders and

followed Rosgen down the creek to examine various features of this complex natural stream. He pointed out evidence of the creek's past meanderings—patterns he had incorporated into his rehabilitation projects.[1]

In addition to listening to this scientist's point of view, the officials listened to other specialists to consider related economic and political issues before making final decisions about upcoming projects related to watersheds in their state.

Just as Rosgen introduced information from hydrology to the state officials, you (with the help of students and other teachers and adults) can introduce experiences designed to foster ideas and skills from various disciplines. During this interdisciplinary approach, your students can study a topic and underlying ideas/theme on an ongoing basis to gain related knowledge and skills from a variety of disciplines/subject areas. For instance, you can develop language arts skills through an ITU by stimulating communication skills through creative writing and other reading, writing, listening, and speaking activities. Throughout the unit, you can guide your students in exploring ideas related to different disciplines to integrate their learning.

CHAPTER INTRODUCTION

By now, you probably understand that students' personal inquiries are central to learning by interdisciplinary thematic instruction. How is that learning assessed? That is the topic of this chapter, but before we begin, take time to review some of the important aspects of **assessment**—the purposes, some guiding principles, and terms related to assessment.

REVIEWING PURPOSES OF ASSESSMENT

Assessment of achievement in student learning is designed to serve in the following ways:

1. **To assist in student learning.** This purpose is the first one considered when speaking of assessment, and it is the principal topic of this chapter. For you, a classroom teacher interested in using interdisciplinary thematic instruction,

this purpose and the one that follows are (or should be) the most important purposes.

2. **To assist in identifying strengths and weaknesses in student learning.** Identification and assessment of students' strengths and weaknesses are necessary for two reasons: (a) to structure and restructure the learning activities and (b) to restructure the curriculum. Concerning the first reason, data on student strengths and weaknesses in conceptual and procedural understandings are important in planning activities appropriate for both skill development and intellectual development. This identification results in diagnostic assessment (also known as **preassessment**). Related to the second reason, data on student strengths and weaknesses in conceptual and procedural understandings are useful for making appropriate modifications in activities/lessons/content both during the process of the ITU in particular and to the curriculum in general.

3. **To assess and improve the effectiveness of a particular instructional strategy.** It is important for you to know how well a particular strategy helped accomplish a particular goal or objective. Competent teachers continually reflect on and evaluate their strategy choices and use several sources to do this: student achievement as measured by assessment instruments, their own professional teaching intuition, informal feedback given by the students, and sometimes informal feedback given by colleagues such as members of a **teaching team** or mentor teachers.

4. **To assess and improve the effectiveness of curriculum programs.** Components of the curriculum are continually assessed by committees of teachers and administrators. The assessment is done while students are learning (formative assessment) and afterward (summative assessment). For example, some schools have restructured their programs and changed from a traditional to a nontraditional schedule; from traditional instructional methods to integrated learning; and from traditional report cards with grades of ABC to reporting **procedures** that identify the extent to which students have mastered state standards. Schools have compared or are comparing student achievement data to determine the effectiveness in learning that has resulted either directly or indirectly from the restructuring.

5. **To assess and improve teaching effectiveness.** To improve student learning, teachers are periodically evaluated on the basis of (a) their commitment to working with students at a particular level, (b) their ability to interact with students at a particular age or grade level, and (c) their ability to show mastery of appropriate instructional techniques and their willingness to risk trying new techniques.

6. **To provide data that assist in decision making about a student's future.** Assessment of student achievement is important in guiding decision making about course and program placement, promotion, school transfer, class standing, eligibility for honors and scholarships, and career planning.

7. **To communicate with and involve parents and guardians in their children's learning.** Parents/guardians, communities, and school boards all share in an accountability for the effectiveness of the children's learning. Today's schools are reaching out and engaging parents, guardians, and the community in their children's education. All teachers play an important role in the process of communicating with, reaching out to, and involving parents.

GUIDING PRINCIPLES OF AN ASSESSMENT PROGRAM

Because the welfare and, indeed, the future of so many people depend on the outcomes of assessment, it is impossible to overemphasize its importance. For a learning endeavor to be successful, the learner must have answers to basic questions such as the following: Where am I going? Where am I now? How do I get where I am going? How will I know when I get there? Am I on the right track for getting there? These questions, or similar ones, can be integral to a good program of assessment. Of course, in the process of teaching and learning, the answers may be ever-changing as the teacher and students continue to assess and adjust plans as appropriate and necessary.

These questions are the basis for the following principles that guide an assessment program and that are reflected in the discussion in this chapter.

1. **Reciprocal process.** Assessment, from a variety of sources and types of data-collective devices, is a reciprocal process and includes assessment of teacher performance and student achievement. Teachers need to know how well they are doing. Students need to know how well they are doing. Thus, assessment should provide evidence and input data that show how well both the teacher and students are doing.

2. **Ongoing process.** Assessment should be an ongoing process that includes the continual monitoring and assessment of the selection and implementation of plans and activities to check student progress and to change or adopt instructional strategies to promote desired outcomes. With this monitoring, assessment can aid teaching effectiveness and contribute to the intellectual and psychological growth of children.

3. **Ownership process.** Assessment can be an ongoing student responsibility—an ownership process—when it includes the components of student reflection and self-assessment. These two features help the students develop the skills necessary for them to assume increasingly greater ownership of their own learning.

4. **Accountable process.** Assessment is an ongoing teacher responsibility. A teacher's responsibility is to facilitate student learning and to assess student progress in that learning, and to do that, the teacher is, or should be, held accountable.

CLARIFYING TERMS USED IN ASSESSMENT

When discussing the assessment component of learning and teaching, it is easy to be confused by some of the terminology. The following clarification of terms is offered to aid your reading and comprehension.

Assessing and Evaluation

Although some authors distinguish between the terms **assessment** (assessing is finding out what the students are learning, a relatively neutral process) and **evaluation** (making sense of what was found, a subjective process) —for the purposes of this guide, we do not. We think the difference too slight and therefore consider the terms to be synonymous.

Assessing and Measurement

Measurement refers to quantifiable data about specific behaviors. Tests and the statistical procedures used to analyze the results are examples. Measurement is a descriptive and objective process, relatively free from human value judgments.

Assessment includes objective data from measurement but also other types of information—some of which are more subjective such as information from anecdotal records and teacher observations and ratings of student performance. In addition to the use of objective data (data from measurement), assessment also includes arriving at value judgments made on the basis of subjective information. Consider the following example:

A teacher may share information that Jeff Bright received a score in the 90th percentile on the eighth-grade statewide achievement test in reading (a statement of measurement) but may add that "according to my assessment of his work in my language arts class, he has not been an outstanding student" (a statement of assessment).

Validity and Reliability

The degree to which a measuring instrument actually measures that which it is intended to measure is the instrument's **validity.** For example, when we ask if an assessment instrument has validity, key questions concerning that instrument are as follows: Does the instrument adequately sample the intended content? Does it measure the cognitive, affective, and psychomotor knowledge and skills that are important to the unit of content being tested? Does it sample all the instructional **objectives** of that unit?

The accuracy with which a technique consistently measure a procedure is its **reliability.** If, for instance, you know that you weigh 114 pounds, and a scale consistently records 114 pounds when you stand on it, then that scale has reliability. However, if the same scale consistently records 100 pounds when you stand on it, we can still say that the scale has reliability (because it is producing similar results when you use it repeatedly) but it is not necessarily valid (because you know you weigh 114 pounds, not 100 pounds). In this situation, the scale is not measuring what it is supposed to measure—so although it is reliable, it is invalid. To consider a similar situation in your classroom, a technique must have reliability before it can have validity. The greater the number of test items or situations on a particular objective, the higher the reliability. The higher the reliability, the more consistency there will be in students' scores measuring their understanding of that particular objective.

ASSESSING STUDENT ACHIEVEMENT: A THREE-STEP PROCESS

As discussed in Chapter 3, assessing student achievement is a three-step process. These three steps are as follows:

1. **Diagnostic assessment.** (sometimes called pre-assessment) The assessment of the student's knowledge and skills before the new instruction.
2. **Formative assessment.** The assessment of learning during the instruction, usually represented by grades or ranks shown on chapter tests, progress reports, or even the presence of deficiency notices.
3. **Summative assessment.** The assessment of learning after the instruction, ultimately represented by the student's final term, semester, or year's achievement grade or rank related to selected standards. Note that an end-of-the-chapter test or a unit test can be summative when the test represents the absolute end of the student's learning of material for that instructional unit.

ASSESSING STUDENT LEARNING: SOME APPROACHES

Each step of the three-step process mentioned previously can include three approaches for assessing a student's achievement in learning. The approaches are

1. **Saying.** What the student says—for example, the quantity and quality of a student's contributions to a class discussion.

2. **Doing.** What the student does—for example, a student's performance (e.g., the quality of a student's participation in the culminating activities of the ITU).
3. **Writing/Drawing.** What the student writes or draws—for example, as shown by items in the student's **portfolio** (e.g., **assignments,** project work, and written tests). These approaches of assessment will be discussed in more detail later in this section.

Although your own situation and personal philosophy will dictate the levels of importance and weight you give each *approach* of assessment during each *step* of assessment, you should have a strong rationale if you value and weight the three approaches for assessment differently than one-third each.

Assessing Authentically

When assessing for student achievement, it is important that you use procedures that are compatible with the **instructional objectives.** As mentioned in earlier chapters, this measurement is referred to as authentic assessment. Other terms used for authentic assessment are *accurate, active, aligned, alternative,* and *direct.* Although performance assessment is sometimes used, this term refers to the type of student response being assessed, whereas authentic assessment refers to the assessment situation. Although not all performance assessments are authentic, those that are authentic are most assuredly performance assessments.

In English/language arts, for example, it may seem fairly easy to develop a **criterion-referenced test** (assessing the progress of a student toward meeting a learning objective/outcomes/preset standard), administer it, and grade it, but tests often measure language skills rather than language use. It is extremely difficult to measure students' communicative competence with a paper-and-pencil test. For example, paper tests often do not measure listening and talking very well. In addition, a test on punctuation marks does not indicate the students' ability to use punctuation marks correctly in their own writing. Instead, these tests typically evaluate a student's ability to add punctuation marks to a set of sentences created by someone else or to proofread and spot punctuation errors in someone else's writing. An alternative and far better method is to examine how students use punctuation marks in their own writing.[2] An authentic assessment of punctuation, then, would be an assessment of a performance item that involves students in writing and punctuating their own writing. For the authentic assessment of the student's understanding of that which

the student has been learning, you would use a performance-based assessment procedure.

In still another example of teacher decision making related to authentic assessment, consider this: "if students have been actively involved in classifying objects using multiple characteristics, it sends them a confusing message if they are then required to take a paper-and-pencil test that asks them to define classification or recite a memorized list of characteristics of good classifications schemes."[3] Note that an authentic assessment technique would be a performance item that actually involves the students in classifying objects. In other words, to obtain an accurate assessment of a student's learning, the teacher uses a performance-based (outcome-based) assessment procedure—a procedure that requires students to produce rather than select a response.

Advantages and Limitations. Advantages claimed for the use of authentic assessment include (a) the direct (also known as performance-based, criterion-referenced, outcome-based, standard-based) measurement of what students should know and can do, and (b) an emphasis on higher order thinking. Conversely, limitations on using authentic assessment include a higher cost, difficulty in making results consistent and usable, and problems with validity, reliability, and comparability.

Assessing What a Student Says and Does

When evaluating what a student says, you should (1) listen to the student's interactions with others, oral reports, questions, and responses and (2) observe the student's attentiveness, creativeness, involvement in class activities, and responses to challenges. Notice that we say you should listen and observe. While listening to what the student is saying, you should also be observing the student's nonverbal behaviors. For this observation, you can use checklists and rating scales, behavioral growth record forms, observations with scoring rubrics, and scoring guides of the student's performance in learning activities. You will see sample checklists and sample scoring guides/rubrics later in this chapter and in the units in Chapter 5.[4]

To see a sample generic form for recording and evaluating teacher observations of a student's verbal and nonverbal behaviors, see Figure 4.1. The form allows space for you to record what the student said, did, and wrote and what outcome/behavior was expected related to the learning objective. If you duplicate the form, you can carry copies with you in your pocket or on a clipboard to record your observations. If you are interested in recording student observations electronically anywhere and at any

FIGURE 4.1 Evaluating and Recording Student Verbal and Nonverbal Behaviors: Sample Form

Student _____   School _____

Teacher _____   Date _____

Subject _____   Period _____

_____

What student did, said, wrote   Desired Outcome   Objective/Standard

Teacher's or observer's comments:

time, consider updated software such as the program *Learner Profile,* which allows you to record your observations in a different way.[5]

With each technique used, you must proceed from your awareness of anticipated learning outcomes (the instructional objectives linked to standards) and assess a student's progress toward meeting those objectives. The process is called **criterion-referenced assessment.**

Debriefing for a Specific Experience. A debriefing for a specific experience is a "what we learned" type of discussion with the purpose of assessing a single event or happening, such as a lesson related to place-based education (field trip), a visit by a resource person to the classroom, or the culmination of an ITU through a special activity or final project. For a debriefing in a class meeting, the students usually summarize the information and activities they thought were important and any new learning they acquired. A teacher usually has the students record their remarks on a class chart, the writing board, or an overhead transparency while also recording the same remarks they hear in notebooks or on individual sheets of paper. If a class meeting is held *before* the specific experience to allow students to discuss what they wanted to learn from the event, then the debriefing *after* can focus on comparing (looking for similarities) and contrasting (looking for differences) what the students had anticipated learning with what they actually learned.

Guidelines for Assessing What a Student Says and Does. Regardless of the grade level you teach, there are several guidelines and steps to follow when assessing a student's verbal and nonverbal behaviors in the classroom, including the following:

- List the desirable behaviors/outcomes for a specific activity; check the list against the specific instructional objectives (linked to standards if appropriate for your class/school/district/state).
- Maintain an anecdotal record book/folder and identify a section in it for your records of each student. Record your observations as quickly as possible following your observation. Audio or video recordings (with permission in some cases) and, of course, computer software programs and small self-adhesive notes can help you keep records and check the accuracy of your memory. You can schedule time during school or after school to record your observations while they are still fresh in your thoughts. Record your professional judgment about the student's progress toward the desired outcome/behavior, but consider it carefully before making it part of a permanent record. Write reminders to yourself such as *Check validity of observation by further testing* or *Discuss observations with student's parent/guardian/mentor* (adult representative from the community) or *Discuss observations with the student or with other teachers on the teaching team*.
- Encourage students to write about their experiences in school and especially about their experiences related to what is being learned in the ITU. This provides students with practice in expressing themselves in written form and in connecting their learning through writing.
- Talk individually with students about their journals to seek clarification about their responses. Each student's journal will be useful to you in understanding her/his thought processes and writing skills (part of your diagnostic assessment/evaluation). Later, for grading purposes, you can simply record the outcome that the student is maintaining a journal and perhaps write a judgment about the *quantity* of writing in it—but not about the *quality* (see Figure 4.2). We recommend that you do not place letter grades in student journals.
- Review the students' portfolios and discuss with them individually the progress they are making in their learning that is shown by the materials in the portfolio. Remind them that a major purpose of the portfolios is for student self-assessment and to show progress in learning. For this to happen, the students should keep all or major samples of materials related to a particular study in their portfolios. We recommend that you do not place letter grades in student portfolios.

Assessing What a Student Writes or Draws

When assessing what a student writes or draws, you can use peer conferences, selected student journal writing and sketching, student writing and illustrating projects, student portfolios, tests, worksheets, written homework, papers, and teacher-student conferences. In many schools, homework assignments, portfolios, and worksheets are the tools primarily used for the formative evaluation of each student's achievement. Tests, too, can be a part of this formative evaluation, but note that tests are often a first-choice tool selected for ongoing diagnostic purposes and for summative evaluation at the end of a unit.

Peer Conference Group.   A peer conference group normally consists of five or six students who meet to assess the reports related to the ITU written by the group members. Each student takes a turn telling the others what he/she needs in the way of help, feedback, and ideas. The students hand their papers to their peers on the left and silently read the papers they receive. Each member writes his or her suggestions for improvement on duplicated response sheets, using such phrases as *Can you explain . . . ?* or *Can you tell more about . . . ?* or *I like . . .* and *I thought this was interesting because. . . .* The response sheets are given to the appropriate authors of the reports so each student gets feedback from all the other group members before rewriting.

Student Journal.   A **journal** (sometimes called a **learning log**) usually takes the form of a spiral notebook that contains a student's writings. In general, journal entries indicate what is being learned related to a current study or ITU. A journal also might include personal writing about the students' interests and experiences, in which case it is sometimes called a **life-writing journal,** or it might include a student's personal reaction to material related to learning, in which case it is sometimes called a **thinkbook.** A journal might also contain entries written by the student every afternoon before leaving school about what he or she has learned that day, in which case, it is sometimes called a **cooperative teacher-student log.**

You can communicate in writing with each student through any type of journal—but it is crucial for you to write comments for each student when the approach taken is the cooperative teacher-student log. In this type of journal, the student writes about what he or she thinks has been accomplished for the day, what was personally interesting during the day's

FIGURE 4.2 Scoring Guide for Assessing Students in Cooperative Learning: Sample Form

	9–10	8	7	1–6
Goals	Consistently and actively helps identify group goals; works effectively to meet goals.	Consistently communicates commitment to group goals; carries out assigned roles.	Sporadically communicates commitment to group goals; carries out assigned role.	Rarely, if ever, works toward group goals or may work against them.
Interpersonal Skills	Cooperates with group members by encouraging, compromising, and/or taking a leadership role without dominating; shows sensitivity to feelings and knowledge of others.	Cooperates with group members by encouraging, compromising, and/or taking a leadership role.	Participates with group, but has own agenda; may not be willing to compromise or to make significant contributions.	May discourage others, harass group members, or encourage off-task behavior. Makes significant changes to others' work without their knowledge or permission.
Quality Producer	Contributes significant information, ideas, time, and/or talent to produce a quality product.	Contributes information, ideas, time, and/or talent to produce a quality product.	Contributes some ideas, though not significant; may be more supportive than contributive; shows willingness to complete assignment but has no desire to go beyond average expectations.	Does little or no work toward the completion of group product; shows little or no interest in contributing to the task; produces work that fails to meet minimum standards for quality.
Participation	Attends daily; consistently and actively utilizes class time by working on the task.	Attends consistently; sends in work to group if absent; utilizes class time by working on the task.	Attends sporadically; absences/tardies may hinder group involvement; may send work when absent; utilizes some time; may be off-task by talking to others, interrupting other groups, or watching others do the majority of the work.	Frequent absences or tardies hinder group involvement; fails to send in work when absent; wastes class time by talking, doing other work, or avoiding tasks; group has asked that member be reproved by teacher or removed from the group.
Commitment	Consistently contributes time out of class to produce a quality product; attends all group meetings as evidenced by the group meeting log.	Contributes time out of class to produce a quality product; attends a majority of group meetings as evidenced by the group meeting log.	Willing to work toward completion of task during class time; attends some of the group meetings but may arrive late or leave early; may keep inconsistent meeting log.	Rarely, if ever, attends group meetings outside of class or may attend and hinder progress of the group; fails to keep meeting log.

Source: (Courtesy of Susan Abbott and Pam Benedetti, Elk Grove School District, Elk Grove, CA.) Explanation for use: Possible score = 50. Scorer marks a relevant square in each of the five categories and student's score for that category is the small number in the top right corner within that square.

study, and what he or she wants to read, write, sketch, or study next. Schedule time to read the logs often and write meaningful responses back to the students.

If you want to include the cooperative teacher-student log as part of the ITU, you may want to read the logs as part of the overall assessment of the unit and recognize the students for the effort that they have put into their journal entries with some type of awards and bonuses. In addition, the students can reread their journals at the end of an ITU to focus on an end-of-the-unit review of what they have learned. The students might number their journal pages, write titles for the different entries on different pages, create a table of contents page, decorate a cover and a title page, insert illustrations or sketches, develop a glossary or index, and write a self-evaluation as a summary on the last page of the journal to establish a closure for the ITU.

Teacher-Student Conferences. A teacher-student conference is an arranged 10- to 15-minute meeting that you have with an individual student during the school day. The purpose is to help guide the student to self-assess his or her own educational progress, with a focus on the student's self-direction in learning. During the conference, one or two elements from the student's educational materials may be reviewed such as a learning log, various recordings, a writing folder, and a daily journal. The atmosphere should remain friendly and helpful (i.e., nonjudgmental), and the student can be encouraged to do most of the talking—focusing on any difficulties the student is having, discussing his or her feelings about the assignments, and telling about any problems in the school environment that may be threatening or interrupting the student's learning progress.

Conference Log. This is a notebook in which you write notes about each student's conference. It also contains a time schedule of meetings with the individual students. Using a sheet with the student's name and conference date on it, you can record what was discussed and what elements from the student's educational materials were reviewed. For instance, if a portion of the student's writing was discussed, you could make notes about the student's work and, if mentioned by the student, what the next writing project would concern. Notes might also be made in the conference log about the student's invented spelling (if any) and about the teacher's suggestions related to grammar and structure for the student's final revision.

Writing Folder. A **writing folder** is usually a three-ring binder containing a number of cardboard

pockets, labeled to show the different styles of writing the student accomplishes. For example, the pockets may be labeled *First Drafts* for all the beginning writing a student does, *Current Writing* for the ongoing pages of writing, and *Finished Drafts* for the final products. A fourth pocket might be labeled *Writing Ideas* for a list of topics for future writing and a fifth pocket *Personal* for a student's reflections on any matters related to learning in general and the unit in particular. If appropriate, you can ask the students to begin a list of independently published classroom books that each has developed through the unit. Inside the back cover, you can place a checklist of writing skills (linked to standards) to indicate what each student has accomplished and maintained through the unit of study.

Guidelines for Assessing Student Writing. When assessing what a student writes, consider the following guidelines:

- Correlate student writing assignments and test items with specific instructional objectives (i.e., objectives should be **criterion** referenced and can be standard-based).
- Encourage students to write about their experiences in school and especially about their experiences related to what is being learned. In a free, nonthreatening environment, engage them in thinking about their thinking and in writing their creative thoughts. By doing this, you provide the students with practice in expressing themselves in written form and in connecting their learning.
- Provide positive written or verbal comments about the students' work. Consider a comment before writing it on a student's paper or journal page by asking yourself how you think the student (or parent/guardian/mentor) will interpret or react to it and if that is a correct interpretation or reaction to your intended meaning. Respond with statements of empathy instead of value judgments. Empathic statements such as *I understand your point of view* and *Thanks for sharing your thoughts* can be written instead of a letter grade or an evaluative sentence. Gibbs and Early[6] have some suggestions about teacher responses to journals; they mention that a teacher should (1) initially ignore correcting spelling and grammar; (2) resist probing and asking for more than the student wants to share and resist asking students to share entries with you or with their peers; (3) indicate that pages marked *Personal* will not be read; and (4) resist writing evaluative statements or giving grades in journals.

- As mentioned, talk individually with students about their journals to get more clarification. Each student's journal will be useful to you in understanding the student's thought processes and writing skills (part of your diagnostic evaluation). For future assessment and evaluation, you can record the extent to which the student is maintaining a journal and perhaps record a judgment about the *quantity* of writing in it but no judgment should be made about the *quality* of writing (see Figure 4.2 Scoring Guide for Assessing Students in Cooperative Learning: Sample Form). We recommend that no grades be entered into student journals.
- As mentioned, review the students' portfolios and discuss individually the progress in their learning as shown by the materials in their portfolios. Remind them that the purpose of the portfolios is for student self-assessment and to show his or her progress in learning. For this to happen, the students should keep all, or major samples of, papers related to the study or ITU in their portfolios. We recommend that no grades be entered into student portfolios.

ASSESSING FOR AFFECTIVE AND PSYCHOMOTOR DOMAIN LEARNING

Whereas evaluation of cognitive domain objects often lends itself to written tests of achievement, the evaluation of affective and psychomotor domains often requires the use of checklists where student outcomes/behaviors can be observed in action. However, as mentioned earlier, educators today are encouraging the use of alternative assessment procedures (alternatives to traditional paper-and-pencil testing). As also mentioned in preceding chapters, in regard to learning that is most important and that is most meaningful to students, the domains are interconnected. Learning that is meaningful to students is not as easily compartmentalized as the taxonomies of the domains might indicate or that the taxonomies of educational objectives would imply (see Chapter 3). Alternative assessment approaches include the use of group projects, oral presentations, papers, performance tests, portfolios, and skits.

In schools where you work in groups or teams of teachers who remain with the same cohort of students for more than a year, you will probably have the opportunity to observe the positive changes in your students' values and attitudes.[7] Unfortunately, if you work in an educational situation where you only see a student for a given school semester or year, then you may never see the effects you had on a student.

ASSESSING STUDENT INVOLVEMENT

The students' continuous self-assessment should be planned as an important component of your unit. If the students are to progress in their understanding of their own thinking (**metacognition**) and in their intellectual development, they must receive instruction and guidance in how to become more responsible for their own learning. During the empowerment process, they learn to think better of themselves and of their individual capabilities. To achieve this self-understanding and improved self-esteem requires the experiences afforded by successes, with guidance in self-understanding and self-assessment.

To support this student involvement with assessment, you can provide opportunities for students to think about what they are learning, how they are learning it, and how far they have progressed. Several ways to accomplish this professional responsibility are to involve the students in cooperative group learning; to engage the students in maintaining journals; to have them keep portfolios of their own work; and to use scales, scoring guides/rubrics, or checklists periodically to self-assess their learning progress.

Using Cooperative Group Learning

Group learning, including cooperative group learning, can be an integral part of learning by ITUs. The purpose of a cooperative learning group is for the group to learn, which means that individuals within the group must learn. Group achievement in learning, then, depends on the learning of individuals within the group. Rather than competing for rewards for achievement, members of the group cooperate by helping each other learn so that a group's recognition of their achievement will be a positive one. It is well documented in research studies that when small groups of students of mixed backgrounds, skills, and capabilities work together toward a common **goal,** they increase their liking and respect for one another. As a result, each student's self-esteem and academic achievement also increase.

When recognizing the achievement of a cooperative learning group, both group and individual achievement are recognized and rewarded. Remembering that the emphasis must be on peer support rather than peer pressure, a teacher needs to be cautious about giving group grades.[8] Some teachers give bonus points to all members of a group to add to their individual scores when everyone in the group has reached preset criteria. Preset standards can be different for individuals within a group, depending on each member's ability and past performance. It is important that each member of a group feel rewarded and successful. Other teachers give subjective grades to individual students on their role performances within the group (See Figure 4.2 Scoring Guide for Assessing Students in Cooperative Learning: Sample Form). To determine students' report card grades, individual student achievement can be measured later through individual results on tests and other sources of data. The final grade can be based on those results and the student's performance in the group. Still other teachers do not assign letter grades of ABC but give indications of individual student achievement with terms of *satisfactory progress, consistent achievement,* and so on, related to a standard-based performance.

Using Checklists

One item maintained by students in their portfolios can be a series of checklists. Items on the checklist will vary depending on your purpose, subject, and grade level (see Sample Forms in Figure 4.3, Assessing a Student's Oral Report: Sample Checklist and Figure 4.4, Student Self-Assessment of Writing: Sample Form). Checklist items can be used easily by

a student to compare with previous self-assessment. Open-ended questions such as those found in the checklist in Figure 4.4 allow the student to provide additional information and do some expressive writing. After a student has demonstrated each of the skills satisfactorily, a check is made next to the student's name, either by you independently or in conference with your student.

Using Portfolios

Student **portfolios** fall into three general categories; the purpose in a given situation may transcend some combination of these or use all three categories. The categories are (1) the **selected work portfolio** in which students maintain samples of their work after a teacher prompt; (2) the **longitudinal portfolio** in which student work samples are oriented toward outcome-driven goals and represent work from the beginning to the end of a specified period (such as the start-to-finish of an ITU or a semester or term) to exemplify achievement toward the goals; and (3) the **career portfolio** in which samples of student work will document the student's

FIGURE 4.3   Assessing a Student's Oral Report: Sample Checklist[*]

Oral Report Assessment Checklist

Did the student . . .	Yes	No	Comments
1. Speak so that everyone could hear?			
2. Finish sentences?			
3. Seem comfortable in front of the group?			
4. Give a good introduction?			
5. Seem well informed about the topic?			
6. Explain ideas clearly?			
7. Stay on the topic?			
8. Give a good conclusion?			
9. Use any visuals/effective visuals to make the presentation interesting?			
10. Give good answers to questions from the audience?			

*This checklist can become a self-assessment form for older students by changing the initial heading of *Did the Student* . . . to *Did I* . . . and giving it to the students to complete. Also, you can rearrange a checklist similar to this into a scoring guide to show levels of satisfactory completion for selected performance. As an example, a scoring guide rearranged with the behaviors just listed could indicate levels of performance (i.e., for strong speaker [3 points]: finishes sentences, seems comfortable in front of group and gives good introduction; for capable speaker [2 points]: usually is informed on the topic and usually explains ideas clearly; for developing speaker [1 point]: has difficulty staying on the topic and difficulty giving a good conclusion).

FIGURE 4.4 Student Self-Assessment of Writing: Sample Form

Student _____ Date _____

Teacher _____ Class/grade level _____

Draft title of paper _____

Answer the following questions about the draft of your own paper after all group members have shared their papers by reading them aloud to others in the group.

		Yes	No
1.	In my introduction, I put forth my thesis.	_____	_____
2.	In the beginning, I orient the reader by providing relevant background information and sources.	_____	_____
3.	I support my interpretive claims by providing (circle those that apply): textual evidence, specific quotations, personal experience, related readings.	_____	_____
4.	I explain how my examples support my claim by using words such as demonstrates, illustrates, proves, and shows.	_____	_____
5.	My supporting evidence provides the bulk of my composition.	_____	_____
6.	I take a strong, consistent stance and maintain it.	_____	_____
7.	I convince my readers that my interpretation is valid.	_____	_____

8. What I like best about my paper is:

_____

_____

_____

_____

9. A part where I need more information is:

_____

_____

_____

_____

10. Other revisions I might make are:

_____

_____

_____

_____

Source: Adapted from unpublished material by Pam Benedetti. *Using Portfolios to Strengthen Student Assessment in English/Language Arts (Grades 6–12).* Copyright 1991 by Pam Benedetti, p. 29.

readiness to move forward in his or her education career, such as moving from one school grade level to another, from high school to a work situation, or on to postsecondary education.

Student portfolios should be well organized chronologically and, depending on the grade level, contain some of the following: anecdotal records, which are useful for recording spontaneous events; assignment record sheets; class worksheets; checklists or inventories, which are useful for recording development of skills; forms for student self-assessment and reflection on the work done; scoring guides or rating scales; the students' responses to questions; records of homework; project binders that include a project record and successive drafts of the students' work; and any other class materials thought important by the students and the teacher.[9] If appropriate for your students, send their writing portfolios home periodically with a "response paper" for the parent or guardian. If any writing needs further work, add the words *work in progress* so an adult will understand why errors are still found in the writing. Ask the adult in the home to look through the portfolio with the student and sign your enclosed response paper, which indicates that the adult has seen the student's work. The response paper also asks for feedback about the student's writing using questions similar to these:

- What is your favorite piece of writing in the portfolio? Why?
- Where do you see that your child is doing well in the enclosed work?
- Where have you seen improvement in your child's writing in the enclosed work?
- What were some of the surprises (if any) that you found in the portfolio?

Request that *both* the student and the adult sign the paper before it is returned to you. To engage the adult in the home further, you may develop a student portfolio in thirds, which means the adult in the home selects from the student's work sent home and inserts it as one-third of the portfolio; the student selects material for another third; and you select the remaining one-third of the material.

Although portfolio assessment as an alternative to traditional methods of evaluating student progress has gained momentum in recent years, setting standards has been very difficult. Research on the use of portfolios for assessment indicates that **validity** and **reliability** of teacher evaluation are often quite low. Before using portfolios as an alternative to traditional testing, you will want to clearly understand the reasons for doing it, carefully decide on portfolio con-

tent, establish **scoring guides/rubrics** or standard-based expectations, anticipate grading problems, and consider parent and guardian reactions.

When emphasizing the criteria for assessment, scoring guides/rubrics, rating scales, and checklists provide students with a means of expressing their feelings and give you as the teacher still another source of input data for use in assessment. To provide students with reinforcement and guidance that will improve their learning and development, you can meet with individual students to discuss their self-assessments. Such conferences can provide your students with understandable and achievable short-term goals and help them develop and maintain adequate self-esteem.[10]

Although almost any instrument used for assessing student work can be used for student self-assessment, in some cases it might be better to construct specific instruments with the student's understanding of the instrument in mind. Student self-assessment and self-reflection should be done on a regular and continuing basis so comparisons can be made periodically by the student. You will need to help students learn how to analyze these comparisons during your individual conferences, because they should provide a student with information previously not recognized about his or her own progress and growth.

Guidelines for Using Portfolios.   Following is a summary of guidelines for using student portfolios in the assessment of learning:

- Contents of the portfolio should reflect course/grade level goals, learning standards, and **target objectives.**
- Contents should be determined and announced clearly and in writing (perhaps also post a schedule in the classroom) about when, how, and by what criteria the portfolios will be reviewed by you.
- Students should be given the responsibility for the maintenance of their portfolios, should date everything that goes into them, and keep them in the classroom.
- Contents in the portfolios should not be graded/compared in any way with those of other students. Remind students that the portfolios are for student self-assessment and for showing progress in learning. Encourage them to keep major sample papers related to the study or ITU in the portfolios. For assessment, you can record the extent to which the portfolio was maintained and use a checklist to show which required materials related to standard-based objectives are in the portfolio.

MAINTAINING RECORDS OF STUDENT ACHIEVEMENT

You must maintain well-organized and complete records of student achievement, perhaps in a written record book or on an electronic record book (i.e., a computer software program, either commercially developed or one you have developed yourself by using a program spreadsheet). At the very least, the record book should include attendance records and all records of scores on tests, homework, projects, and other assignments. At the high-tech end of record keeping, a record-keeping and learner profile system is available that uses a computer; Apple Newton material;[11] or a bar code scanner to help you plan, customize assessment criteria, observe and collect data anywhere without interrupting the learning process, make reports, and assist in student self-assessment.

Daily interactions and events occur in the classroom that may provide informative data about a student's intellectual, emotional, and physical development. Maintaining a dated record of your observations of these interactions and events can provide important information that might otherwise be forgotten. At the end of a unit, and again at the conclusion of a grading period, you will want to review your records. During the course of the school year, your anecdotal records (and those of other members of your teaching team) will provide important information about each student and ideas for attention to be given to each individual student, as well as changes that you and your team might want to make in the future use of the ITU or of a different one.

GRADING AND MARKING STUDENT ACHIEVEMENT

If conditions were ideal (which they are not), and if you and your teaching colleagues did your jobs perfectly well (which many of us do not), then all students would receive top marks (the ultimate in **mastery** or quality learning), and there would be less need to talk about grading and marking. Master learning implies that some end point of learning is attainable, but that end point probably does not exist. In any case, because conditions for teaching never are ideal and we as teachers are mere humans, although limited by the nature and scope of this guide, let us continue to discuss this topic of grading. It is undoubtedly of special interest to you; to your students; to their parents or guardians; and to school counselors, administrators and school boards, potential employers, providers of scholarships, and college admissions officers.

As educators, we frequently use the term **achievement,** but what is meant by this term? Achievement means accomplishment, but is it accomplishment of the instructional objectives against preset standards, or is it simple accomplishment? Most teachers probably would choose the former, during which you as the teacher establish a standard or select a state/national standard that must be met for a student to receive a certain rating or grade for an assignment, project, test, quarter, semester, or course. Achievement, then, is decided by degrees of accomplishment.

Preset standards usually are expressed in percentages (degrees of accomplishment) needed for marks or ABC grades. On one hand, if no student achieves the standard required for an A grade, for example, then no student receives an A. On the other hand, if all students meet the preset standard for the A grade, then all receive As. As mentioned, determining student grades on the basis of preset standards is referred to as **criterion-referenced grading.**

Criterion-Referenced versus Norm-Referenced Grading

Whereas criterion-referenced (or competency-based) grading is based on preset standards, norm-referenced grading measures the relative accomplishment of individuals in a group (e.g., one classroom of chemistry students) or in a larger group (e.g., all students enrolled in the same chemistry course) by comparing and ranking students. It is commonly known as *grading on the curve.* Because it encourages competition and discourages cooperative learning, **norm-referenced grading** is *not* recommended for the determination of student grades. After all, each student is an individual and should not be converted to a statistic on a frequency distribution curve. Grades for student achievement should be tied to performance levels and determined on the basis of each student's achievement toward preset standards.[12]

In criterion-referenced grading, your aim is to communicate information about an individual student's progress in knowledge and work skills in comparison with that student's previous attainment, or his or her progress in the pursuit of an absolute, such as content mastery. Criterion-referenced grading is featured in continuous-progress curricula, competency-based curricula, and other programs that focus on **individualized** learning.

Criterion-referenced grading is based on the level at which each student meets the specified objectives (or standards) for the unit/course or grade level. The objectives/standards must be clearly stated to represent important student learning outcomes. This approach implies that effective teaching and learning results in high marks/rankings or high grades (As) for most students. In fact, when a mastery concept is used, the student must accomplish the objectives before being allowed to proceed to the next learning task. In this approach, the comparison is between what Brittany the student could do yesterday and what she can do today and how well these performances compare with the preset standard.

Most schools use some sort of combination of both norm-referenced and criterion-referenced data usage. Sometimes, both kinds of information are useful. For example, a report card for Brittany in the eighth grade might indicate how she is meeting certain criteria, such as an A grade for her skill in addition of fractions. Another entry might show that this mastery, however, is expected in the sixth grade. Both criterion- and norm-referenced data may be communicated to Brittany's parents or guardians and to Brittany herself. Appropriate procedures include the following:

- A criterion-referenced approach to show the extent to which the student can accomplish the task and, if so, to what degree.
- A norm-referenced approach to show how well a student performs compared with the larger group to which the student belongs. The latter, for instance, is important data for college admissions officers and for committees that offer academic scholarships.

Determining Grades

Once entered onto school transcripts, grades have a significant impact on the students' future. When determining achievement grades for student performance, you must make several important and professional decisions. These decisions relate to your school's policy about giving marks such as E, S, and I or pass/no pass, or about using percentages of accomplishment and letter grades for courses taught in middle schools and high schools.[13] Consider what decisions you will make related to the guidelines shown in Figure 4.5, Guidelines for Determining Grades.

TESTING FOR ACHIEVEMENT

Competent planning, preparing, administering, and scoring of tests is an important set of professional skills for you to develop. The paragraphs that follow provide guidelines that will be a reference to you as a student teacher, and again during your initial years as an employed teacher.

One source of information for determining grades is data obtained from testing for student achievement. In this section about testing, we briefly consider the difference between standardized and nonstandardized tests, then discuss the purposes and frequency of testing, test construction, and administering tests.

Using Standardized and Nonstandardized Tests

Standardized tests are those that have been constructed and published by commercial testing bureaus and are used by districts and states to determine and compare student achievements, principally in the subjects of mathematics, reading, science, and social studies. Standardized norm-referenced tests are best for diagnostic purposes and should not be used for determining student grades. Space in this guide does not allow our consideration of standardized achievement testing so our focus here will be on **nonstandardized tests** that are designed by you or by your teaching team for your own unique group of students.

Commercial materials—textbook publishers' tests, test item pools, and standardized tests—are available from a variety of sources because schools, teachers, and students are different. Teacher-designed materials are those tests that you will be designing (or collaboratively designing) and preparing for your own purposes for your distinct cohort of students.

Purposes for Testing

Tests can be designed for several purposes. Employing a variety of tests and alternative test items will keep your testing program interesting, useful, and reliable. Remembering your beginning college or university days when you were a first-semester student, you will probably recall taking tests that measured your knowledge and achievement in a particular course—but now as the teacher you will want to use tests for other reasons as well. You can use tests to assess and aid in your curriculum development or to help you determine your teaching effectiveness. You can use tests to help your students develop positive attitudes, appreciations, and values; to help them increase their understanding and retention of facts, concepts, principles, and skills; to provide diagnostic information for planning individualized instruction; to motivate, provide a review, or replace a drill to enhance their learning; and, finally, to serve as ongoing informational data for the students and their parents/guardians.

FIGURE 4.5 Guidelines for Determining Grades

Guidelines	Decisions to make about . . .
Be as objective as possible.	*Converting accomplishments to letter grades or rankings.* When converting your interpretation of a student's accomplishments to a letter grade, be objective. For the selection of criteria for ABC grades, you can select a percentage standard such as 92 percent for A, 85 percent for B, 75 percent for C. Cutoff percentages are your decision, although your school/district may have guidelines that you are expected to follow.
Clarify your terms for others.	*Using variety of sources of data.* You'll want to make decisions about using a variety of sources of data for the determination of a student's final grade (assessment), and see that grades are one aspect of evaluation about educational progress that you communicate to a student and to his/her parents or guardian.
Develop your grading policy on accomplishment.	*Considering degrees of accomplishment.* Build your grading policy around degrees of accomplishment rather than failure, and around the idea that students proceed from one accomplishment to the next.
Explain your grading/marking policies.	*Determining your policies and having examples to show others.* At the start of the school term, clearly discuss your policies for grading—first to yourself, then to your students and their parents/guardians at back-to-school night or through a written explanation that you send home. Or, you might want to use both methods to contact the student's home. Share examples of scoring guides/rubrics and grading with students and parents.
Use a system and preset standards.	*Selecting a system and standards.* To determine the students' final grades, we recommend a point system, where responses that students write, say, and do are given points and the possible point total determines the grade. If 92 percent is the cutoff for an A and 500 points are possible, then any student with 460 points or more (500 × .92) has achieved an A. With a point system and preset standards, at any time during the grading period you and the students know the current points possible and can easily calculate a current grade standing related to grade level, unit of study, or course.

Frequency of Testing

Assessment of student learning should be continual—it should be ongoing every minute of every class day. To clarify this concept, Brookhart points out that assessment means how you gather evidence of your students' achievement in the context of your classroom instruction, and says that what you should know about assessment can be organized into words represented by the three Ps—pervasive, pivotal, and primary. Assessment is pervasive be-cause you are always doing it; it is pivotal because it provides data for your decisions that affect the students; and it is primary because it is central and important to your teaching.[14]

For grading or marking purposes, it is difficult to generalize about how often to formally test for student achievement, but we believe that testing should be cumulative and frequent. Cumulative indicates that the items for each assessment should measure for the student's understanding of previously learned materials and for the current unit of study. Frequent means as often as once a week. Assessments that are cumulative include any review, reinforcement, or articulation of previously learned material with the most recent material. The advantages of frequent assessment include a reduction in student anxiety over tests and an increase in the validity of the final summative assessment.

Test Construction

After determining the reasons for which you are designing and administering a test, you need to identify the specific instructional objectives/standards the test is being designed to measure. As emphasized in Chapter 3, your written instructional objectives are specific so you can write assessment items to measure against these objectives. That is referred to as **criterion-referenced assessment.** When the objectives are aligned with specific curriculum standards, as they usually are or should be, it also can be referred to as standards-based assessment. So we suggest that the first step in test construction is identifying the purpose(s) for the test. The second step is to identify the standards and specific objectives to be measured, and the third step is to prepare the test items. The best time to prepare draft items is after you have prepared your instructional objectives—while the objectives are fresh in your mind, which means before the lessons are taught. After teaching a lesson, you will want to rework your first draft of the test items that are related to that lesson to modify any draft items as a result of the instruction that occurred.

Administering Tests

The actual administration of a test involves several factors including test-taker's anxiety and the planning of a formative assessment program. These two factors are discussed as follows:

- **Reduce test anxiety.**   For some students, test taking can be a time of high anxiety. Students demonstrate test anxiety in several ways. For instance, just before and during testing, some students are very quiet and thoughtful while others are noisy and disruptive. To more accurately measure student achievement, you will want to take steps to reduce their anxiety. To reduce some student anxieties, review what will be the focus of the test and/or test items, give them time to study in small groups or individually, and let them write their own test items for a topic of study and perhaps "take" a test composed of their own test items to review the material.
- **Plan a routine for a formative assessment program.**   Because students often respond best to a

familiar routine for testing purposes, plan your formative assessment program so tests are given at regular intervals and administered at the same time and in the same way—perhaps on Friday afternoon.

PREPARING ASSESSMENT ITEMS: GENERAL GUIDELINES

As you plan the assessment component of your ITU of instruction, consider the following general guidelines, suggestions to help you organize your teaching responsibility in this area and prepare for assessment of the students:

- Include several kinds of items and assessment instruments (see more types that follow).
- Ensure that content coverage is complete (i.e., that all objectives or relevant standards are being measured).
- Ensure that each item is reliable—that it measures the intended objective (one way to check item reliability is to have more than one item measuring the same objective).
- Ensure that each item is clear and unambiguous to all students.
- Plan each item to be difficult enough for the poorly prepared student but easy enough for the student who is well prepared.
- Maintain a bank of items with each item coded according to its matching instructional objective and its domain of learning (cognitive, affective, or psychomotor), and whether it requires recall of information, processing of information, or the application of information.
- Consider using ready-made test banks available on computer disks that accompany many programs or textbooks. If you use them, be certain that the items match your instructional objectives/standards and that they are well written. Just because they were published does not mean that the items are well written or are appropriate for you and your students.

Every test that you administer to your students should represent your best educational effort—clear and without spelling and grammatical errors. A test that has been quickly and poorly prepared can cause you more grief (and loss of respect) than you can imagine. A test that is sprinkled with mistakes in grammar and misspelled words will be frowned upon by well-prepared students and discerning parents/guardians. If you are a teacher candidate, it will certainly bring about an admonishment from your cooperating teacher and your university supervisor.

ATTAINING CONTENT VALIDITY

To ensure that your test measures the appropriate objectives, you can construct a table of specifications. A two-way grid indicates behavior in one dimension and content in another (see Figures 4.6 and 4.7). In the grid in Figure 4.6, behavior relates to the cognitive, affective, and psychomotor domains. In this figure, the **cognitive domain** is divided according to Bloom's taxonomy (see Chapter 3) into the six categories of knowledge—simple recall, comprehension, application, analysis, synthesis (often involving an original product in oral or written form), and evaluation. The specification table of Figure 4.7

does not specify levels within the affective and psychomotor domains.

To use a table of specifications, you can examine objectives/standards for the unit and decide what emphasis should be given to the behavior and to the content. For instance, if vocabulary development is a concern for a sixth-grade study of *Civilizations: Ancient Greece,* then probably 20 percent of the test on vocabulary would be appropriate, but 50 percent would be unsuitable. This planning enables you to design a test to fit the situation rather than have a haphazard test that does not correspond to the objectives either in content or behavior emphasis. Consider the following example: You realize that recall questions are

FIGURE 4.6   Table of Specifications I: Behavior Related to Cognitive, Affective, and Psychomotor Domains

CONTENT	BEHAVIORS								TOTAL
Social Studies Grade 6	Cognitive						Affective	Psychomotor	
Ancient Greece	Knowledge	Comprehension	Application	Analysis	Synthesis	Evaluation			
I. Vocabulary development		2 (1, 2)	1 (2)						3
II. Concepts		2 (3, 4)	2 (4)						4
III. Applications	1 (5)	1	1 (5)	1 (5)	1 (5)	1 (5)			6
IV. Problem solving		1 (6)		1 (6)					2
TOTAL	1	6	4	2	1	1			15

FIGURE 4.7   Table of Specifications II: Behavior Related to Cognitive, Affective, and Psychomotor Domains

CONTENT	BEHAVIORS							TOTAL
	Cognitive			Affective		Psychomotor		
	Input	Processing	Application	Low	High	Low	High	
I.								
II.								
III.								
IV.								
TOTAL								

easy to write and note that tests often fail to go beyond this level even though the objectives/standards state that the student will analyze and evaluate. The sample table of specifications for an ITU on *Civilizations: Ancient Greece* indicates a distribution of questions on a test. Since this test is to be an objective test and it is considered unnecessary to test for affective and psychomotor behaviors on this test, this table of specifications calls for no test items in these areas. If these categories are included in the unit objectives/standards, often assessment devices can be used to test student learning in these domains. As the teacher, you could also show the objectives tested, as indicated in parenthesis in Figure 4.6. Then a later check on inclusions of all objectives (and a check on which standards are linked to the included objectives) is easy to perform.

Preferred by some teachers is the alternative table shown in Figure 4.7. Rather than differentiating among all six of Bloom's cognitive levels, this table separates cognitive objectives into three levels: (1) those that require simple low-level recall of knowledge, (2) those that require information processing, and (3) those that require application of the new knowledge. In addition, the affective and psychomotor domains are each divided into low-level and high-level behaviors.

PERFORMANCE TESTING: EXPENSIVE AND TIME INTENSIVE

As you might conclude from our preceding discussion, performance testing is usually more expensive and time-consuming than verbal testing, which in turn is more time-demanding and expensive than written testing. However, a good program of assessment will use alternative forms of assessment and not rely solely on one form (such as written) or one type of written item (such as multiple choice). You also should avoid using one form of assessment when assessing student learning during and at the conclusion of an ITU of instruction.

The type of test and the items that you use depend on your purpose and objectives/standards. Carefully consider the alternatives within that framework. To provide validity checks and to account for the individual differences of students, a good assessment program should include items from different types, which is what writers of articles in professional journals are referring to when they talk about **alternative assessment.** They are encouraging the use of multiple assessment items, as opposed to the traditional heavy reliance on such items as multiple-choice questions only.

Performance Type Assessment Item

Description. Provided with certain conditions or materials, the student solves a problem or accomplishes some other action.

Example. Write a retelling of your favorite ancient Greek fable or myth on the computer and create a diorama to accompany it.

Advantages. This type of item comes closer to direct measurement (authentic assessment) of certain expected outcomes than most other types. As indicated in the discussions about other question types that follow, some items can actually be prepared as performance type items; that is, when the student actually does what he or she is being tested for—for example, the student actually arranges items in a sequence or order because he/she is being tested for his/her knowledge of sequence/order. You also will note that essay type questions can be used in performance assessment when students are involved in making predictions given certain conditions in selected situations.

Limitations. This type can be difficult and time-consuming to administer to a group of students. Scoring may tend to be subjective. It could be difficult to give makeup tests to students who were absent on test day.

Guidelines for use. Use your creativity to design and use performance tests, as they tend to measure well the important objectives. To establish a performance assessment situation, see the instructions in Figure 4.8, Steps for Establishing a Performance Assessment Situation: Samples of Listening Scoring Guide and Checklist.

PREPARING AND USING MORE ASSESSMENT ITEMS: DESCRIPTIONS, EXAMPLES, AND GUIDELINES

Arrangement Type

Description. Terms, sentences, or realia (hands-on objects) are to be arranged in a specified order to assess performance of knowledge of sequence and order.

Example. Arrange the following list of events on a time line in order of their occurrence: The *Mayflower* anchored in the harbor. The crew and the passengers of the *Mayflower* assembled for a meeting to determine their self-government. The pilgrims on the *Mayflower* signed the Mayflower Compact to establish a government of just and equal laws and promised to obey such laws.

Advantages. This type of item tests for knowledge of sequence and order and is valuable for initiating reviews, for starting discussions, and for performance assessment.

FIGURE 4.8   Steps for Establishing a Performance Assessment Situation: Samples of Listening Scoring Guide and Checklist

---

I. Specify the performance objective/standard.

II. Specify the test situation.

III. Establish the criteria (scoring guide/rubric) for judging the excellence of the process and/or product. Here is a sample scoring guide for assessing a student's skill in listening.

   A. Strong listener:

      Responds immediately to oral directions

      Focuses on speaker

      Maintains appropriate attention span

      Listens to what others are saying

      Is interactive

   B. Capable, competent listener:

      Follows oral directions

      Is usually attentive to speaker and to discussions

      Usually maintains attention span

      Usually listens to others without interrupting

      Is usually interactive without interrupting

   C. Developing listener:

      Has difficulty following directions

      Relies on repetition

      Is often inattentive

      Has short attention span

      Often interrupts the speaker

IV. Make a checklist to score the performance or product. The checklist includes criteria you established in Step III. For example, the following is a brief checklist for listening. Check the item if the behavior reaches the standard in a particular category listed as A, B, or C above.

   Category of strong listener:

   _____ 1. Responds immediately to oral directions.

   _____ 2. Focuses on speaker.

   _____ 3. Maintains appropriate attention span (and so on).

V. Prepare your directions in writing for expected listening skills, and outline the expected outcomes with instructions for the students.

Limitations.   Scoring can be difficult, so be cautious and meticulous when using this type for grading purposes.

Guidelines for use.   To enhance reliability, you may need to add instructions to the students to include the rationale for their arrangement, making it a combined arrangement and short explanation type of assessment. Allow space for explanations on an answer sheet. This is useful for small, heterogeneous group assessment to allow students to share and learn from their combined thinking and reasoning.

Completion Type

Description.   This type is sometimes called a fill-in item in which an incomplete sentence is presented and the student is to complete it by filling in the blank space(s) or is to complete an incomplete drawing. This item assesses comprehension through a **cloze type procedure.**

Example. To test their hypotheses, social scientists conduct _____.

(Write your reason(s) for your word choice here:_____.)

Advantages. This type of item requires less time than a complete answer or drawing, which might be required in an essay type item. This type is easy to design, take, and score.

Limitations. Take care with the instructions to students, do not misinterpret the expectation, and be flexible in accepting the response. Your answer key may have "experiments" as the correct answer for the item in the example, but a student might answer with *investigations* or *tests* or some other equally valid response.

Guidelines for use. This is useful for small, heterogeneous group assessment to allow students to share and learn from their group thinking and reasoning and to measure conceptual knowledge. You can make the item a combined drawing-completion and short explanation type and engage the students in including their rationales for their thinking behind their completions. Allow additional space for explanations or for responses of students with motor control difficulties. For sentence completion, use one blank per item and keep the blanks equal in length.

Correction Type

Description. This is similar to the completion type with the following variation: patterns, complete sentences, or paragraphs are given with underlined or italicized words that are to be changed to make the sentences/paragraphs correct.

Example. After the settlement of Jamestown, Virginia, in 1607, Plymouth Colony was the second English *sand castle* in North America. The *sand castle* was established on the rocky shore of Cape Cod Bay in 1620. The colonists called their new *sand castle* Plymouth after the English *fortress* Plymouth from which they had set sail on the *Mayflower* to North America.

(Explain your word choices here: _____.)

Advantages. This type of item is very useful for introducing procedures, patterns such as the Fibonacci number series (1,1,2,3,5,8, . . .), words with multiple meanings, or information. Writing of this type can be entertaining for the teacher (and for the students who read the item). It is useful for preassessment of student knowledge or for starting a review. When it is used occasionally, students enjoy the test-taking relief of light humor given by the incorrect absurdities.

Limitations. As with the completion type, the correction type tends to measure for low-level recall and rote memory—except in cases where a student is unfamiliar with the patterns or information. Then it becomes a relatively high-level question. Note that the italicized/underlined items also could be so humorous that they might cause more classroom disturbance than you want.

Guidelines for use. Use occasionally for test-taking diversion and for discussion purposes. When possible, write items that measure for higher-level cognition or consider making this type of item a combined correction and short explanation type. If appropriate for your students, allow space for student explanations.

Essay Type

Description. This is used when a question or problem is presented and the student is asked to compose a response in the form of sustained prose using the students' own words, phrases, and ideas within the limits of the question or problem.

Example. Related to the pilgrims' Mayflower Compact, what contributions about self-government would you have made to the compact if you had been a pilgrim on the *Mayflower* in 1620? Justify your contributions (this means to show some reasons with an emphasis on advantageous, correct, and positive points of view).

Advantages. This type of item measures conceptual knowledge and higher mental processes, such as the ability to synthesize material and to express ideas in clear and precise written language. It is especially useful in thematic teaching. It provides practice in written expression and can be used in performance assessment such as predicting how long a plant will live after seeing that it is growing in certain conditions of soil, light, and temperature.

Limitations. An essay item requires a good deal of time to read and to score. It can provide an unreliable sampling of achievement and is vulnerable to teacher subjectivity and unreliable scoring. Further, an essay item tends to punish the student who writes slowly and laboriously or has limited proficiency in the written language, but who may have achieved as well as a student who writes faster and is more proficient in the language. An essay item tends to favor students who have fluency with words but whose achievement may not necessarily be better. In addition, do not assume that all students understand all the verbs unless you have given instruction in the meaning of key directive verbs. If appropriate for your group, you can give *ad hoc* lessons in the meaning of key verbs for essay item responses. The students can then discuss the verbs, draw cartoons about them, write definitions,

FIGURE 4.9 Meaning of Directive Verb Pairs and Essay Cues for Essay Responses

Directive Verb Pairs, Meanings, and Essay Cues

Compare or contrast: Compare asks for an analysis of similarity and differences but with a greater emphasis on similarities or likenesses; *contrast* asks more about differences than similarities. Essay cue: *Compare* one of your belongings given to you by a friend with a gift you gave to your friend. *Contrast* one gift you received from a friend last year with one gift you received this year.

Criticize or evaluate: Criticize asks for the good and bad of an idea or situation; *evaluate* asks for an expression of judgment of value or worth. Essay cue: *Criticize* receiving letter grades of ABCs. *Evaluate* the idea of using scoring guides/rubrics for assessment.

Define or identify: Define means to express clearly and concisely the meaning of a term in the student's own words or from a dictionary; *identify* means to state recognizable or identifiable characteristics. Essay cue: *Define* the meaning of *friendship* from your point of view. *Identify* some characteristics of what a friend means to you.

Describe or relate: Describe means to give an account of something in words; *relate* means to tell how specified things are connected or brought into some kind of relationship. Essay cue: *Describe* which of your belongings given to you by a friend is your favorite. *Relate* what keeps you and your friends together as friends.

Diagram or illustrate: Diagram means to put quantities or numerical values into the form of a chart, drawing, or graph; *illustrate* means to describe by means of diagrams, examples, figures, pictures, or sketches. Essay cue: *Diagram* on a chart of the number of friends each class member states he/she has. *Illustrate* at least two times that you attended an event or outing with a friend.

Discuss and explain: Discuss means to present various sides of events, ideas, or situations; *explain* means to describe with an emphasis on cause and effect. Essay cue: *Discuss* which of your belongings given by a friend would be painful for you to lose. *Explain* what caused you to change your mind about a friend you first liked, then disliked.

Enumerate or list: Enumerate means to name or list one after another and is different from the direction to *explain briefly* or *tell in a few words; list* means to simply name items in a category or to include them in a row or column without much description. Essay cue: *Enumerate* which of your belongings, given to you by a friend, that you like best. *List* any belongings you have with wheels.

Generalize and summarize: Generalize means to arrive at a valid generalization from specific information; *summarize* means to recapitulate the main points without example or illustrations. Essay cue: *Generalize* which of your acquaintances could become a best friend to you. *Summarize* what caused you to trust someone as a friend.

Infer or interpret: Infer means to forecast what is *likely* to happen as a result of information provided; *interpret* means to *describe* or *explain* a given fact (theory, principle, or doctrine) within a specific context. Essay cue: *Infer* what might happen when your best friend moves away. *Interpret* what the meaning of friendship does for you when you are sad.

Justify or prove: Justify means to show reasons with an emphasis on advantageous, correct, and positive ones; *prove* means to present materials as evidence, proof, and witnesses. Essay cue: *Justify* which of your friends is the best friend from your point of view. *Prove* what caused you to change your mind about a friend you first disliked, then liked.

Outline or trace: Outline means to give a short summary with headings and subheadings; *trace* means to follow a history or a series of events, step by step, by going backward over the information. Essay cue: *Outline* what you and your friend did yesterday. *Trace* the events that you and your friend did yesterday.

or sketch scenes to illustrate some of the differences in verb meanings that are indicated in Figure 4.9 on page 114.

Guidelines for use. When preparing an essay-only test, prepare many questions that require a relatively short prose response (similar to the short explanation type). Short response questions are preferable to a smaller number of questions that require long prose responses. Briefer answers tend to be more precise and the use of many items provides a more reliable sampling of student achievement. When you prepare short prose response questions, be sure to avoid using words verbatim from the student textbook. Also consider the following hints:

Before the test

1. Give instruction and practice to students in responding to key directive verbs that will be used in the test before giving this type of test item. (See list in Figure 4.9.) Additional discussion and practice can introduce sample questions such as the ones that follow to the students for their brief written responses:
   • Recall a time when you changed your mind, attitude, or feelings about a person, place, or event.
   • Consider a favorite person, place, or thing that you would not want to lose or be parted from or give up.
   • Consider a favorite person, place, or possession that you consider very meaningful to you and tell how you came in contact with it and why you remember it in a special way.
2. Prepare the essay items, make a tentative scoring guide (see Figure 4.10), and decide the key

ideas you expect the students to identify. Decide the number of points that will be allotted to each item.

During the test

3. Have the students write their names on the backs of the papers or use a number code rather than having students put their names on the front of essay papers. This practice will keep you unaware of whose paper you are reading and will nullify the **halo effect** that can occur when you know whose paper you are correcting.
4. Inform the students about the relative test value for each item. Point values, if different for each item, can be listed in the margin of the test next to each item.
5. Consider having the students all answer the same questions rather than letting them select essay items from a list. This continuity will give you different qualities of achievement and students' responses that you can compare.
6. Allow students adequate test time for a full response.

After the test

7. Read all student papers for one essay item response at a time in one sitting, and while doing that, make notes to yourself; then repeat and while reading that item again, score each student's paper for that item. Repeat the process for the next essay item, but change the order of the pile of papers so you are not reading them in the same order. While scoring the essay responses, keep in mind the nature of the objective/standard being measured, which may include the qualities

FIGURE 4.10 Scoring Guide for Student Essay Writing: Sample Form

Category 1: Outstanding Competence	Category 2: Definite Competence	Category 3: Competence	Category 4: Deficiencies	Category 5: Basic Deficiencies
10–9 Well organized, clear explanations and details, displays varied language use with no errors in mechanics, structure of sentences, usage, and word choices.	8–7 Well organized generally, has explanations and details, displays varied language use and word choices with few errors in mechanics, structure of sentences, and usage.	6–5 Organization adequate, some explanations and details, displays facile language use with some errors in mechanics, structure of sentences, and usage.	4–3 Organization inadequate, inadequate explanations and details, displays limited language use with many errors in mechanics, structure of sentences, and usage.	2–1 Organization not coherent, explanations and details are undeveloped, writing skills show basic deficiencies, many errors in writing mechanics, usage, and sentence structure—sometimes in repetitive patterns.

of grammar, handwriting, neatness, punctuation, and spelling.

8. Mark the papers with positive and constructive comments and show students how they could have explained or responded better. Remember the three **P** words in marking students' papers— be patient, positive, and prescriptive—understanding that while having some knowledge of a concept, some students will not yet be facile with written expression. To reduce subjectivity in scoring, you can prepare distinct scoring guidelines as shown in Figure 4.11, Scoring Guide for Student Research Paper: Sample Form.

Grouping Type

Description.   Several items are presented and the student is to select and group those that are related in some way.

Example.   Separate the following words into two groups: Place those that are related to Plymouth Colony in Group A; place those that are not in Group B. Words: pilgrims, sand castle, compact, jet, self-government, automobile, *Mayflower.*

Advantages.   This tests knowledge of grouping and can be used to measure conceptual knowledge and higher levels of cognition, and to stimulate discussion. It can also be similar to a multiple-choice type item.

Limitations.   Remain alert for the student who has an alternative but valid rationale for her or his grouping.

Guidelines for use.   To allow for an alternative correct response, consider making the item a combination grouping/short explanation type, being certain to allow adequate space to encourage student explanations.

Identification Type

Description.   Unknown *specimens* are to be identified by name or some other criterion.

Example.   Identify each of the food specimens on the table by its common name.

Advantages.   This type of item is useful for authentic and performance assessments and allows students to work with real materials or symbolizations. It can measure high-level learning, procedural understanding, and identification of steps in a process.

Limitations.   This takes more time than many of the other types—both for the teacher to prepare and for the students to complete. Because of a special familiarity with the materials, some students may have an advantage over others. Therefore, be fair by ensuring that the specimens used are equally familiar or unfamiliar to all students.

Guidelines for use.   Whatever specimens are used, they must be familiar to all or to none of the students, and they must be clear and not confusing (e.g., fuzzy photographs or unclear photocopies, dried specimens, incomplete plant specimens, and garbled music recordings can be frustrating for students to discern). Consider using this item for a dyad or team rather than for individual testing.

Matching Type

Description.   Several items are presented in a list of numbered items and the student is to match the items to a list of lettered choices, or in some way to connect the items that are the same or related.

Example.   In the blank space next to each description in column A (stem or premises column) put the letter of the correct answer from column B (the answer or response column).

A (stem column)	B (answer column)
_____1. 20th century U. S. President	A. Bill Clinton
_____2. U. S. past president	B. Thomas Jefferson
_____3. First U.S. president	C. George Washington
	D. George W. Bush

Advantages.   Matching items can measure for ability to judge relationships and to differentiate between similar facts, ideas, definitions, and concepts. These items are easy to score and can test a broad range of context. They reduce guessing, especially if one group (e.g., the answer column) contains more items than the other, are interesting to students, and are adaptable for performance assessment.

Limitations.   Although the matching item is adaptable for performance assessment, the items are not easily adapted to measuring for higher cognition. Because all parts must be homogeneous, it is possible that clues will be given, thus reducing the validity.

Guidelines for use.   The number of items in the response or answer column should exceed the number in the stem column, but keep the number of stem items to 10 or less. Matching sets should have high homogeneity (i.e., items in both columns or groups should be of the same general category) and avoid mixing dates, events, and names. The answers in the response column should be short, about one or two words each and should be ordered logically, perhaps alphabetically or chronologically. If answers from the response column can be used more than once, which can help to avoid guessing by elimination, the directions should state that fact. Be prepared for the student who can legitimately defend a response you might deem incorrect. To eliminate the paper-and-pencil aspect and make the item more direct, use a

FIGURE 4.11 Scoring Guide for Student Research Paper: Sample Form

	14–15	12–13	11	1–10
Parenthetical Reference	All documented correctly. Paper's references document a wide variety of sources cited—at least five from bibliography.	Most documented correctly. Few minor errors. At least three sources from bibliography are cited.	Some documented correctly. Some show no documentation at all. May not correlate to the bibliography.	Few to none are documented. Does not correlate to the bibliography. May be totally absent.
Bibliography and Sources	Strong use of library research. Exceeds minimum of five sources. Bibliography is correctly formatted.	Good use of library research. Exceeds minimum of five sources. Bibliography has few or no errors in format.	Some use of library research. Meets minimum of five sources. Bibliography is present but may be problematic.	Fails to meet minimum standards for library research. Bibliography has major flaws or may be missing.
Mechanics/Format	Correct format and pagination. Neat title page, near perfect spelling, punctuation, and grammar.	Mostly correct format and pagination. Neat. Few errors in title page, spellings, punctuation, and grammar.	Errors in format and pagination. Flawed title page. Distracting errors in spelling, punctuation, and grammar.	Incorrect format. Title page is flawed or missing. Many errors in spelling, punctuation, and grammar. Lack of planning is obvious. Paper is difficult to read.
Thesis	An original and comprehensive thesis for essay or research paper that is clear and well thought out. All sections work to support it.	Comprehensive and well-focused thesis, which is clearly stated. All sections work to support it.	Adequate thesis that is understandable but may be neither clear nor focused. It covers the majority of the issues found in the sections.	Inadequate thesis that is disconnected from the research or may be too broad to support. May be convoluted, confusing, or absent.
Completeness/Coherence	Paper reads as a unified whole. There is no repetition of information. All sections are in place, and transitions between them are clearly developed.	Paper reads as a unified whole with no repetition. All sections are in place, but transitions between them are not as smooth.	Paper has required sections. Repetitions may be evident. The paper does not present a unified whole. Transitions are missing or inadequate.	Paper lacks one or more sections and makes no attempt to connect sections as a whole unit. Sections may be grossly repetitive or contradictory.
Thinking/Analyzing	Strong understanding of the topic. Knowledge is factually relevant, accurate, and consistent. Solutions show analysis of research discussed in paper.	Good understanding of the topic. Uses main points of information researched. Solutions build on examination of research discussed in paper.	General understanding of topic. Uses research and attempts to add to it. Solutions refer to some of the research discussed.	Little understanding of topic. Uses little basic information researched. Minimal examination of the topic. Solutions may be based solely on own opinions without support.

Source: Elk Grove School District, Elk Grove, California. Possible score = 100. In this adaptation, the scorer marks a relevant entry in each of the six categories. The score for that category is the lowest number of the entry.

direction such as *from the materials on the table, pair up those that are most alike.*

Multiple-Choice Type

Description.   This type is similar to the completion item in that statements are presented (the stem) and are sometimes incomplete or have several options or alternatives. This type requires recognition or even higher cognitive processes than mere recall.

Example.   Which one of the following is a pair of antonyms?

   a. loud/soft
   b. halt/finish
   c. absolve/vindicate
   d. procure/purchase

Advantages.   This type of item can be answered and scored quickly. A wide range of content and higher levels of cognition can be tested in a relatively short time. This type is excellent for all testing purposes—motivation, review, and assessment of learning.

Limitations.   Unfortunately, because multiple-choice items are relatively easy to write, test authors tend to write items measuring only for low levels of cognition. Multiple-choice items are excellent for major testing, but questions should be of high quality and measure higher levels of thinking and learning.

Guidelines for use. Consider the following:

1. If the item is in the form of an incomplete statement, then it should be meaningful in itself and imply a direct question rather than merely lead into a collection of unrelated true and false statements.
2. Use a level of language that is easy enough for even the poorest readers and those with limited proficiency in English to understand; avoid unnecessary wordiness.
3. If there is much variation in the length of alternatives, arrange the alternatives in order from shortest to longest (i.e., first alternative is the shortest, last alternative is the longest). For single-word alternatives, the consistent use of the arrangement of the alternatives is recommended, such as by length of answer or in alphabetical order.
4. Arrangement of alternatives should be uniform throughout the test and listed in vertical (column) form rather than in horizontal (paragraph) form.
5. Incorrect responses (distracters) should be plausible and related to the same concept as the correct alternative. An occasional humorous distracter may help relieve test anxiety, but in general, they should be avoided in this type of item. They offer no measuring value and increase the likelihood of the student guessing the correct response.

6. It is not necessary to maintain a fixed number of alternatives for every item, but the use of less than three alternatives is not recommended. Although it is not always possible to develop four or five plausible responses, that number reduces chance responses and guessing, thereby increasing reliability for the item. If you cannot think of enough plausible distracters, include the item on a test the first time as a completion item. As the students respond, wrong answers will provide you with a number of plausible distracters that you can use the next time to make the item multiple choice.
7. Some mainstreamed students may work better when allowed to circle their selected response rather than write its letter or number in a blank space.
8. Responses such as *all of these* or *none of these* should be used only when they will contribute more than another plausible distracter. Be sure that such answers complete the item. *All of the above* is a poorer alternative than *none of the above* because items that use it as a correct response must have four or five correct answers; also, if it is the right answer, knowledge of any two of the distracters will provide the clue.
9. Every item should be grammatically consistent. For example, if the stem is in the form of an incomplete sentence, it should be possible to complete the sentence by attaching any of the alternatives to it.
10. The stem should state a single and specific point, mean the same thing to every student, and not include clues to the correct alternative. Here's an example: A four-sided figure whose opposite sides are parallel is called _____. (Use of the word parallel clues the answer.)
    a. an octagon
    b. a parallelogram
    c. a trapezoid
    d. a triangle
11. The item should be expressed in positive form. A negative form can present a psychological disadvantage to some students. Negative items are those that ask what is *not* characteristic of something, or what is the *least* useful. Discard the item if you cannot express it in positive terminology.
12. There must be only one correct or best response, which is easier said than done. You might consider providing space between test items for students to include their rationales for their responses, thus making the test a combination multiple-choice and short-explanation type item.

This form provides for the measurement of higher levels of cognition and encourages writing. It provides for the students who can rationalize an alternative that you had not considered plausible, which is especially possible today with the diversity of cultural experiences represented by students. For example, recall the story about a math test question that asked, "If a farmer saw 8 crows sitting on a fence and shooed away 3 of them, how many would be left on the fence?" According to the answer key, the correct response would be 5. However, one critical thinking student chose *none* as the answer and was marked wrong by the teacher. The student thought that the crows that were not shooed away would be frightened by the farmer's action and would fly away too—thus none would remain on the fence.

13. Understanding of definitions is better tested by furnishing the name or word and requiring a choice between alternative definitions than by presenting the definition and requiring a choice between alternative words.

14. Avoid using alternatives that include absolute terms such as *never* and *always*.

15. Multiple-choice items need not be entirely verbal. Consider the use of charts, diagrams, realia, videos, and other visuals. They will make the test more interesting, especially to students with low verbal abilities or those who have limited proficiency in English, and consequently, they will make the assessment more direct.

16. Once you have composed a series of multiple-choice items or a complete test of this test item, tally the position of answers to be sure they are evenly distributed, to avoid the common psychological habit (when there are four alternatives) of having the correct alternative in the third position. In other words, when alternative choices are A, B, C, and D or 1, 2, 3, and 4, unless the test designer is aware and avoids it, more correct answers will be in the C or 3 position than in any other.

17. While scoring, tally the incorrect responses for each item on a blank copy of the test. Analyze incorrect responses for each item to discover potential errors in your scoring key. If, for instance, many students select B for an item for which your key says the correct answer is A, you may have made a mistake on your scoring key or in teaching the lesson.

Short Explanation Type

Description. The short explanation question is like the essay type but requires a shorter answer.

Example. Briefly explain in a paragraph how you would end the story.

Advantages. This type of item, like the essay type, assesses student understanding, but takes less time for you to read and score. By using several questions of this type, a greater amount of content can be queried than with a lesser number of essay questions. This type of question provides valuable opportunities for students to learn to express themselves succinctly in writing.

Limitations. Some students will have difficulty expressing themselves in a limited fashion orally or in writing. They need practice, coaching, and time (see suggestions in the essay type section).

Guidelines for use. This type is useful for occasional reviews and quizzes and as an alternative to other types of questions. For scoring, establish a scoring guide/rubric and follow the same guidelines as for the essay type item.

True-False Type

Description: A statement is presented and students are asked to judge its accuracy.

Example. True or False? Plymouth Colony was established in 1620 near the bay now known as Cape Cod.

Advantages. This type of item allows many items to be answered in a relatively short time, making queries of broad content possible. Scoring is quick and simple. True-false items are good as discussion starters, for review, and for diagnostic evaluation (preassessment) of what students already know or think they know.

Limitations. This type can sometimes be difficult to write as purely true or false without qualifying them in such a way that clues the answer. Another difficulty is writing an item that tests only one or two ideas with

In a peer conference, students hand their papers to peers on the left, who offer suggestions for improvements.

which the student should be familiar. In the previous example, a student has to consider more than one idea—Plymouth Colony, concept of establishment, 1620, and Cape Cod Bay. Also, a student may question whether the colonists actually *established* a distinct colony or just built a settlement or may misunderstand the meaning of the term *established* or the meaning of the word, *colony*. Questions about the example could include, *Where, exactly, was the colony established?* and *What is meant by Cape Cod Bay?*

Other limitations are (1) much of the content that lends itself to the true-false type of test item is trivial; (2) guessing might be encouraged; and (3) this type of item lacks data about why a student misses an item. Students have a 50 percent chance of guessing the correct answer, thus giving true-false items both poor validity and poor reliability. In addition, scoring and grading will give you no clue about why a student missed an item. Consequently, the limitations of true-false items far outweigh the advantages. *Therefore, we suggest that pure true-false items not be used for arriving at grades.*

Guidelines for use. For grading purposes, we suggest that you use modified true-false items (see guideline 11 that follows) where space is provided between items for students to write their explanations, thus making the item a combined true-false/short explanation type. Consider the following hints for use:

1. To prepare a false statement, first write the statement as a true sentence, then make it false by changing a word or phrase.
2. Include only one idea in each true-false statement.
3. Try to have an equal number of true and false statements.
4. Proofread your items (or ask a friend to do it) to be sure that the sentences are well constructed and are free from typographical errors.
5. Try to avoid words that may have different meanings for different students.
6. Try to avoid using verbatim language from the student textbook.
7. Avoid trick items such as a reversal of numbers in a date.
8. Try to avoid using negative statements as they tend to confuse students.
9. Try to avoid using specific determiners (e.g., always, all, or more), because these words usually clue that the statement is false; also avoid words that may clue the statement is true (e.g., often, probably, and sometimes).
10. Rather than using symbols for the words *true* and *false* (sometimes teachers ask students to use symbols such as + and −, which might be confusing) or having students write the letters T and F (confusing when a student does not write the letters clearly enough for the teacher to be able to distinguish between them), have students write out the words *true* and *false* or have the students simply circle T or F in the left margin of each item.
11. To avoid wrong answers caused by variations in thinking and to make the item more valid and reliable, encourage the students to write in their rationales for selecting true or false and make the item a modified true-false item. Here's an example: (Circle one) T or F? When a farmer saw 8 crows sitting on the fence surrounding the corn field, he shooed 3 of them away. Five were left on the fence. Explanation: _____.

As stated earlier, for grading purposes, you may use modified true-false items, thus making the item a combined true-false/short explanation type and allowing for divergent and critical thinking. Another form of a modified true-false item is the *sometimes-always-never* item in which a third alternative, *sometimes*, is introduced to reduce the 50 percent chance of guessing correctly.

Now do Exercise 4.1 to begin the preparation of assessment items for your ITU.

ASSESSING YOUR ITU BY FIELD TESTING

Once the ITU is completed, you may want to assess it through field testing, either on your own or as a member of a teaching team. You can begin by reviewing the teaching lessons you planned to initiate the ITU. When working as a member of a teaching team for an ITU, on an agreed-upon date each team member should present a synopsis of results of the lesson(s) each has taught. As the unit continues, the team can field test the ITU in various ways—members could trade classes or participate in team teaching. As an example, two members could combine their classes for instruction in the ITU, if the situation is possible within the school's facilities and scheduling arrangements.

Ongoing formative evaluation. As the unit continues, consider the ITU from daily perspectives. Write down the successes and failure experiences *each day* so you can make gradual, daily adjustments to your teaching, which is part of your formative evaluation of the unit. Gather information about the students' progress in the unit in various ways as discussed in this chapter. Collect information that relates specifically to your learning objective and standard. For instance, you might consider developing an overall checklist about the information related to the unit for your assessment record. It can be a place for recording notes about a student's participation, behavior, and development of conceptual and procedural knowledge, and about affective behaviors. The sample checklist in Figure 4.12 would need

FIGURE 4.12 Student Learning Assessment: Checklist Sample

Learning Assessment Checklist

Student _____ Date _____

Teacher _____ School _____

_____ **1.** Can identify main idea, theme, topic of the unit.

_____ **2.** Can identify contributions of others to the theme.

_____ **3.** Can identify problems related to the unit of study.

_____ **4.** Has developed skills in:

_____ Applying knowledge	_____ Problem identification
_____ Assuming responsibility	_____ Problem solving
_____ Categorizing	_____ Reading maps/globes
_____ Classifying	_____ Reading text
_____ Decision making	_____ Reasoning
_____ Discussing	_____ Reflecting
_____ Gathering Resources	_____ Reporting to others
_____ Inquiry	_____ Self-assessing
_____ Justifying choices	_____ Studying
_____ Justifying others	_____ Summarizing
_____ Listening to others	_____ Thinking
_____ Locating information	_____ Using resources
_____ Metacognition	_____ Working independently
_____ Ordering	_____ Working with others
_____ Organizing information	_____ Others unique to the unit

Additional teacher/student comments:

Facts on Praxis and Other Teacher Tests

Praxis and other tests for beginning educators take into account the view that writing skills are crucial to educational professionals and are a major part of the work that teachers do related to teaching and learning. Thus, many of the tests for credentialing assess writing tasks that ask the educator to recognize a particular purpose for writing a short essay or a brief response. The writing task will probably ask the writer to organize and develop related ideas and use eye-catching, ear-catching words, proper mechanics, and appropriate sentence structure in an essay or short response. Adopting the guidelines previously written in this chapter about the essay type assessment item as your *own* guidelines before you write an on-target essay or brief answer will give you the opportunity to practice/demonstrate your competence in writing effectively before you are asked to respond through an essay/short response format in a test situation (See Exercise 4.2).

Further considering teacher credentialing tests, you'll note that some of them measure classroom performance. These measurements take place in the classroom and are made by a school administrator or trained assessors who use a set of nationally validated criteria. This guide is a useful resource for supporting your performance when developing and teaching an ITU.

Further, if you are being observed in the classroom as part of a first year teaching situation or a pretenure/posttenure ongoing evaluation process, it is possible that the observation will include a reference to curriculum standards. As an example, the following observation guide is connected to selected literacy/English/language arts standards and can provide suggestions for you as you prepare for an observation. You can review other standards related to other areas as appropriate. In your teaching, are you doing the following?

- **Grouping/Eliciting Oral Responses.** Accepting students' invented spelling while composing writing but assisting students later for correct spellings? Facilitating group discussions? Giving skills instruction for students who need it? Giving time for individual, independent work by students? Promoting discussion, divergent thinking, and multiple responses? Using questioning that promotes dialogue, inquiry, and critique? Using different grouping situations such as cooperative learning groups, flexible small groups, literature circles, dyads/partners, and whole class?

- **Listening/Oral Response Times.** Planning opportunities for students to listen to others' responses? Planning some structured language with choral reading, debates, discussion time, drama, sharing time, oral reports, and speeches?

- **Modeling.** Modeling and sharing your pleasure in reading, writing, and listening related to the theme? Modeling the writing process that includes prewriting, drafting, sharing, revising, editing, and publishing? Suggesting books to interest students?

- **Providing Genres/Variety of Responses.** Providing a variety of genres with biographies, essays, informational books, magazines, novels, poetry, and short stories—fiction and nonfiction? Encouraging a variety of responses including writing in divergent and creative ways?

- **Providing Listening Tasks.** Modeling and encouraging students to keep eye contact, paraphrase to demonstrate understanding, and summarize what was heard? Providing listening situations such as reports, readers theater, and rehearsed oral reading? Reading aloud to students daily from a variety of texts?

- **Providing Daily Reading/Writing.** Giving daily time for writing? Providing time for daily, self-selected silent reading and oral and silent reading practice?

- **Scheduling Peer Conferences/Self Assessment/Portfolio Reviews.** Collecting portfolio assessment information that is selected by student, the parent/guardian, and teacher that helps assess progress? Conferring with students? Promoting peer conferences and self-assessment?

to be modified to fit your purposes but it is an example of a checklist that could be used in your ITU (to make additional copies, use Planning Master 4.1).

During a common planning period (and periodically, if needed), members should meet as a group to assess the progress of the ITU. During this time you will want to discuss recent pluses and minuses in the lessons, which is part of the team's ongoing formative assessment of the unit. Together, team members can brainstorm what they to change in the ITU, how the changes should be introduced, and when such changes should occur.

Ongoing summative evaluation. Each day you can reflect on that day's experience and consider what went well and what needs to be changed, how it can be changed, and how soon the changes can be made. *After* the ITU has been taught, you should write what, if any, revisions you will make in the future, which is part of your summative evaluation of the unit. As mentioned in Chapter 2, the best ITUs are never set in concrete but are ever-changing.

After the ITU has been completed, the teaching team should convene to discuss what revisions in the ITU should be made for future use. This, too, is part of the team's summative assessment of the unit.

SUMMARY

At this point in the guide, you have learned the importance of the assessment component of teaching and learning, of its ongoing nature, and of various techniques by which you and your students can discover what they are learning and have learned. Many of these devices are information data-collecting techniques (such as checklists, reading student essays, journals, portfolios, and teacher logs), but other devices such as tests are more formal. You realize the effective assessment begins with what students know or what they think they know about a topic and you will develop clear considerations about what the students should learn and then observe them as they are learning (see Exercise 4.2). Additionally, you will make judgments about the quality and quantity of their work both during and at the completion of their study. For scoring guides that will help in making these judgments, see Exercise 4.3. Quality assessment means "kid watching" and your observations and informal methods of assessment are central to the evaluation of meaningful learning. This means that for each student you must keep carefully annotated and well-organized records.

You have thought about and planned some of your assessment strategies. Now it is time for you to complete the development of your ITU, which you will do in Chapter 5.

IF A COLLEAGUE, COMMUNITY MEMBER, OR PARENT ASKS YOU ABOUT . . .

1. **Alternative testing techniques.** What would be your response to a colleague who asked you to identify three alternative techniques for testing student learning during or at completion of an interdisciplinary thematic unit? Further, what would be your response to a parent who asked you, "What student learning activities, if any, should not be graded?" When, if ever, would you use non-graded activities for assessment of student learning?

2. **Equivalent disciplines.** What would be your response to a community member if you were asked if you thought that all disciplines were equal in importance? Some critics argue that different disciplines are not equivalent in importance and value or in the manner of learning involved. In your opinion, are all disciplines equivalent? Why or why not? What helped you form your opinion? What methods would you use to determine which disciplines to include in an ITU? Discuss your suggestions with others in your group and review what you would tell a parent, colleague, or community member about this.

3. **Plagiarism.** How would you explain to a parent the ways you agree or disagree with the following? In a student handbook in a Missouri school system in Hickory county, a statement on plagiarism reports that in addition to disciplinary action, any student who plagiarizes materials from any source shall receive an F for the project (Minkel, 2002).

4. **Prior concepts.** What would be your response if an educational colleague asked you to describe any prior concepts about assessment that changed as a result of your experience with this chapter? How would you describe the changes?

5. **Updated tests.**   If a parent asked you if you agreed or disagreed with the following statement, what would you reply? In some states, districts/schools are replacing their annual exams with three types of exams— (1) updated achievement tests that are nationally normed, (2) more standard tests, and (3) school exit exams. With this in mind, parents often express that we need to be teaching kids the standards; if we're teaching them the standards, they'll do well on any norm-referenced test. To what extent do you agree or disagree with the statement? Discuss your view with others.

6. **Questions about the chapter.**   Do you have any questions generated by the content of this chapter? If so, list them and share the list with your colleagues. See if the answers to your questions can be obtained from them.

EXERCISE 4.1

Preparing Assessment Items for My ITU

Instructions.   The purpose of this exercise is for you to practice your skill in preparing different types of assessment items, as you think about the various ways you will assess for student learning in your ITU. Select one objective from your ITU instructional objectives/standards (as in Exercise 3.5), make sure it is linked to a standard, focus on the anticipated learning, and then write assessment items for the objective for each category:

Category I: preassessment—diagnostic assessment of what students know or think they know prior to your instruction

Category II: formative assessment—assessment of learning in progress

Category III: summative assessment—assessment of learning after instruction is completed

If you decide that a particular item is not applicable for your particular grade level or for the assessment category, write NA next to the item. Then, while reviewing one another's exercises, talk about your decision to obtain group consensus on it. Perhaps others may see how an item could be used. When complete, share this exercise with your colleagues for their feedback. If you need more space than provided here, use separate paper.

Tentative title of ITU:

Grade level:

Objective:

For Preassessment

1. Arrangement item:

2. Completion item:

3. Correction item:

4. Essay item:

5. Grouping item:

6. Identification item:

7. Matching item:

8. Multiple-choice item:

9. Performance item:*

10. Short explanation item:

11. True-false or *modified* true-false item:

For Formative Assessment

1. Arrangement item:

2. Completion item:

3. Correction item:

4. Essay item:

5. Grouping item:

6. Identification item:

7. Matching item:

8. Multiple-choice item:

9. Performance item:[*]

10. Short explanation item:

11. True-false or *modified* true-false item:

For Summative Assessment

1. Arrangement item:

2. Completion item:

3. Correction item:

4. Essay item:

5. Grouping item:

6. Identification item:

7. Matching item:

8. Multiple-choice item:

9. Performance item::[*]

10. Short explanation item:

11. True-false or *modified* true-false item:

[*]Note that some of the other types listed can be performance items as the teacher observes students when they are asked to arrange objects in a sequence or pattern, to complete a pattern or sequence, to predict something in writing in an essay, to group objects together according to characteristics, to match real objects, to orally give a short explanation of how something works, and so on.

EXERCISE 4.2

Writing a Brief Reflective Essay about Teaching an ITU: A Self-Check

Instructions.   Now that you have reached this point in this guide about developing ITUs, consider the way you would express the value of developing and teaching an ITU for a grade level of your choice. Consider a response to this brief reflective essay topic: Teaching through an interdisciplinary thematic unit is an educational procedure that results in increased learning benefits for students.

If you need a particular approach to essay writing, consider the following three-paragraph approach to coordinate your writing interests and skills in responding to the essay topic:

Three-Paragraph Approach: Try a triad approach—a minimum of three paragraphs—and include an introductory paragraph, a transitional paragraph, and a concluding paragraph.

- First, your introductory paragraph sets your purpose (i.e., One might think there isn't much value in the teaching idea of involving students in an interdisciplinary thematic unit, but as a matter of fact. . . ,).
- Second, your transitional paragraph can summarize one idea and/or introduce another idea.
- Third, your final paragraph presents your conclusion.

Write your essay draft here:

NOTES

EXERCISE 4.3

Writing a Scoring Guide for a Skill or Lesson of Your Choice

Instructions.   Now that you have reviewed the topic of assessment in this chapter, consider the way you would develop your own scoring guide for a skill/lesson of your choice to show some degrees of satisfactory completion for the desired characteristics, behavior, or performance of a skill or lesson. After you write your draft, share it with a colleague to get feedback about making changes.

Here is an example of a scoring guide with degrees of development for a student's skill in listening:

- *For a developing listener* (score point 5): has difficulty following oral directions; has short attention span; inattentive; often interrupts the speaker; relies on repetition.
- *For a capable listener* (score point 10): follows oral directions; has longer attention span than a developing listener; usually attentive; listens to speaker and others in discussion without interrupting; does not rely on repetition.
- *For a strong listener* (score point 15): responds immediately to oral directions; has appropriate attention span; focuses on speaker and others in discussions and listens to what is being said without interruptions; does not rely on repetition; interacts with others.

Write your draft of a scoring guide here:

Show your guide to a member of your group and ask for feedback. What changes will you make?

CHAPTER NOTES

1. J. Little, "Forum," *The Sacramento Bee* p. 4 (November 28, 1993).
2. G. E. Tompkins and K. Hoskisson, *Language Arts: Content and Teaching Strategies* (Upper Saddle River, NJ: Prentice Hall, 1991), p. 63.
3. S. J. Rakow, "Assessment: A Driving Force," *Science Scope 15*(6), 3 (March 1992).
4. H. Goodrich, "Understanding Rubrics," *Educational Leadership 54*(4), 14–17 (December 1996/January 1997).
5. For more information, contact Sunburst, 101 Castleton Street, PO Box 100, Pleasantville, NY 10570-0100.
6. L. J. Gibbs and E. J. Earley, *Using Children's Literature to Develop Core Values* (Bloomington, IN: Fastback 362, Phi Delta Kappa Educational Foundation, 1994).
7. E. A. Wynne and H. J. Walberg, "Persisting Groups: An Overlooked Force for Learning," *Phi Delta Kappan, 75*(7), 527–528, 530 (March 1994).
8. S. Kagan, "Group Grades Miss the Mark," *Educational Leadership, 52*(8), 68–71 (May 1995); see also D. W. Johnson and R. T. Johnson, "The Role of Cooperative Learning in Assessing and Communicating Student Learning," Chapter 4 in R. T. Guskey (ed.), *Communicating Student Learning* (Alexandria, VA: ASCD Yearbook, Association for Supervision and Curriculum Development, 1996).
9. Software packages for the development of student electronic portfolios are becoming increasingly available; for example, *Classroom Manager* from CTB Macmillan/McGraw Hill, Monterey, CA; *Electronic Portfolio* from Learning Quest, Corvallis, OR; and *Grady Profile* from Aurbach and Associates, St. Louis, MO.
10. For a discussion of the educational benefits of positive feedback, use of student portfolios, and group learning, see R. Sylvester, "The Neurobiology of Self Esteem and Aggression," *Educational Leadership 54*(5), 75–79 (February 1997).
11. See information about Apple Newton at the nearest Apple outlet, contact the nearest address of Apple Computer, Inc., or write to 20525 Mariani Ave., Cupertino, CA 95014.
12. That grading and reporting should always be done in reference to learning criteria and never on a curve is well supported by research studies and authorities on the matter. See, for instance, the further readings at the end of this chapter, such as pages 18–19 in T. R. Guskey, and pages 436–437 in R. J. Stiggins.
13. For a presentation of other methods being used to report student achievement, see T. R. Guskey in footnote 12.
14. S. M. Brookhart, "Classroom Assessment: Pervasive, Pivotal, and Primary," *National Forum, 77*(4), 3, 5, 8 (Fall 1997). (Baton Rouge, LA: The Honor Society of Phi Kappa Phi.) See also M. Schmoker, *Results: The Key to Continued School Improvement* (Alexandria, VA: Association for Supervision and Curriculum Development, 1996), for a presentation on the importance of scoring guides/rubrics.

FOR FURTHER READING

Airasian, P. W. (2001). *Classroom assessment: Concepts and applications* (4th ed.). Boston: McGraw-Hill.

Andrade, H. G. (2000, February). Using rubrics to promote thinking and learning. *Educational Leadership, 57*(5), 13–18.

Arter, J., & McTighe, J. (2001). *Scoring rubrics in the classroom: Using performance criteria for assessing and improving student performances.* Thousand Oaks, CA: Corwin Press.

Asp, E. (2000). Assessment in education: Where have we been? Where are we headed? In R. S. Brandt (Ed.), *Education in a new era* (pp. 123–157). Alexandria, VA: ASCD Yearbook, Association for Supervision and Curriculum Development.

Azwell, T. (Ed.). (1995). *Report card on report cards: Alternatives to consider.* Portsmouth, NH: Heinemann.

Bracey, G. W. (2000). *A short guide to standardized testing.* Fastback 459. Bloomington, IN: Phi Delta Kappa Educational Foundation.

Carr, J. F., & Harris, D. E. (2001). *Succeeding with standards: Linking curriculum, assessment, and action planning.* Alexandria, VA: Association of Supervision and Curriculum Development.

Chen, Y., & Martin, M. A. (2000, Spring). Using performance assessment and portfolio assessment together in the elementary classroom. *Reading Improvement, 37*(1), 32–38.

Demers, C. (2000, October). Beyond paper-and-pencil assessment. *Science and Children, 36*(2), 24–29, 60.

Martin, B. L., & Briggs, L. J. (1986). *The affective and cognitive domains.* Englewood Cliffs, NJ: Educational Technology Publications.

Marzano, R. J. (2000). *Transforming classroom grading.* Alexandria, VA: Association for Supervision and Curriculum Development.

Minkel, W. (2002, April). Web of deceit. *School Library Journal,* 50–56.

Montgomery, K. (2000, July/August). Classroom rubrics: Systematizing what teachers do naturally. *Clearing House, 73*(6), 324–328.

Moskal, B. M. (2000). *Scoring rubrics part I: What and when.* Washington, DC: Assessment and Evaluation. (ED446110)

Nitko, A. J. (2001). *Educational assessment of students* (3rd ed.). Upper Saddle River, NJ: Prentice Hall.

Oosterhof, A. (2001). *Classroom applications of educational measurement* (3rd ed.). Upper Saddle River, NJ: Merrill/Prentice Hall.

Ronis, D. (2000). *Brain compatible assessments.* Arlington Heights, IL: Skyline.

Skillings, M. J., & Ferrell, R. (2000, March). Student-generated rubrics: Bring students into the assessment process. *Reading Teacher, 53*(6), 452–455.

Smith, J. K., Smith, L. F., & De Lisi, R. (2001). *Natural classroom assessment: Designing seamless instruction & assessment.* Thousand Oaks, CA: Corwin Press.

Stiggins, R. J. (2001). *Student-involved classroom assessment* (3rd ed.). Upper Saddle River, NJ: Merrill/Prentice Hall.

Thompkins, G. E., & Hoskisson, K. (1991). *Language arts: Content and teaching strategies.* New York: MacMillan.

CHAPTER 5

Completing Your ITU: Finalizing Activities, Lessons, and Units

Everything should be made as simple as possible, but not simpler.

—Albert Einstein

INTERDISCIPLINARY THEMATIC UNIT EXAMPLE FOR PRIMARY GRADE STUDENTS: THEME, EMERGENCY; TOPIC, WAITING FOR TREATMENT, SERVICE LEARNING IN THE COMMUNITY

Service learning—a teaching approach integrated with community service and academics to enrich learning and teach civic responsibility—can be addressed in a simple, straightforward way through an interdisciplinary thematic unit. In one such unit, the theme *emergency* was selected along with the topic of *waiting for treatment* (at an emergency room at a local hospital). In this unit, a kindergarten teacher asked the students to explore how they felt—being bored or afraid—when they had to wait for treatment for themselves and others. With input from the hospital staff, the students decided to create a special waiting place for children in one of the emergency treatment rooms. The teacher linked the theme to various disciplines and the students participated in the following:

- *Art and language arts.* Students used their artistic skills to decorate the treatment room with murals, create self-portraits to hang on the walls, and make quilts. They also designed a Get Well book for other children to read.

- *Communications and social studies.* The students gave their input about activities they thought would make children less afraid during an emergency and discussed contributing toys, videos, and a chalkboard.

- *Math.* First, students initiated a toy drive and completed math lessons to calculate the funds they had collected to buy toys. Later, when they decided to design/equip the children's room themselves, they used math to study the floor plans, take measurements for their art works, and rearrange the furniture on paper.

- *Science and health.* Students used criteria to determine the safety features related to the toys and other items that they wanted to introduce into the room for the children.

- *Sociology.* After the students designed and equipped the treatment room, community members sent letters to thank them for making their hospital visits more comfortable.[1]

CHAPTER INTRODUCTION

You'll recall that Chapter 4 was on various assessment techniques that can be used to enable you and your students to discover their progress in learning, generally by comparing what they are learning, or did learn, with what they were expected to learn. Students' personal inquiries are central to the process and much of the assessment of students' learning is done informally and continuously. It is now time for you to further consider activities and lessons and complete your ITU. Then, we suggest you try it out with students for whom it is designed. Your further focus for this chapter is to prepare your lessons and put your ITU into its final shape for implementation, although you will make many modifications during its implementation and after. Like any good lesson plan, the best ITUs are flexible and never set in concrete.

Organization of This Chapter with Units. To assist you in completing your unit, this chapter is organized around three main topics. The first topic discusses learning activities—initiating activities, then developmental activities and culminating ones to incorporate into a unit. The second topic provides step-by-step guidelines and examples for preparing lessons for an ITU. The third part provides sample interdisciplinary units. From the unit examples provided here for your study, referral, and potential use, you will see the ways that different teachers have planned their thematic units. Rather than reading and studying all three units, you may want to concentrate on the one of most interest to you. See Exercise 5.1, Examining Units. Note that certain aspects of each sample ITU may be incomplete or omitted due to publishing space constraints or to the nature of ITUs in general, which reflects the idea that one learning activity may lead to another unforeseen activity. The three sample ITUs are

1. *Early Civilizations: Dawn of a New Age in Ancient Greece.* For use in middle and secondary grades, the unit is divided into 11 lessons that may occur over a period of several weeks.

2. *Migrations: Early Newcomers in North America.* Adaptable for use in upper elementary, middle, and secondary grades, the unit is divided into 10 lessons and may occur over a period of more than two weeks.

3. *Changes: Spring as a Time of Growth, Beauty, and Transformations.* For use in first through third grades, the unit is divided into five lessons that may extend over a period of more than a week.

PLANNING LEARNING ACTIVITIES

Learning activities or instructional strategies that engage the students in learning constitute the educational engine of the ITU. Some activities start a unit in motion and are called *initiating activities.* Those that make up the day-to-day momentum of the unit are the *ongoing developmental activities,* and those that bring the unit to a natural close are *culminating activities.* Although nearly limitless, the list in Figure 5.1 gives you an idea of the many options from which you can choose activities for any of these three categories. Some, of course, may overlap in some way or another and others might naturally fit one category better than another.

Connected Components

Central to the selection and development of learning activities for interdisciplinary thematic instruc-

tion is a connection among four close components: (1) instruction is centered around a large meaningful idea (perhaps a theme of emergency care such as the one in the unit about "Waiting for Treatment: Service Learning in the Community" at the beginning of this chapter) rather than on fictitious subject areas; (2) decision making and responsibility for learning is shared by the students and the teacher; (3) the learning activities are selected so that the students are actively engaged—that is, they are physically active with hands-on learning and mentally active with minds-on learning; and (4) there is reflection and sharing about what is being done and what is being learned.

Initiating Activities

An ITU can be initiated in countless ways. You must decide which ways are appropriate for your educational goals and objectives; for your own identified group of students with their abilities, interests, needs, and skills; and for the time considerations that you have. You could begin with an artifact, a book, a community concern, a current event, or something interesting on the Internet.

Consider some additional approaches to initiating a unit:

display	activity center	problem as focus
current event	painting	question wheel
inquiry	place-based education	role-play

FIGURE 5.1 Examples of Instructional Strategies

Assignment	Group Work	Problem solving
Autotutorial	Guest Speaker	Project
Brainstorming	Homework	Questioning
Coaching	Individualization	Review and practice
Collaborative learning	Inquiry/Internet	Role-play
Cooperative learning	Interactive media	Script writing
Debate	Journal writing	Self-instruction module
Demonstration	Lab investigation	Simulation
Diorama	Laser videodisk	Study guide
Discovery	Lecture	Symposium
Drama	Library/resource center	Telecommunication
Drill	Metacognition	Term paper
Expository	Mock-up	Textbook
Field trip	Multimedia	Think-share-pair
Game	Panel discussion	Tutorial

Points of View of Several Disciplines to Initiate Study.

Often, to help students recognize the connections between selected content areas, the initial ITU activities are designed to allow the students to assume roles of real-world professionals. One initiating activity for elementary students could be centered around introducing them to points of view from various disciplines. Such an introduction does not have to be deadly dull. For instance, you and the students might begin a particular study by reading books related to an underlying guiding question (idea/problem/topic/theme), a process that perhaps lasts for two or three sessions. Then, the students might plan an ITU or review a proposed plan that includes individually reserving "ownership" of some inquiries. Over the next few sessions, you and the students first might approach the unit from the point of view of a particular discipline and then move on to a different discipline every day or two.

On subsequent days, you can encourage students to see things from the vantage point of various other disciplines—anthropology, economics, history, and so on. Through this process, you get the students involved in thinking about what can be explored and what inquiries can be made from the perspective of various disciplines. Once the students are introduced to some of the knowledge and skills of different disciplines, they can use what they have learned as they make their own interdisciplinary inquiries through an ITU.

Point of View of One Discipline to Initiate Study.

One effective way to introduce students to the perspective of a discipline is to encourage them to assume the role of a professional in that discipline as they examine some topic or content. Figure 5.2 can give you several ideas about how to help students assume such roles (see also Planning Master 5.1).

Suppose the perspective of an archeologist is needed for an ITU. As the teacher, you could first solicit and introduce questions an archeologist would ask and discuss, and then demonstrate how an archeologist would organize and share information about the topic. To help your students understand an archeologist's perspective, you could briefly and succinctly introduce knowledge and skills unique to that discipline. For example, you might choose to do this by reading excerpts aloud from your favorite book about archeology or from *You Can Be A Woman Egyptologist* (New York: Cascade Press, 1993) by B. M. Bryan and J. L. Cohen. In the book, an Egyptologist explains how she became interested in the profession, what work she does, and what discoveries she has made.

If the point of view of a paleontologist is needed for an ITU, you might consider reading aloud excerpts from the novel *My Daniel* (New York: Harper & Row, 1989) by P. Conrad. In this story, 80-year-old Julia Creath Summerwaite takes her grandchildren to New York's Museum of Natural History to see the dinosaur exhibit. She also tells them about her brother, Daniel, a paleontologist; his passion for fossils; and how he engaged in fierce competition with other paleontologists for treasures in Nebraska.

Place-based Education to Initiate Study.

Some teachers use place-based education (field trips) in the community to stimulate interest in a particular unit of interdisciplinary thematic instruction.[2] Possibilities include

- fast-food fact finding
- local pollution problem
- nature in the city
- one city block
- places, faces, things at mall
- reading a cemetery story
- starting a homestead
- urban predator-prey relationships

Questions to Initiate Study.

At Marquette Middle School (Madison, WI), students initially were asked to list questions about themselves and their world. They then were asked to identify a number of themes suggested by their questions. From their list of possibilities, the students then selected one theme: Living in the Future. Next, they began listing activities they might use to find possible answers to their questions related to their selected theme.[3]

Ongoing Developmental Activities

Once the ITU has been initiated, the students can become occupied with a variety of ongoing activities such as those listed in Figure 5.1. When working with students in selecting and planning the ongoing learning activities, you will want to keep in mind the concept represented by the learning experiences ladder (see Chapter 2) and your predetermined goals and objectives.

If there are specific curriculum requirements/standards from the state, district, or school that must be addressed in your ITU, you can reference the requirements by activity in your scope-and-sequence plan. If desired, you may also reference which sections of the standards of professional organizations, the state framework, the district curriculum documents, and local school documents are being ad-

FIGURE 5.2   Assuming Roles as a Way to Introduce Students to Various Disciplines

Anthropology

In the role of an anthropologist. The students can ask, "How can we investigate the cultures and the ways of organization of a society and make generalizations about the society's life?" or "How can our experience(s) in our culture help us understand the way other people live?" or "How might ethnocentric views and limited experiences hinder someone's understandings of other cultures?" When the students take this role, they show that they are getting involved in direct observation/participation as a primary way to gather data. They focus on a relationship between people's behaviors and their beliefs. While taking this role, students can see each culture as one variety of human behavior among many possibilities and can inquire, "What direct observations can we make to see a relationship between the behavior of people and their beliefs?"

Economics

In the role of an economist. The students can ask, "What economic problems can be identified related to scarce resources and unchecked human wants?" and "What resolutions to the problems can be identified?" or "What work is done in the economy by the people?" and "What changes happen in the economic system and in the people's values as the people respond to new needs and problems?" In this role, the students can show that they are interested in an economic system and in the resolution of problems (such as assistance for the unemployed and the need for conservation of limited resources) that exist in our society.

Expressive Arts

In the role of an artist. The students can ask, "How can we show what we know about the theme (topic/subject) through the visual and performing arts such as drawing, painting, music, dance, and sculpture?" Taking this role, the students can demonstrate they are interested in art, artists, and the messages that can be sent through visual and auditory representations.

Geography

In the role of a geographer. The students can ask, "How has geography influenced the theme (topic/subject) and what we know about it?" In this role, the students show that they are interested in several aspects: (1) the land-human relationship—the features of the earth's surface and the effects of nature and humans on the features; (2) the cause-and-effect relationship of land inhabited by humans; and (3) the relationship of urban geography to other areas.

History

In the role of an historian. The students can ask, "How has information about this theme (topic/subject) changed over time?" and "How have ways we receive information about this theme changed over time?" In this role, the students can demonstrate that they are interested in a record of facts about a person, place, or event, including ancestry, environment, and past experiences.

Mathematics

In the role of a mathematician. The students can ask, "How can we express what we know about the theme through mathematics?" and "How can mathematics help us learn more about this?" In this role, the students can demonstrate that they are interested in a record of relations about known quantities related to the theme/topic/subject.

Political Science

In the role of a political scientist. The students can ask, "How have people organized themselves to express their values/information about the theme?" or "How well does the political system under study work in resolving problems/issues/conflicts related to the theme? and "How close a match is there between the selected theme, people's values, and the functioning of the governing system?" In this role, the students expand their knowledge about government with its processes, institutions, and values.

Science

In the role of a scientist. The students can ask, "What problem do we know about and what is our guess about explaining its cause?" and "What experiment can we design to test the hypothesis, and how can we collect and analyze the data and arrive at a conclusion?" In this role, the students expand their understanding of ways science helps them learn more about the theme and discover which scientists operate to help them get information about the theme/topic/subject.

Sociology

In the role of a sociologist. The students can ask, "What groups operate in the society to bring us information about the theme?" and "How can we help in the community to resolve a real problem related to the theme?" In this role, the students can show ways they understand aspects of sociology that show the relationship between humans and their communities.

Other Disciplines

Disciplines selected by the students and teacher.

dressed through each activity. Your reference notes may look like the following:

Activities in Scope-and-Sequence Plan	References from Professional Standards, State, District, and School Documents
1. Activity A	1. References for Activity A

Theme, Extinction; Topic, Dinosaurs.   Supported by ongoing learning activities, the theme of extinction is one that is common to some elementary school teachers and teachers in middle schools. Often the topic centers around dinosaurs. After determining a theme, teachers, with student input, plan instruction around a sequence of activities that focus on the theme.[4] Whatever its selected title might be in a given situation, a thematic unit about dinosaurs can encompass any number of multidisciplinary activities related to the topic. Following are some examples:

- *History.* Students develop a graphic time line, using a variety of texts, showing the long time frame that dinosaurs were dominant on the earth and write about what the animals did. They visit a museum that features dinosaur exhibits to discover answers to questions they have and to write or draw sketches about their museum visit or their visit to the Jurassic Classroom, a virtual tour of the Dinosaur Hall at the Carnegie Museum of Natural History through www.carnegiemuseums.org/cmnh. *Links to standards:*[5] reading a range of literature and texts; writing with different writing process elements, perhaps procedural writing about what they did first, second, and third during a field trip, or narrative writing to tell a story about what happened; using a variety of resources—databases, computer sites, libraries—to gather information and communicate knowledge.
- *Mathematics.* Students in dyads, in small groups, and independently categorize the types of dinosaurs and create graphs illustrating the variety and proportional sizes of dinosaurs. *Links to standards:* constructing and applying math ideas; using variety of instructional formats like pairs, triads, small groups; communicating math ideas with others.
- *Reading, writing, and art.* Students create and write illustrated stories about a favorite dinosaur. *Links to standards:* applying knowledge of language, spelling, capitalization, punctuation, figurative language, and media techniques to create/critique.
- *Science.* Students speculate about why the dinosaurs were so successful and how some events led to their rather quick disappearance. *Links to standards:* leading students to inquiry; providing for discussion and debate; focusing on student understanding and use of scientific knowledge.

In another example, Kristie Darras (Elk Grove, California), teacher in a primary grade classroom, guided her students in a thematic unit centered around dinosaurs.[6] Learning activities integrated science and math, drawing and crafts, and music and reading, and included publishing original books to support the study. Connecting reading to music, the students listened to a song about each dinosaur being studied. Students read sentence strips with the words of the song. They added sound effects, sang the song several times, and added a rhythmic beat with their fingers and hands. Additionally, the students prepared their own dinosaur-shape books, wrote original pages, and drew illustrations. To survey favorite dinosaurs, graphing was introduced. The students built their own line graph in the classroom by drawing a favorite dinosaur on a small slip of paper and adding it to a line on a large graph to show their favorites—line 1 was tyrannosaurus rex, line 2 another favorite, and so on. Students used individual copies of the graph to record what was added to the large graph and marked Xs with their pencils in the appropriate places. When the class graph was finished, the students read it with guidance from the teacher and talked about the information they had gathered.

Culminating Activities

The ITU discussed previously was brought to closure with a culminating activity. The final event took place at the school's spring open house. The students' assignment for open house was to bring one adult and explain to that person what they had been learning at school. Confidently, the students told their visitors about dinosaurs and proudly displayed their dinosaur books, dinosaur mobiles, dinosaur clay models, and dinosaur body shapes made from felt.

A culminating activity should incorporate sharing the product of the students' study. You can accept the students' suggestion for a final event if it engages them in summarizing what they have learned with others. Guide them toward a culminating activity that brings closure to a unit to give the students an opportunity for synthesis (by assembling, constructing, creating, inventing, producing, or incorporating the product of their studies) and perhaps even an opportunity to present that synthesis to an audience by establishing an Internet website or sharing their product on an existing school website. See Figure 5.3 for examples.

Olé! This culminating activity provides students with a fun and interesting way to end a unit on Mexico.

With a culminating activity, you can provide an opportunity for the students to move from recording information to reporting on their learning. Examples of additional culminating activities include the following:

- At the end of an ITU taught by an interdisciplinary core team of teachers (mathematics, science, social studies, and reading), seventh graders developed an earthquake safety guide to share with others.

- At the end of an ITU with a focus on immigrants, middle school students assumed the roles of immigrants who became naturalized citizens by completing a required assignment. The assignment included going through processing and naturalization as immigrants to encounter the problems faced by many real immigrants, participating in a group presentation, telling a fairy tale from the home country, showing a natural resource map of the home country, and receiving an "official" document that contained "visas."

- Another culminating activity asked students to "reserve" early in the study an aspect of the unit's theme/topic for his or her own individual study. Then during a class period reserved for the final

activity, each reported on the individual project to the whole group.

- You can introduce a final activity with a puppet show that offers facts about the topic with suggestions from *Leading Kids to Books Through Puppetry* (American Library Association, 1998) by C. F. Bauer.

- As still another culminating activity, place-based education can synthesize the students' learning in a way that culminates the study. During the ride/walk to the site, students can discuss the questions they have and tell what they would like to learn from the trip. Distribute small note pads and short pencils and ask students to make notes of the questions. At the site, have them take further notes about what they learn and make lots of detailed sketches of what they see—objects that catch their interest. After the visit to the site, encourage students to choose something interesting they saw at the site, and then build a scale model of it. The teacher and students can devote a full class period or more to working with cardboard, clay, rulers, yardsticks, and other materials to make the models. To share their learning further, the students can design invitations to send to other classes to invite them to inspect the scale models and to listen to their reports about what object caught his/her attention. Students can also present an art show of drawings about the unit's theme/topic, with a narration that informs the other classes about their study.

If you turn back to the beginning of Chapter 3 and review the ITU called Changes: Chromatography, you'll note that the teacher captured the attention of the students with the development of a question map to launch the ITU. To have the experience of using questions on a question map as this teacher did, and just as you would do in your own classroom, finish reading this chapter and then complete Exercise 5.2, Connecting Questions and Activities for an ITU. After you do this exercise, complete Exercise 5.3, Combining Objectives, Resources, and Learning Activities for

FIGURE 5.3 Examples of Culminating Activities

Audiovisual presentations	Learning centers	Replicas
Children's book	Newspaper displays	Resource people
Computer simulations	Paintings	Retelling a story
Creating games	Performing play	Role-playing
Dioramas	Performing with puppets	Transparencies
Displays	Problems	Writing music
Dramatic activities	Reading reader scripts	Others by students

a Teaching Plan, to write a specific plan for 1 day. After Exercise 5.3 is finished, do Exercise 5.4, Planning Culminating Activities, to develop a natural closure for a unit.

PLANNING LESSONS FOR INTERDISCIPLINARY THEMATIC INSTRUCTION

You will develop a personal system of lesson planning that works best for you. If you are a beginning teacher, however, you may need a substantial framework from which to work. For that reason, this section provides a suggested lesson plan format (see Figure 5.4), which is the format used for the sample lesson plan in Figure 5.5. As you read this part of the chapter, several references will be made to the lesson plan in Figure 5.5.

In addition to the sample lesson plan that is provided, you will find alternative formats in the sample ITUs. Nothing is sacred about any of these formats and each has worked for some teachers. As you review the suggested format and the alternatives, determine which appeals to your purposes and style of presentation and use it with your own modifications until you find or develop a better model. All else being equal, we encourage you to begin your teaching by following as closely as possible our format in Figure 5.4.

All plans should be written in an intelligible style. You have good reason to question teachers who say they have no need for a written plan because they have their lessons planned "in their heads." How many lessons will have to be planned in one's head for the periods in a school day that range from several to many, and for the numbers of students in each class? When multiplied by the number of school days in a week, a semester, or a year, the task of keeping so many plans in one's head becomes mind-boggling. Few persons could effectively accomplish such a feat. Until you have considerable experience, you will need to write and keep detailed plans for guidance and reference.

You are now going to engage in learning how to prepare a lesson plan, one that could possibly guide you for a day or more. We do not use the term *daily lesson plan* but rather the term *lesson plan*. In some instances, as shown in the sample lesson in Figure 5.5 and in the first lesson of *Early Civilizations: Dawn of a New Age in Ancient Greece* that is shown later in this chapter, a single lesson plan may run for more than one class period or day, perhaps two or three or even more. In other instances,

the lesson plan is, in fact, a plan for the day and may run for an entire class period, or in instances of block scheduling, for less than a 2-hour block of time. In the latter case, more than one lesson plan may be used during that time.

PREPARING ELEMENTS OF A LESSON PLAN

A written lesson plan should contain the following basic elements: (1) descriptive data; (2) goals, objectives, and (if appropriate for your grade, school, district) standards; (3) rationale; (4) procedure; (5) assignments and assignment reminders; (6) materials and equipment; and (7) a section for assessment, reflection, and revision. These components are neither required in every written lesson nor presented in any particular or standard format. Also, you can choose to include additional components or subsections or choose to delete a formal rationale for an ITU. However, we suggest that you develop one since it is the presentation of the worthiness of your unit and can be a creation statement—the "reason(s) for being" for your unit. Note that Figure 5.4 illustrates a format that includes the seven components and sample subsections of those components. The figure is placed alone on its page so you can remove it and make copies to use in planning the lessons for your ITU. Following are the descriptions of seven major components or elements in a basic lesson plan with explanations about why each is important and an example for each element/component.

Descriptive Data

This information represents demographic and logistical data that identify details about the class. Anyone reading this information should be able to identify when and where the class meets, who is teaching it, and what is being taught. Although the teacher knows this information, someone else may not. Members of the teaching team, administrators, and substitute teachers (and, if you are the student teacher, your university supervisor and cooperating teacher) appreciate this information, especially when asked to substitute, even if only for a few minutes during a class session. Most teachers find out which items of descriptive data are most beneficial in their situation and then develop their own identifiers. Remember that the mark of a well-prepared, clearly written lesson plan is the ease with which someone else (such as another member of your teaching team or a substitute teacher) could implement it. If you'll return to

FIGURE 5.4 Preferred Lesson Plan Format with Seven Components[*]

1. Descriptive Data

Teacher _____ Class _____ Date _____ Grade level _____

Room number _____ Period _____ Lesson number _____ Topic _____

Anticipated noise level (high, moderate, low)

2. Goals, Objectives, and Standards
Instructional Goals:

Standards:

Specific Objectives:
  Cognitive domain:

  Affective domain:

  Psychomotor domain: (Note: All three domains not always present in every lesson.)

3. Rationale (Note: New and different rationale not always present in every lesson, especially during reteaching.)

4. Procedure (Procedure with introduction, modeling examples, planned transitions, enrichment work for students who master the objective(s) quickly, or remedial work for struggling students who need a restructured lesson)

_____ minutes. Activity 1 (Set, introduction)

_____ minutes Activity 2

_____ minutes Activity 3

_____ minutes Activity 4 (Final lesson conclusion or closure)

If time remains:

FIGURE 5.4 Continued

5. Assignments and Reminders of Assignments

Special notes and reminders to myself:

6. Materials and Equipment Needed

Audiovisual:

Other:

7. Assessment, Reflection, and Revision

Assessment of student learning; how it will be done:

Reflective thoughts about the lesson after taught:

Suggestions for revision if used again:

*This blank lesson plan format is placed alone so, if you choose, you may remove it from the book and make copies for use in your teaching.

FIGURE 5.5 Lesson Plan Sample: Multiple-Day, Project-Centered Interdisciplinary and Transcultural Lesson Using Worldwide Communication via the Internet

---

1. Descriptive Data

Teacher _____ Class ___English/Language Arts/Science___ Date _____

Grade level ___Adaptable for grades 4–12___ Room number _____ Period _____

ITU ___Changes: The Atmosphere_____ Lesson number _____

Topic: __Writing Response and Peer Assessment via Internet as Part of Investigative Research and__

___Generative Writing___ Anticipated noise level (high, moderate, low)

2. Goals, Objectives, and Standards

Instructional Goals

2.1 One goal for this unit is for students to collaborate and prepare response papers to peers from around the world who have shared the results of their own experimental research findings and research papers about ozone levels in the atmosphere with peers on the Internet.

2.2 A second goal for this unit is for students to prepare and publish worldwide a final paper about global ozone levels in the atmosphere to peers on the Internet.

Specific Objectives:

Cognitive domain:
a. Through cooperative group action, students will conduct experimental research to collect data about the ozone level of the air in their environment. (application)
b. In cooperative groups, students will analyze the results of their experiments. (analysis)
c. Students will compile data and infer from their experimental data. (synthesis and evaluation)
d. Through collaborative writing groups, students will prepare a final paper that summarizes their research study of local atmospheric ozone levels. (evaluation)
e. Through sharing via the Internet, students will write response papers to their peers in other locations in the world. (evaluation)
f. From their own collaborative research and worldwide communications with their peers, students will draw conclusions about global atmospheric ozone levels. (evaluation)

Affective domain:
a. Students will respond attentively to the response papers of their peers. (attending)
b. Students will willingly cooperate with others during the group activities. (responding)
c. Students will offer opinions about the atmospheric level of ozone. (valuing)
d. Students will form judgments about local, regional, and worldwide ozone levels. (organizing)
e. Students will communicate their findings accurately and diligently to their worldwide peers. (internalizing)

Psychomotor domain:
a. Students will give commands on the computer so that their e-mail communications are transmitted accurately. (manipulating)
b. In a summary to the study, students will describe their feelings about atmospheric ozone concentrations and possible solutions. (communicating)
c. Students will ultimately create a proposal for worldwide dissemination. (creating)

Standards (here paraphrased and related to science[7]; other standards from other disciplines may be added):
a. Students will develop their abilities of inquiry to understand scientific concepts more fully and process their skills in context.
b. Students will study subject matter in the context of inquiry, technology, and science in personal and social perspectives and participate in an integration of many aspects of science content.
c. Students will participate in activities that investigate and analyze science questions, engage in investigations over extended periods of time, and use evidence and strategies for developing or revising an explanation.

3. Rationale

3.1 Important to improving one's writing and communication skills are the processes of selecting a topic, decision making, arranging, drafting, proofing, peer review, commenting, revising, editing, rewriting, and publishing the results—processes that are focused toward the context of the writing aspect of this unit.

3.2 Related to personal and social perspectives, student writers need readers to respond to their work. Through worldwide communication with peers and dissemination of their final product, this need can be satisfied.

3.3 Students learn best when they are actively pursuing a topic of interest that has meaning for them. This unit provides an opportunity for students to brainstorm potential problems and arrive at their own topic(s) for problem solving/investigations.

3.4 Real-world problems are interdisciplinary and transcultural. The problems involve writing (English/language arts), science, mathematics (data collecting, graphing, etc.), other disciplines as needed, and intercultural communication.

FIGURE 5.5 Continued

4. **Procedure** (includes modeling examples, transitions, practice, and content where the exact number of activities in the procedures will vary):

At the beginning of this unit, collaborative groups were established via intercultural e-mail with other classes from schools around the world. These groups of students conducted several scientific research experiments on the ozone level of their local atmosphere. To obtain relative measurements of ozone concentrations in the air, students set up experiments that involved stretching rubber bands on a board, then observing the number of days until the bands broke. Students maintained daily journal logs of the temperature, barometric pressure, and wind speed/direction and of the number of days that it took for bands to break.[8] After compiling their data and preparing single-page summaries of their results, students exchanged data with other groups via the Internet. From data collected worldwide, students wrote a one-page summary about what conditions might account for the difference in levels of ozone. Following the exchange of students' written responses and their subsequent revisions based on feedback from the worldwide peers, students prepared a final summary report about the world's atmospheric ozone level. The intention is to disseminate worldwide (to newspapers and via the Internet) this final report.

Activity 1: Introduction, 10 minutes
Today, in **think-share pairs,**[9] you will prepare initial responses to the e-mail responses we have received from other groups around the world. (Teacher shares the list of places from which e-mail has been received.)

Any questions before we get started?

As we discussed earlier, here are the instructions: In your think-share pairs (each pair is given one response received via e-mail), prepare written responses according to the following outline: (a) note points or information you would like to incorporate in the final paper to be forwarded via the Internet; (b) comment on one aspect of the written response you like best; and (c) provide questions to the sender to seek clarification or elaboration. I think you should be able to finish this in about 30 minutes, so let's try for that.

Activity 2: 30 minutes
Preparation of dyad responses

Activity 3: Undetermined minutes
Let's now hear from each response pair. Dyad responses are shared with the whole class for discussion of inclusion in response paper to be sent via the Internet.

Activity 4: Undetermined minutes
Discussion, conclusion, and preparation of final drafts to be sent to each e-mail correspondent by cooperative groups (the number of groups needed to be decided by the number of e-mail correspondents at this time).

Activity 5: Undetermined minutes
Later, as students receive e-mail responses from other groups, the responses will be printed and reviewed. The class will then respond to each using the same criteria as indicated and return this response to the e-mail sender.

Closure:
The process continues until all groups (from around the world) have agreed upon and prepared the final report for dissemination.

5. **Materials and Equipment Needed**

School computers with Internet access, printers, copies of e-mail responses.[10]

6. **Assessment, Reflection, and Revision**

Assessment of student learning for this lesson is formative; journals, daily checklist of student participation in groups are used; writing drafts are initiated.

Reflective thoughts about lesson and suggestions for revision:

Special notes and reminders to myself:

the sample lesson plan in Figure 5.4, you'll find the following descriptive data:

1. Name of course or class and grade level. These serve as headings for the plan and facilitate orderly filing of plans. Example: English/Language Arts/Science; Adaptable for grades 4–12.
2. Name of the unit. Inclusion of this detail facilitates the orderly control through topics and subtopics related to the hundreds of lesson plans a teacher constructs. Example: ITU: Changes: The Atmosphere.
3. Topics to be considered within the unit. Also useful for control and identification. For example: Topic(s): Writing Response and Peer Assessment via Internet as Part of Investigative Research and Generative Writing.

Anticipated Noise Level.   You might include in the descriptive data the category of anticipated classroom noise level such as high, moderate, or low. Its inclusion is useful to you during the planning phase of instruction when thinking about how active and noisy students might become during the lesson, how you might prepare for that, and whether you would alert an administrator and teachers of neighboring classrooms. Inclusion of this item is requested sometimes by cooperating teachers and university supervisors.

Goals and Objectives

The instructional goals are general statements of intended accomplishments from that lesson. They usually are related to state- and/or district-mandated curriculum standards. Teachers and students need to know what the lesson is designed to accomplish. In clear, understandable language, the general goal statement provides that information. From the sample in Figure 5.5, the goals are

- For students to collaborate and prepare response papers to peers from around the world who have shared the results of their own experimental research findings and research papers about ozone levels in the atmosphere with peers on the Internet.
- For students to prepare and publish worldwide a final paper about global ozone levels in the atmosphere to peers on the Internet.

Because the goals are also in the unit plan, sometimes a teacher might include only the objectives in the daily lesson plan (as shown in Figure 5.5). For a beginning teacher, it is a good idea to include both.

Objectives of the lesson are included as specific statements detailing precisely what students will be able to do as a result of the instructional activities. Teachers and students must be aware of the objectives. Performance objectives provide clear statements of what learning is to occur. In addition, from clearly written objectives, assessment items can be written to measure whether students have accomplished the objectives. The type of assessment item used (discussed in Chapter 4) should not only measure for the instructional objective but should also be compatible with the objective being assessed. As discussed earlier, your specific objectives might be covert or overt or a combination of both. Note that from the lesson shown in Figure 5.5, selected sample objectives are as follows:

- Through cooperative group action, students will conduct experimental research to collect data about the ozone level of the air in their environment. (cognitive, application)
- Through the Internet, students will write and share response papers to their peers in other locations in the world. (cognitive, evaluation)
- Students will form judgments about local, regional, and world ozone levels. (affective, organizing)
- Students will create a proposal for worldwide dissemination. (psychomotor, creating)

Setting specific objectives is a crucial step in the development of any lesson plan. It is at this point that many lessons weaken. Teachers sometimes mistakenly list their intentions, such as "cover the next five pages" or "do the next 10 problems," and fail to focus on just what the true learning objective in these activities is—what the students will accomplish (performance) as a result of the instruction. When you approach this step in your lesson planning, ask yourself, "What should students learn as a result of this lesson?" Your answer to that question is your objective!

Standards

Standards are criteria that are established as models or examples of quality or are statements of what something should be. With an increasing interest on curriculum standards (and related exams to validate effective teaching of identified standards), educators are encouraged to consider the effectiveness of writing standards in lessons as general statements of curriculum standards. They can be state- and/or district-mandated curriculum standards and can be connected to state exams. Related to this, you'll discover that administrators, other teachers, students, and parents often have an interest in any identified standards that support a particular lesson. In clear, understandable language, the standards provide the foundation for the lesson. You will see from the sample lesson in Figure 5.4 that certain selected, adapted, and paraphrased standards from the science area are identified and that other standards from other disciplines may be added. Read the standards from science that follow; note their general nature and recognize their ability to connect to many of the lessons that you will teach:

- Students will develop their abilities of inquiry to understand scientific concepts more fully and process their skills in context.
- Students will study subject matter in the context of inquiry, technology, and science in personal and social perspectives and participate in an integration of many aspects of science content.
- Students will participate in activities that investigate and analyze science questions, engage in investigations over extended periods of time, and use evidence and strategies for developing or revising an explanation.
- Other standards from other discipline areas may be added to the lessons.

Rationale

The rationale is an explanation of why the lesson is important and why the instructional methods chosen will achieve the objectives. Parents, students, teachers, administrators, and others have the right to know why specific content is being taught and why the methods employed are being used. Teachers become reflective decision makers when they challenge themselves to think about *what* they are teaching, *how* they are teaching it, and *why* it must be taught. Sometimes teachers include the rationale statement at the beginning of the interdisciplinary thematic unit plan, but not in each daily lesson. At other times, the rationale is included in the introduction and goals of the unit.

Procedure

The procedure consists of the instructional activities for a scheduled time frame. You worked on this activity at the end of Chapter 3 and you will focus on it again in this chapter as you complete your ITU plans. You may want to refer back to your work at the end of Chapter 3 as you continue through this chapter.

The substance of the lesson—the information to be presented, obtained, and learned—is the content. Appropriate information is selected to meet the learning objectives, the level of competence of students, and the requirements of the course. To be sure your lesson actually covers what it should, write exactly what content you intend to present. This material may be placed in a separate section or combined with the procedure section. Having written the information, you now have a quick and easy reference tool. If, for instance, you intend to lead the lesson using discussion, you can write the key discussion questions. Or, if you plan to introduce new material to older students in high school using a 12-minute lecture, then an outline of the content of that lecture is helpful to you.

The word *outline* is not used casually. You need not have pages of notes to sift through; nor do you need to read declarative statements to your students. You should be familiar enough with the content that an outline (as detailed as you believe necessary) will be sufficient to carry on your lesson. Examine the following example of a content outline.

Causes of Civil War

A. Primary Causes
   (1) Economics
   (2) Abolitionist pressure
   (3) Slavery
   (4) Other

B. Secondary Causes
   (1) North-South friction
   (2) Southern economic dependence
   (3) Other

The procedure or procedures to be used, sometimes referred to as the instructional components, comprise the major component of the lesson plan. Appropriate instructional activities are chosen to meet the objectives, to match students' learning styles and special needs, and to ensure that all students have equal opportunity to learn. The procedure is the section in which you establish what you and your students will be doing during the lesson. Ordinarily, you should plan this section of your lesson as an organized entity having a beginning (an introduction or set), a middle, and an end (often called the closure) to be completed during the lesson. This structure is not always needed if you plan the lessons to be simply parts of units or long-term plans and will carry on the activities mentioned in the units and plans. Still, most lessons need to include the following in the procedure section:

- An **introduction,** which includes the process used to prepare students mentally for the lesson; sometimes referred to as the *set* (to bring into play, into use, into practice, or into the students' notice), the *initiating activity* (instructions or actions marking the beginning of the lesson), or the *stimulus* (incentive or something that rouses the student's mind/spirit or his/her interest in an activity).
- A **lesson development** section that details the activities that occur between the beginning and the end of the lesson; includes the transitions that connect the activities.

- **Coached practice,** which details ways that you intend for students to interact in the classroom; sometimes referred to as the follow-up and can include individual practice, dyad practice, small group work, and conferences or mini-lessons during which the students receive guidance and coaching from you and their peers.
- The **lesson conclusion** or **closure,** which is the planned process of bringing the lesson to an end, thereby providing students with a sense of completeness; with effective teaching, it also provides for student accomplishment and comprehension by helping them synthesize the information learned from the lesson.
- A **timetable,** which serves simply as a planning and implementation guide.
- A **lesson extender** activity, which is a plan of action used when some or all of your students finish the lesson and time remains.
- **Assignments,** which are what students are instructed to do as a follow-up to the lesson, either as homework or as in-class work, providing students an opportunity to practice and enhance their learning.

Now read further to consider some of these elements in more detail.

Introduction to the Lesson.   Like any good performance or piece of writing, a lesson needs an effective beginning. In many respects, the introduction sets the tone for the rest of the lesson by alerting students that the business of learning is to begin. The introduction should be the attention getter. If the introduction is exciting, interesting, or innovative, it can create a favorable mood for the lesson, which is sometimes referred to as a "hook." In any case, a thoughtful introduction serves as a solid indicator that you are well prepared. Although it is difficult to develop an exciting introduction to every lesson taught each day, you can implement a variety of available options to spice up the beginnings of your lessons. You might, for instance, begin the lesson by briefly reviewing the previous lesson, thereby helping students connect the learning. Another possibility is to read aloud just a few brief comments, called your own top ten list, written by students about their favorite or best learning time from the previous day (save the rest of the comments for other lessons). Still another is to review vocabulary words from previous lessons and introduce new ones. An additional possibility is to use the key point of the day's lesson as an introduction and then again as the conclusion. Yet another possibility is to begin the lesson with a writing activity on some controversial aspect of the ensuing lesson.

Sometimes teachers begin a lesson by demonstrating a discrepant event (i.e., an event that is contrary to what one might expect). Teachers might select artifacts, audiovisual presentations, and stories from children's books to start a lesson. Computer simulations, displays, or newspaper articles can help launch the learning. Sometimes, paintings, problems, role-playing, resource people, or replicas initiate a student discussion. The important thing is they are all attention getters. Here are more examples:

- For American history—a study of westward expansion: Ask, "Who has lived somewhere other than (name of state)?" After the students show their hands and answer, ask individuals why they moved to the state. If appropriate, write the reasons in a list on the writing board or overhead transparency. Then ask the students to recall some of the reasons why the first European settlers came to the United States. Record those reasons in a second list and have students compare the two lists for similarities. Have students read aloud the information as a transition before the next activity about the westward expansion. During the study, collect reasons why people moved westward to prepare a third list for students to use to identify similarities/differences.
- For science—a study of adhesion or the process of predicting: The teacher takes a glass filled to the top with colored water and asks the students to meet in groups of two and discuss and predict how many pennies can be added to the glass before any water spills over the edge.
- For social studies/language arts—a study of interpretations: As students enter the classroom, the state song is playing softly in the background. The teacher begins class by showing the state seal on the overhead, and then asks the students to get together in dyads to discuss the object and write down what they believe it is, what they think it is used for, what meaning they think it has in today's world, and what changes they would make to the design. They can report back to the whole group.

Note that you can use the introduction of the lesson to perform several educational responsibilities: to review past learning, to tie the new lesson to the previous lesson, and to introduce new material. Additionally, the introduction can help you point out the objectives of the new lesson, help students connect their learning with other disciplines, or connect with something reported in the news. An introduction can also help you show students what they will learn and why the learning is important, help you build motivation, and provide students with a mindset favorable to the new lesson.

The Lesson Development. The developmental activities comprise the bulk of the plan and are the specifics by which you intend to achieve your lesson objectives. They include activities that present information, demonstrate skills, provide reinforcement of previously learned material, and provide other opportunities to develop understandings and skills. Furthermore, by actions and deeds during lesson development, the teacher models the behaviors expected by students (e.g., during a period of Drop Everything and Read, the teacher reads quietly, too). Students need such modeling. By effective modeling, you exemplify the anticipated learning outcomes. Activities of this section of the lesson plan also should be described in some detail so (1) you will know exactly what it is you plan to do and (2) so you will stay focused during the class meeting and not forget important details and content. This is why you should consider, for example, noting answers (if known) to questions you intend to ask and solutions to problems you intend for students to solve.

Lesson Conclusion.   Having a clear-cut closure to the lesson is as important as having a strong introduction. The closure complements the introduction. The concluding activity should summarize and bind together what has ensued in the developmental part of the lesson and should reinforce the principle points of the lesson. One way to accomplish these ends is to restate the key points of the lesson (then have the students turn to their partners and restate them to one another) or to briefly outline the points on the board and have the students read them aloud to partners. Still another method is to repeat the major concept (what we learned today) and have the students repeat the concept to you (or a classroom aide or another student) at the door as they leave the classroom. Sometimes the closure is not only a review of what was learned but is also the summarizing of a question left unanswered that signals a change in your plan of activities for the following day. Regardless of the plan, the concluding activity is usually brief and to the point.

The Timetable.   Estimating the time factors in any lesson can be very difficult. A good procedure is to gauge the amount of time needed for each learning activity and note that time alongside the activity and strategy on your written plan, as shown in the sample lesson plan. You'll want to give information to older students about how much time they have for a particular activity such as a quiz, a class meeting, or a group discussion. Placing too much faith in your time estimate the first time you teach the lesson may be foolish—an estimate is more for your guidance

during the preactive phase of instruction than for anything else. Beginning teachers sometimes find that their discussions and presentations do not last as long as expected. To avoid being embarrassed by running out of material, try to make sure you have planned enough meaningful work to consume the entire class period. For example, during the final minutes of class time you can read aloud selected passages of text from an informational book or a biography or autobiography of a person eminent in the field/main discipline or related to the theme that is major to your lesson/ITU unit. Here are some books from which to select brief text passages to read aloud that would relate to the three units at the end of the chapter:

1. *Civilizations:* Your favorite book on the topic or *The Walls of Windy Troy* (Harcourt, 1960) by M. Braymer; select text passages about Heinrich Schliemann, the archeologist who did research on the site of ancient Troy.
2. *Migrations:* Consider your favorite about the Pilgrims' journey or choose *Where Do You Think You Are Going Christopher Columbus?* (Putnam, 1980) by J. Fritz; select text passages about difficulties of a ship's journey and set the stage for the later arrival of the Pilgrims.
3. *Changes:* Read aloud your favorite book about the weather or read a rhyme about each season's weather from *Season Song* (Harper, 2002) by M. Barack or give information about the vernal equinox from *The Spring Equinox: Celebrating the Greening of the Earth* (Millbrook, 2002) by E. J. Jackson. In America's hemisphere, this equinox occurs the third week in March, a time when some people celebrate Earth Day along with other festivals and celebrations.

Assignments

When giving an assignment, make sure to note it in your lesson plan. When to present an assignment to students is optional, but never yell an assignment as an afterthought to students as they exit the classroom at the end of the period. When giving assignments—whether in-class or out-of-school assignments—it is best to write them on the writing board, in a special place on the bulletin board, or on a handout. Take extra care to be sure that assignment specifications are clear to the students.

It is also important that you understand the difference between assignments and procedures. An assignment tells students *what* is to be done, and procedures explain *how* to do it. Be sure to explain *how* to do something during a procedural time *before* you give students an assignment about *what* is to be done. Although an assignment may include specific procedures, spelling out procedures alone is not the same thing as an academic assignment. When the students are given an assignment, they need to understand the reasons for doing it and to have some notion of ways the assignment might be done.

Some teachers give assignments to their students on a weekly basis, requiring that students maintain an assignment schedule in their portfolios. When given on a periodic basis, rather than daily, assignments should still show in your daily lesson plans so you can remind students of them. Once assignment specifications are given, it is a good idea to *not* make major modifications to them, and it is especially important to not change assignment specifications several days after an assignment has been given. Last-minute changes (you probably don't like them either) in assignment requirements and procedures can be very frustrating to students who have already begun or completed the assignment; making changes shows little respect for those students.

Assignments and Benefits of Coached Practice.
Allowing time in class for students to begin work on homework assignments and long-term projects is highly recommended; when students begin their work during the final minutes of class it ensures that you have planned enough meaningful work to consume the entire class period and it also provides an opportunity for you to give individual attention—coached practice—to students. Being able to coach students individually or in small groups is the main reason for using in-class time to begin assignments. The benefits of coached practice include being able to (1) monitor students' work so students do not go too far in the wrong direction, (2) help students to reflect on their own thinking, (3) assess the progress of individual students, (4) provide for peer tutoring, and (5) discover or create a "teachable moment." For the latter, for instance, while observing and monitoring student practice, you might discover a commonly shared student misconception. You then stop the action and discuss that point and attempt to clarify the misconception or collaborate with students to plan a subsequent lesson or learning activity centered around the common misconception.

Special Notes and Reminders
Some teachers provide a place in their lesson plan format for special notes and reminders. Most of the time, you will not need such reminders, but when you do, it helps to have them in a regular location in your lesson plan so you can refer to them quickly. In that special section, you can place notes to yourself concerning such things as announcements to be made; participation in school programs; names of students who have to leave for special instruction, requirements, or other reasons; or makeup work for certain students.

Materials and Equipment
Materials of instruction include the textbook, supplementary readings, media, and other supplies necessary to accomplish the lesson objectives. You must be certain that the proper and necessary materials and equipment are available for the lesson, which certainly takes planning. If you are busy during instructional time looking for materials that should have been ready before class began, then you may have to face some classroom control problems as a result.

Assessment, Reflection, and Revision
You must include in your lesson plan details of how you will assess how well students *are* learning (formative assessment) and how well they *have* learned (summative assessment). For formative assessment, you can include informal checklists and comprehension checks that include both the questions you ask and those the students ask during the lesson. Questions you intend to ask (and possible answers) can be included in the developmental section of the lesson plan. For summative assessment, you can use tests, independent practice, or summary activities at the completion of a lesson. You also can use review questions at the end of a lesson (as a closure) or at the beginning of the next lesson (as a review or transfer introduction). We suggest again that your major questions for checking for comprehension should be detailed in your lesson plan.

In most lesson plan formats, there is also a section reserved for you to make notes or reflective comments about the lesson. Sample reflective questions you might ask yourself are as follows:

- How did I feel about my teaching today?
- If I feel successful, what student reactions made me feel that way?
- Would I do anything differently next time? If so, what and why?
- What changes to tomorrow's lesson need to be made as a result of today's lesson?

Writing, and later reading, your reflections can spark new ideas for a future lesson or lead to modifications of subsequent activities in the ITU. This type of reflection also offers a catharsis, which eases the stress from teaching. To continue working effectively at a challenging task requires significant amounts of reflection. Proceed now to Exercise 5.5 at the end of the chapter where you will analyze a lesson that failed;

then, if appropriate for your group as indicated by your instructor, do Exercise 5.6 titled Preparing Lesson Plans for My ITU, and 5.7, Evaluating Lesson Plans for My ITU, also found at the end of this chapter. Save Exercise 5.8 for your reflection about preparing an ITU when you complete your ITU.

SAMPLE INTERDISCIPLINARY THEMATIC UNITS

The remaining pages of this chapter provide three sample interdisciplinary units, namely:

1. *Early Civilizations: Dawn of a New Age in Ancient Greece* (adaptable for grades 6 and up).
2. *Migrations: Early Newcomers in North America* (adaptable for grades 4 and up).
3. *Changes: Spring as a Time of Growth, Beauty, and Transformations* (for grades 1–4).

From these three examples, you will see ways that different teachers have planned their thematic units. Again, we emphasize that to conserve space in this guide and to reflect the serendipitous nature of ITUs in general, certain aspects of each sample ITU may be incomplete or omitted. Sometimes, when teaching an interdisciplinary thematic curriculum, you will find that your best prepared lesson may go untaught as the interests of students lead to uncharted areas, unforeseen discussions, or quickly planned activities.

As you review these sample ITUs, pay special attention to the margin notes, which are provided to help you focus your attention, to fill in possible gaps, and to provide additional information and resources. When related to management, the margin note is coded (**M**). *M is for management in the classroom.* An example follows:

M

The actual time length of each lesson and number of class periods it takes will depend on the intellectual level of your students and the nature of the scheduling at your school. Many of the activities will consume full class periods. You can incorporate any of the ideas in the margin notes for teaching diverse students and facilitating cooperative group activities or instituting the technology ideas. Note that some schools have a looping schedule where teachers stay with students for two or more years.

T is for technology. When the marginalia is related to technology and resources, it is coded (**T**). Here is an example:

T

With *Connecting Kids and the Internet* (New York: Neal-Schuman, 1999) by A. C. Benson & L. M. Fodemski, use the CD-ROM to locate lesson plans and Web learning activities that include home pages, links to high-interest sites, pen pals, safety online, talking with experts, virtual bookstores, and virtual field trips.

D is for diversity. When the margin note is related to student diversity, it is coded (**D**). Here is an example:

D

To meet heritage interests. Issues of diverse cultures with interdisciplinary teaching strategies are arranged by themes for grades K–8 in *Promoting a Global Community Through Multicultural Children's Literature* by S. F. Steiner (Englewood, CO: Libraries Unlimited, 2001). Activities you select should be varied and represent a holistic approach to the unit theme.

Now, enjoy reading the following interdisciplinary thematic units—each one unique and differently planned—as you look for the supplementary marginalia and appreciate the hard work of the individual teachers who created and contributed these lesson plans. When you have completed your reading, turn to the final exercise, a self-check on developing interdisciplinary thematic units.

SAMPLE ITU I
Early Civilizations: Dawn of A New Age in Ancient Greece*

Middle and Secondary Grades. This ITU revolves around several disciplines including geography, literature, mathematics, physical education, science, and social science. It was developed to facilitate and motivate students' learning about ancient Greece and to make comparisons between life today and life 2,000 years ago in Greece. As presented here, the unit could be taught by one teacher or, with modifications, by a team of teachers.

Unit Overview. This ITU includes a variety of multisensory activities involving language arts, mathematics, science, art, drama, social studies, health, and physical education. As presented, each lesson requires from 45 to 75 minutes, but lesson I and II each require at least 2 consecutive days. This unit

---

* *Source:* Adapted by permission from unpublished contribution of Nancy Mortham.

will take at least 3 weeks. In addition to the 11 lesson plans, there are additional suggested activities. Originally designed for grades 5–9, it is adaptable for any grades 5–12.

The unit contains several cooperative learning activities that assume students have had prior experience working in cooperative groups. If students have not had such prior experience, then these lessons should be preceded by a discussion of the expected behaviors and responsibilities when working cooperatively with others. It is recommended that students be in teams of four at the start of the unit because this size group will facilitate an easy transition into group work and allow for a team-based behavior management system, if so desired.

To visually show the emphasis and the contributions of a particular discipline to some of the lessons in the unit, you can develop a web to focus on the integration of the different disciplines selected for the unit, such as the one that follows. It can

be drawn on the writing board to discuss with the students, if appropriate for your group.

To support the unit, an arranged environment should be created in the classroom(s). This supportive environment might include artifacts, Greek music, posters, simple toga costumes that can be worn during specific activities, and trade and resource books. Bulletin boards could be created using students' myths from Lesson 4 and the vase art activity.

To visually show the emphasis and the connections of selected curriculum standards to some of the lessons in the unit, you can develop a web as an advance organizer or orientation set to focus on the integration of the different standards selected for the unit. See the one in Figure 5.6. It can be drawn on the writing board to discuss with the students, if appropriate for your group.

Unit Goals.   From California's History/Social Studies curriculum, the unit is designed to incorporate these goals.

FIGURE 5.6   Unit Lessons and Connections to Selected Standards

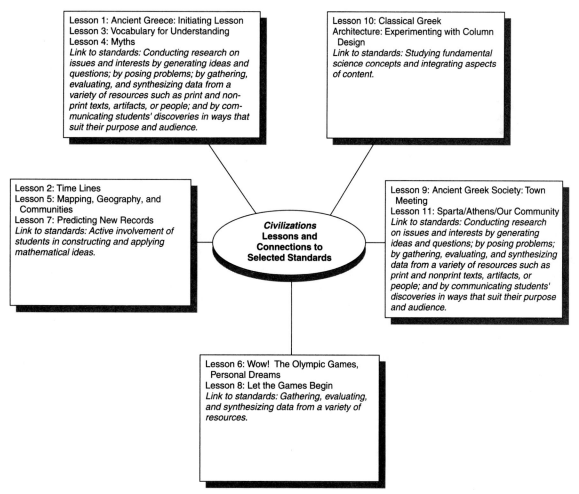

- Knowledge and cultural understanding
- Democratic understanding and civic values
- Skills attainment and social participation

   More specifically, the unit is designed to explore the following:

- The changes in Greek society from 2000 B.C. to 400 B.C.
- Greek mythology
- The effects of Greece's geography on its people and their way of life
- How the early Olympic Games differ from those held today

- The social class structure in early Athenian society
- Greek architecture
- Two very different city-states: Sparta and Athens

Assessment of Student Learning.   For this unit, there are three components for assessment of student learning: (1) students' portfolios, which include a unit assessment checklist; (2) a unit test; and (3) teacher's anecdotal notes. Additionally, students are encouraged to assess their own performances through self-assessment and group assessments.

LESSON 1

Ancient Greece: Initiating Lesson

Objective

Students will demonstrate and share their learning about Grecian times by creating small-group presentations, which will be performed for the class. Standards are found in the web in the unit overview (Note that additional standards may be added).

Materials

Resource books, posters, artifacts, and student texts

Procedure

"Today we are beginning an exciting unit about ancient Greece. We will participate in a wide variety of activities and have many opportunities to work in cooperative groups on special presentations and projects." Assess prior student knowledge by eliciting what they know about ancient Greece. Write their responses in a list. Then, with students, review the list and group similar entries, such as those related to clothing, shelter, and activities. Let the students "reserve" topics for personal inquiry. "Today we are going to form groups that will be in place for the remainder of the unit."

1. Put the students in teams of four (or three) students per team. Assign each team a topic to research from one of the following (depending on the number of students in your class, more than one team could have the same assignment): the Minoan Age, the Mycenaen Age, the First Olympics, the Age of Expansion, or the First Use of Coins.

   Student teams create presentations to be performed in front of the class the next day, or later, depending on the grade level, the complexity of their presentations, and the research needed. This may be done in the form of a play, newscast, report, discussion, and so forth.
2. Present and discuss assessment forms for the unit assessment, group presentations, and listening skills checklists (not included here but modified forms are found in figures in Chapter 4 of this guide).
3. The following day (or a later day), students present to the class.
4. Before, during, or immediately following each presentation, team members prepare an outline on the board to include who, what, when, where, and why or how.
5. Presenters respond to questions as the class takes notes on the information presented.
6. After the presentations, students evaluate their own listening behavior.

M

To enrich content, students can create banners to hang from the ceiling over their study groups. Each group decides on an appropriate name for their group and creates a banner made of art paper that depicts objects, mythological characters, or some other representation of ancient Greece. Students could research items for banners or the procedures used in creating vases (see Lesson 3).

M

Students' ideas can be solicited about procedures for their research and presentations; task outcomes should be clearly identified and understood by students. Creating a visual graphic on the board can help you record students' prior knowledge (use graphic again to review before a brief essay test or to add to what they have learned at the close of an ITU).

M

At various times, class meetings can be used to discuss goals and to establish class expectations, procedures, and consequences for inappropriate behavior.

(Continued)

LESSON 1

Ancient Greece: Initiating Lesson—Cont.

Closure

"What is something interesting that you learned from the presentations that you didn't know before? Did your group have any problems while researching information or putting together your presentations?" Discuss cooperation when working in groups and the importance of giving each member of the group a chance to contribute ideas.

Assessment

Group presentations are teacher evaluated according to scoring guides/rubrics presented. Students individually self-assess their listening behavior using a checklist form.

Note that annual testing to measure student performance is now authorized in the updated Elementary and Secondary Education Act (January, 2002). The act also holds poorly performing schools responsible, provides funds for local schools to purchase resources and technology, and allows parents to bar for-profit firms from gathering data about their children at school.

T

To enrich content, consider the video, *Conversations with Ancient Greeks* (Cinema Guild, 1992, grades 9 and up). It brings Socrates, Odysseus, Euripides, and others from ancient history into the present as figures who share their ideas in a conversation. They tell how their contributions affect the present and includes breaks for student discussions.

T

The video, *Effective Listening Skills; Listening to What You Hear* (Cambridge Career Products, 1992, grades 10–12), delivers information through the acronym DRIVE about the related skills for which the letters stand—deciding to listen, reading all stimuli, investing time wisely, verifying what was heard, and expending energy to listen. These skills, along with recognizing a student's individuality in the process, can become part of a scoring guide for listening.

LESSON 2

Time Lines

Objective

Students will demonstrate and share their understandings of significant events and their time frame by creating and drawing time lines documenting significant events of ancient Greece.

Materials

Texts as a resource; white, unlined paper; rulers; masking tape line on the classroom floor

Procedure

"As groups, you completed your presentations of information based on what was read about different events in early Greece. Today we are going to create a time line to give us a visual experience of the progression of events as they occurred over time in Greece."

1. Discuss the purpose of the time line, how to read it, and the meaning of B.C. and A.D.
2. Create a sample time line on the board using important personal dates offered by members of the class.
3. Point out the masking tape time line on the floor, and ask each group to select one person to stand at the spot on the time line that represents the event or period they presented the day before, thus creating a "people time line."
4. After students are in place, they give a brief review of the information they presented the day before. Stress the very long span of time covered compared with the history of the United States.
5. Students individually create their own time lines on paper, including all of the dates represented by students on the people time line. These time lines, then, include dates for the Minoan Age, the Mycenean Age, the first Olympics, and so on. Students place their completed time lines in their portfolios.

Closure

"We have been talking about events in Greece dating back to 2000 B.C. Raise your hand if you can tell us how many years ago that was. If a time line was written the same way as the number lines we see in math, how would we write the numbers that we refer to as B.C.?" (Those numbers would be negative numbers.)

Assessment

Observe students as they form the people time line and as they create their own time lines with the given information. Individual time frames from students' portfolios will be reviewed during individual conferences.

M

To support a goal of interesting students in becoming readers and integrating choice into the study, read aloud books that are interesting, give students a choice of books to read for a book report, and provide daily time to read.

D

To meet diverse individual student needs or class needs, help students become successful and accommodate differences in the backgrounds of students by assessing their prior knowledge with K-W-L,[11] have students write about their backgrounds.

M

To present the contributions of Greeks of the past, incorporate information about their accomplishments into as many subject areas in the integrated unit as possible.

D

To meet diverse needs and provide an accurate portrayal of a student's progress, have students develop working portfolios to hold all of a student's work on a specific ITU or subject. Use the portfolio to show progress that has been made and to identify areas in which the student still needs to grow and develop.

M

More than 100 assessment tools are available in *Practical Aspects of Authentic Assessment: Putting the Pieces Together* (Norwood, MA: Christopher-Gordon, 1998) by B. C. Hill & C. A. Ruptic.

LESSON 3
Vocabulary for Understanding

Objective
After completing a vocabulary coding exercise, students will define and illustrate relevant vocabulary words.

Materials
Vocabulary coding; textbook as resource

Procedure
"Early Greeks stored grain in large vases. Examples of these are displayed in pictures around the room. Today you are going to color-code a vase based on the vocabulary from our unit."

1. Describe how students may color-code the vase (Figure 5.7), with the word and its definition colored the same color. Students may suggest other ways to match words with definitions.
2. Students can use the text as a resource.
3. Allow students to complete the activity (about 15–20 minutes).
4. As students complete their coding, they may begin writing definitions and creating illustrations for each word. After beginning in class under the teacher's guidance, this activity should be completed as homework.

Word List

barter	democracy	tragedy	ephor
comedy	monarchy	sanctuary	turant
helot	oligarchy	city-state	

Closure
Questioning review: "Which of these words define a form of government? Which of these words are nouns that describe a person in ancient Greece? Two of the words are still used today to describe the plays and other entertainment. Which are they?

Assessment
The vocabulary coding and the definitions and illustrations are included in each student's portfolio.

D

When students have difficulty reading unfamiliar words, finish reading the sentence and use context clues as a strategy to help students comprehend the word. Vocabulary words that are difficult will vary depending on the grade level, English language skills, and intellectual maturity of students.

D

Students can research the procedures for creating vases. Also, the "coding with coloring" activity asks students to complete a higher-level task—to match terms and their definitions. This activity supports a higher-level thinking task for LEP students and supports conceptual growth in building knowledge about ancient Greece.

M

Related to assessment, you can model the expected behavior and send messages to students that acknowledge students' feelings, invite cooperation, give appropriate directions, and express feelings about a situation rather than about a student's character.

M

Class management includes having plans for boundaries, consequences, group work, routines, signals, rules, and rule enforcement (Batesky, 2002).

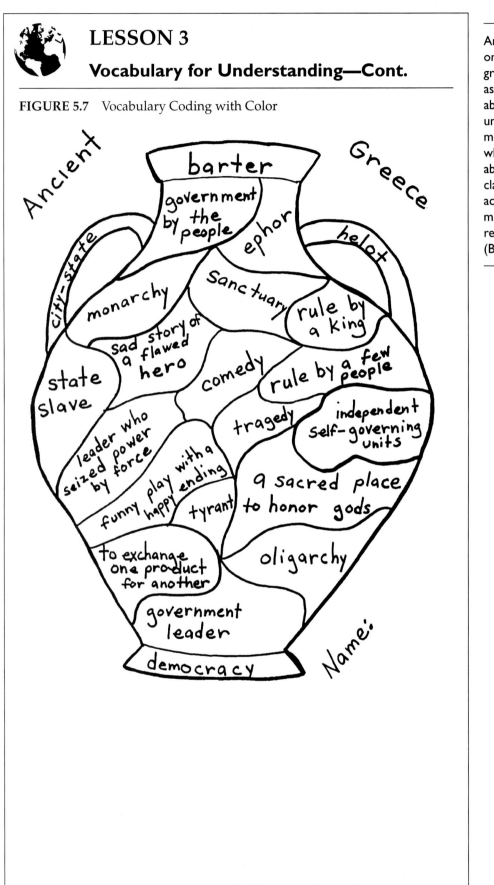

LESSON 3

Vocabulary for Understanding—Cont.

FIGURE 5.7   Vocabulary Coding with Color

M

An effective teacher has ongoing year-by-year growth as a professional; asks reflective questions about lessons; understands students; meets needs of students who have a wide range of ability levels; adapts to class reality—acknowledges changes, mistakes, reteaching, and replanned presentations (Batesky, 2002).

LESSON 4
Myths

Objective
After listening to and reading Greek myths and discussing what constitutes a myth, students will create their own myths.

Materials
Prometheus and the Story of Fire by I. M. Richardson (New Jersey, Troll Associates, 1983); overhead transparency of "Perseus Meets the Medusa" adapted by Lanette Whitnell from *D'Aulaires Book of Greek Myths;* visual display that illustrates the components of a myth.

Procedure
"I'd like to show you a poster that will help you remember the major components of a myth." Present and discuss a poster depicting a large map of Greece, titled "A Country and a Myth." On the map are cards that read Imagination, Mystery, Pre-Science Explanation of Nature, and Belief in Supernatural Powers. Have students listen for the components as a myth is read aloud.

1. Read aloud *Prometheus and the Story of Fire.* Discuss story components in a brainstorming activity.
2. While brainstorming, students can compare/contrast myths and legends with which they are familiar. Teacher records student ideas on the board and then encourages students to add to the descriptions on the myth map of Greece.
3. Students participate in a choral reading of "Perseus Meets the Medusa." Discuss the reading.
4. Students begin their rough drafts of their own myths.

Closure
"Raise your hand if you think you can explain why the stories we heard and read today are classified as myths rather than as legends." Students may refer to the myth poster for assistance.

Assessment
After the students complete their rough drafts, they receive feedback from their peers using a myth checklist as a guide (Figure 5.8). Final drafts are teacher-evaluated using a scoring guide/rubric similar to the following:

—M—

Recommended educational practices for effective teaching include preparing quality lesson plans; becoming familiar with content; and establishing a learning environment that includes a class management plan that gives students opportunities to learn about high expectations (Batesky, 2002).

To enrich content, listen to excerpts from the ancient story about Odysseus and his adventures with the Cyclops and others in the recorded audiobook *The Odyssey* by Homer narrated by N. Dietz (Recorded Books, LLC, 270 Skipjack Road, Prince Frederick MD 20678); also, read brief encounters between Athena, Hercules, Asclepius, and others in *From Atlanta to Zeus: Readers Theater from Greek Mythology* (Englewood, CO: Libraries Unlimited, 2000, grades 4–8) by S. L. Barchers.

—T—

To encourage higher-order thinking skills by students, include activity center material of your choice or material from *Greek Mythology* (Tapes 'n Books for Gifted Education, 314–350 Weinacker Ave., P.O. Box 6448, Mobile, AL 36600, grades 5–12). Include task cards with activities keyed to Bloom's taxonomy.

LESSON 4
Myths—Cont.

The myth demonstrates the Greeks' belief in higher
powers (Greek gods/goddesses)   12.5 points
The myth explains something in nature   12.5 points
The myth demonstrates writing skill   60.0 points
The myth shows student's individuality in
the study
    depth   5.0
    breadth   5.0
    unique direction of the writing   5.0

Assessment of the writing skill considers purpose, mode, audience, effective elaboration, consistent organization, clear sense of order and completeness, and fluent and effective language (see criteria in figures in Chapter 4 of this guide).

FIGURE 5.8 Myth Assessment Checklist

Myth Checklist

1. Does this myth demonstrate a belief in
higher powers (Greek gods/goddesses)?   yes _____   no _____

2. Does this myth try to explain something
in nature?   yes _____   no _____

3. In this myth, I like:

4. Suggestions:

5. Author of the myth:

Peer reviewer:

(Continued)

D

More advanced literature can be substituted according to students' reading level (i.e., an interdisciplinary approach through thematic chapters is found in *Ancient Greece*, Greenhaven, 2001, grades 10 and up by D. Nardoo).

M

Communicate to students that you know what is occurring in the classroom through nonverbal interactions (handshakes, smiles, signals) and emphasize expectations, procedures, rewards, and consequences with the stated understanding that the responsibility for good behavior rests with each student individually.

M

Consider multiple assessment of one piece of writing. To do this, grade the students' open-ended response questions, essays, or paragraph writing by first targeting just a few specific skills in the written work. For example, after reading a student's essay about a particular person based on an autobiography or biography, you may want to grade just for the skills in the category of mechanical skills—spelling, punctuation, and so on (Palardy, 2001).

LESSON 4
Myths—Cont.

Option. After evaluating a student's writing on a few skills, file the work in the student's portfolio and use it again later for the student's self-editing (and then your second evaluation) toward another grade in a previously unaddressed category such as the student's style and use of paragraph structure, topic sentence, relevant details, logical sequence, and conclusion. Again, file the work and use it still another time to assess the student's use of content with emphasis on details, good descriptions, and cited references. Thus, a student's essay might be examined by you and self-edited by the student several times and assessed in one, two, or three different categories at different times (Palardy, 2001).

LESSON 5

Mapping, Geography, and Communities

Objective

Students will demonstrate further understanding of ancient Greece as they create a physical map of Greece, discuss how geography played an important role in the development of Greek society, and complete information retrieval charts. Through Socratic questioning, students will make connections about their own communities with what they have learned about early Grecian communities.

Materials

One map per cooperative learning group (CLG), papier maché, glue, retrieval charts

Procedure

"Today in your cooperative learning groups, you are going to make a physical map of Greece. Each of you can contribute. When the map is complete, place it on the display table. Show the locations of city-states on the map."

1. Groups complete their maps.
2. In groups, students read the section of the text (or other sources) that deals with the geography of Greece.
3. As a class, students begin writing information on individual retrieval charts and brainstorm how the geography affected the following:
   a. farming (only a quarter of the land was suitable for growing grain; Greeks also grew grapes and olives)
   b. development of city-states (isolated, close-knit communities developed because of mountains and sea)
   c. trade (people traded by sea for goods they could not grow or make)
   d. culture (trade led to extensive contact with people from other cultures, which led to the spread of products and ideas)
4. Students complete their individual retrieval charts (see Figure 5.9).

Closure

"Let's share our ideas from the retrieval charts." Have students volunteer to share their responses. "I am going to pretend that I know nothing about the subject and you are going to give me information. As you each give information, ask questions to help others discover some connections between our community today and those in early Greece."

(Continued)

M

Related to subject-specific skills for the ITU, there will always be some skills/lessons that resist integration, that are definitely worth teaching, and that might best be taught in a conventional setting.

M

Promote cooperative group work and support students' interactions with one another's work. Your goals in using a cooperative-learning approach may include motivating students to help one another, having students communicate what they are learning to others, and acknowledging that each has an effect on one another's successful progress.

M

Rather than creating a physical map, you may prefer that students draw individual maps of Greece. If a student is too immature to work in a cooperative group, consider working with the student on an individual basis with intervals of returning to the group to try out his or her developing participation skills. If a student is thinking silently in response to a question, consider giving additional encouragement by waiting and giving extra time for the student to respond.

LESSON 5

Mapping, Geography, and Communities—Cont.

FIGURE 5.9   Retrieval Chart: Ancient Greece

> How did geography and climate influence ancient Greece in the following areas?
>
>   a. Farming?
>
>
>   b. Development of city-states?
>
>
>   c. Trade?
>
>
>   d. Culture?
>
>
>
> Use the following space to record any important ideas you discover during this discussion:

If appropriate, discuss Socrates' instruction, known as the Socratic Method. It is a form of cross-examination during which Socrates would pretend to know nothing of the subject under discussion. It consists of a series of carefully directed questions to make the other person find out the truth independently. He used inductive argument and arrived at general conclusions through examples from the lives of the common people.

M

Students can be instructed in small groups primarily where academically related discourse can be encouraged. There can be assigned academic tasks with intermittent teacher assistance.

T

For references, resources, and brain teasers about Greece, see CD-ROM *Geopedia* (Encyclopedia Britannica Ed. Corp, 1993, grades 5–8).

M

Socratic seminars are discussed as performance assessment in *The Performance Assessment Handbook, Volume 1* by B. Johnson (Larchmont, NY: Eye on Education, 1997).

LESSON 5

Mapping, Geography, and Communities—Cont.

Continue: "Although both the geographic terrain and climate affect a culture, it takes people working together to build a community. The people who successfully settled in the Aegean region formed tightly knit communities to build and shape their civilization. How does the geography of the Aegean region compare with our own? In what way is your community a tightly knit one? Why or why not? What kinds of things determine how close members of a community feel?" Extend the activity with other questions generated by the students.

Assessment

The geography retrieval charts are added to students' portfolios. Students' responses and thinking that they demonstrated are informally evaluated.

—**M**——

If your students so choose, the closure of this lesson could lead students into a long-term study of their own community.

—**T**——

To see the effects of the Mediterranean Sea on the climate of the region, discuss the video *Europe: Southern Region* (EBED, 1994, grades 6–12). It has an overview of Greece and southern Europe and complements science as students make connections of geographic locations and climate that affect suitability for farming.

LESSON 6

Wow! The Olympic Games, Personal Dreams

Objective

After comparing and contrasting the early Olympic Games with the present day and watching a video of Olympic heroes, students will brainstorm to determine qualities they deem important in an Olympic athlete.

Materials

A favorite video on the topic or *Wilma Unlimited: How Wilma Rudolph Became the World's Fastest Runner* (Harcourt, 1996) by K. Krull

Procedure

"What did you hear in the book that was read aloud, *Wilma Unlimited*, (or see in the video) about the personal qualities of the athletes? Krull's biography emphasizes Rudolph's achievement as the first American woman to win three gold medals in a single Olympics. Raise your hand if you can tell us something about the attitudes of the athletes you heard about (or saw on the video)."

1. Ask students how many have watched the Olympic Games. What are their thoughts about the games?
2. Discuss with students these aspects of the ancient Olympic Games:
   a. The purpose was to honor the gods.
   b. War ceased while the games were played.
   c. Only men participated.
   d. Games were held every 4 years.
   e. The Olympics began with just a 200-yard footrace and later included other races, boxing, wrestling, discus throw, horse racing, and chariot races.
3. Write the following question on the board and ask students to think about it as they listen to more excerpts from the book (or see a video): "What personal qualities are often found in Olympic athletes?"
4. Students listen to excerpts or view the video and take notes if appropriate for the group.
5. Make a list on the board as students share the qualities that make an Olympic athlete (e.g., dreams, goals, perseverance, talent, pride, dedication, determination, courage, endurance, failure, fear).

M

To enrich the learning environment, have students create an arranged classroom that includes artifacts, Greek music, trade and resource books on the topic, and simple toga costumes to wear during specific activities. Bulletin boards could be created to show students' myths from Lesson 4 and the vase "color and code" activity.

M

Information from a recent Olympics such as the games in Athens in the year 2004 can be useful for this lesson and can be compared with facts about the first modern Olympic games in Athens in 1896 from *Coubertin's Olympics: How the Games Began* (Lerner, 1995) by K. Davida or from *Olympism: A Basic Guide to the History, Ideals and Sports of the Olympic Movement* (Gareth Stevens, 2001, grades 4–5) by the U.S. Olympic Committee.

M

Use a think-share pair activity so students can brainstorm their perceptions of the personal qualities of Olympic athletes.

LESSON 6

Wow! The Olympic Games, Personal Dreams—Cont.

Closure

"Many of the qualities that make a successful Olympic athlete are also the qualities of any successful person. What do you think that means?" Discuss goal setting, dreams, and so on. Mention to students that Michael Jordan did a television commercial talking about how many times he has failed. Discuss events in the life of Wilma Rudolph where you think she first failed/was successful. Perhaps students would like to pursue projects related to the dreams, trials, failures, and successes of famous people.

Assessment

The quantity of student contributions and the level of student thinking are recorded in the teacher's log.

M

Locate the standards for student achievement and learning in your state. You'll note that some criterion-referenced tests may be administered in your state with the standards as the criteria.

LESSON 7

Predicting New Records

Objective

After observing you create a bar graph on the board as a model, students will design a bar graph that graphically displays Olympic discus records.

Materials

Graph paper, overhead transparency, list of Olympic records

Procedure

"Let's take a vote to find out which athlete on our local professional baseball (basketball, football, hockey) team is the favorite of most class members. Raise your hand if _____ is your favorite. _____. _____. I'll write the information on the board and show how to create a bar graph to display the results. I'm going to think out loud to tell you what I am thinking and doing as I create the graph. The neat thing about a bar graph is that we don't have to look at the actual numbers to know at a glance which athlete is the favorite. We only need to compare information on the bar graph."

1. After watching the teacher, students work individually to create a bar graph of Olympic discus records, given the following figures:

Year	Distance in Feet	Year	Distance in Feet
1896	96	1972	211
1912	148	1988	226
1932	162	1996	227.6
1956	185	2000	227.3

2. Students make a prediction for the next summer Olympic Games based on previous years and then graph their predictions.
3. Students write a brief response or short essay to explain the reasons for their predictions. Ask volunteers to read their writing aloud to partners.
4. Students discuss making further predictions, collect more data, and make more bar graphs.
5. If appropriate, repeat the previous graph activity or engage students in developing a variety of graphs with selected information about the top three medal-winning countries in the summer Olympic Games.

LESSON 7

Predicting New Records—Cont.

Past Medal Winners

1928: United States with 22 gold medals (G), 18 silver (S), and 16 bronze (B); Germany with 10 G, 7 S, and 14 B; Finland with 8 G, 8 S, and 9 B.

1932: United States with 41 G, 23 S, and 30 B; Italy with 12 G, 12 S, and 12 B; Finland with 5 G, 8 S, and 12 B.

1936: Germany with 33 G, 26 S, and 30 B; United States with 24 G, 20 S, and 12 B; Italy with 8 G, 9 S, and 5 B.

1948: United States with 38 G, 27 S, and 19 B; Sweden with 16 G, 11 S, and 17 B; France with 10 G, 6 S, and 13 B.

1952: United States with 40 G, 19 S, and 17 B; Soviet Union with 22 G, 30 S, and 19 B; Hungary with 16 G, 10 S, and 16 B.

1956: Soviet Union with 37 G, 29 S, and 32 B; United States with 32 G, 25 S, and 17 B; Australia with 13 G, 8 S, and 14 B.

1960: Soviet Union with 43 G, 29 S, and 31 B; United States with 36 G, 26 S, and 28 B; Germany with 12 G, 19 S, and 11 B.

1964: United States with 45 G, 28 S, and 34 B; Soviet Union with 30 G, 31 S, and 25 B; W. Germany with 7 G, 14 S, and 14 B.

1968: United States with 45 G, 28 S, and 34 B; Soviet Union with 29 G, 32 S, and 30 B; Hungary with 10 G, 10 S, and 12 B.

1972: Soviet Union with 50 G, 27 S, and 22 B; United States with 33 G, 31 S, and 30 B; E. Germany with 20 G, 23 S, and 23 B.

1976: Soviet Union with 49 G, 41 S, and 35 B; United States with 34 G, 35 S, and 25 B; E. Germany with 40 G, 25 S, and 25 B.

1980: Soviet Union with 80 G, 69 S, and 46 B; E. Germany with 47 G, 37 S, and 42 B; Bulgaria with 8 G, 16 S, and 17 B.

1984: United States with 83 G, 61 S, and 30 B; W. Germany with 17 G, 19 S, and 23 B; Romania with 20 G, 16 S, and 17 B.

1988: Soviet Union with 55 G, 31 S, and 46 B; E. Germany with 37 G, 35 S, and 30 B; United States with 36 G, 31 S, and 27 B.

1992: Unified Team (Soviet Union) with 45 G, 38 S, and 29 B; United States with 37 G, 34 S, and 37 B; Germany with 16 G, 22 S, and 16 B.

(Continued)

—**M**———
Point out to students that they can visually represent information with graphs and they need to select the best way to show the data. Mention that a bar graph (or line graph) is best for showing changes over time (i.e., changes over time in the distance of a discus thrown by an athlete) and a "whole" circle graph or pie graph is best for showing the relationship between the "whole" and its parts (i.e., comparing/contrasting).

—**T**———
Useful internet resources are found in *K–12 Resources on the Internet: An Instructional Guide* (New York: Library Solutions, 1998) by G. Junion-Metz and its accompanying disk with more than 350 connections to web resources.

LESSON 7

Predicting New Records—Cont.

Closure

"When we create and read bar graphs, we are more interested in seeing changes over time and observing any trends than in knowing the exact numbers that are graphed. Let's talk about the following:

a. How do the previous medal records help us in predicting what will happen in next summer's games?

b. What is the number of years between each discus record? Do you think you should make your prediction about the games that took place in 2000 by taking into account that there is a difference of 8 years from the 1992 to the 2000 Olympics? In what way could you use the Internet to research the actual discus record for 2000?

c. What else would you like to predict on the basis of your collection of data and the creation of a bar graph?"

Assessment

The bar graphs are included in each student's portfolio. Students also respond to the open-ended question, "Can discus records continue to increase indefinitely?" If appropriate, ask students to write a short essay to respond to the question after discussion. Note that before asking students to write essay-type responses, they should engage in an initial lesson or review of one or more of the features in a top-notch essay—correct use of grammar, idioms, mechanics, verb tense, and punctuation; addressing a purpose; organization; presentation of ideas; development; and interesting syntax.

M

Since writing involves a valuable set of skills for every student, ask students throughout the study to write brief responses or short essays to questions (perhaps writing about developing a graph) at different intervals. A scoring guide can reflect addressing a purpose; correct use of grammar, development, idioms, mechanics, organization, punctuation, presentation of ideas, verb tense, and interesting syntax; and recognizing a student's individuality in the study of the depth, breadth, and direction of the subject.

M

Sample writing topic: A student often believes that a lesson is particularly interesting or deadly dull. Later, the student may come to see that lesson differently. Have a student recall a lesson that was thought to be either boring or interesting and explain what caused him or her to change his or her mind about the lesson.

LESSON 8

Let the Games Begin

Objective

After discussing proper exercise procedures, computing target aerobic heart rates, and creating pulse-rate graphs, students will monitor and record their pulse rates while voluntarily participating in movement activities and drawing conclusions about what it means to be physically fit and how regular exercise helps maintain fitness.

Materials

16 Frisbees; straws; participation awards; graph papers; target heart rate bulletin board; watch with second hand; blue, red, green markers or crayons

Procedure

"When is the last time you participated in a physical activity for at least 15 minutes that made your heart beat faster and your body sweat? Today we are going to learn how to exercise safely and effectively so that we can be physically fit."

1. Students brainstorm the meaning of physical fitness, and why it is important to exercise regularly.
2. Introduce the physical activity sequence; warm-up, stretch, aerobic activity, cool down.
3. Explain how maximum heart rates and target heart rates are calculated:

   maximum rate = 220 − age
   target heart rate = 60%–80% of maximum rate

4. Students calculate their target heart rates, and then you introduce the target heart rate bulletin board (see Figure 5.10).

M

Teachers who are most effective are those who specify task outcomes, have high expectations for students, and use active teaching behaviors. Top ten qualities of outstanding educators that have been identified by African American students include the following: (1) explains things well, (2) makes work interesting, (3) gives extra help, (4) has patience, (5) is fair, (6) is friendly, (7) has sense of humor, (8) challenges students academically, (9) is intelligent, and (10) makes the work relevant (Thompson, 2002).

M

To promote vocabulary development and comprehension, students can develop their own vocabulary word lists related to the lesson and work in cooperative groups for a few minutes to write words related to the lesson/unit/theme. Back in the whole group, they can categorize the words and explain the associations among the words in a visual way on the board or overhead.

(Continued)

LESSON 8

Let the Games Begin—Cont.

FIGURE 5.10   Target Heart Rate Bulletin Board Display

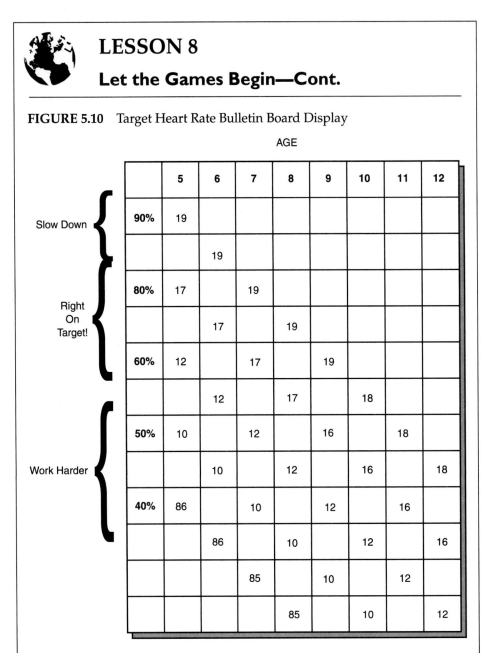

AGE

		5	6	7	8	9	10	11	12
Slow Down	**90%**	19							
			19						
	80%	17		19					
Right On Target!			17		19				
	60%	12		17		19			
			12		17		18		
	50%	10		12		16		18	
Work Harder			10		12		16		18
	40%	86		10		12		16	
			86		10		12		16
				85		10		12	
					85		10		12

5. Students create line graphs (Figure 5.11) to record the following color-coded data:

   Resting pulse rate (in blue)
   Aerobic pulse rate (in red)
   Recovery pulse rate (in green)

6. Teach students the proper procedure for taking and recording a 10-second pulse and record resting pulse rates.

M

To integrate more reading/language arts, have brief mini-lessons with a student-developed word list: a lesson can focus on an unfamiliar word to determine its meaning (context clues) in text; on patterns of words in the list that have prefixes, suffixes, and syllabication (word analysis skills); or on the use of the dictionary to determine the appropriate definition of a word on the list for a given context (dictionary skills).

LESSON 8

Let the Games Begin—Cont.

FIGURE 5.11   Sample Line Graphs of Pulse Rates

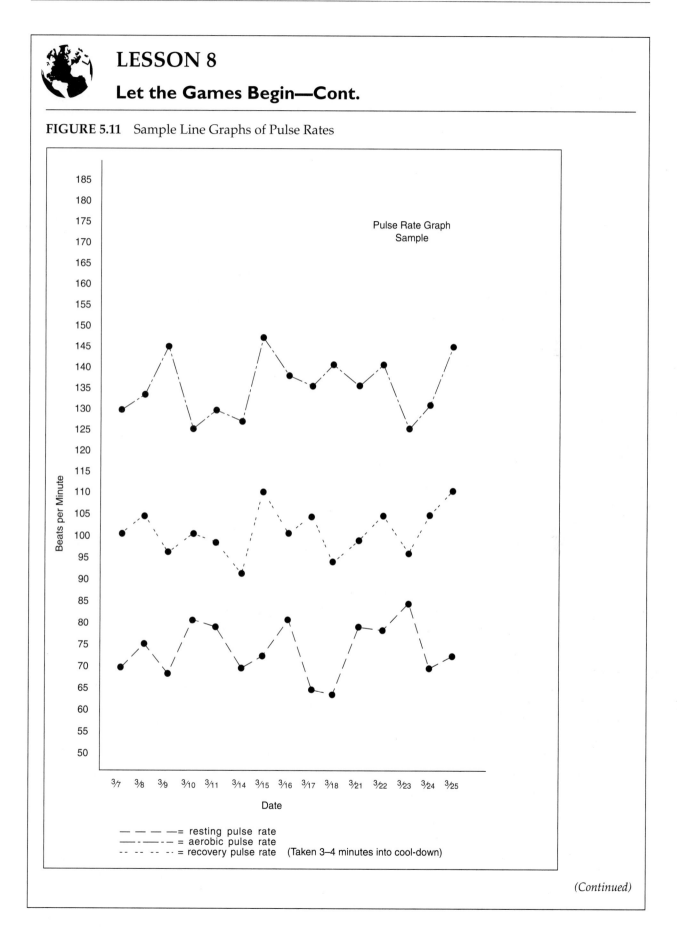

(Continued)

LESSON 8

Let the Games Begin—Cont.

7. Students voluntarily participate in the following activities: (Note: students who choose not to, or who cannot, participate in the exercises can serve as teacher helpers—keeping time, recording information, being reporters of events who participate in outside writing activities in their Olympic journals)

   warmup—fast walk around 0.1 mile course
   stretch—legs, arms, back
   aerobic—modified kickball, in which one entire team runs the bases while the outfield passes the ball and runs to form a circle at a designated place

8. During activity, students take their aerobic pulse rates.
9. After a cool-down walk of about 5 minutes, students take their recovery pulse rates.
10. Both pulse rates are recorded on students' graphs (example in Figure 5.11).
11. Students participate in a fun Olympic activity:

    javelin throw using straws
    discus throw using Frisbees

Closure

"Raise your hands if you can tell us the proper sequence of physical activity. Why is it important to warm up and stretch before an aerobic activity?" Who can explain how we calculate our target heart rates? We will be keeping track of our pulse rates for the rest of this month as we participate in physical education activities. As you begin to exercise regularly, what do you hypothesize we will discover? We should find that your resting pulse rate will become lower and your recovery rate will be quicker."

Assessment

Pulse rate graphs are added to each student's portfolio. Students are encouraged to monitor their own improvement. Students who participate in the movement activities receive an award for participation, which is worth points at the end of the unit (Figure 5.12). An alternate award activity will be decided for students who cannot participate in the movement activities.

M

For word study, have students keep individual vocabulary notebooks of words they do not know and record the pronunciation or definitions for the words as they gain the information they need. They can use the K-W-L approach in their notebooks with the headings, "What do I know about this word?" "What do I want to know?" and "What did I learn about this word after the lesson/unit?"

M

To incorporate more writing into content, review the writing process of prewriting, drafting, revising, editing, and sharing and then provide opportunities for students to use the process in the content such as writing advertisements for the Olympics, composing brief biographies of athletes, and explaining charts of data.

M

Using the writing process can include writing descriptions of an athlete in an event, essays about the Olympics, letters to one another to tell what was learned about pulse rate, news articles about athletes, poetry, records of procedures, rules related to a sport, reports, or writing from the perspective of an athlete, coach, or family member.

LESSON 8

Let the Games Begin—Cont.

FIGURE 5.12 Sample of Participation Award

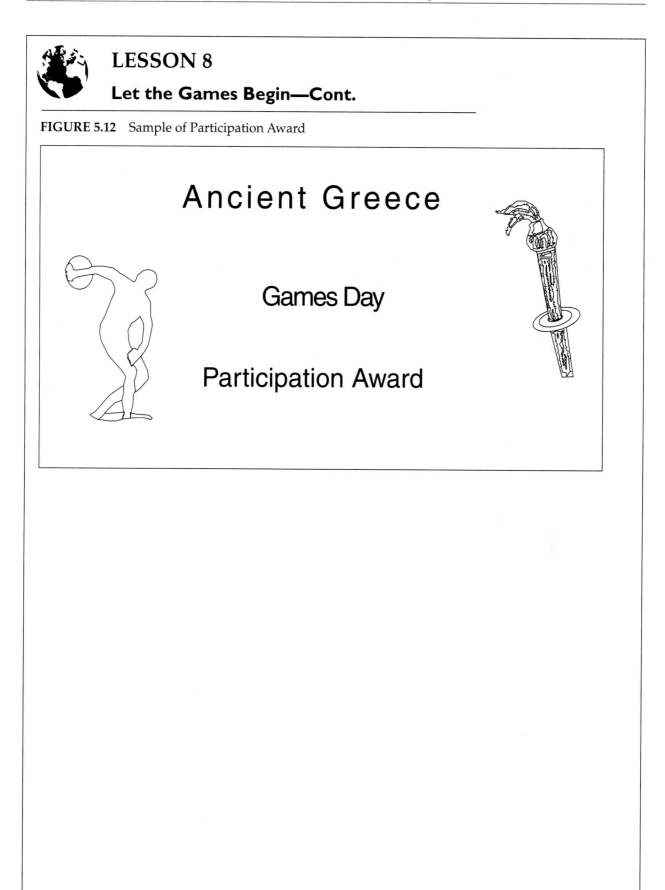

LESSON 9

Ancient Greek Society: Town Meeting

Objective

After discussing the four classes of Athenian society, students demonstrate their knowledge as they participate in a simulated town meeting and complete their retrieval charts.

Materials

Retrieval charts; role-play description sheet; game cards for citizen, family of citizen, metic, slave; identification necklaces for children, accused slave, accusing metic, and wife of citizen.

Procedure

As students enter the room, hand each a game card, which will identify his or her role in the simulation. Explain briefly that the students will be participating in a role-play and that they are to stay in character until the town meeting is finished. (Note: Depending on the number of students in your class, cards should be divided proportionately as follows: 15% citizens, 48% family of citizens, 12% metics, and 25% slaves.)

1. Arrange the classroom for a town meeting.
2. Explain the following four levels of ancient Greek society:
   Citizens. Men over 18 years of age. They may vote, hold office, speak at town meetings, and own slaves, and they are protected by laws.
   Family members of citizens. Wives and children. They may not vote or speak at town meetings and have no rights, privileges, or protection under the law.
   Metics. Foreigners, craftsmen, shopkeepers, and tradesmen. They may not vote or hold office, but they may speak at town meetings and are protected under the law.
   Slaves. Prisoners of wars and other captives. They may not vote or hold office. They have no protection under the law and no job choice, and they may have a family only with their master's permission.
3. Students read the scenario from the role-play description sheet (Figure 5.13).

T

To incorporate real-place education into content, perhaps students can participate in a community service project or attend a town meeting or similar meeting in their community.

T

Some tour buses that teachers used to take students to sites for real-place education now have TVs and VCRs for the students to watch while on the bus. The copyright term *fair use* allows teachers to show videos *directly related to the curriculum and not for entertainment purposes* to their students in the teaching environment without the prior permission of the copyright holder.

M

In discussion, point out that prosecution against Socrates was based on his view that there were weaknesses in the Greek democracy (i.e., that it did not require proof of special knowledge of its leaders; that it surrendered people's destinies to those without adequate experience in democratic government; and that it treated all opinions of citizens as equal in value and neglected the morality or justice of a particular policy).

LESSON 9

Ancient Greek Society: Town Meeting—Cont.

FIGURE 5.13 Role-Play Description Sheet

Town Meeting in Ancient Greece

Setup

Eight chairs should be placed in the front of the room for the key characters in this simulated town meeting: five citizens, one metic, one wife of citizen, and one slave. Other chairs can be arranged in circular rows (as in a small amphitheater) for those members of the town not allowed to speak in the meeting. Other metics should sit closest to the key characters in case they wish to speak.

Scenario

While at the busy town center where metics were selling their wares earlier in the day, turmoil erupted. A slave who was accompanying the family members of a citizen was accused of stealing food from one of the metics. The only one who said he actually saw this happen was the metic who accused the slave of stealing. The wife of the slave owner claimed it was not the slave but another thief who was at fault. Since slaves have no legal rights and are not citizens, a crime such as stealing can result in severe fines for the slave owner and possible banishment or even death for the accused slave.

The slave owner is called to a town meeting accompanied by the rest of his family. All other citizens and people of the town are present at this meeting. They listen to arguments from both the metic's and the slave owner's points of view. The slave owner's wife quietly supplies her husband with information but is not allowed to speak to the assembly. The accused slave is not allowed to speak. The slave owner, since he is a citizen, is the only one who can speak on behalf of the slave. The metics may speak, but they cannot vote as to the guilt or innocence of the accused slave.

After all arguments have been heard, the citizens take a vote to determine the verdict.

---

4. Reiterate the roles and powers.
5. Students hold the town meeting.
6. Students form groups of three or four to complete the information on the retrieval chart (Figure 5.14).

(Continued)

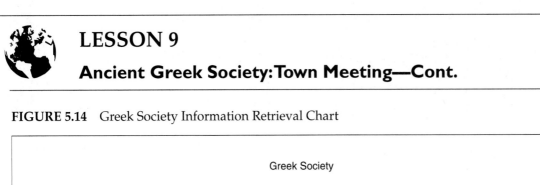

LESSON 9

Ancient Greek Society: Town Meeting—Cont.

FIGURE 5.14 Greek Society Information Retrieval Chart

Greek Society

Level	Description	Rights	Responsibilities
Citizens			
Family of Citizens			
Metics			
Slaves			

Compare democracy in United States today with the democracy of ancient Greek society. List the similarities and differences.

Similarities	Differences

LESSON 9

Ancient Greek Society:
Town Meeting—Cont.

Closure

"Using your retrieval chart, how would you differentiate among the roles of citizens, family members of citizens, metics, and slaves? Which would you prefer to be? Why? How would you compare and contrast the democracy of ancient Greece with democracy in the United States? Are there town meetings held in our country? Have you or someone you know ever attended one? What are the meetings like? Are they similar to those of ancient Greece? Different? How?

Assessment

The retrieval chart is a required element for the student folder. Students will also be assessed according to participation in the simulation.

LESSON 10

Classical Greek Architecture: Experimenting with Column Design

Objective

Students will demonstrate skill in hypothesizing and experimenting to determine which column designs will support the most weight.

Materials

9″ × 12″ construction paper, tape, rulers, supplemental teaching information form, pictures illustrating the three architectural styles

Procedures

"Let's take a minute to look around the room at the pictures of ancient Greece that show us examples of their architecture. Raise your hand if you think you can tell the rest of us something about how the early Greeks built structures. Where are there examples of that kind of architecture today?"

1. Encourage students to share what they already know or think they know about architectural design.
2. Using the supplemental teaching information (Figure 5.15) as a resource, discuss the three orders of Greek architecture: Doric, Ionic, and Corinthian. Show examples of each.
3. Discuss the scientific method and why it should be thought of as a cyclic rather than a linear process (i.e., as new data come in, an earlier conclusion may be thrown out, and the process repeats or cycles all over again).
4. Describe the experiment students will conduct and clarify any questions they may have about it. Then give students the instructions for the column experiment (Figure 5.16).
5. Put the students in their cooperative learning groups and assign the following roles: recorder, facilitator, thinker.
6. Allow students enough time to conduct their testing and to record their results.

T

For assistance using the Internet, turn to *The 21st Century Teachers' Guide to Recommended Internet Sites* (Neal-Schuman, 2001) by M. DiGeorgio & S. Lesage and insert the accompanying CD-ROM into a disk drive. It leads you to more than 400 sites with exercises, interactive lessons, multimedia use, and quizzes.

M

To find classroom applications in art education, review national standards for arts education, and integrate art into the curriculum, turn to *Artworks for Elementary Teachers*, 9th ed. (McGraw-Hill, 2002) by D. & B. Herberholz.

LESSON 10

Classical Greek Architecture: Experimenting with Column Design—Cont.

FIGURE 5.15   Classical Greek Architecture: Supplemental Teaching Information Sheet

Classical Greek Architecture

General Information

The earliest buildings of Greece were made of sun-dried bricks, timber, and decorative terra-cotta. Later, stone and marble became the chief materials. Mortar was rarely used, the finely cut blocks being held by metal dowels and clamps. Although Greek architects were aware of the arch and vault, their approach was relatively conservative. The megaron, with its portico entrance and low-pitched roof, was the model for Greek temples. The earliest temples were timber; their forms were later translated into mud-brick and, finally, stone. The two basic elements of timber structures, vertical supports (columns) and horizontal members (entablatures), were transformed into the three carefully proportioned orders, or styles, of Greek architecture: the Doric, Ionic, and Corinthian.

The Doric: The earliest and simplest of the classical orders. The fluted columns stand firmly on their platform without intermediate bases. The abacus is deep and plain.

The Ionic: This elegant order is recognized by the capital (head of the column) of spiral-shaped scrolls called volutes.

The Corinthian: The last and most elaborate order. The tall fluted column was capped by an elaborate stylized carving of acanthus plants. The decorative character of this order made it popular.

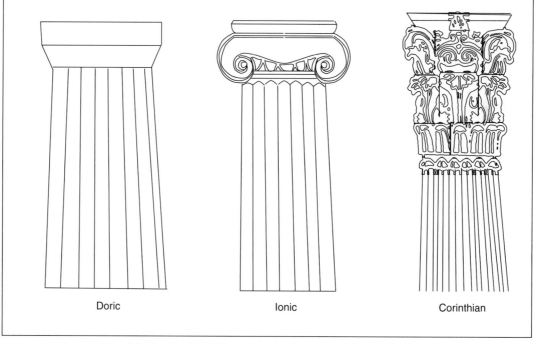

| Doric | Ionic | Corinthian |

Source: Adapted from *The Book of Buildings: A Traveler's Guide* by Richard Reid, Michael Joseph Limited, 1980.

(Continued)

LESSON 10

Classical Greek Architecture: Experimenting with Column Design—Cont.

FIGURE 5.16   The Column Design Experiment

Column Experiment

Focus question: Will a single sheet of paper support a heavy book? Try this experiment to find out.

Purpose: What do I want to find out?

Which of the tested columns will support the most weight?

Experiment:

1. Roll a 9" x 12" piece of construction paper so that it is 9 inches long and has a diameter of 1 inch.
2. Stand the paper on end to form a 9-inch high column.
3. Add math books to the column until the column collapses.
4. Repeat with the following column specifications: 9 inches long with a 2-inch diameter; 6 inches long (folded in half) with a 1-inch diameter; and 6 inches long (folded in half) with a 2-inch diameter.

Analysis: Collect and interpret data

Relative Strengths of Various Columns

Number of math books

	9 x 1	9 x 2	6 x 1 (doubled)	6 x 2 (doubled)	
12					
11					
10					
9					
8					
7					
6					
5					
4					
3					
2					
1					
0					

Conclusions: What did I learn?

What questions do I now have? (This will lead to a new purpose, perhaps a new experiment)

LESSON 10

Classical Greek Architecture: Experimenting with Column Design—Cont.

Closure

Ask groups to share their results and write those results on the board. Discuss the need to make multiple trial tests when conducting an experiment. Ask students to calculate the average result for each tested column using the data from the board.

Assessment

The completed experiment forms are included in each student's portfolio. Each student's level of understanding is assessed by reviewing the student's conclusions and by further questioning, perhaps in individual conferences.

LESSON 11

Sparta/Athens/(name of our community)

Objective

After discussing selected terms, students will do team research on an assigned or selected topic and report on it to the class.

Materials

Text, resources already available in classroom; examples:

For middle grade students (grades 4–8), special education, and ESL students:

- *Favorite Greek Myths,* a Scholastic Smart Book (Scholastic) by M. P. Osborne, with illustrations by M. Howell, on CD-ROM for Macintosh computers. Available from Educational Software Institute, 4213 South 49th Street, Omaha, NE 68127.
- *Ancient Lands* by Microsoft, for grades 5–8, CD-ROM for Mac or Windows.
- *Early Civilizations* by BFA, for grades 4–8, Laserdisc or VHS videotape.
- *Recess in Greece* by Electronic Arts/Morgan Interactive, for grades 5–8, CD-ROM for Mac.
- *Aesop Alive & Well* by D. Ferlatte Storyteller, 6531 Chabot Rd., Oakland, CA 94618, for grades 4–6, CD. Has fables told and sung.
- *Olympia: Warrior Athletes of Ancient Greece* (New York: Walker, 2001, grades 5–8) by D. Blacklock. Note that it includes a well-defined map and illustrations of naked warriors in events related to warfare and honoring Greek gods.
- *I Wonder Why Greeks Built Temples and Other Questions about Ancient Greece* (Kingfisher, 1997, grades 2–4) by F. Macdonald. It is suitable for reluctant readers and has sections on customs, government, everyday life, military, famous people.
- Selections for reading aloud can come from *Pandora* (Harcourt/Silver Whistle, 2002, grades 3–5) by R. Berleigh or *Folktales from Greece* (Libraries Unlimited, 2002, all grades) by C. Mitakidou, L. Manna, & M. Kanatsouli.

For older students (grades 9 and up):

- *Theseus: Caught in the Maze of Minoa* by Compton's new Media/Westwind, CD-ROM for Mac computers. Tales of heroes with narration, music, sound effects, maps, charts, and a giant database for in-depth study. Available from Educational Software Institute, 4213 South 49th Street, Omaha, NE 68127.
- *The Story of Civilization* by Compton's/World Library, for grades 9–12, CD-ROM for IBM or Windows.
- *World History Illustrated: Ancient Greece* by Queue, for grades 9–12, CD-ROM for IBM or Mac.

To students writing reports, pass along information about copyright use by defining it, and talking about the concept of public domain and the term *fair use.*

M

For effective teaching, it is important for teachers to be familiar with various materials, technologies, and resources available to them.

LESSON 11

Sparta/Athens/(name of our community)—Cont.

Procedure

"When we discussed the geography of Greece, we talked about the development of city-states. What is a city-state? Are there any in existence today?" (Note: Singapore was, until 1997, a modern city-state.) "In your opinion, which city would have been a better place to live, Athens or Sparta?"

1. Discuss these terms: *democracy, economy, government, lifestyle, monarchy,* and *oligarchy.* For background, use the information sheet in Figure 5.17.
2. Assign or have each cooperative learning group select one of the following topics. There are 15 topics listed; depending on the number of students in your class, you may want to modify the topics or assignment.

Arts/Athens	Arts/Sparta	Arts/our town
Government/Athens	Government/Sparta	Government/our town
Education/Athens	Education/Sparta	Education/our town
Economy/Athens	Economy/Sparta	Economy/our town
Lifestyle/Athens	Lifestyle/Sparta	Lifestyle/our town

3. Student teams research their topics, perhaps over a period of several days.
4. Groups present their information to the class with a visual outline. The focus should be on comparing and contrasting Athens and Sparta.
5. Students ask questions of the presenters and take notes on the information given. If appropriate, students can use their notes to write brief paragraphs about what they learned about Athens and Sparta.

Closure

"What were some of the ways that Athens and Sparta differed? How might we account for these differences? In what ways did they differ from our own community? Where would you rather live—Sparta, Athens, or our town? Why?" Closure can also include time for students to use their notes to write brief paragraphs about where they would rather live and why.

Assessment

As part of assessment, students complete their first paragraphs about what they learned about Athens and Sparta and their second paragraphs about where they would rather live and why. The paragraph writing is evaluated by a teacher-prepared scoring guide. Students can also complete self-assessments and group assessment (Figure 5.18) on

(Continued)

M

A teacher-of-the-year in a western state makes world history come alive in his high school classes by appearing before his TV-oriented students each day in costumes portraying historical characters to tell stories from history. For example, to tell a story about the Greek city-state and the council of 500, he wears a toga as the students take notes on the information (King, 1998).

M

To provide a common experience for students in grades 5–8 interested in ancient Greece, show diagrams of ancient buildings and drawings of individuals related to Athens and Sparta found in *Ancient Greece* (New York: Oxford Univ. Press, 2001) written by A. Solway and illustrated by P. Connolly. It covers topics such as daily life, government, sports, and theater.

M

To support developing essay writing skills, consider the following topics for a student response: (1) As a Greek citizen, which of your rights would be the most difficult for you to give up? Discuss why. (2) As a Greek citizen, describe an object in your life in Greece that is valuable to you. Tell how you acquired it and why you consider it valuable.

LESSON 11

Sparta/Athens/(name of our community)—Cont.

FIGURE 5.17   Athens and Sparta: Supplemental Teacher Information Sheet

Athens

Government. In ancient Greece, Athens was a monarchy, ruled by one king. In time, the nobles were depended on more and more to help defend the land and thus began to demand more power in return. By the end of the Dark Ages, an oligarchy developed with power in the hands of a few. As the population grew in this society where much of the land was unsuitable for farming, food shortages occurred and people began to look for change. After a period of tyranny, an early form of democracy appeared, around 510 B.C. The entire process took several centuries. The democracy included a council of 500 members, who were chosen at random each year. The council proposed new laws and were paid for their service. An assembly that included all citizens met every 9 days to vote on laws. Courts were made up of citizens who were paid to serve as jurors.

Economy. The main activity in the Athens area was farming. Most citizens had just enough land to support their families. The wealthy few had estates with slaves. Some tenant farmers rented land. Until 500 B.C., trading depended on bartering; later, the government began to make gold and silver coins. Still later, Athens had an international trade center. The monetary system and trade led to wealth, but the wealthy were expected to give large sums of money to the government to support projects resulting in a flow of money back to the citizens.

Education. Boys from wealthy families began their formal education at age 7. They lived at home, unlike the Spartans. They were taught reading, writing, math, poetry, music, dance, and athletics. They had a much more liberal education than the Spartans. At age 18, men joined the army for 2 years of military service. The wealthy men attended academies and studied throughout their lives. Girls received no formal education in Athens.

Lifestyle. Boys were more prized than girls. Upon birth, infant girls were sometimes left abandoned outside the city gates. Men managed farms and estates and participated in the government. Boys lived at home during their schooling. Girls received no training and often were married by age 15. Women cared for the home and raised the children. Athenians enjoyed greater freedom than the Spartans and entertained themselves with myths, plays, and poetry.

Sparta

Government. The government of Sparta began as a monarchy with two kings and gradually moved toward an oligarchy with power in the hands of a few. The 30-member senate consisted of men who were over the age of 60. The senators were elected by the citizens, who were male landowners over the age of 30. Members of the citizens' assembly could not propose laws but could vote yes or no on the laws proposed by the senate or the ephors. The senate and the ephors actually had the power to ignore a vote if they chose, and power was concentrated in the hands of a few families.

Economy. Sparta had a military economy and the men were required by law to be soldiers. As a result, people in the surrounding communities provided trade and craft items, although luxury goods were forbidden. Every citizen was given a plot of land by the government, and helots (state slaves) were assigned to farm the land. The helots were given crops as payment. The owner was required to give the government crops in exchange for daily meals; if he was unable to do so, he lost his rights as a citizen.

Education. Because Sparta was a militaristic city-state, education focused on military training, athletics (jumping, boxing, and wrestling), discipline, reading, and writing. At age 7, boys left their families to live in military barracks. Conditions in school were very harsh, as it was believed that hardship would create stronger character.

Lifestyle. Much can be understood by knowing that government inspectors were sent upon the birth of a child to determine whether the child would live or be abandoned in a cave to die. Male children lived in barracks from the age of 7 and at age 18 were expected to devote their lives to the army. At the age of 30 they gained full citizenship but were expected, even if married, to eat all meals with the soldiers in the mess hall. It can be inferred from this that family life was not as strong a value as military life. Entertainment consisted of religious festivals, chorus contests, and dance contests.

LESSON 11

Sparta/Athens/(name of our community)—Cont.

FIGURE 5.18　Form for ITU Student Self-Assessment and Group Assessment

Unit Self-Assessment and Group Assessment

Please evaluate your contributions to your group by placing an X at the location that most accurately reflects your own performance.

1. While creating the group banner, I
did not take part　　　　　　　took responsibility for some
　　　　　　　　　　　　　　　part of the project

　1　　2　　　　　3　　4　　　　5

2. During the paper column experiment, I
did not work cooperatively or share　　worked cooperatively with
with others　　　　　　　　　　　others

　1　　2　　　　　3　　4　　　　5

3. When working with my group, I
usually failed to stay on task　　　worked to the best of my
　　　　　　　　　　　　　　　ability
　1　　2　　　　　3　　4　　　　5

4. In a few sentences, explain what you enjoyed most about the ancient Greece unit.

5. Which activity did you like the least? Why?

6. List some problems you and your group experienced while working on the assigned projects.

7. List some successes you and your group enjoyed while working on the assigned projects.

(Continued)

Related to assessment, scoring guides/rubrics can be the key to assessment standards that evaluate a student's development along a continuum of skills that are current and definitive or within a range of prescribed knowledge in a particular area. However, some critics say that scoring guides can dictate conformity in direction, depth, and breadth of subject area. Think of ways to add a feature to a scoring guide that would recognize a student's individuality in the study of the depth, breadth, and direction of the subject.

LESSON 11

Sparta/Athens/(name of our community)—Cont.

their presentations. The student presentations are evaluated with another teacher-prepared scoring guide that includes content accuracy and completeness and, if appropriate, a student's individuality in the writing.

Summative Unit Assessment

Summative assessment of student learning for this unit will be based on the teacher's anecdotal records, each student's unit assessment checklist from the student's portfolio (see Figure 5.19), and the student's performance on the unit test (Figure 5.20) that follows in this lesson.

FIGURE 5.19   Unit Assessment Checklist

Item	Point Value	Student Self-Evaluation
Write your own myth	10	_____
Myth checklist (you are the reviewer)	5	_____
Group banner with clear theme	5	_____
Vocabulary scribble	5	_____
Definitions and illustrations	5	_____
Retrieval chart (geography)	10	_____
Participation in games day	10	_____
Discuss bar graph	10	_____
Paper column experiment	10	_____
Retrieval chart (levels of Greek society)	10	_____
Debate (knowledgeable participation)	10	_____
Self-assessment and group assessment	10	_____
Total	100	_____

M

You'll recall from some of your other courses that when you are comparing a student's score with the scores of other students in the same class, you are establishing a locally norm-referenced score; that when you are comparing a student's score with the scores of a national group of students who have taken the same test, you are establishing a nationally norm-referenced score; and that when you are comparing a student's score with the scores of other students in the same grade/age and month, you are establishing a developmentally referenced score.

LESSON 11

Sparta/Athens/(name of our community)—Cont.

FIGURE 5.20　Example of Unit Test

Unit Test

1. Compare the Olympic Games in ancient Greece to the Olympic Games held today. How are they alike? How are they different?

2. Write the letter of the correct definition after each vocabulary word.

oligarchy	_____	a. rule by a few people
barter	_____	b. independent self-governing unit
helot	_____	c. government by the people
sanctuary	_____	d. state slave
democracy	_____	e. sad story of a flawed hero
city-state	_____	f. sacred place to honor Greek gods
monarchy	_____	g. rule by a king
tragedy	_____	h. exchange one product for another

3. How did the geography of Greece affect the following (choose any two and explain):

a. farming

b. the development of city-states

c. culture

d. trade

4. We learned that there were four classes of people in ancient Athens. What type of people belonged to each class and what rights did people of each class have?

5. Compare life in Athens with life in Sparta. Outline the differences. Where would you rather live? Explain why.

SAMPLE ITU 2
Migrations: Early Newcomers in North America*

Middle and Secondary Grades. This ITU about native people, early explorers, and colonists in North America can be adapted for students in middle and secondary schools as part of an integrated program about the development of the United States of America.

Unit Overview. Through selected learning activities, students can develop a meaningful understanding of the United States as they study about people with different backgrounds, ideas, and ways of life. In this unit, students become better acquainted with the people who first lived in the area, early explorers, the early settlement of the colonies, and some of the reasons newcomers came to North America. You can guide students as they compare that time period with present-day events, developing new insights that for a selected group of students can be expanded for whatever period of time that seems appropriate. By necessity, some of the lessons will last several days.

To visually graph the emphasis and show the connections of a particular lesson to some selected curriculum standards suitable for the unit, you can develop a web such as the following one to show the links between standards and the different lessons selected for the unit. It can be drawn on the writing board to discuss with the students if appropriate for your group. This graphic can also be an advance organizer or orientation set that shows the unit lessons and the connections to selected language arts standards. Standards from other disciplines can be added.

Unit Goals. From History/Social Studies Framework in a western state, this unit is designed to explore

- selected early explorers
- early settlement of colonies, the people who lived there, the reasons they came to North America, and how those reasons are similar to and different from the reasons newcomers today come to America
- effects of the environment on people and their food, clothing, and shelter
- how the concept of migration or colonization compares with that of today

Standards.
- Adjust spoken and written language vocabulary and style to communicate effectively with audiences for different purposes.
- Use spoken and written language for enjoyment, exchanging information, and learning about a particular topic of interest.
- Develop competence in English and understanding of content across the curriculum.
- Read a range of literature to build an understanding of human experience.
- Use different writing process elements to communicate with different audiences for a variety of purposes.

*Source: Adapted from A *Guide for Developing Interdisciplinary Thematic Units,* 2nd Ed. (Merrill/Prentice Hall, 2000) by R. D. Kellough and P. L. Roberts.

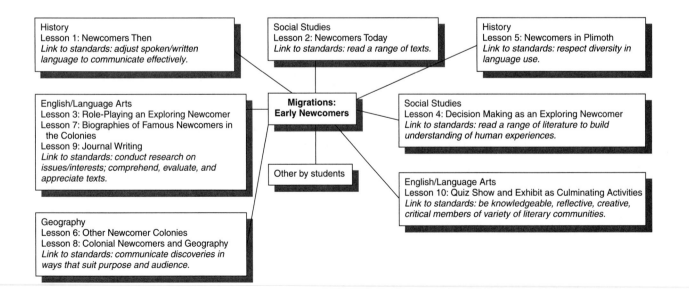

- Gather, evaluate, and synthesize data from different sources and communicate their discoveries in ways that suit their purpose and audience.

Student Diversity.   To provide additional classroom service to diverse students and their needs in the classroom, a teacher can consider the support services found in Figure 5.21.

FIGURE 5.21   Classroom Services for Diverse Students

Diverse Students	Classroom Services
For students with attention deficit disorder	Adjust to the diverse needs of students with attention deficit disorder in the classroom by posting the rules, supervising writing down assignments, making eye contact, giving signals, seating a student in a quiet area, and providing a notebook with dividers and folders for work. Encourage cooperative learning tasks with others, let the student stand at times to work, provide desk breaks, compliment positive behavior, place near good role models, send positive notes home, and talk alone often with the student (Barkley, 1990).
For blind and visually impaired students	To provide additional service to blind and visually impaired students, consider requesting Braille materials, talking books, raised relief maps, magnifiers, and large-type printed materials. For information about products, reports, films, and publications, write to the American Foundation for the Blind, Consumer Products Department, 15 West 16th Street, New York, NY 10011.
For deaf and hearing impaired students	To provide additional service to deaf and hearing impaired students, consider requesting assistance from a signing adult, classroom aide, or interpreter as needed. Use visuals and the overhead projector for writing questions and responses.
For ESL students	To provide additional service to ESL students, invite the students to work with those who have strong oral skills. Strategies to help introduce nonreaders to reading in English include the use of real objects, talking about pictures, reading aloud, demonstrating meaning, reciting poetry in choral groups, creating chart stories, playing word games, and making class dictionaries and word files. When appropriate, children's books related to the unit can present people of different ethnic and cultural groups and can be read aloud. For instance, selections to read aloud can be made from a source such as *Cultural Cobblestones: Teaching Cultural Diversity* (Scarecrow, 1994) by L. Miller, T. Steinlage, and M. Printz. In addition, provide the students with bilingual materials as needed and, when appropriate, bicultural materials. Request information from the National Clearinghouse for Bilingual Education, 11300 Wilson Boulevard, Suite B2-11, Rosslyn, VA 22209 and Gryphon House, 37 Otis House, P.O. Box 217, Mount Rainier, MD 20822 (for multiethnic books).

(Continued)

FIGURE 5.21 Continued

Diverse Students	Classroom Services
For gifted education students	To provide additional service to gifted and talented students, help build their critical thinking and problem solving skills with exercises using the text they read. Have them transform text from prose to free verse poetry (or vice versa), elaborate on text, and rearrange syntax. Provide them with computer programs and extensive reading (references, texts, and library books) related to the topic and, if appropriate, to the diversity of heritages bibliography in Figure 5.23 found later in this ITU. Engage the students in using their extensive reading to lead to independent inquiry, biographical research about key figures, and class reports. Have one student respond to questions in a unit study guide prepared by another student. Other activities for grades K-8 are suggested in N. J. Polette's *Gifted Books, Gifted Readers: Literature Activities to Excite Young Minds* (Englewood, CO: Libraries Unlimited, 2000). For more resources for both physically impaired and gifted students, contact the Council for Exceptional Children, 1920 Association Drive, Reston, VA 22091.
For students' learning modalities	Adjust to the needs of students' learning modalities and provide them with access to a wide range of materials at room sites (perhaps study centers at tables or desks). Allow scheduled time for individual free choice at the centers. For example, audio-centered students could select the audiovisual table and gain information about the topic of early settlers as newcomers with the filmstrip *The Pilgrims of Plimoth* (Weston Woods, Weston, CT) by M. Sewall. Visual learners might be helped by organizing information in a visual manner. Using a graphic web, chart, overhead diagram, or chalk display might make it easier for them to see relationships and, thus, better understand concepts being learned.
For physically impaired students	To give additional service, provide the students with a buddy system to help them use materials, equipment, and other resources. To inquire about special reading programs, contact the National Library Service for the Blind and Physically Handicapped, Library of Congress, Washington, DC 10542 or Telesensory Systems, Inc., 3408 Hillview Avenue, P. O. Box 10099, Palo Alto, CA 94304.

LESSON 1

Newcomers Then

Objectives

- Given a biography, the student will interpret a concept of *newcomer,* describe the ideas of others, and demonstrate active listening skills.
- Students will willingly cooperate with others during group activities.
- Students will describe their feelings about the topic. Standards in unit overview.

Materials

My Name Is Pocahontas (Holiday House, 1992) by William Accorsi or *The Double Life of Pocahontas* (Putnam, 1983) by Jean Fritz; paper, pencils, writing board or overhead transparency; students' portfolios

Procedure

"Today, you are going to hear about newcomers to the culture of a Native American princess, Pocahontas. Listen to find out what the princess did to help in events that happened between her culture and the newcomer's culture."

1. Introduce the concept of early English settlers as newcomers by reading aloud excerpts from *My Name Is Pocahontas* (Holiday House, 1992) by William Accorsi. This fictionalized biography is told by the princess beginning in her childhood. She tells of her friendship with Captain John Smith, her marriage to John Rolfe, and her trip to England as Rolfe's wife. Another read-aloud choice is *The Double Life of Pocahontas* (Putnam, 1983) by Jean Fritz. This biography focuses on the role the princess played in the events between two cultures. Discuss ways Smith and Rolfe were newcomers in Pocahontas's culture.

2. Write the word *newcomers* on the board or overhead transparency. Ask the students to identify new ideas (understandings, concepts, or feelings from their own points of view or from reference material) related to the topic of newcomers. Write their suggestions on the board in a list and invite students to write/copy their own lists at their desks or in small groups.

You may want to guide students toward an interdisciplinary focus with such questions as, "What in the biography tells us someone used math in a certain way? Art? Science? Music?"

M

Class expectations, matters of behavior, and consequences can be established with student input through class meetings. To develop the students' understanding of content in history/social studies, sequence the topics of instruction in a chronological order so concepts and facts strengthen one another.

T

Enrichment comes from outside sources such as *Pocahontas: Powhatan Peacemaker* (Chelsea, 1993) by A. Holler or *Multicultural Friendship Stories and Activities for Children, Ages 5–14* (Scarecrow Press, 1998) by P. L. Roberts.

M/D

Working in small groups supports students' understanding of a particular concept and contributes positively to their understanding of self and their acceptance of others. Also, research suggests that teacher subject matter presentation and knowledge have significant effects on student learning (Goldhaber and Brewer, 1999).

(Continued)

LESSON 1

Newcomers Then—Cont.

3. Ask students to rank order the concepts from the most general to the most specific (ranking from area of mathematics).

4. Arrange the general concept words in a graphic design on the writing board or in a web format. Invite the students to draw their own concept web at their desks. If appropriate, circle the general concept words and arrange them so that the most specific concept words and related ideas can be connected to them with radiating lines (as in a web).

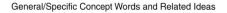

General/Specific Concept Words and Related Ideas

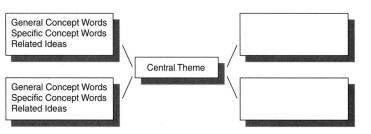

5. To integrate reading skills, the teacher can turn to a chart with the heading "We Read at Different Speeds" to ask questions of students, such as "when we want to find out _____, what should be our reading speed?" The chart contains information for the whole group: *Our Reading Chart*
We Read at Different Speeds

   a. *We read rapidly* when we want to find out if a page or book has information we can use.
   b. *We read at a moderate speed* when we want to find an answer to a question.
   c. *We read slowly* when we want to study to understand the information.

6. Invite students to discuss and define the connections between the related ideas. Have them define selected terms from the visual graphic of the theme/topic and use the word *PAID* as a guiding device: **P** means a student will pantomime (or silently demonstrate) something about the term that helps define it; **A** means a student will demonstrate actions (act out something with dialogue) related to the term; **I** means a student will show illustrations related to the term; and **D** means a student will define a term by reading a definition from a dictionary, glossary, thesaurus, or textbook, or will describe something about the term.

—**M**————————
Educational standards in the arts are linked to concentration exercises, rhythmic dialogue, and other activities in *Creative Drama and Music Methods: Introductory Activities for Children* by J. E. Rubin and M. Merrion and language arts standards are identified for the activities in *Language Arts and Environmental Awareness: 100+ Integrated Books and Activities for Children* by P. L. Roberts (both books from North Haven, CT: Shoestring Press/Linnet Professional Publications, 1996 and 1998 respectively).

LESSON 1

Newcomers Then—Cont.

More Interdisciplinary Aspects

If appropriate to emphasize various discipline further, discuss with students any or all of the following:

1. What can we see in the story of Pocahontas that shows a relationship between one's behavior and his or her beliefs? (anthropology)

2. What economic problems can we see in the story? What resolutions of the problems? (economics)

3. How could we show what we know about Pocahontas through the visual and performing arts? (art, music, dance, sculpture, and so on)

4. In what ways do you believe geography influenced the life of Pocahontas? (geography)

5. How have ways we receive information about this topic changed over time? (history)

6. In what ways could we express what we know about newcomers through numbers? (mathematics)

7. What scientists bring us more information about this topic? (science)

8. How did the people in this time period organize themselves? (political science)

9. In what ways can we participate to resolve a real problem related to the topic of migrations and newcomers? (sociology)

Closure

"Let's share our ideas about the concept of newcomers." Invite students to volunteer the information they gained about this concept and have them describe the ideas of others that they hear. To encourage them to demonstrate their listening skills, engage students in expanding some of the sentences they hear, in clarifying others, and if appropriate, in challenging still others.

(Continued)

M

To enrich the theme of early newcomers in colonies, introduce the flute and invite the students to sing several songs related to the time period. Perhaps display the long maple fife banded with brass ferrules that comes with the book *Amy, Ben and Catalpa the Cat* (Colonial Williamsburg Press, 1990, grades 1–2) by A. S. Owens, a story of children in 18th century Williamsburg that includes several tunes of the times and flute instructions.

M

Introduce the concept of cardinal points. With a small compass, have a volunteer walk in different directions; draw a compass shape in chalk on the floor, label the directions, and call out names of students to sit or stand by a particular direction.

M

Engage students in independent reading with A. Blackwood's book *Beethoven*, M. B. Goffstein's *A Little Schubert*, and D. Lasker's *The Boy Who Loved Music*. Use a time line on a transparency to show the era and country in which each lived to connect the composer with events in that period. To extend content, ask students to prepare drawings of a favorite composer of the period, play samples of musical scores, or write background facts on transparencies.

LESSON 1

Newcomers Then—Cont.

Assessment and Reflection

- Engage students in individual written assessments of what they have learned from listening to (or reading aloud) the biography and have them sketch or finish incomplete sentences with their own words. The following sentences are examples that the students could complete individually with their words or sketches:

  My idea of the concept of a newcomer is _____.

  What I learned most about newcomers was _____.

  Here is one idea about newcomers that I heard from someone else: _____.

- Have students place their written assessments in their portfolios.

- Keep a checklist of teacher observations regarding student participation in developing a visual map, in ranking the big ideas (concepts), and in defining terms. Have students begin a journal related to this unit and describe the most important facts, information, or skills they learned from the lesson and how they could apply what they learned to their lives in some way.

- Prepare a guideline related to assessing a student's skill in listening. You can assign a score if needed. Example: _____ (student name) is a strong listener who demonstrates the following:

  a. an immediate response to oral directions. (5 points)

  b. a focus on the one who is speaking.

  c. an appropriate attention span.

  d. an attention to what others are saying; expanding, clarifying, or questioning.

M

To further enrich content, have students sing the Shaker abecedarium from *A Peaceful Kingdom* (Viking, 1976, all grades) by the Provensons to the tune of "The Alphabet Song." Sing the story-songs that have historical significance from *Pop! Goes the Weasel and Yankee Doodle: New York in 1776 and Today with Songs and Pictures* (Harper, 1976) by Robert Quackenbush.

M

When students protest against a teacher-suggested activity—like singing—a teacher can use positive reinforcement and offer the students the opportunity to do something they like if they will first do something they don't like. Musically challenged learners can be asked to participate in musical games that involve listening to identify sounds of instruments or matching tones.

LESSON 2

Newcomers Today

Objective

- Students will demonstrate further understanding about the concept of the words *newcomers today* as they look for news articles about the contemporary newcomers.
- Students will make connections of similarities and differences about today's newcomers and early newcomers and report their findings back to the group.

Materials

Copies of different newspapers, paper, pencils, Venn diagram

Procedure

"Just as John Smith and John Rolfe were newcomers to the culture of Pocahontas, there are people today who are newcomers to your culture. Look at the newspaper you are given and with your partner look for articles and photographs, and read headlines of today. Get ready to tell the whole group about something similar and different about today's newcomer and a colonial newcomer."

1. Distribute copies of different newspapers to the students and ask them to work with partners and look for articles about newcomers today. Younger students can look for photographs and read headlines. Older students can read the articles and look for similarities and differences between the newcomers of today and the colonial newcomers. Have the students report back to the whole group about the similarities and differences they find.

2. Demonstrate the use of a Venn diagram (two circles that intersect) to show the similarities (written in intersection) and differences between colonial newcomers (written in circle A) and contemporary newcomers (written in circle B). Have the students develop the diagram as a group. If appropriate, have students work with partners to complete their own diagrams to show similarities and differences in the two groups of newcomers.

M

To assess students' overall knowledge about a theme/topic, have students brainstorm as a group what they know about the theme/topic. Record the information on classroom charts.

M

Engage students in the responsive structured practice of Morning Meetings Circles (part of a Responsive Classroom practice developed by Northeast Foundation for Children) with the components of greeting, sharing, having a group activity, reporting news, and giving announcements (Bondy, 2002). Have students share information with one another to gain a sense of classroom community, a sense of value and significance, and a sense of social skills, and to prepare for the school day. Over time, the circle helps the teacher observe improvement in individual student behavior in these areas.

(Continued)

LESSON 2

Newcomers Today—Cont.

3. Invite students who developed their own diagrams to show them and report on what they wrote about similarities and differences. As students report, make decisions about what ad hoc groups are needed, if any.

4. To integrate ad hoc groups to attend to learning or to structure learning groups around selected skills or content for special assistance, consider any or all of the following:

   a. *Capitalization.* Checking capitalization related to your ITU: Write sentences on the writing board or overhead transparency and ask students to identify which word/words need a capital letter. Include sentences with proper names, names of books, and names of cities and states. Examples to be corrected: william bradford was the governor of the pilgrim colony in the cape cod area. william bradford's journal is called homes in the wilderness.

   b. *Comprehension.* For multiple meanings related to your ITU: With the students, identify words with multiple meanings (e.g., duck, fair, top, train) and ask them to contribute sentences related to the ITU and write them using the words. Then write a pair of sentences leaving out a selected word that has multiple meanings. Ask students to select the appropriate word. Example for *duck:* Sentence 1: The Pilgrims watched the _____ swimming in the water. Sentence 2: The tree branch hit the Pilgrim because he didn't _____. Example for *top:* Sentence 1: The Pilgrim father climbed to the _____ of the hill. Sentence 2: The Pilgrim baby liked to play with his wooden _____.

   c. *Comprehension.* For context clues related to your ITU: Select sentences from any text related to the ITU and write them on the writing board leaving out a noun. Write four nouns as choices and ask the students to read the sentence and select a noun that fits the context. Repeat to develop skill in recognizing context clues.

   d. *Reading.* Revising Reading Passages related to ITU: Write a short passage (with some misspellings in several phrases) from a newspaper or text on the board or overhead transparency and identify one phrase at a time. Give students four spelling choices for each phrase and ask them to identify a correct spelling choice for each phrase.

T

To enrich the theme, show a related video such as *The English Come to America: Jamestown and Plymouth* (Chariot Productions/AGC/United Learning, 1560 Sherman Avenue, Suite 100, Evanston, IL 60201; grades 2–5) about where the colonists came from, reasons why they migrated, their ocean crossing, and the building of their settlements, or *Early Settlers* (100% Educational Videos, 4921 Robert J. Mathews Parkway, El Dorado Hills, CA 95762; grades 1–3) that explains what life was like for the early settlers in the United States hundreds of years ago.

M

To assess students' comprehension after reading, consider after-reading activities such as comparing what is read with another story, creating an alternate ending, integrating art with a project based on the story, engaging in brief drama or role play, or writing an entry in a journal about one's feelings about the character in the story.

LESSON 2

Newcomers Today—Cont.

e. *Rewriting.* For rewriting paragraphs related to your ITU: With the students, select a short paragraph from text related to your ITU and write it on the board or overhead transparency making these changes: *Change 1:* Rewrite a sentence to make it say the same thing twice. *Change 2:* Rewrite a sentence so it is incomplete. Ask the students to locate the sentence that says the same thing twice and to locate the incomplete sentence. Ask them for the best ways to rewrite these sentences. Reread the paragraph as rewritten. Repeat with other paragraphs.

f. *Spelling.* Checking spelling related to your ITU: Identify words that are often misspelled by the students and use them as word choices to complete sentences related to the ITU. Some words that are often misspelled are *before, knew, sugar.* Example: The Pilgrim mother put _____ in her hot tea (spelling choices: shugar, sugar, suger, shugir).

g. *Study skills.* For ad hoc study skills related to your ITU: Photocopy one page of an index of a book related to the theme of your ITU and make a transparency with it for the overhead projector. Show the transparency and ask students questions about the use of the index. Examples:
  - This book does *not* include information about . . . (give three or four choices written on the writing board).
  - On what page would you begin reading about . . . (give several page choices on writing board)?
  - To find out about _____, you would begin reading on page . . . (give multiple choices).
  - On which pages would you look to find out about _____ (give multiple choices)? Discuss with the group.

h. *Vocabulary.* For synonyms related to your ITU: Ask the students to read a sentence you have written on the writing board or overhead and then find a word from four choices you have written that has the same or almost the same meaning as a word you underlined in the sentence. Example: The Pilgrim mother had a <u>regular</u> time for supper (usual, normal, early, secret). The Pilgrim father put on his <u>cloak</u> (robe, collar, jacket, hat). The Pilgrim leader was a <u>feeble</u> old man (rich, famous, ugly, weak). Repeat with other examples.

i. *Word Analysis.* For ad hoc word analysis related to your ITU: With the students, identify words and make class charts to review. What word begins with the same sound as . . . (g as in gem, c as in circus, and so on)? What word has the same sound as the letters "oo" in _____? as the letters "ea" in _____? As the letters "se" in _____? What word rhymes with the word _____? What word ends with the same sound as _____?

(Continued)

M

Check your school's/district's scope and sequence for curriculum for your grade level to determine which activities are developmentally appropriate for your students.

LESSON 2

Newcomers Today—Cont.

Interdisciplinary Aspects

To integrate various disciplines, discuss any of the following for whole group work or ad hoc group work as needed:

1. *To integrate writing.* In a Pilgrim newsletter, students can pass along the survey results and then use different types of writing to share information—including informational writing (to tell of dangers in the Pilgrim's time), advertisement writing (with samples of advertisements about items Pilgrims needed), newswriting (stories about people and events), persuasive writing (editorials about debatable points), expository writing (topics such as ways to protect health of people), sidebar writing with graphs and charts, and caption writing to explain illustrations and sketches.

2. *To integrate language arts/expressive arts.* How can we show what we know about these newcomers to America through art, dance, music, and sculpture (expressive arts) and through reading, writing, listening, and speaking (language arts)? Consider using body and facial expressions to bring a character/Pilgrim to life through a group-dictated story.

- To depict the environment for the Pilgrims, have students bring to class plant leaves that are descendants of plants from an earlier time period, such as leaves of the gingko, willow, maple, and others. Have them talk about what they observe, and reproduce the leaves in the mural.
- Help students create, understand, and appreciate art forms by exploring various characteristics of an artist with the *Art for Children* series (Lippincott, 1990)

3. *To integrate social studies.* How can we participate in our community today to resolve a problem related to today's newcomers? (sociology)

- Consider a comparative theme such as families at work now and long ago (kindergarten) and have students discuss a story with the dilemma of working/not working together. Have the students substitute the name and personality of a Pilgrim child for a child in the story and discuss what happens when family members (whether Pilgrim or contemporary) don't work together.

4. *To consider themes.* Consider a theme of children in time and space (suitable for first grade) and have students explain some information they have found.

- Consider a theme of people who make a difference and have students read selected stories about Pilgrims and tell others one of the ways the main character made a difference. Consider a theme of continuity and change and have students select a variety of examples from reading biographies, folk tales, legends, songs, and realistic stories.

5. *To consider history.* How can we find out what newcomer groups settled in our area? How is their influence shown today? (history)

M

For alternative math experiences for younger students, count with rhymes or songs, do finger-play activities, move replicas (perhaps pilgrim shapes) around to arrange and rearrange them in groups/categories; count up to X number; review the pattern of one-more-than and one-less-than (numbers).

T

Introduce students to some of the basics of geography with your choice of suitable filmstrips. They help review the effects of climate, water, and land types on people; ways to locate places; and the use of natural resources.

LESSON 2

Newcomers Today—Cont.

- *To consider changes over time.* Consider a theme of our changing state and interest children in talking about cultural diversity in the past and in current times.

6. *To integrate basics of geography.* In what ways did geography influence the newcomers? (geography)
   - Consider a theme of our area's/state's/nation's geography and have students better understand people and where they live by learning some of the basics of geography.

7. *To integrate student ownership of text.* Use a reader's script where the story is read aloud and the students make sound effects and chime in on repetitive lines.
   - Give students ownership of the text by doing a second reading of a story about Pilgrims and stopping to allow students time to imagine the setting, then stopping to have them talk among themselves as they feel Pilgrims would do. Write new words for familiar songs. Change well-known rhymes, finger plays, or verses of songs with newly contributed words about Pilgrims ("Yankee Doodle went to town" becomes "Pilgrim Bradford went next door." Chant a refrain of poetry, predict meanings of words in poems, or make oral interpretations.

8. *To integrate anthropological science.* What experiences related to science could we have that would help us understand the way these newcomers lived? (science) Tell students that one way to find out what the Pilgrims were like and how they lived is to use resources to study the artifacts of their lives and to locate items that Pilgrims used.
   - *To gather and organize data.* Students can also look at the types of plants and insects and animals that lived during the time period that the Pilgrims did to learn more about life during this time.
   - *To integrate a survey.* Students can write questions on a survey sheet that they want to ask others about what they believe about Pilgrims. They can put a tally mark in the right place on the sheet, count tallies, and discuss the meaning of the survey.

9. *To integrate math.* In what way could we use math to show something we have learned about the topic/theme? To integrate mathematics, consider one or more of the following experiences appropriate for the students:
   - *For addition.* Make up addition situations about Pilgrim life. Place felt or flannel pieces side by side and recognize the signs for + and =. Write math sentences in vertical or horizontal format.
   - *For differences.* Find books that do or do not have further information about a theme/topic being studied and place titles on a bar graph with categories for "Has Information" and "Does Not Have Information." See Figure 5.22 for further integration activities.

(Continued)

M

To integrate art, have students make clay or papier mache items that resemble items used by the early newcomers.

LESSON 2

Newcomers Today—Cont.

FIGURE 5.22   Examples of Math Activities for Integration in ITU

Math Activity	Integrated Activity in Migrations Unit
For subtraction	Use the idea of one of the Pilgrim children moving along a number line. Draw a number line on the board to show the math sentence of 12 − 7 =_____ . The movement of a paper cutout of a Pilgrim child along the number line taking 7 steps of the 12 steps that are needed to get to a certain spot can illustrate the math sentence.
For division	Show groups in arrangements such as 3 cabins in each of two rows (ask how many 3s are in 6 and write math sentence 6 divided by 3 = 2) or complete a table to find the number of small wild two-legged turkey fossils in an early Pilgrim area. To do this, students divide each number in the following first line by 2.

How many small wild two-legged turkey fossils?

Number of fossilized turkey feet

10	8	6	4	2

Number of turkeys   5

Math Activity	Integrated Activity in Migrations Unit
For commutative property	Distribute paper strips (8″ × 3″) and self-adhesive circular white-paper hole reinforcements to each student. Show two groups (perhaps 4 and 3) of Pilgrims' models (or cabins, wild animals, or vegetables) and have students count and glue the same number of the reinforcements at one end of the strip (4) and the same number at the other end (3) to show the number in each of the two groups. Students count again and write the math sentence 4 + 3 = 7 on strip. Have students turn right end of strip to left, count again, and write the commutative math sentence 3 + 4 = 7.
To use measurement	Students can make individual calendars to understand the continuous measurement of time by days, weeks, and months. With scales, students can weigh individual books to understand the continuous measurement of weight of objects. Students can use metric rulers to measure off the lengths of Pilgrims' cabins, household utensils, and tools or to estimate the length, height, and weight of animals the Pilgrims domesticated.
To use enlargement and ratio	Use a cut-apart photocopy of a drawing of a cabin. Have each student take a 1-inch part of the cabin shape and use a ruler to enlarge the piece by drawing it to 10 inches on a larger sheet of paper. Each can cut out the enlarged pieces and all can assemble the cabin shape on a class wall to make an enlarged picture of the Pilgrim's shelter.
To use geometry	Students can look at illustrations related to the topic with the purpose of recognizing common geometric shapes. Students can search for geometric shapes in the forms and shapes of domesticated/wild animals or make paper models of plants or small creatures with paper, scissors, and glue by measuring, marking, connecting, and folding required shapes and using circles for eyes, a triangle for nose, rectangles for teeth, and cylinders for body tubes.

M

For more multiplication, count cabins in two or more groups (4 groups of 3 cabins) and write math sentences that tell the number of cabins in all groups or draw four rows of cabins with 6 cabins in each row and write math sentences (4 × 6) to show what is going on.

M

For more graphing, make a graph to show books about the theme read by students during the days of the week and use multiplication to determine the total read by students A, B, and C.

LESSON 2

Newcomers Today—Cont.

FIGURE 5.22   Continued

Math Activity	Integrated Activity in Migrations Unit
To show function	Show the one-to-one relationship of numbers (function) by showing the relationship of an early Pilgrim to her or his country of origin by writing a sentence (i.e., Pilgrim 3 came from Y) or by drawing separate lines from the Pilgrim's name (list A) to the name of the Pilgrim's original country (list B).
To use graphs, statistics, and probability	Students make simple block graphs that represent stories they know about Pilgrims or types of household utensils or tools found in informational books about this time period. Students can also draw, color, and cut out a small Pilgrim to show the clothing being worn in the story being read and each can paste the shape on a chart that has headings on it, (i.e., wearing cloak, not wearing cloak, and so on). Have students look at the chart to discover the patterns or types of dress that authors have written about or illustrators have shown in the stories and help students see the graph as a useful device for collecting information. Also, a pie chart can be made for contrasting and comparing different categories of clothing worn by the whole Pilgrim population that the students find in the stories.
To use logical thinking	Ask students "Was William Bradford a Pilgrim? And if you guessed, predicted, or hypothesized (had a hunch) that William Bradford *was* a Pilgrim, then can you use what you know about Pilgrims to answer questions? Let's find out. Our questions are related to *who, what, where,* and *when* (i.e., the term *who* asks *who he was*). Can you use what you know to say that William Bradford would be a person/man/Pilgrim who traveled with the other Pilgrims on early ships such as the *Mayflower*? (The term *what* asks *what he did*). Can you use what you know to say that William Bradford would be a person who did Pilgrim chores (and what would those chores be?) and lived in a Pilgrim shelter (and what would the shelter be like)? The term *where* asks *where he would have lived.* Can you use what you know to say that he would have lived in the early Plymouth Rock area? The term *when* asks for a time period (would he have lived in the 1600s?). You can search for information from sources to support your statements."
To use problem solving	Students can use math sentences to express a problem situation (e.g., if the number of students in class represents the number of Pilgrims in an imagined situation, what is the number of Pilgrims/students in school? the number not in attendance? the number eating lunch not brought from home (cafeteria)? the number who brought their lunches from home? the number walking home for lunch?)

M

For further logical thinking, ask students to generate statements from another point of view using *if-then* words, that is, If William Bradford was *not* a Pilgrim, then William Bradford would *not* be a person/man who traveled with the other Pilgrims on early ships such as the *Mayflower*.

(Continued)

LESSON 2
Newcomers Today—Cont.

Closure

Engage students in discussing newcomers and, "What meaning does this have for us today?" Have them dictate a paragraph about the two newcomer groups for a group chart. If appropriate, engage more able students in writing individual paragraphs about the similarities and differences of the two groups.

Assessment and Reflection

In a group, ask students an oral assessment type question, "Now that you've thought about what it was like to be a colonial newcomer and what it is like to be a contemporary newcomer, what could we do in the future to assist newcomers?" List all of the responses on a class chart, overhead transparency, or bulletin board, for later reference. Have students copy the list and place their copies in their portfolios.

    Teacher observation on student participation:

a. While developing a group diagram (or written paragraph), the similarities and differences of two newcomer groups can be noted and recorded. Have students place copies of the diagram (or individual paragraphs) in their portfolios.

b. While recording responses to oral assessment questions, consider a teacher observation checklist such as the one that follows on page 205.

c. While students are reading and reporting on newspaper articles, you can develop a checklist about a student's reporting to the group. See the following checklist on page 205.

d. Have students write in a journal and describe the most important thing they learned about newcomers and how they can use the information to relate better to newcomers who come into their lives.

M

To engage students in sorting data, the teacher can model how to place information in categories, how to take notes, and how to put notes in a paragraph form.

LESSON 2

Newcomers Today—Cont.

Teacher Observation Checklist

Observation Period _____ for _____ Date _____

The following is the number of times the students demonstrated participation in group work:

Student name   **in group**   **in response to questions**

1.

Checklist of a Student's Oral Report to a Group

Date _____ Student _____

	sometimes	always	needs work
spoke up so all could hear			
finished sentences			
appeared confident before group			
gave good introduction			
was informed about topic			
explained clearly			
stayed on topic			
gave good ending			
was interesting			
gave good answers to questions			

LESSON 3

Role-Playing an Exploring Newcomer

Objective

After discussing the role, or what it means, to be an exploring newcomer, students will participate in role-playing activities and draw some conclusions about what it means to be in that role.

Materials

Samples of edible foods/plants (ordered from a local produce business) that are unique and unfamiliar to the students, writing journals, pencils, sketch paper, crayons

Procedure

"We can play the part of exploring newcomers who have the responsibility of finding some edible plants for the rest of the colony. To begin, who will suggest some ways we can play the roles of newcomers who are exploring the area and looking for plants for food that the colonists can eat."

1. With the whole group, discuss some ways of portraying the role(s) related to being exploring newcomers. Elicit suggestions about playing the roles from the students and write their ideas on the board.

2. Discuss questions such as those that follow that are related to role-playing for information purposes and problem solving before students are asked to play the roles. You can list the questions for the students to use during the role-playing exercise. Later the list can be reused by the students as a reference for their class discussion after the role-playing events.

Role-Playing Questions

What's your persona?	What do you look like?	Where are you?
What does the setting look like?	Why are you there?	What could happen?
How are you feeling?	What are you thinking?	What will you say?
How will you act?	How can you make the relationship stronger with someone?	

3. Invite two partners to role-play two exploring newcomers looking for edible plants. Give each partnership one of the unique and unfamiliar foods or plants to use in the role-playing exercise. Have two other partners be the audience. Then have them change roles so each student can play the part of an exploring newcomer.

To enrich the topic for future role-playing, show laser disc *The First Thanksgiving* (Clearvue/eav, grades 1–3) or *Pilgrims at Plymouth* (Clearvue/eav, grades 4–6).

LESSON 3

Role-Playing an Exploring Newcomer—Cont.

4. *Stop-the-action Activity 1 for Journal Writing.* Stop the students in the middle of role-playing and ask them to write in their journals what they are thinking and feeling. As part of the study of the theme/topic, invite them to include any words and actions they particularly liked during the role-play.

5. After writing, invite the students to meet with new partners and resume the role-play with two other partners as an audience. Have them trade roles again.

6. *Stop-the-Action Activity 2 for Sketching.* Stop the role-play and engage the partners in making a sketch of a Pilgrim's personal possession related to the role-play—have them make the object lifesize or larger on large art paper. Ask them to write a dedication to a friend in the class for their sketches: "To _____ from your exploring newcomer friend, _____." Let students give their sketches to the person to whom they wrote the dedication.

7. After sketching, invite the students to trade partners still another time and resume role-playing again. Have them trade roles so each student can be an exploring newcomer.

8. *Stop-the-Action Activity 3 for Discussion.* Ask the partners to meet with another pair of partners and discuss ways the role-playing stimulated their curiosity about wanting to know more about being an exploring newcomer. Have them each make a copy of their list:

> What We Are Curious About
> 1.

9. After list-making, have the students trade partners and resume role playing again. Have them trade roles so each student gets to play all the roles in this situation.

10. *Stop-the-Action Activity 4 for Suggestions.* Back in the whole group, debrief the role-playing by having students suggest ways it helped them learn more about what it was like to be an exploring newcomer. Ask volunteers to tell the ways the role-playing stimulated their curiosity about the theme, topic, or particular event that was selected. They can refer to their lists titled "What We Are Curious About." Elicit any additional experiences that the students have had related to the role-playing. Discuss.

More Interdisciplinary Aspects

Discuss any or all of the following:

1. How can we show through expressive and language arts what these newcomers did as they searched for edible plants? (expressive and language arts)

(Continued)

D

To guide student learning through verbal interactions, the teacher can facilitate effective instructional conversation. This means that students should be encouraged to build on what others say so each statement expands, clarifies, or challenges previous statements. This type of dialogue has been demonstrated to be highly relevant to the linguistic, cognitive, and academic development of linguistically and culturally diverse students.

LESSON 3

Role-Playing an Exploring Newcomer—Cont.

2. What experiences have we had to help us understand the new-comers' need to search for food? (anthropology)
3. In what ways did geography influence the plants the newcomers found? (geography)
4. What scientists can we invite to class to tell us about edible plants? (science)
5. Who could lead us on a real-place educational trip to investigate the quantity of edible (safe) plants in our area? (science)

Closure

"All the items in our role-playing list are items to help us understand what it means to be an exploring newcomer. Which item helped you the most? Why?" Discuss ways students participated in the role-playing activities and engage them in drawing some conclusions about what it means to be in that role.

Assessment and Reflection

* Ask students to record what they learned about the topic by writing paragraphs in their journals to tell what they learned from the role-playing activity. Encourage them to write about ways in which they learned more than mere facts (about attitudes, body language, facial expressions, feelings, personalities, points of view).
* In addition, encourage students to refer to their lists of "What We Are Curious About" and follow their curiosity into areas related to this unit that interest them by engaging in independent research when they finish class assignments or during library time. The lists and paragraphs can be placed in the students' portfolios.
* Teacher observations of student participation in role-playing can take the form of a checklist such as the one that follows:

M

For an authentic account of what went on, read aloud excerpts from *Homes in the Wilderness: A Pilgrim's Journal of Plymouth Plantation in 1629* by W. Bradford et al. and edited by M. W. Brown (North Haven, CT: Shoestring Press/Linnet Professional Publications, 1988 repr. 1939). It describes the Pilgrims' first encounter with Native Americans and ways they survived their first winter.

Teacher Observation for Role-Playing

Observation Period _____

Student name   **cooperates**   **contributes**   **is consistent**

1.

LESSON 4

Decision Making as an Exploring Newcomer

Objectives

- Students will participate in decision making, cooperate in discussion and small-group work, and sketch what they have learned about testing an unfamiliar food for edibleness.
- Students will respond attentively, willingly cooperate with others during group activities, and create a proposal for decision making related to the safety of eating unfamiliar foods.

Materials

People of the Breaking Day (New York: Atheneum, 1990) by M. Sewall or *Squanto and the First Thanksgiving* (New York: Carolrhoda, 1983) by J. K. Kessel; samples of edible foods/plants (perhaps from previous lesson or ordered from a local producer) that are unique and unfamiliar to the students; writing journals, pencils, sketch paper, crayons

Procedure

"Squanto, a Patuxet Indian, taught the Pilgrims ways to live through the harsh winter in Massachusetts. They relied on Squanto's knowledge to help them survive. Suppose they did not have Squanto to help them and were exploring newcomers who had to search for food among unfamiliar plants. What would they have done to determine which foods were safe for them to eat?"

"We can imagine we are colonists and have no one—not even Squanto—to tell us which food is safe to eat. We can play the part of exploring newcomers who have the responsibility of finding some edible plants for the rest of the colony. We can show how we made decisions as the colonists who had the responsibility of finding safe, edible plants for the others in the colony."

1. Read aloud excerpts related to the Native Americans' survival skills from *People of the Breaking Day.* Discuss what the Native Americans did to survive and to gather food in their environment.

2. Have students reread the story independently or get in small groups to discuss the story and then have them imagine they are exploring newcomers who do not have the knowledge that the Native Americans had, but who have the responsibility of finding some edible plants for the rest of the colony.

3. Distribute some unfamiliar edible foods to the groups. Suggestions include bok choy leaves, watercress leaves, cilantro, star fruit, radicchio, artichokes, and kiwi fruit. Ask the groups to act out finding their food items. Have the students play the role of exploring newcomers

(Continued)

M

To provide students with enrichment activities that require critical thinking skills; give students illustrations, drawings, or sketches of Pilgrims from informational books; and ask students to write brief stories that tell about the lives of these people.

M

If suitable for students who are to read independently, introduce purposeful prereading activities such as having students predict what the story is about based on the title and cover illustration; or ask the students to reflect on their knowledge about Native Americans of this time period and what they might learn from the story.

LESSON 4

Decision Making as an Exploring Newcomer—Cont.

who have not seen the foods before and are concerned about eating them. Their challenge is to make decisions about the safety of eating the unfamiliar food their group has been given. They should discuss what they would do to determine the food's safety for the colony. What would they do? Have the groups engage in making decisions about testing the safety of the food.

4. Back in the whole group, have a reporter from each group tell the group's decisions about determining the safety of the food for the colony. Write the group's decision-making proposals on the board or on an overhead transparency. Discuss each proposal.

5. Ask the students to brainstorm additional ways that the exploring newcomers could have "tested" an unfamiliar food to determine the extent to which it was safe for humans to eat. Write their suggestions on the board or transparency.

6. Have the students make posters depicting the most interesting and valuable information to turn into "rules or guidelines" about testing unfamiliar foods. On the back, ask them to write (or tell) an explanation about what they learned.

More Interdisciplinary Aspects

Discuss:

1. How can we show what we know about the Native Americans of this period through expressive and language arts? (expressive/language arts)
2. What experiences have we had to help us understand the way the Native Americans lived? (anthropology)
3. In what ways did geography influence the food of the Native Americans? (geography)
4. What can we do to find out which Native Americans lived in our area? (history)
5. How can we participate in our community today to resolve a real problem related to Native Americans? (sociology)

Closure

Invite students to offer suggestions in regard to improving any future decision-making activity, cooperating in discussion and small-group work, and making sketches about what was learned when testing an unfamiliar food.

M

As an instructional comprehension strategy during reading, stop at points in the reading and ask students to make inferences, summarize, retell the events in sequence, or identify problems first and then come up with possible solutions.

M

When reports are to be in writing, review stages of writing with students— prewriting, drafting, editing, and publishing. Point out that prewriting activities include discussion, interviewing, researching, note-taking, and brainstorming. Drafting activities include writing ideas on paper, and editing means sharing a draft with someone for further discussion, proofing, correcting, and refining.

LESSON 4

Decision Making as an Exploring Newcomer—Cont.

Assessment and Reflection

If desired for your group, introduce the idea of circle assessment, during which the members of each group sit in a circle and respond in turn to your assessment questions. Possible questions include, "What did you learn from this activity?" and "What do you still want to know?"

- Teacher observation can be kept on a checklist of student participation in role-playing an exploring newcomer, in discussing the decisions, and in drawing their posters to show information. Also include information about students participating in decision making, cooperating in discussion and small-group work, and making sketches about what was learned when testing an unfamiliar food.
- Have students also write in their journals about this unit and draw pictures or describe the most important things they learned from the lesson and how they could apply what they learned to their lives in some way.
- Have students place their work in their portfolios.

M

After using a variety of methods of assessing individual student performance, a teacher can make a formative assessment by giving individuals feedback to increase their skills.

LESSON 5

Newcomers in Plimoth

Objectives

- Given information, students will identify responsibilities of the colonists, discuss and describe their lives, and demonstrate listening skills in partnership and group work.
- Students will offer opinions and justify their ranking choices about the topic.
- Students will describe their feelings about the topic.

Materials

The Pilgrims of Plimoth (Macmillan, 1986) by M. Sewall

Procedures

"You are going to hear about the children, women, and men who were the newcomers who lived at Plimoth Colony. Listen to find out what their lives and responsibilities were like."

1. Divide the class into three groups. Have one group listen and report back on the responsibilities of the children; a second group on the lives and responsibilities of the men; and third, the lives and responsibilities of the women at Plimoth.

2. When the groups report, list their responses on the board. From the list, have students identify or infer any problems the colony newcomers had.

3. Review the problems and help students classify similar problems together under student-suggested headings such as "Problems of Shelter" and "Problems Getting Food." Ask the students to list the problems on paper and then rank order them with the greatest problem being number one, and so on.

4. Ask students to meet with partners and justify their choices and their rankings to one another. Ask the partners to give written feedback about their agreement or disagreement with any of the rankings.

5. Back in the whole group, discuss the rank ordering and what was needed to help resolve some of the problems the colonial newcomers had.

More Disciplinary Aspects

Consider:

1. Related to the topic of newcomers in Plimoth, discuss with the students ways they can show some of the daily responsibilities of the newcomers through reading, writing, listening, and speaking (English literacy/language arts) and through art, music, sculpture, dance (expressive arts)? Examples include the following:

M

To extend decision making, help students explore modern-day decision making about establishing colonies in space with the computer software, *Colonization* (Tom Snyder Productions, grades 5–12).

LESSON 5

Newcomers in Plimoth—Cont.

- Create an artistic work with costumes, music, and dance and let students write scripts, compose music, and design sets.
- Look for symbolic language in dance through a video of dance and then transfer what was learned back to a Pilgrim topic. Students can locate music that represents movements of the Pilgrims and plan body language that has meaning to go along with the music.
- Look for artists' works and show examples of ways different artists show Pilgrims in books.
- Have students design projects such as making an informational diorama of a scene with a Pilgrim whose background has been researched by writing and drawing about a favorite event, time, or place.
- Have students illustrate an original booklet to show their research, or dramatize certain events in a Pilgrim's life.
- Have students select a theme, use available rhythm instruments, and work together to compose a brief rhythmic selection. They can play it for others and tell how they tried to keep to their theme.

2. What experiences have you had that help you understand the newcomers' problems of getting shelter and food? (anthropology) How can you share this experience with others? What are your feelings about this?

3. In what ways can you show others how geography influenced the shelter available to the newcomers? (geography)

4. How can we participate in our community today to resolve a real problem related to getting food and shelter for those who need it? (sociology)

Closure

"Many of the responsibilities of the colonists are also the responsibilities people face today. What do you think some of these responsibilities are?" Have students identify responsibilities of the colonists. Encourage them to expand on what they say and discuss and describe what went on in the colonists' lives (i.e., in what ways did the colonists organize?) Encourage them to demonstrate listening skills toward others in the group.

To further extend closure, have students recreate some of the Pilgrims' utensils and tools through invisible sculptures by having students sculpt with "invisible clay." Students work with pretend motions, make something out of the clay, and then, as a Pilgrim, show how he/she would use it to a partner. If the partner understands the actions and guesses the object's name, then the partner receives the invisible clay and makes another object. Repeat the activity by changing partners.

(Continued)

T

Have students create class bulletin boards by getting information from a video such as *Creative Bulletin Boards* (American School Publisher, 1990) and ask students to plan a good display with colors and shapes and prepare artwork related to their unit theme.

M

Help students recognize a theme in music by listening to a favorite music education video or to *Adventures in Listening* (Merit Audio Visual, 1990). Ask students to discuss a theme in a musical composition that they think evokes the topic/theme.

T

Engage students in choral conversations with calls and answers from *Beats: Conversations in Rhythm for English as a Second Language* (Educational Activities, 1990, grades 2–5).

LESSON 5

Newcomers in Plimoth—Cont.

Assessment and Reflection

- Ask students to place their list of problems, rankings, and written feedback in their portfolios.
- Teacher assessment can be done by observing the students' participation in the discussion and activity and noting their demonstration of listening skills as they respond to each other.
- Reports that students make back to the group can be assessed with a set of guidelines you have established such as the following:

Teacher Guidelines for Oral Report

Student _____ Date _____ Topic _____

Excellent presentation (5 points for each)
a. Appeared confident
b. Covered important information
c. Introduced report well
d. Made good eye contact with audience
e. Spoke for scheduled time
f. Spoke loudly so all could hear

Adequate presentation (3 points for each)
a. Appeared uneasy and not always confident
b. Covered information but not always important
c. Introduced report in vague way
d. Made eye contact sometimes with audience
e. Spoke but not for allotted time
f. Spoke but not all could hear all of the time

Disorganized presentation (1 point for each)
a. Appeared uneasy
b. Covered unimportant information
c. Failed to introduce report
d. Made no or limited eye contact
e. Spoke for brief time
f. Spoke but not all could hear most of the time

- Have students write in a unit journal describing what they learned about the lives and responsibilities of the newcomers at Plimoth and how they could apply what they learned to their lives.

LESSON 6

Other Newcomer Colonies

Objectives

- Students will transform information into an art form, will research reasons for the establishment of colonies, and will organize and summarize information.
- Students will cooperate with others during the activities and demonstrate communication skills.

Materials

Map, reference materials, paper, pencils

Procedure

"You are going to read about newcomers who lived in other colonies. Read to find out several reasons why newcomers started their colonies."

1. With a map, point out the location of the northern, middle, and southern colonies.

2. Ask students to identify one group of colonies to research. In their research, ask them to consider the following questions:

    a. What reason(s) can you give to support newcomers starting the colonies of Rhode Island, Connecticut, and New Hampshire?

    b. Were the middle colonies started by newcomers for the same (or different) reasons?

    c. For what reasons were the southern colonies started by newcomers?

    d. What main idea or statement can you make from this information?

3. Have small groups of students support one another and follow their individual inquiries about their colony group with class resources, the school library, computer programs, and so on.

4. Ask the group members to work together to organize and summarize the information they have gained.

5. In the whole group, have students from each group report on the main idea or statement related to the previous study questions.

6. Back in small groups, have students transform their information into an art form and make a mural to illustrate the information each student considers the most valuable. Have students display the mural to others and answer any questions the other students might have about the mural and its information. Ask for feedback about cooperation of group members during the group work.

7. Engage students in suggesting individual or group projects related to the topic of newcomer colonies, such as How can you show some of the similarities or differences of the northern, middle, and southern colonies through art and sculpture, dance, or music?

(Continued)

T

Enrichment from outside sources can come from such media as *Native American Lifestyles 1500–1820* (Cherokee Heritage Indian Educ. Foundation. Dist. by Lucerne Media, 16 Woodmill Road, Chappaqua, New York, 10514, grades 4–8); It examines the lifestyles of Native Americans hundreds of years ago. A teacher's guide is available.

T

To enrich the content, make available the laser disc *The Geography of the New England States* (SVE, grades 4–8) or the video *Map Skills for Beginners* and *Map Skills* (Coronet/MTI, grades K–5 and 3–6 respectively); or *Latitude and Longitude* (National Geographic, grades 4–9).

LESSON 6

Other Newcomer Colonies—Cont.

8. As an option for a mini-lesson, suggest to students that they gather additional information about the colonies from reading maps: "Let's locate some major places and use the rulers to measure/estimate distances. Let's review map symbols to locate latitude lines and match a color code to locate specific colonies." Help the student respond to a worksheet designed to help them work on their map skills. Guide those

---

Map Skill Worksheet for Individual Activity

Student _____ Date _____

Teacher _____ Period _____

Map I

Find the map on page _____ of your textbook (atlas, information sheet). Complete the following items:

1. Locate the English colony of Roanoke Island. Write the name of the ocean that surrounds the island. _____

2. Calculate the miles to the inch with your ruler and measure the distance from the colony of Roanoke Island across the ocean to Raleigh Bay.

Map II

Find the map. Complete the following items:

3. Locate the colony on Roanoke Island again. Between which two lines of attitude was this colony located? _____ and _____.

4. Study the map symbols to find out which group had the rights to the land where this colony started.

Map III

Find the map on page _____ of your textbook. Complete the following items.

5. Review the color code on the map and write the names of the colonies that were known as the New England Colonies

_____

6. Which colonies were known as the Middle Colonies?

7. Which colonies were known as the Southern Colonies?

LESSON 6

Other Newcomer Colonies—Cont.

who need assistance as they respond to information. Assessment of this mini-lesson can be based on students' responses to the worksheet and on the ways they demonstrate that they can locate places, determine distance, identify latitude, and read map symbols and color codes.

9. To help students interpret graphic representations, a teacher can ask students to answer questions based on a map of the area of the colony. In the event that students do poorly on this (or any other activity), a teacher can reteach. To reteach students about map interpretations, have students interpret a map orally with teacher guidance in lessons and then interpret graphic representations again by individually answering questions based on a map of the colony's area.

More Interdisciplinary Aspects

Discuss:

1. How can we show the similarities/differences in the northern, middle, and southern colonies through expressive and language arts? (expressive/language arts)
2. What experiences have we had to help us understand how the colonists lived? (anthropology)
3. In what ways did geography influence the newcomers? (geography)
4. What can we do to find out which newcomer groups lived in our area and how their influence is shown today? (history)
5. What can we do in our community today to improve our own relationships with newcomers? (sociology)
6. How can we express what we know about newcomers through math (e.g., collect data about ethnic groups)?

Closure

"Some of the reasons the colonists had to establish their colonies are also the reasons people immigrate to other countries today. What do you think some of these reasons are?" Have the students identify reasons for the establishment of the colonies and write them on the board. Encourage them to expand on what they hear others say in the discussion. Encourage them to demonstrate communication skills toward others in the group.

Assessment and Reflection

- Teacher observations are recorded and kept as to the students' participation in individual inquiry; organizing summarizing information with a small group; reporting on a main idea; and illustrating valuable information on a group mural.

(Continued)

T

To extend the topic of the physical development of a colony, show the video *Colonial Williamsburg* (Videotours, 19930, grades 7 and above) or multimedia CD-ROM *PilgrimQuest* (Decision Development Corporation, grades 4–12) or software titled *National Inspirer and Geography Search* (Tom Snyder Productions, grades 4–12 and 5–9, respectively).

M

Students make progress in the expressive arts when they use materials and supplies efficiently, enjoy the different processes in the expressive arts, and can see some relationships between their art work and their world or between their art work and their creative thoughts.

M

You may prefer to teach selected skills, such as map skills, in mini-lessons for ad hoc groups as a break-out instructional technique. Historic maps can be obtained from the U.S. Geological Survey website at (http://www.usgs.gov/)

LESSON 6

Other Newcomer Colonies—Cont.

- Have students write in a journal about ways their own relationships with newcomers could improve, about the colonies they would have liked to belong to if they had lived during this period, and about how they could apply what they learned to their lives.
- Make a checklist of students' names to indicate which students transformed information into the mural art form, which ones researched and recorded reasons for the establishment of colonies, which organized and summarized information, which cooperated with others during the activities, and which demonstrated communication skills.

LESSON 7

Biographies of Famous Newcomers in the Colonies

Objectives

- Students will identify specific events in a biography as most important, and will participate in partnership and group activity.
- Students will describe their feelings about the contributions of this famous person.

Materials

Biographies of famous newcomers in the colonies (some choices are Peter Stuyvesant, William Penn, Anne Hutchinson, John Smith, John Rolfe)

Procedure

"You are going to read about famous newcomers who made contributions to the people's lives in the colonies. As you read, write some specific events in the person's life that you found to be important to you and put the information in a letter to the famous person. Then, you'll meet with a partner and read your letter aloud and ask for questions."

1. Ask each student to choose and read a biography about a famous newcomer who lived in one of the colonies.

2. After reading, have students engage in the individual activity of writing a letter to that person, mentioning specific events in the person's life that were most important to the student. Then, have students meet with partners to read their letters aloud to one another and to ask their partner if they have any questions about the famous newcomer in the colonies.

3. Have students describe the biography they read to their partners and have them tell what contributions the newcomer made to life in the colonies. Have them conclude their partnership activity by telling one another what they learned that helped them appreciate the contributions of the famous newcomer.

4. Back in the whole group, have students tell what they learned from each other during their partnership activity.

More Interdisciplinary Aspects

Ask the students for their suggestions about individual or group projects related to any or all of the following:

1. How can you show the contributions of some famous newcomers in the colonies through art and sculpture, dance, or music (expressive arts) or through reading, writing, listening, and speaking (language arts)?

(Continued)

D

The more diverse the students, the greater the need for integrated curriculum and active learning with partners and small groups (Garcia, 1994).

M

To encourage creative writing in a procedural way, ask students to write directions for making a creative item related to the theme—perhaps a Fall Harvest Moon Pie for this unit about newcomers. Students can create imaginary ingredients if they wish and tell what they would do first to start the pie. Remind them to tell about all the steps (first, second, third, last) for making the creative dish.

LESSON 7

Biographies of Famous Newcomers in the Colonies—Cont.

2. What experiences have you had that help you appreciate the contributions of some of the famous colonists? (anthropology)
3. In what ways can you apply what you learned about these famous colonists to your own lives? (sociology)

Closure

"Many of the contributions of famous colonists are contributions people also make to their communities and the people around them today. What do you think some of these contributions are?" Have the students identify contributions of some famous newcomers. Write the students' ideas on the board, a chart, or overhead transparency. Encourage students to expand on what they hear others say by writing a paragraph to report what they learned that helped them appreciate the contributions of the famous newcomers in the colonies.

Assessment and Reflection

- Have students write a paragraph to report what they learned that helped them appreciate the contributions of the famous newcomer in the colonies.
- Keep teacher observations on a checklist of student participation related to reading a biography, writing a letter to a famous person, meeting with a partner, and participating in asking and answering questions.
- Have students write about the unit in a journal and describe the most important thing they learned from reading the biography and how they could apply what they learned to their own lives.
- Have students place their final summarizing paragraphs in their portfolios.

LESSON 8

Colonial Newcomers and Geography

Objectives

- Students will willingly cooperate in small groups to research and report on the geography of the colonies—the New England colonies, the middle colonies, or the southern colonies.
- Students will offer opinions and judgments about the topic.

Materials

Maps related to the sites of selected colonies

Procedure

"Imagine that you are one of the colonists who is to choose a land site for the new settlement. You will read maps to make decisions about selecting a site. What kind of land site will your colony need? What clues on the map will help you make a decision?" Students can brainstorm responses.

1. Have students research and report back to the group which colonies were known as the New England colonies, which ones were known as the middle colonies, and which were known as the southern colonies.

2. Divide students into six groups. Distribute a map of the New England colonies to two groups, a map of the middle colonies to two groups, and a map of the southern colonies to two groups.

3. When the students have their maps, ask them to use the information on the map (legend, color code, etc.) and imagine that they are the council members who will decide on a site for their colonies. Have them use the maps as a basis for a discussion about the best site for the colonies to build (near water, building materials, land to grow crops, etc.).

4. Have them report back to the whole group and announce the selected sites on their maps and the reasons for the selection.

5. Back in the small groups, have students research the sites of the original colonies and compare the sites they selected with the actual sites of the colonies.

6. Ask students to write individual paragraphs about what they learned from this activity about selecting a site for a community (colony, city).

7. Ask the students for their suggestions about individual or group projects for further individual inquiry about colonial newcomers and geography.

—M—

One way to identify and assess what students know is to have them brainstorm and contribute their responses to a question without any judgment about the responses.

—M—

An effective teacher has different ways to instruct students; this includes cooperative learning where the students create something together or demonstrate something together to produce a group result.

(Continued)

LESSON 8

Colonial Newcomers and Geography—Cont.

More Interdisciplinary Aspects

Ask the students for their suggestions about individual or group projects related to any or all of the following:

1. How can we demonstrate what we know about the geography of the sites of the colonies through expressive and language arts?
2. What experiences have we had that help us understand the decisions the colonists made in selecting a colony site? (geography)

Closure

"Many of the effects of geography on the colonists are similar to effects that people feel today in their communities. What do you think are some of these effects?" Have the students identify effects of geography on the newcomers. Write the students' ideas on the board, a chart, or overhead transparency. Encourage students to expand on what they hear others say by writing a paragraph to report what they learned that helped them appreciate the effect of geography on the people in the colonies.

Assessment and Reflection

Have students place their paragraphs in their portfolios. Teacher observation on a checklist of student participation can be kept. Have students write about the unit in a journal and describe the most important thing they learned from the lesson and how they would apply what they learned to their lives.

M

A teacher is effective when he/she helps students connect learning from one discipline to another and apply what is learned, and when he/she is aware of materials/resources and has a satisfactory use for them in the classroom.

LESSON 9
Journal Writing

Objectives

- Students will demonstrate interest in bookmaking (journal making).
- Students will interpret information in an analysis/synthesis and demonstrate communication skills.
- Students will respond attentively to the writing of their peers.

Materials

Students' journals, writing materials, materials for bookmaking (journal making)

Procedure

"You are going to have time to analyze what you have learned in this unit of study by rereading your journals. To show that you took time to analyze what you read, you are to write a final paragraph as a synthesis about what you have learned about early newcomers in North America. First, I'll show you how I would write a brief paragraph—a synthesis—about what I learned. Then, when your paragraph is finished, you can complete your journals in a bookmaking (journal making) activity by making covers, writing in page numbers, writing a table of contents, sketching any extra illustrations you want to add, and putting an index in the back of your journal."

1. Have students write a description of what they have learned in their journals. You can model writing a brief analysis on the writing board or on an overhead transparency. Have students read and study the entries they wrote or sketched in their journals on the topic. Ask them to analyze and then write a final paragraph about what they learned. If needed, guided practice to help students write their paragraph of analysis can be scheduled.

2. Have the students meet with partners and trade their paragraphs. Have them read one another's work and write one question concerning something in the paragraph that they do not understand. Have each student give the question to his/her partner who can attempt to answer it, and who, in turn, can respond with another question about the paragraph he or she has just read. Repeat the question/answer activity until students run out of questions or class time ends. The paragraphs are then returned to the original authors.

3. To enrich the journal experience, have students make covers for their journals, write in page numbers, develop a table of contents, sketch additional illustrations, and add an index of their topics at the back of the journal.

—**M**————

To determine the extent to which a student understands something and can explain it, consider asking him/her to write a brief essay on the topic. Short response writing gives a student an opportunity to tell what is known, to show a deep understanding of the topic, to show relationships between main ideas/concepts, and to analyze the information by thinking clearly and writing concisely.

—**M**————

To extend a topic, you can select books that are well written, emphasize human relations, and cause a student to consider the actions of the characters.

(Continued)

LESSON 9

Journal Writing—Cont.

4. When appropriate throughout the unit, an individual student can "reserve" an inquiry and report on a topic of his or her choice related to a diversity of heritages reflected by people's lives during this time period. Figure 5.23 is a bibliography of multiethnic children's books that emphasizes the diversity of heritages with selections from a range of grade levels that provides multitext reading. Due to limited space in this guide, the list is not an exhaustive, comprehensive compilation of all the books on the topic and you and the students are encouraged to add related books that you discover.

Several activities for these books include the following:

a. Have the students read more than one book to promote more than the traditional view of this time period. For example, engage the students in discussing the time period from the perspectives of Native Americans, Latino-Hispanics, Asians, and Africans.

b. Encourage the students to read and compare stories of families of diverse heritages set in the time period of this bibliography (1600s with some overlap to the 1700s) with stories of families today. Have the students note the differences and similarities in societies and personal attitudes. To enrich multitext reading, display additional resources in books such as *African-American Voices in Young Adult Literature: Tradition, Transition, Transformation* (Scarecrow, 1994) edited by K. P. Smith; *The Best of the Latino Heritage: A Guide to Best Juvenile Books about Latino People and Cultures* (Lanham, Maryland: Scarecrow, 1996) by I. Schon; *Tales from Gold Mountain: Stories of the Chinese in the New World* (New York: Macmillan, 1990) by P. Yee; and *The Native American in Long Fiction: An Annotated Bibliography* (Lanham, Maryland: Scarecrow, 1996) by J. Beam and B. Branstad.

c. Encourage the students to suggest other books about life in the 1600s that they have found in their library searches and ask them to mention books written by authors of various heritages. Add the titles to Figure 5.23.

T

To enrich content and introduce quotations and songs of American Indians in tribal languages, discuss the video, *Catch the Whisper of the Wind* (Horizon 2000, 1993, grades 7 and above).

LESSON 9

Journal Writing—Cont.

FIGURE 5.23   Multitext Reading: Diversity of Heritages

Accorsi, W. *My Name Is Pocahontas*. Ill. by author. (Holiday House, 1992). This is the story of the Indian princess who was the daughter of the Indian leader Powhatan. Biography. Grades K–2.

Anderson, J. *The First Thanksgiving Feast*. Ill. by G. Ancona (Clarion, 1984). This book gives first person accounts of life at Plymouth in the 1620s. The photographs are taken at Plimoth Plantation, a Living History Museum. Nonfiction. Grades 3–6.

Asimov, I. & E. Kaplan. *Henry Hudson: Arctic Explorer and North American Adventurer*. (Gareth Stevens, 1991). Henry Hudson (?–1611), a British sea captain, is sent to search for a northwest passage (1607, 1609, 1611). In 1611, the crew mutinies and places Hudson, his son, and loyal sailors adrift in a small boat and they are never heard from again. Labeled drawings of Hudson's ships and glossary are included. Biography. Grades 2–5.

Bowen, G. *Stranded at Plimoth Plantation, 1626*. (HarperCollins, 1994). This book is the fictionalized diary of a young colonist, Christopher Sears, who writes about the problems of living at Plimoth Plantation. Woodcuts for illustrations. Historical fiction. Grades 4–7.

Brebeuf, Father J. de. *The Huron Carol*. (Dutton, 1993). This is the story of the birth of Christ as set in the Huron world that was recorded by a missionary, Father Jean de Brebeuf in the 1600s. Folk literature. Grades 1–4.

Bulla, C. R. *Squanto, Friend of the Pilgrims*. (Scholastic, 1988). This life story presents a brief picture of the native American who helped the Pilgrims at Plymouth Colony. Biography. Grades 2–4.

Christian, M. B. *Goody Sherman's Pig*. (Macmillan, 1990). This story is based on historical facts about Goody Sherman, who started a legal battle over her runaway pig in 1636. Historical fiction. Grades 3 and up.

Fisher, L. E. *Colonial Craftsman*. (Marshall Cavendish Corporation, 1997). This informational text explores the lives, times, and occupations of colonists in America and presents history through illustrations. One of a series that includes *The Glassmakers, The Silversmiths, The Cabinetmakers, The Schoolmasters, The Doctors, The Shipbuilders, The Peddlers, The Shoemakers, The Weavers,* and *The Homemakers*. Nonfiction. Grades 4 and up.

Fleischman, P. *Saturnalia*. (HarperCollins, 1990). Set in December 1681, a 14-year-old Indian boy from the Narragansett people search for evidence of his past. Historical fiction. Grades 7 and up.

Fradin, D. *Anne Hutchinson*. (Enslow, 1990). This book is the life story of Hutchinson who preaches that true religion is the following of God's guidance through an "inner light." Biography. Grades 3–5.

Fritz, E. I. *Anne Hutchinson*. (Chelsea, 1991). This life story describes Anne's early life, education, and finally her banishments from the colony. Biography. Grades 3–5.

Fritz, J. *Who's That Stepping on Plymouth Rock?* (Putnam, 1980). This portrays the history of early settlers landing on Plymouth Rock. It seems that in moving the rock in 1740, the townspeople split the rock in half but left part of it on the beach. Historical fiction. Grades 3–5.

Iannone, C. *Pocahontas: The True Story of the Powhatan Princess*. (Chelsea, 1995). This text details the princess's brief life and includes original sketches, paintings, and quotes from primary sources that include *The General Historie of Virginia, New England and the Summer Isles* by John Smith. Biography. Grades 4–7.

(Continued)

M

To create interest and discussion leading to further investigations, read aloud a motivating, well-written book related to the theme/topic; emphasize human emotions in the story and have students consider the actions of the characters.

D/M

Students of diverse heritages are affirmed by seeing members of their heritages pictured or described in literature. Note the story of Japanese colonists experiencing the dangers of establishing a colony in the 1600s in Namioka's *The Coming of the Bear*.

D/T

To enrich the concept of diverse heritages, make available CD-ROM, *Black American History: Slavery to Civil Rights*. (Queue, Inc., 1994). Grades 7 and up.

LESSON 9

Journal Writing—Cont.

FIGURE 5.23   Continued

Kagan, M. *Vision in the Sky: New Haven's Early Years 1636–1783*. (Linnet Press, 1989). This story portrays the early Colonists with a focus on the strict Puritan values they live by and their relations with Original Native Americans. The book ends with the defeat of the British Redcoats in the Revolutionary War. Historical fiction. Grades 3 and up.

Lasky, K. *A Journey to the New World: The Diary of Patience Whipple.* (Scholastic, 1996). Based on facts, this text narrates what the experience of journeying on the *Mayflower,* settling in Plymouth, and attending Thanksgiving was like for a young girl. Historical fiction. Grades 4 and up.

Namioka, L. *The Coming of the Bear.* (HarperCollins, 1992). In a parallel colonization in the 1600s, two samurai, Zenta and Matsuzo, escape to Ezo (now Hokkaido) and confront the warlike tension between the Aimu who live there and Japanese colonists who try to settle the land. Historical fiction. Grades 5 and up.

Petry, A. *Tituba of Salem Village.* (HarperCollins, 1991). Tituba, an intelligent black slave is vulnerable to suspicion and attack from the witch hunters in Salem. Historical fiction. Grades 5 and up.

Raphael, E. & D. Bolognese. *Pocahontas: Princess of the River Tribes.* Ill. by authors (Scholastic, 1993). This life story is a brief account that lists facts about selected events in the life of the Indian princess who died in England in 1617. Biography. Grades 1–3.

Sewall, M. *King Philip's War.* (Atheneum, 1995). The fictionalized story is told in two voices, one a Wampanoag and the other, a Pilgrim. The two points of view explain the adverse relations between the English settlers in Plymouth and the native people that grow into King Philip's War and eventually leads to the destruction of the Wampanoags and their allies. Map included. Historical fiction. Grades 2–4.

Sewall, M. *People of the Breaking Day.* (Atheneum, 1990.) This book portrays the Wampanoag people as a proud industrious nation in southeastern Massachusetts before the settlers arrived. Life in the tribe and the place of each member in the society is explained along with details about hunting, farming, survival skills, and the value of a harmonious relationship with nature. Includes recreational and spiritual activities. Nonfiction. Grades 2–4.

Sewall, M. *The Pilgrims of Plimoth.* (Atheneum, 1986.) This book is based on the writings of Governor William Bradford of the Plymouth Colony in 1620. It describes the lives and responsibilities of the children, women, and men who lived there. Nonfiction. Grade 3 and up.

Spier, P. *Father, May I Come?* (Bantam, 1993). Two young Dutch boys, both named Sietze Hemmes, participate in sea rescues, the first in 1687 and the other 300 years later in a similar parallel story. Cutaway diagrams included. Historical fiction. Grades 1–3.

Van Leeuwen, J. *Across the Wide Dark Sea.* Ill. by Thomas B. Allen. (Dial, 1995). In a search for freedom, soon-to-be colonists and 9-year-old Love Brewster travel in the cramped ship packed with nearly 100 people and the supplies they'll need when they arrive in an unknown land. There are 8 weeks of constant storms; a diet of hard, dry biscuits, and cheese; and chronic seasickness. There are details of the 1620 voyage and the harrowing first year at Plymouth Plantation. Love's father, William, is the religious leader of the colony. Historical fiction. Grades 2 and up.

D/M

To create interest in distant lands in other time periods and the people who lived there, have them take an imaginary journey into history via literature, particularly historical fiction and biography.

D/M

To enrich the concept of heroes, share one of the creative activities/ bibliographies from *Hooray for Heroes! Books and Activities Kids Want to Share with Their Parents and Teachers.* (Scarecrow, 1994). by D. Deneberg and L. Roscoe.

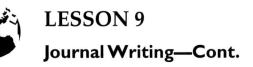

LESSON 9

Journal Writing—Cont.

FIGURE 5.23 Continued

> Walters, K. *Samuel Eaton's Day: A Day in the Life of a Pilgrim Boy.*
> (Scholastic, 1993.) Set in 1627 at Plimoth Plantation, the book shows the
> details of a day in the life of 7-year-old Samuel as he gets dressed, checks
> his animal snare, and gathers wood before he eats his breakfast of curds,
> mussels, and parsley. Doing his chores, he helps the men harvest rye
> despite the pain of his blisters. Historical fiction. Grades 1–3.
> Waters, K. *Tapenum's Day: A Wampanoag Boy in Pilgrim Times.* Ill. by R.
> Kendall. (Scholastic, 1996.) Tapenum, a fictional figure, describes each
> family member's duties as they relate to food, clothing, shelter, and
> weapons, and shares his interest in becoming a respected member of his
> community. Photographs are taken at the recreated Indian homesite at
> Plimoth Plantation in Massachusetts. Author's notes provide background
> information. Glossary of definitions and pronunciation of Wampanoag
> words included. Nonfiction. Grades 2–4.

More Interdisciplinary Aspects

Discuss:

1. What kind of exhibits can be prepared to reflect what we know about newcomers to America? Who can describe this kind of exhibit in journal writing? (expressive arts, language arts)
2. What kind of charts or graphs can be prepared to show some information about newcomers? (mathematics)
3. What other suggestions do you have?

Closure

"Let's meet in small groups and tell one another the information we learned."

Assessment/Reflection

- Teacher reflection can be based on the extent to which you are (1) Modeling and sharing your pleasure in reading, writing, and listening related to the theme; (2) Modeling students to keep eye contact, paraphrase to demonstrate understanding, and summarize what was heard; (3) Planning opportunities for students to listen to others' responses, and planning some structured language with choral reading, debates, discussion time, drama, sharing time, oral reports and speeches; (4) Promoting peer conferences and self-assessment.
- Teacher summative assessment can be based on the portfolios, journal writings, responses to questions during the culminating activity, and ways students demonstrate their interests in their journals and how they shared information about the unit.
- A scoring guide/rubric can be created for any of the previous items. Example:

(Continued)

M

For teacher reflection about language arts in the ITU, consider if you are (1) Accepting invented spelling while composing writing but assisting students later for correct spellings? (2) Conferring with students? (3) Collecting portfolio assessment information? (4) Facilitating group instruction and giving skills instruction for students who need it? and (5) Giving daily time for writing?

LESSON 9

Journal Writing—Cont.

(Worth 5 points each)

1. Highly inventive
2. Presence of characteristics expected (very successful communication of ideas)
3. Presence of predetermined criteria
4. Student's individuality (depth, breadth, and direction of the writing)

(Worth 4 points each)

1. Fairly successful communication of ideas
2. Some details and some predetermined criteria
3. Some presence of expected characteristics

(Worth 3 points each)

1. Communication of ideas is unsuccessful
2. Little or no presence of predetermined criteria
3. Little or no presence of expected characteristics

• In addition, a behavior checklist (see Figure 5.24) based on teacher observations throughout the unit can be developed.

FIGURE 5.24   Sample Checklist for Teacher Observations of Group Work

---

Example of Group Work Checklist

Student _____   Date _____

1. Participated in group task

 _____ always _____ often _____ sometimes _____ seldom _____ never

 Comments:

2. Participated in helping others

 _____ always _____ often _____ sometimes _____ seldom _____ never

 Comments:

3. If appropriate, participated in writing or copying learning plan and giving a copy to the teacher

 _____ always _____ often _____ sometimes _____ seldom _____ never

 Comments:

LESSON 9

Journal Writing—Cont.

FIGURE 5.24   Continued

Example of Group Work Checklist—Continued

4. Participated in decision making

   _____ always   _____ often   _____ sometimes   _____ seldom   _____ never
   Comments:

5. Participated in collecting and recording information

   _____ always   _____ often   _____ sometimes   _____ seldom   _____ never
   Comments:

6. Participated in group discussion

   _____ always   _____ often   _____ sometimes   _____ seldom   _____ never
   Comments:

7. Participated in organizing information collected by the group

   _____ always   _____ often   _____ sometimes   _____ seldom   _____ never
   Comments:

8. Participated in drawing a conclusion by the group

   _____ always   _____ often   _____ sometimes   _____ seldom   _____ never
   Comments:

9. Participated in preparing materials needed for the group to present its findings

   _____ always   _____ often   _____ sometimes   _____ seldom   _____ never
   Comments:

10. Participated in making a presentation to others

   _____ always   _____ often   _____ sometimes   _____ seldom   _____ never
   Comments:

Other added by the teacher or students

LESSON 10

Quiz Show and Exhibit as Culminating Activities

Objectives

- Students will use information gained to prepare questions and answers for a quiz show format, will form judgments related to appropriate questions to prepare, and will demonstrate active listening skills.
- Students will willingly cooperate with others during the group activities.
- Students will create materials for a quiz show or an exhibit. Standards are in the unit overview.

Materials

Materials for a review related to the theme/topic and selected by students

Procedure

"You are going to have an opportunity to prepare for a culminating quiz show. You can make it similar to the TV show *Jeopardy* and choose your own categories. In groups, discuss what you learned about the early newcomers in America. Review any information you need, such as the facts in your journals and portfolios." Model a way to do this and show students how to use some materials to prepare a few categories, questions, and answers.

1. Divide students into small groups for discussion about what they learned related to the unit. Ask students to prepare for the culminating quiz show by preparing clues about famous newcomers, places, or events related to the unit.

2. In a quiz show format, have the students take turns describing or giving clues about a particular famous newcomer, a place, or an event related to the topic. They can select students to answer. A correct answer gives the answering student an opportunity to describe or give clues about something related to the topic.

3. In addition, regarding this unit of early newcomers in North America, ask any students who have prepared individual or group projects to exhibit items for the group. The following questions are suggestions for discussion:
   a. Who has an exhibit that reflects what we know about these newcomers to America and who can describe it in journal writing? (expressive arts, language arts)
   b. Who has charts or graphs that show some information about newcomers? (mathematics)
   c. Others suggested by the students.

T

Visit (http://www.247ref.org) for a list of participating libraries who offer live service by a reference librarian who answers questions from the public over the Internet, 24 hours a day, 7 days a week.

M

Curriculum connections, lesson plans, and introductions to selected concepts from science and social studies through award-winning children's books are available in *Caldecott Connections to Science* and *Caldecott Connections to Social Studies*, both by S. Glandon (Englewood, CO: Libraries Unlimited, 2000).

M

In studying the colonies, students can use math to graph and analyze the number of people involved, the number of domestic animals with them, the miles they traveled, and the quantity of food and water needed. The graphs can be a basis for questions for a quiz show format in a culminating activity.

LESSON 10

Quiz Show and Exhibit as Culminating Activities—Cont.

Closure

"Many of the descriptions and clues related to early newcomers in North America help us understand the way these newcomers lived. The descriptions and clues also helped us understand the following:"

a. How being a newcomer has changed (or stayed the same) over time

b. How newcomers acquire food, shelter, and work in the economy

c. How newcomers organize themselves, especially in conflict situations

d. How people from newcomer groups have contributed to society

e. How newcomers have cultural roots, language, and customs to share with others

Assessment and Reflection

- Teacher reflection includes asking yourself if you (1) provided a variety of genres and encouraged a variety of responses including writing in divergent and creative ways; (2) provided time for daily, self-selected silent reading, oral and silent reading practice, and reading aloud to students daily from a variety of texts; (3) promoted discussion, divergent thinking, and multiple responses; and (4) provided listening situations through reports, readers' theater, and rehearsed oral reading.

- Teacher assessment can be based on the students' participation in group work. You can meet with small groups and observe and make notes. As you meet with groups and observe, make notes that will go in a folder for each student.

- A sample checklist like the one that follows can indicate students' participation in preparing questions and answers, in demonstrating listening skills, and in participating in the quiz show activity. See Figure 5.25.

- Assessment is based also on students' responses to the quiz show and the way(s) they demonstrate that they can share information about the theme/topic.

—M—

You can make a summative assessment to see how well students accomplished the objectives and can use the information to assess them on their learning. If you desire a norm-referenced assessment, you can compare an individual's performance with overall class performance.

—M—

To reflect, have you (1) used questions that promote dialogue, inquiry, and critique? (2) suggested books to interest students? (3) taught the writing process that includes prewriting, drafting, sharing, revising, editing, and publishing? (4) used different grouping situations such as cooperative learning groups, flexible small groups, circles, dyads/partners, whole class? and (5) given time for individual, independent work by students?

(Continued)

LESSON 10

Quiz Show and Exhibit as Culminating Activities—Cont.

FIGURE 5.25   Sample Checklist for Individual and Group Work

Student _____   Date _____

Teacher _____

	often	sometimes	seldom
The student participated in			
the task of the group	_____	_____	_____
decision making	_____	_____	_____
discussing information	_____	_____	_____
discussing positive contributions of others	_____	_____	_____
drawing conclusions	_____	_____	_____
helping others	_____	_____	_____
making a positive contribution to the group	_____	_____	_____
preparing materials to present findings	_____	_____	_____
respecting others' opinions	_____	_____	_____
other	_____	_____	_____

SAMPLE ITU 3

Changes: Spring as a Time of Growth, Beauty, and Transformations[*]

Primary and Middle Grades. This interdisciplinary thematic unit revolves around several disciplines, including science and literature. It was developed to facilitate and motivate students' learning about changes in the environment around them and to make comparisons between seasons they experience. It is hoped the instruction will gradually enlarge the students' perspective of changes from the school's own environment during a selected season to other environments and seasons. As presented here, the unit could be taught by one teacher or, with modifications, by a team of teachers.

Unit Overview. This ITU was developed for use mainly in the primary grades and, as presented, reflects some recommendations of Project 2061, a science literacy project, as published in *Science for All Americans*. Project 2061 and the national Science Teachers' Association's guidelines call for curriculum integration of different disciplines and indicate that science integration can lead students to a better understanding of the world and help them learn effective problem-solving skills. Related to this, the following unit consists of five lessons, the first of which can be taught immediately following a rainstorm or anytime water puddles are on the ground. The unit contains several cooperative learning activities that facilitate developing an understanding of the concept of cycles of changes. This concept relates to several of the national science content standards for grades K–4: characteristics and changes in populations; changes in environments; organisms and environments; and change, constancy, and measurement.

To visually see the emphasis on a discipline and illustrate the contributions of a particular discipline to some of the lessons in the unit, you can develop a drawing similar to the following one under "Assessment of Learning" as an advance organizer or orientation set to show the integration of the different disciplines selected for the spring unit. This graphic drawing will help in making decisions about selecting activities you want to add, change, or delete in the unit.

Unit Goals. Related to national science content standards and Project 2061, this unit is designed to incorporate the following goals:

- To become familiar with the natural world and recognize its diversity and its unity
- To understand some key concepts of science
- To gain skills in predicting and observing
- To understand the connections among water, rain, and evaporation
- To understand how plants grow and what is needed for plant growth
- To understand the importance of water
- To understand the diversity in nature
- To gain knowledge about rainbows
- To understand cycles and change in nature
- To make presentations to others

Standards. (Connected to language arts; standards from other disciplines may be added.)

- Use spoken and written language for the purposes of enjoyment, exchanging information, and learning about a particular topic of interest.
- Develop competence in English and understanding of content across the curriculum.
- Adjust spoken and written language vocabulary and style to communicate effectively with audiences and for different purposes.
- Read a range of literature to build an understanding of human experience.
- Use different writing process elements to communicate with different audiences for a variety of purposes.
- Gather, evaluate, and synthesize data from different sources and communicate their discoveries in ways that suit their purpose and audience.

Assessment of Student Learning. For this unit, individual learning of students is assessed through ongoing (formative assessment) teacher observation of student participation in the activities. Assessment and scoring guides/rubrics are to be developed with the students as the unit progresses.

The culminating activity is designed to be a major feature of this unit. After completing the five lessons, students will select a theme topic for continued pursuit. They can select this topic individually, in pairs, or in small groups. This pursuit can entail further research, investigation, and a presentation to the class at some later date or a community service project by the whole class. The major requirements for the culminating unit activity are that (1) it must be an activity selected by the student(s), and (2) it must deal in some way with the central

[*] *Source:* Adapted by permission from unpublished work submitted by Stephanie Carington, Nancy Giboney, and Suzanne Cantlay, and by Keven MacDonald.

Art
Lesson 1: Changes: Water and Puddles
(transform into art)
Lesson 5: Rainbows: Beauty of Nature
(transform into art)

Science
Lesson 2: Changes: Flowers and Beauty
(senses to gain information)
Lesson 4: Spring Creatures That Creep and Crawl
(observation skills)

Language Arts
Lesson 3: Trees in Bloom
(listening, observation, and discussion skills)

Mathematics
Lesson 4: Spring Creatures That Creep and Crawl
(counting skills)

Changes: Spring as a Time of Growth, Beauty, and Transformations

theme of Changes: Spring as a Time of Growth, Beauty, and Transformations. The culminating activity also involves a summative assessment. Here are some examples of culminating activities; others can be suggested by the students:

making audiovisual presentations

reporting on children's books

showing computer simulations

creating information games

building dioramas

arranging displays

dramatic activities

engaging in learning centers

displaying newspapers/articles

displaying paintings

discussing problems

reading reader scripts

building replicas

interviewing resource people

retelling a story

role-playing

performing a prepared play

performing puppet theater

showing transparencies

writing new words to familiar tunes

LESSON 1

Changes: Water and Puddles

Objective

Students will share their learning about what happens to water in puddles over a period of time; the different aspects of water; and some of the connections among water, rain, and evaporation and they will make comparisons and predictions. Standards are found in previous unit overview.

Materials

Water puddles, plastic bags, chalk, art paper, crayons or markers

Procedure

"Today after the rain, we will go outside to find where the ground is wet and look for water puddles. To keep our feet dry, we will cover our shoes with baggies and fasten the baggies around our ankles with rubber bands or tape." Assess prior student knowledge by eliciting what they know about different aspects of water.

- "What do you think the water in a puddle will do when you walk through it?" (spread out) "Why do you think so?"
- "What do you think will happen when you walk away from the puddle?" (make wet prints) "Why do you think this is so?"
- "Do you think the shoe prints will last forever? Why or why not?"

1. List their responses as predictions (guesses, hunches) on the board, a class chart, or an overhead transparency. Tell students the responses can be confirmed later when they return from outside.

2. Outside, have students walk through the water puddles. (If appropriate, you can spray water from a hand mister or sprayer to make additional puddles.) Ask the students to observe what happens to the puddles when they walk through them and what happens after they walk away from the puddles.

3. Distribute chalk pieces to each student and have them draw around each puddle so they can compare the sizes. Using a measuring tape or ruler, have them determine which is largest, smallest, and about the same size. If time allows, have students use the chalk and sketch the shapes of various puddles on blue or black sheets of art paper.

4. With students back in the classroom, collect the sketches and put them on the chalk rail in the room. Point out the earlier responses they made (their guesses, hunches) and have them check their predictions and confirm the appropriate ones.

M

Active teaching fosters students' engagement in the learning tasks and includes student involvement, appropriate instructional pacing, and monitoring of student participation and progress.

M

One way to determine students' prior knowledge before starting a lesson/unit (or to involve students in developing higher level thinking skills or help them comprehend expository text) is to consider K-W-L (or KWLQ), a teaching method where students recall what they already *know* (K), determine what they *want* to learn (W), and later assess what they *learned* (L) (Schmidt, 1999).

D

Students can be assigned to partners to complete selected activities and ESL students can work with students who model strong oral skills.

(Continued)

LESSON 1

Changes: Water and Puddles—Cont.

5. Invite the students to each draw two additional pictures—one showing what the puddles looked like when they walked through them outside and another showing what they think the puddles will look like in 2 hours.

6. After 2 hours (or as they leave the classroom to walk to the bus or walk home), ask students to look at the puddles and be prepared to discuss what has happened to them the next time you meet. When you meet, explain that the puddles receded as they evaporated, becoming smaller and smaller until they dried up.

7. To begin or close the lesson or unit, read aloud poems or play background songs that relate to the unit. For poems, read aloud "Ocean Rhythms" and other selections from *Splash! Poems of Our Watery World* (Scholastic/Orchard, 2002, grades 2–6) by C. Levy. For songs, invite the students to sing along with such songs as "If Only the Raindrops were Lemon Drops" on Raffi's *Evergreen, Everblue* (Troubadour, 1990, grades K–2), a cassette that includes environmental theme music. Play CD/audiocassette "Sing a Song of Seasons" by Rachel Buchman or "When the Rain Comes Down" on *A Cathy and Marcy Collection for Kids* (both Rounder Records, 1997 and 1994, respectively, grades K–2).

8. Optional rainy day activity to begin the unit:

a. Before the students arrive for the first day of school, videotape the view outside your classroom windows as well as other outside areas of the school campus on a hot, dry day. Later in the semester, during the first rainy day or a rainy week, play the "dry day" tape for your students without interruption.

b. After students see the tape, have them divide into groups to talk about what they saw on the tape and how it differs from the way the environment looks now on the rainy day.

c. If appropriate for the group, remind the students to "listen to one another to make listening work for them" and "focus on the messages someone else is sending" and "ask questions." Encourage them to listen for main ideas and take notes. Encourage them to restate what each one just heard in his/her own words or say it again before sending a different message.

d. Give the student groups about 20 minutes to talk about the "dry day vs. rainy day" topic and then have them list the changes they have observed, with each student making an individual list.

e. When the group members have written down their observations, replay the videotape. Tell the students to revise and make changes to their original lists. After seeing the replay of the tape, discuss what was seen in the second viewing that was not seen in the first viewing and talk about anything that did *not* change in the second viewing.

—**M**————

Relate children's literature to thematic units with *Literature Frameworks: From Apples to Zoos* (Linworth, 1997) by S. L. McElmeel. Each letter of the alphabet is linked to a theme along with background information.

LESSON 1

Changes: Water and Puddles—Cont.

f. Ask the students to return to their groups and tell one another the *changes* they made to their original lists. Back in the whole group, invite volunteers to discuss their lists with others in the class. On the writing board or on a class chart, ask student volunteers to list the changes that each group observed that were the *same* under one heading and, under another heading, list the items on each group's list that were different. Discuss.

Same Observations	Different Observations
1.	1.

More Interdisciplinary Aspects

If appropriate for the group, have the students respond to the following interdisciplinary features:

1. How do scientists share information about weather changes with us? (science, mathematics)
2. What work is done by others to help us study changes in the spring? In different kinds of weather? (economics)
3. How does weather affect rivers and other geographical features around us? (geography)
4. How has our community changed from one spring to another? Over several years? (history)
5. Who (city, country, state, federal governments) cooperates to bring us information and services related to changes (such as floods) in different seasons? (political science) How do artists share information about changes with us?

Closure

"What is something interesting you learned today that you didn't know before? What would you like to continue learning about?" Discuss the idea of a final—culminating—activity and show examples of what might be done. Present the two requirements for the activity: (1) it must be an activity selected by the student(s), and (2) it must deal in some way with the central theme of Changes: Spring as a Time of Growth, Beauty, and Transformations. Have the students announce whether they want to work individually, in pairs, or in small groups and record their announcements. Suggest to them that they can do further research and investigations, prepare a presentation to the class, take part in preparing a class exhibit for the school, or participate in a community service project.

(Continued)

T

Find out if your area has an urban creek council/agency that educates the public on the value of urban creeks and streams and helps people see the creeks as valuable drainage to larger lakes and rivers and as more than dumping grounds. Find out if there are annual creek activities that students might be interested in attending (i.e., bird watching, nature walking, wildflower viewing, joining a creek cleanup team or a volunteers' picnic, seeing exhibits at a local museum or library). Send home pertinent information.

T

For an introduction to the Internet, show students in grades 1–6 your favorite video on the topic or the video *How to be a CyberSurfer* (TV Ontario/Chip Taylor Communications, 2001). It covers issues such as manners on the net, privacy, and accuracy, and discourages sharing personal information to an unknown on the net.

LESSON 1

Changes: Water and Puddles—Cont.

Assessment and Reflection

- A teacher can keep anecdotal records about students and ways they demonstrated and shared their learning about what happens to water in puddles over a period of time.

- A teacher ascertains which students noticed the different aspects of water and connections among water, rain, and evaporation. They can also note students' pictures to determine the extent to which they each predicted a change in the puddle they observed and the extent to which they can make comparisons.

- This is also an opportunity to assess individual psychomotor skills and to record observations on a teacher checklist. If suitable for the group, a teacher can have students begin portfolios to keep samples of their work and can insert their chalk-art paper pictures that showed their observations, and their classroom drawings that predicted changes in water puddles.

D

To emphasize the effect of water on living things, select *What the Animals Were Waiting For* (Scholastic, 2002, grades 1–4) by J. London. This story from the Masai people takes place during the "hungry season," the drought. Also choose *Bringing the Rain to Kapiti Plain: A Nandi Tale* (Dial, 1981) by Verna Aardema, an accumulating story from Kenya that takes place during a drought. Read aloud *A Cool Drink of Water* by B. Kerley (National Geographic, 2002, grades 1–2) to show that water is basic to all human life.

LESSON 2

Changes: Flowers and Beauty

Objective

Students will participate in touching, observing, smelling, and planting flower seeds and sharing their view about what is needed for flower growth. Standards are found in the unit overview.

Materials

Art paper, circles, scissors, printed leaves and stems, glue, seed, soils, cups, various flowers in the room, index cards or squares of paper

Procedure

"Today, look at the examples of flowers here in the room and touch and smell them." Ask the students to raise their hands as soon as they have descriptive words for touching, feeling, and smelling the flowers. Elicit the students' descriptions of the flowers. If desired, write their descriptions on index cards or squares of paper and place the descriptions near each display of flowers.

1. Show the students different types of flower seeds. Place different types of seeds on the stage of an overhead projector so students can discuss the different shapes and sizes. Students can sketch the shapes.

2. Elicit from the students a point of view similar to that of a botanist, one who studies plant life. Ask what they think is important for seeds to grow and develop into flowers (soil, water, sunlight, wind, and other ways of seed dispersement). Write their responses on the board.

3. Students plant their own seeds in paper cups (or clear plastic cups) so they can eventually observe the life phenomena exhibited by the plants (observations botanists use). Point out that since the seeds are all different, each student will eventually have a unique flower that can grow in his or her region (botanists are always interested in plant life in different regions). Discuss the idea that the flower seeds depend on the students for care. Further, you can guide students from a hands-on experience such as this one to an experience that promotes a larger principle/theory (science). As an example, students can grow seeds in paper cups—some in shade, some in sun, some watered daily, some watered on alternate days—and record the daily or weekly growth measurements in a table (mathematics) to help them recognize variables needed for plant growth.

4. After the students have planted the seeds, have them use scissors, glue, and art paper or printed leaves and stems to create their original ideas of blooming flowers and sketch themselves caring for the plant in some way.

(Continued)

D

Through real-life experiences, primary grade students can increase their skill in using their senses to gain information.

M

Effective teaching includes communicating directions clearly, presenting new information clearly, maintaining students' involvement in tasks, communicating expectations, and monitoring students' progress. Ad hoc mini-lessons to facilitate learning for students at different stages of reading can be taught as needed; for example, give instructions on how to use phonics to read unfamiliar words in texts about the topic/theme.

D/T

Diverse children explore ways plants are propagated with cuttings, seeds, leaves, and roots in the videos *Wonders of Growing Plants* (Churchill Media, 1993) and *Look What I Grew: Windowsill Gardens* (Intervideo/Pacific Arts Video, 1992).

LESSON 2

Changes: Flowers and Beauty—Cont.

5. Discuss the many changes in a flower before it blooms (from the students' point of view) and the questions, "Do flowers last forever?" "Why do you think that way?"

More Interdisciplinary Aspects

If appropriate for the group, have the students respond to the following interdisciplinary features:

1. How do artists share information about flowers and their beauty with us? (expressive arts) Students can be introduced to the beauty of nature by reading aloud one of the following and showing the artist's illustrations:

- To show that beauty of nature is appreciated by such artists as Van Gogh and others, read *Katie and the Sunflowers* (Scholastic/Orchard, 2001, K–3) by James Mayher. Katie and her grandmother leave their garden on a rainy day to visit a museum where, fancifully, Katie reaches into Van Gogh's painting of sunflowers and knocks over the vase, and it falls onto the museum floor.

- To show the importance of water to all living things, read *Precious Water: A Book of Thanks* (North/South Books, 2002, grades K–2) by B. Weninger, in which a young girl tells her cat about the value of water; or *Water Hole Waiting* (Greenwillow, 2002, grades K–3) by J. Kurtz and C. Kurtz, a story of a young monkey who carefully waits his turn for a safe time to drink at a busy water hole in a savanna environment.

- If appropriate, connect the concepts related to the content with the format of the presentation of the concepts. For example, discuss with students the main idea of the book (a concept in the content area of art and English/literature) and the format (the arrangement of the book itself, i.e., "Let's identify how this book was made/constructed/arranged to tell us something about the beauty of nature").

2. What work is done by others to help us study changes in flowers? (economics)

3. How does weather affect flowers around us? (geography)

4. How have the flowers in our area changed from one spring to another? Over several years? (history)

5. Who (city, country, state, federal governments) cooperates to bring us information and services related to the care of flowers in different seasons? (political science)

6. How do scientists share information about flowers with us? (science, mathematics)

M

Children's literature can be an interesting way to introduce an ITU, start a lesson, or close a lesson—reading a related book aloud often stimulates children to focus and think about the topic/theme, and helps motivate students to read more.

LESSON 2

Changes: Flowers and Beauty—Cont.

Closure

1. Discuss what was learned today and write high points of the discussion from the students on the board. Remind them of the culminating activity requirements (an activity selected by the student and related to the central theme of Changes: Spring as a Time of Growth, Beauty, and Transformations).

2. Begin brainstorming ideas for this culminating activity. Encourage a flow of ideas by all the students and discourage any judgments of the ideas; keep a record of the ideas and elicit who will work individually, with someone else, or in a small group to display the information; and add to the record during the lessons that follow.

3. As resources for the children, display more children's books related to the theme of changes/topics that have activities. Show the book *Bathtub Science* (Sterling, 2001, grades 2–6), by Shan Levine and Leslie Johnstone to present more than 30 water experiments (not all in the tub) that include making a wave machine, an outdoor water cannon, a burping water bottle, and an outdoor garden of paper flowers that open their petals when they absorb water. You can adapt to the different learning styles of students by engaging them in a variety of activities related to the theme/topic. Some can "reserve" their place in a group to create a mural, write a brief play, or compose and sing a song. Others can meet with the teacher for an ad hoc mini-lesson, discuss text from an informational source, or work alone.

Assessment and Reflection

- A teacher can keep anecdotal notes about students and ways they participate in discussion, plant seeds, and care for their flowers before they bloom.
- With a checklist, a teacher also can assess students' pictures and interpret the data to determine the extent to which they transformed their information into an art form to make their pictures of blooming flowers.

  If students are keeping portfolios, have them insert their pictures of blooming flowers.

T

Introduce students to science experiments including how colored water travels through stems into petals with *My First Science Video* (Sony Kids' Video, 1992, grades K–4) based on *My First Science Book* (Knopf, 1990).

T

A teacher can use various informal assessment strategies such as anecdotal notes, class-based teacher observations, examples of performance, informal checklists or inventories, and work samples in portfolios.

M

Provide opportunities for individual reading, guided reading, and shared reading, and realize there are positive effects related to keeping records of students' oral language and involving students in a variety of reading situations.

(Continued)

LESSON 3

Trees in Bloom

Objectives

- Students will demonstrate listening and observation skills.
- They will share their learning about parts of flowering trees and observing trees in various ways. Standards are found in the unit overview.

Materials

Chart paper, rulers, microscopes or magnifying glasses, samples of tree pieces

Procedure

"Today we are going to arrange parts of flowering trees—such as the almond tree and the cherry tree—on the display table near the rulers and microscopes. Take turns to measure the tree parts, look at the parts through scopes, and then pass around the parts to one another to touch, smell, and observe them with magnifying glasses. As you are passing around the parts of the flowering trees, listen to the story of *The Giving Tree* (HarperCollins, 1964) by Shel Silverstein to find out why he named the tree "a giving tree."

1. Before reading *The Giving Tree* aloud, elicit the students' thoughts about the book title (i.e., what the title means to them) and some of the initial illustrations (i.e., what they think will happen in the story). Write their thoughts on the board and discuss the meaning of the word *predictions* related to what they think might happen in the story.

2. Read the story aloud; then discuss the students' initial thoughts written on the board and compare their thoughts with what happened in the story. See if any of their *predictions* came true. Write their comparisons on the board or on a class chart in two lists:

What we thought:
1.

What happened in the story:
1.

Ask volunteers to tell the group what they heard in the story that told them why the author named the tree "a giving tree."

3. Ask the students to recall how the tree in the story produced its leaves and flowers (and what happened) and then explain that different types of trees do not always produce flowers and leaves at the same time. Ask students why they think that leaves would develop at different times (temperature, sunlight, water, and other environmental conditions). Ask students further questions:

M

To enrich content and show that the beauty of the natural world is appreciated by children, read aloud *Dance Water Dance* (Dutton, 2001, grades K–3) by J. London, where kids explore a watery world, or *The Waterfall's Gift* (Sierra Club, 2001, grades 1–3) by J. Ryder, where a young girl appreciates a waterfall near her grandmother's house.

T/D

Pronunciation and parts of speech are in English and Spanish in the CD-ROM *A World of Plants* (National Geographic Society, 1993, grades K–3), a nature study about seeds, trees, and plants.

LESSON 3

Trees in Bloom—Cont.

a. Do you think that all leaves come out at the same time on the same tree? Why or why not? (Perhaps compare branches and leaves of flowering trees in the classroom to see if all the leaves have come out. You can also show the silhouettes of the branches and leaves on the stage of the overhead projector and ask students to sketch two different branch shapes.)

b. Do you think that all trees produce flowers at the same time? Why or why not? (Perhaps compare flowers of trees shown in the classroom to see if the types of trees have produced blooming flowers. You can also show the difference in the development/ shapes of the flowers on the stage of the overhead projector and ask students to sketch two different flower shapes.)

c. Do you think a tree's flowers are beautiful? Why or why not? (Perhaps hold up branches of flowering trees on the display table.) What makes something beautiful to you?

d. Do you think that tree blooms last forever? Do you think trees last forever? Why do you think that way?

e. What do you think will happen if we put these tree blooms in colored water in a vase in the room for several days? What makes you think that will happen? Not happen?

More Interdisciplinary Aspects

If appropriate for the group, have the students respond to the following interdisciplinary features:

1. How do artists share information about flowers and their beauty with us? (expressive arts)
2. What work is done by others to help us study changes in trees and their blooms? (economics)
3. How does weather affect trees in bloom around us? (geography)
4. How have the trees in our area changed from one season to another? Over several years? (history)
5. Who (city, country, state, federal governments) cooperates to bring us information and services related to care of trees in our area? (political science)
6. How do scientists share information about trees with us? (science, mathematics)

Closure

"Let's share our ideas about what we learned today." Discuss and record the students' remarks on a class chart, overhead transparency, or the writing board. Next, remind students of the culminating activity requirements. If appropriate, elicit students' ideas for their culminating

(Continued)

—M—

To give recognition to a man who restored a natural habitat, read aloud excerpts from *The Shape of Betts Meadows: A Wetlands Story* (Millbrook, 2002, grades 1–3) by M. N. Sayres. This is an account of Gunnar Holmquist who restored a 140-acre pasture to its original wetlands.

—M—

Involve students with their own learning by asking them to meet in groups to tell what they liked/did not like about a story they read/heard and then ask them to justify the main character's decision (higher level thinking skills).

LESSON 3

Trees in Bloom—Cont.

activities and record their ideas on a class chart. Have each student tell the group what they are going to work on and if they will work individually or with someone else. Record the information they give the group.

Name of student(s)	Topic related to Changes: Spring as a Time of Growth, Beauty, and Transformations
1.	1.

Assessment and Reflection

- Informally, assessment can be conducted by observing students participating in group activities and by listening to their contributions to the discussion. This information can be recorded in anecdotal notes in a teacher's log.
- Further, a checklist can provide a record of those students who demonstrated listening and observing skills and who shared their learning about parts of flowering trees and observing trees. Students can copy the group's remarks about what they learned on a given day from the board, class chart, or overhead, and place the remarks in their portfolios.
- If appropriate for reteaching to help students in future lessons, look for errors, especially consistent ones, made by students, such as errors in using pronouns, spelling, syntax arrangement, and use of verbs.

LESSON 4

Spring Creatures that Creep and Crawl

Objectives

- Students will participate in acting out the movements of different animals/creatures seen in the area in spring, and in observing specimens of earthworms, ants, and spiders (non-poisonous).
- Students will participate in sharing what they have learned, including counting, and in telling why the creatures seem to be quite active in spring. Standards are in unit overview.

Materials

Earthworms in soil, spiders in jar, ants in ant farm, and miscellaneous object such as pebbles or seashells for counting

Procedure

"Today, let's act out the movements of some springtime creatures that creep and crawl." Elicit suggestions from students—ants, spiders, worms—and have them act out the movements of different creatures seen in the region in the springtime. For instance, a student can crawl to portray a crawly creature moving across the floor in the front of the room and ask the others to predict the name of the creature being portrayed. (Note: You can put down clear plastic drop cloths—the kind used by painters—for this floor activity). If appropriate, ask the moving student to exaggerate the motions and invite the rest of the students to join in and mimic the motions of the leader. After identifying creatures seen in the spring, ask the students to get into small groups and observe some actual specimens.

1. Divide the students into small groups and distribute specimens of worms in soil, ants, spiders, and other creatures in inexpensive plastic glasses covered with clinging plastic wrap. Ask them to observe and discuss the different creatures.

2. Ask a student-facilitator in each group to pass around the creatures in the plastic glasses, one by one, for students to observe. If appropriate, have the facilitator write the group's observations on index cards.

3. Back in the whole group, have the students respond to the following:
   a. What did the earthworms seem to do when they were in the soil. Why do you think they were showing this behavior?
   b. What did the ants seem to do in the soil in their ant farm?
   c. What did the spider seem to do in the plastic glass?
   d. What else would you like to know about these creepy crawly creatures? How could you find out?

D

Positive cross-cultural interactions take place when students work together to complete their learning tasks, and you can arrange part of the day so students work on activities in small groups. For example, they can develop a bar graph about favorite spring creatures by placing sketches of favorite spring creatures on 2" squares of paper in lines with labels of "Earthworms in soil," "Spiders in jar," and "Other."

(Continued)

LESSON 4

Spring Creatures that Creep and Crawl—Cont.

4. Invite students to go outside with small plastic shovels (or spoons) and dig for similar small creatures to bring back to the classroom for display and discussion. Have students sort out and count the classroom creatures—ants, earthworms, spiders, and so on. You can have the children use art paper squares as counters.

5. At the completion of the counting and discussion about what was found, have students return their small creatures to their original habitat and replace all dirt and grass as it was originally.

More Interdisciplinary Aspects

If appropriate for the group, have the students respond to the following interdisciplinary features:

1. How do artists share information about creatures that creep and crawl with us? (expressive arts)
2. What work is done by others to help us study creatures that creep and crawl? (economics)
3. How does weather affect creatures that creep and crawl? (geography)
4. How have the creeping and crawling creatures in our area changed from one season to another? Over several years? (history)
5. Who (city, country, state, federal governments) cooperates to bring us information and services related to creatures that creep and crawl? (political science)
6. How do scientists share information about these creatures with us? (science, mathematics)

Closure

Continue discussing what has been learned; remind students of the culminating activity requirements; and continue eliciting the students' ideas about what they will be preparing for their final activity.

Assessment and Reflection

- Assessment of student learning can be conducted by monitoring the students, eliciting their responses to questions, and observing their participation in the lesson activities.
- Checklists can record the students' behaviors related to acting out movements of different animals seen in the spring; observing specimens of earthworms, ants, and spiders; counting; discussing; and participating in group work.

M

Depending on the students' interests, longer-term, student-centered projects (such as a culminating activity) might develop as a result of this type of discussion.

M

To extend content, read aloud selections from a favorite informational book or from *Army Ant Parade* (Holt, 2002, grades 1–3) by A. P. Sayre, a story of campers in a Central American rain forest who see an army ant swarm and the creatures who evade the swarm.

M

A discussion about disturbing and not disturbing natural habitats could lead to an extended project study of the students' choice.

M

Have students observe, classify, and count plant and animal life in their backyards/safe area. Each student, with parent's permission, could be responsible for observing a square meter of his/her backyard or other nearby area. Have them draw sketches of what they see and report back to class to tell their findings.

LESSON 5

Rainbows: Beauty of Nature

Objectives

- Students will name the colors seen in a rainbow and transform information about rainbows into artwork representing the colors.
- Students will read color words in sentences and construct individual books of sentences. Standards are in the unit overview.

Materials

Art paper, tempera paints, brushes, white construction paper (18 inches wide), sentence strips, and pocket chart

Procedure

"Who will tell us when they have seen a rainbow and what time of year they saw it? What is the 'prettiest' feature of a rainbow from your point of view? Why do you think that way? What are the names of the colors you saw in the rainbow?"

1. With the whole group, use art paper to show the seven primary colors found in a rainbow. Discuss the color names. Ask the students to use paints, crayons, or markers to draw rainbows using the seven colors. Display the art work in the room or in a class book.

2. Have the students suggest sentences about the colors in the rainbow and write their lines on cardboard sentence strips. Read the lines aloud individually and then as a group. For another reading, invite all of the students to read along chorally and ask them to suggest loud, soft, high, or low volume for different sentences.

3. If appropriate for the level of the group, prepare photocopied or computer print-out duplicates of the sentences and have students construct individual books with sketches to illustrate the sentences.

4. Have students work on their culminating activity projects. Here is a suggestion for a culminating event for any student who cannot think of anything to do. The student's project can be to keep a science journal and write down information after every lesson related to the unit. As a culminating project, the student can turn the information in his/her science journal into a self-published science nonfiction/informational book. The student can develop a title and an illustration for the cover, number the pages, write a table of contents (simple or complex), draw at least five inside illustrations, and write a final index (simple or complex). If time allows, the student can tell about the finished product to a small group. The completed journals can be taken home and proudly given to an adult/parent/guardian in the home to show what the student learned at school.

M

You can introduce a puppet presentation that offers facts about the topic or unit theme with suggestions from *Leading Kids to Books Through Puppets* (American Library Association, 1998) by C. F. Bauer.

D

To identify and assess each student's skills in observation and drawing conclusions, have each student sketch the effects of weather changes through the day/week.

(Continued)

LESSON 5

Rainbows: Beauty of Nature—Cont.

More Interdisciplinary Aspects

If appropriate for the group, have the students respond to the following interdisciplinary features:

1. How do artists share information about rainbows and their beauty with us? (expressive arts)
2. What work is done by others to help us study rainbows? (economics)
3. How does weather affect rainbows? (geography)
4. When have rainbows been seen in our area? Over several years? (history)
5. Who (city, country, state, federal governments) cooperates to bring us information and services related to rainbows (and other weather) in our area? (political science)
6. How do scientists share information about rainbows with us? (science, mathematics)

Closure

With the group, engage students in summarizing what they learned in the lesson and connect it back to information they learned in previous lessons about changes and other topics about spring. Further, discuss the process for finalizing the culminating unit activity and announce which student(s) will share their study/project on what day and at what time. Set a time line for the activity's completion.

Assessment and Reflection

- Assessment of student learning relates to the students' participation in rainbow artwork, choral reading of the sentences, and completion of the students' book of sentences.
- Summative assessment of student learning for this unit will be based on teacher's anecdotal records, the student's performance during activities through the unit, and each student's unit assessment checklist from the student's portfolio. Figure 5.26 is an example of a unit assessment checklist. Figure 5.27 is an example of a scoring guide for student group project presentation.

M

To enrich content and show the journey of water from the sky, through mountains, in rivers, and along a canyon, read aloud *Canyon* (Mikaya, 2002, grades K–5) by E. Cameron or *Rivers: Nature's Wondrous Waterways* (Boyds Mills, 2002, grades 1–4) by D. L. Harrison.

M

Teachers who support activities related to caring for the environment may benefit from the language arts standards-based resource *100+ Integrated Language Arts Environmental Awareness Books and Activities for Children, Ages 5–14* (Hamden, CT: The Shoe String Press, 1998) by P.L. Roberts.

LESSON 5

Rainbows: Beauty of Nature—Cont.

FIGURE 5.26   Sample Changes Unit Assessment Checklist

_____

_____ unit

_____ student name _____ date

	yes	**no**	**sometimes**

I Participated in the following:
1. Sharing my knowledge about what happens to water in puddles over a period of time
2. Discussing the different aspects of water
3. Discussing water, rain, and evaporation
4. Making comparisons and predictions
5. Touching, observing, and smelling flowers
6. Planting flower seeds
7. Sharing my view about what is needed for flower growth
8. Learning to listen
9. Using magnifying glass to observe items
10. Copying remarks of what I learned
11. Acting out movements of different animals/creatures seen in the area in the spring
12. Observing specimens of earthworms, ants, and spiders
13. Counting creatures active in spring
14. Transforming information about rainbows into artwork
15. Choral reading of a book of sentences
16. Using color words
17. Preparing a culminating final activity
18. My comments about what I learned during the unit:

(Continued)

LESSON 5
Rainbows: Beauty of Nature—Cont.

FIGURE 5.27   Scoring Guide for Student Group Project Presentation: Sample Form
Source: Elk Grove School District, Elk Grove, California. Possible score = 100. In this adaptation, the scorer marks a relevant entry in each of the six categories. The score for that category is the lowest/smallest number of the entry.

Professional Presentation	**14–15** Well organized; smooth transitions between sections; all enthusiastically participate and share responsibility.	**12–13** Well organized with transitions; students confer/present ideas; group shows ability to interact; attentive discussion of research.	**11** Shows basic organization; lacks transitions; some interaction; discussion focuses mostly on research.	**1–10** Unorganized; lacks planning; no transitions; reliance on one spokesperson; little interaction; disinterest; too brief.
Engagement of Audience	**14–15** Successfully and actively engages audience in more than one pertinent activity; maintains interest throughout.	**12–13** Engages audience in at least one related activity; maintains attention through most of presentation.	**11** Attempts to engage audience in at least one activity; no attempt to involve entire audience; may not relate in significant way.	**1–10** Fails to involve audience; does not maintain audience attention; no connection with audience; no relationship between activity and topic.
Speaking Skills	**9–10** Clear enunciation; strong projection; vocal variety; eye contact with entire audience; presentation posture; solid focus with no interruptions.	**8** Good enunciation; adequate projection; partial audience eye contact; appropriate posture.	**7** Inconsistent enunciation; low projection with little vocal variety; inconsistent posture.	**1–6** Difficult to understand; inaudible; monotonous; no eye contact; inappropriate posture; interruptions and distractions.
Knowledge of Subject	**18–20** Strong understanding of topic; knowledge factually relevant, accurate, and consistent; solution shows analysis of evidence.	**16–17** Good understanding of topic; uses main points of information researched; builds solution on examination of major evidence.	**14–15** Shows general understanding; focuses on one aspect, discusses at least one other idea; uses research, attempts to add to it; solution refers to evidence.	**1–13** Little understanding or comprehension of topic; uses little basic information researched; forms minimal solution; relies solely on own opinions without support.
Use of Literature	**18–20** Strong connection between literature and topic; significant, perceptive explanation of literature; pertinent to topic; at least two pieces used.	**16–17** Clear connection between literature and topic; clear explanation; appropriate to topic; two pieces used.	**14–15** Weak connection to topic; unclear explanation; one genre; one piece used.	**1–13** No connection to topic; no explanation; inappropriate literature; no literature.
Use of Media	**18–20** Effectively combines and integrates three distinct forms of media with one original piece; enhances understanding; offers insight into topic.	**16–17** Combines two forms with one original piece; relates to topic; connection between media and topic is explained.	**14–15** Includes two or three forms but no original piece; media relates to topic. Explanation may be vague or missing.	**1–13** One form; no original piece; connection between media and topic is unclear.

FACTS ON PRAXIS AND OTHER TEACHER TESTS

Performance assessment. Indeed, teachers are concerned about credentialing tests that are part of the licensing process and about what the tests reflect. As mentioned, these tests are based on current educational research, important tasks and skills required of teachers, and, in some cases, classroom performance. According to the National Association of State Directors of Teacher Education and Certification (2001), 14 states now require tests to assess teaching performance (Cross and Rigden, 2002). Performance assessments can focus on essay writing about classroom procedures, identification of opportunities for students' oral responses, identifying listening responsibilities, portfolio reviews, video stimuli (and response), and actual in-class observations. Related to these foci, this guide has included knowledge/planning skills needed for incorporating some of these types of activities in an interdisciplinary thematic unit approach. Much of this information has been highlighted in Chapter 4 and in the marginalia in Chapter 5 for the three ITUs.

State standards. Also, the interested teacher will want to know that beyond teacher credentialing tests, some states have their own published state standards. You are encouraged to get acquainted with the standards for your state. For example, Florida lists its standards for teachers as *accomplished practices.* One of these practices says that the teacher *engages in continuous quality improvement for self and school* (Bondy, 2002). This practice could be interpreted by your school/district/state to mean that engaging in educational research and classroom field testing to develop an ITU could be one way that a teacher improves herself/himself and the school professionally. Additionally, a teacher's ITU involvement could generate further educational dialogue about quality improvement by contributing information about ITUs through educational conferences, newsletters, publications, and teacher websites.

National Board for Professional Teaching Standards. Beyond credentialing tests are voluntary teacher assessments by the nonprofit National Board for Professional Teaching Standards created in 1987 and governed by a board of teachers, administrators, higher education officials, teacher union representatives, and legislative and community leaders. The establishment of this national board was recommended in *A Nation Prepared: Teachers for the 21st Century* (Carnegie Corporation's Task Force on Teaching as a Profession, 1986), along with a call to set teaching standards and to certify accomplished teachers who volunteer to prepare a teaching portfolio and take a computer-prompted test to meet those standards (Childers-Burpo, 2002). After achieving National Board certification, the teacher receives a National Board Certificate as a generalist/specialist in a particular area of teaching/educational expertise. For more information, contact the National Board for Professional Teaching Standards at (http://www.nbpts.org).

To retain teacher certification. After initial credentialing, recognizing your state's standards and adhering to them, and possibly engaging in voluntary teacher assessment through the *National Board for Professional Teaching Standards,* you may discover that your state is one of the many states that requires teachers to obtain about six semester hours of academic credit every five years in order to retain their licenses (National Association of State Directors of Teacher Education and Certification, 2000). Find out what your state requires.

Now that you have reviewed the previous material about the units that the teachers worked into an integrated curriculum, turn your attention to Exercise 5.1, Examining Units, and to some other examples of units—perhaps units that have been supplied by your course instructor or another educator, or ones that you have borrowed from teachers in the elementary, middle, or high schools. This review is designed to help you refine and polish your own individual unit. You'll see various ways that the teachers have interpreted the unit in the integrated curriculum in their classes. When you have completed your unit, you can turn to the final exercise to assess your reflections about what went into the development of your ITU for an integrated curriculum.

SUMMARY

This resource guide for developing an ITU began by providing an introduction to the value of integrated curriculum and, within that concept, teaching through ITUs. It then proceeded to provide you with data about initiating an ITU, developing objectives, and selecting learning experiences and assessment tools for a unit. The text guided you through a review of learning activities, lesson plans, and three examples of ITUs and identified various ways that you can develop a unit for an integrated curriculum. The information took you to this point where you are now ready for the application level on your own—as a teacher who wants to develop and implement an ITU for your students.

- To further support your interest in this and gain additional information, turn your attention to se-

lected sources related to ITUs in the section *For Further Reading* at the end of this chapter.

- Additionally, now complete Exercise 5.8. Share your results with the instructor. From your reflection and self-check in Exercise 5.8, in what ways do you feel you are ready? Not ready?

Finally, we wish you the best during your educational adventure developing an interdisciplinary thematic unit and implementing interdisciplinary instruction, and in the continued use of integrated curriculum. Occasionally, you may want to return to this guide for reference.

P. L. R.
R. D. K.

IF A COLLEAGUE, COMMUNITY MEMBER, OR PARENT ASKS YOU ABOUT . . .

1. **Learning style/strengths.** If a parent asks you about one of the ways you have attended to student learning styles and student learning strengths (or limitations) in your ITU, what would you respond? Tell your response to a partner in your group.
2. **Questions about ITUs.** If a colleague asked you if you had any questions developing ITUs, what would you respond? Offer your question(s) to peer volunteers to write on a question map on the board. Copy the final map and use one of the questions to start your own individual inquiry about ITUs. Report what you find to others in a culminating group meeting.
3. **ITUs and diverse students.** If a colleague asks you for one way you address needs of diverse students (e.g., gifted and talented, students at risk, and students with special needs) through an ITU, what resources would you suggest to help another teacher find out more about this approach?
4. **ITUs and community resources.** If a community member asked you to suggest one way that a community resource could add a great deal to your students' background of knowledge and frame of reference for learning, what would you say? What suggestions for community involvement in an ITU for your students can you offer?
5. **ITUs and standards.** If a colleague asked you for an example to show how to translate a state standard into classroom instruction, what would you use as your example? To prepare for

this, locate your state's standards for social studies to see what purposes are listed for teaching social studies. Find one standard that relates to the ITU of your choice and translate the standard into classroom instruction for a lesson in the unit.
6. **ITUs and disciplinary soundness.** If a colleague asked you if you supported disciplinary soundness in an interdisciplinary thematic study in your classroom, how would you assure your colleague that you had a firm grasp on what was current in each of the disciplinary fields in your unit? To respond to this, team up with others to collect information about what is current in various disciplinary fields. Select disciplines that you may need when developing an ITU. What suggestions do you have for getting started on this research project? Plan a brief report about what you found and present it to others during a culminating group meeting.
7. **Some theoretical bases for classroom teaching.** What would you say if a colleague asked you which authorities for theoretical bases you referred to in planning your teaching? in recognizing children's cognitive development? in using cooperative learning? in keeping records of oral language? in developing lesson plans? Here are some useful resources:
   - To review children's cognitive development, some teachers reread the writings of Jean Piaget in *Science of Education and the Psychology of the Child* (New York: Orion, 1970) and *The*

Psychology of Intelligence (Totowa, NJ: Littlefield Adams, 1972).

- Teachers who are interested in cooperative learning and conflict resolution turn to the work of Roger and David Johnson in *Reducing School Violence through Conflict Resolutions* (Alexandria, VA: Association for Supervision and Curriculum Development, 1995).

- For the value of keeping records of oral language and supporting wholeness in language learning, still other teachers turn to the work of Donald Holdaway, as well as to Marie Clay's writing for the importance of experimenting actively in early writing. See two early articles for the original views of Holdaway and Clay in "The Big Book Trend—A Discussion with Don Holdaway" (*Language Arts* 59, [November/December 1982] and *What Did I Write?* by Marie Clay (Auckland, NZ and Exeter, NH: Heinemann Educational Books, 1975).

- Further, to consider the importance of various components of a lesson plan, many teachers review the work of Madeline Hunter in *Enhancing Teaching* (New York: Macmillan, 1994).

NOTES

EXERCISE 5.1

Examining Units

Instructions.   The purpose of this exercise is to examine selected instructional units—either the ones that are in this chapter, ones that have been supplied by your course instructor or another educator, or ones that you have borrowed from teachers in the elementary, middle, or high schools. Meet with others in small groups and review the instructional unit by identifying and discussing the features that follow. Talk about the features in your small group and then share information about the unit with others in your whole class.

1. Grade level and theme/main idea/topic/guiding question being studied:

2. Time duration estimate for the unit:

3. Give examples in the unit of the following:
    a. Theme/main idea/topic/guiding question(s):

    b. Specific activities that are identified:

    c. Resources (materials and audiovisual needs):

    d. Assessment and evaluation procedures found:

4. What changes, if any, would you make in this unit? Why?

5. Other features you would incorporate/not incorporate into your own teaching that you want to discuss:

EXERCISE 5.2

Connecting Questions and Activities for an ITU

Instructions. The purpose of this exercise is to work to connect the questions related to your theme and to ongoing learning activities in specific detail. Learning activities can be planned around some central questions (and subquestions) about the theme. The investigative activities needed to inquire about the questions can provide various opportunities for you to respond to the learning styles and needs of your students.

With your partners, create another "we want to know" question map similar to one that was created in Exercise 3.6. Use the information to design some learning activities for the unit (Figure 1.3 shows some examples of questions and related activities).

List of learning activities related to the questions and subquestions:

1.

2.

3.

4.

5.

6.

EXERCISE 5.3

Combining Objectives, Resources, and Learning Activities for a Teaching Plan

Instructions. The purpose of this exercise is to write a specific teaching plan for a minimum of 1 day, incorporating what you have done to prepare goals, write objectives, select resources, and select and plan learning activities. You may want to reference the learning activities to state frameworks, district documents, and local school curriculum. Ask a peer to read and react to your teaching plan. Does your plan convey what you intended to say? What new questions came to mind as you wrote the plan and as it was reviewed by others?

Teaching Plan

Interdisciplinary unit theme:

Main focus question:

Related subquestions:

Objectives

What will the students learn?

What thinking skills such as observing, communicating, comparing, categorizing, inferring, and applying will the students develop?

What attitudes will be fostered?

Resources (media, display visuals, artifacts, computer, and software)

Specifics of Learning Activity/Activities

Preassesssment of Student Learning (How will you determine what students know or think they know about the subject at the start of the unit? Note the following examples.)

Example 1. Consider introducing the strategy of think-share pairs, in which the topic/question is written on the board and the students are asked to think about the topic in pairs, discuss it between themselves, take notes, and then share their thoughts with the whole group about what they know or what they think they know about the topic while the teacher writes the major thoughts on the board, perhaps in the form of a graphic web.

Example 2. Consider using the KWL reading comprehension strategy, with the teacher directing the discussion. Label three columns on the board or on a transparency for the overhead projector. The left-hand column contains what students already know or think they know about the topic; the middle column contains a list of what the students want to learn about the topic; the right-hand column is left blank and filled in at the end of the study or during certain times during the study with what is learned or has been learned about the topic.

Formative Evaluation (What techniques will you use to assess student learning in progress to ensure that they are on the right track?)

Check Discipline Areas Used   *Provide a brief description of how areas were used.*

_____ 1. Sciences

_____ 2. Social sciences/history

_____ 3. Mathematics

_____ 4. Reading and language

_____ 5. Poetry and prose

_____ 6. Music and dance

_____ 7. Painting and sculpture

_____ 8. Health and physical education

_____ 9. Other

Feedback

1. What was the reaction of your peer to your teaching plan?

2. In your opinion, does your plan effectively convey what you originally envisioned?

3. Does it need more detail or revision?

4. Do your selected learning activities appropriately address the varied learning styles of your students?

5. What new questions came to mind as you wrote the plan and as it was reviewed?

EXERCISE 5.4

Planning Culminating Activities

Instructions.   The purpose of this exercise is to develop a closure for the unit (even though inquiry can be lifelong and has no official closure). In this exercise, you must determine what will affect the length of your unit—the interest of your students in the topic; the resources that are available or unavailable; the school holidays; the academic calendar for your school year; and any competing events such as picture day, assemblies, athletic events, and field trips.

1. Which of the following would you incorporate into the culmination of a unit? Explain why.

    a. Creating new problems related to the topic and demonstrating a way to resolve them.

    b. Designing a chart, map, time line, classroom museum of exhibits, an interdisciplinary thematic fair, or a classroom "main street" with booths (learning centers) and reporting on the data the design represents.

    c. Preparing an oral and written presentation on an aspect of the topic; using such creative ways to present data as sketches, sculpture works, cartoons, popular songs, a comic strip format, costume props, a story board, puppets, flannel board figures, rhymes, limericks, and other forms of poetry.

    d. Creating and producing a drama.

    e. Writing and publishing a newsletter or brochure on the topic.

f. Writing and publishing a book.

g. Creating a class or student cohort web page regarding the unit.

h. Presenting data with one or more of the following:

advertisements	fables and myths	poetry
albums and books	fairy tales/folk tales	puppet shows
artworks	family trees	scrapbooks
book jackets	filmstrips/slides	scripts for skits
bulletin boards	greeting cards	songs and instruments
card/board games	illustrations for stories	stencils
collages	maps and murals	tape recordings
costumes	pantomimes	video recordings

i. Other

2. What activity/activities could you plan that would permit your students to synthesize what they have learned in the unit and then report the synthesis to a selected audience?

3. From the activities suggested in question 2, evaluate each suggestion and narrow the choices to two options by considering various needs in your classroom (i.e., diversity and learning value of the activity). Record the two choices here.

EXERCISE 5.5

Analysis of a Lesson That Failed

Instructions. You'll recall that the planning and structure of a lesson can be a predictor of the success of its implementation. The purpose of this exercise is to read the following report of a lesson implementation and to use the report as a basis for class discussion about its outcome.

The setting: Seventh-grade biology class; 1:12-2:07 P.M.; spring semester.

Actual events as they took place:

1:12	Bell rings.
1:12–1:21	Teacher directs students to read from their text, while he takes attendance.
1:21–1:31	Teacher lectures on "parts of a flower," showing pictures of flower parts by holding up pages from a college botany text.
1:31–1:37	Teacher distributes to each student a ditto; students are to now "label the parts of a flower."
1:37–1:39	Teacher verbally gives instructions for working on a real flower (e.g., compare with ditto); can use microscopes if they wish.
1:39–1:45	Teacher walks around room distributing a real flower to each student.
1:45	Chaos. Teacher writing referrals, sends two students to the office. Much confusion, students wandering around, throwing flower parts at each other.
1: 45–2:07	Teacher flustered, directs students to spend remainder of period reading text. Two more referrals written during this time.
2:07	End of period (much to the delight of the teacher).

Questions for Discussion:

1. Do you believe this teacher had a prepared lesson? If it appears so, what (if any) were the good points of it? the problems with it?

   Good Points: _____

   _____

   _____

   _____

   _____

   _____

   _____

   _____

Problems: _____

_____

_____

_____

_____

_____

_____

_____

2. From what you can infer from the scenario and from what you can infer about this lesson plan, was chaos predictable? Why or why not?

_____

_____

_____

_____

_____

_____

_____

3. How might the lesson plan have been prepared to more likely avoid the chaos?

_____

_____

_____

_____

_____

_____

_____

4. Choosing to use this "traditional" lesson plan format, what behaviors could the teacher have performed that might have avoided the chaos?

_____

_____

_____

_____

_____

_____

5. Within this 55-minute period, students were being expected to operate high on the learning experiences ladder. Consider this: 9 minutes of reading; 10 minutes of hearing; 6 minutes of reading and labeling; 2 minutes of hearing; 6 minutes of action (the only direct experience); and 22 minutes of reading. In all, about 49 minutes (89%) of abstract verbal and visual symbolization. Is that a problem?

_____

_____

_____

_____

_____

_____

_____

NOTES

EXERCISE 5.6

Preparing Lesson Plans for My ITU

Instructions. Using a lesson plan format that is approved by your instructor, prepare two _____ -minute lesson plans. The length should be decided in your class according to grade level and other factors. Prepare the lessons for a grade level of your choice and plan them to be the first and second lessons of your ITU. As you prepare these plans, you will want to refer to work you have done for previous exercises, especially the exercise about planning culminating activities (Exercise 5.4). After completing your lesson plans, evaluate them yourself, modify them, and then have the modified versions evaluated by three peers using corresponding Exercise 5.7 (Evaluating Lesson Plans for My ITU).

After completing these two exercises, 5.6 and 5.7, you are ready to proceed in the development of the remainder of the lessons for your ITU.

NOTES

EXERCISE 5.7

Evaluating Lesson Plans for My ITU

Instructions.   You may duplicate this form for evaluation of the lessons you developed previously. Have one or both (to be agreed upon by your group) of your lesson plans evaluated by at least three of your peers and your instructor. For each of the following items, evaluators should check either *yes* or *no* and write instructive comments. Compare the results of your self-evaluation with the evaluation of the others.

	No	*Yes*

1. Are descriptive data adequately provided?   _____   _____

Comments _____

_____

_____

2. Are the goals clearly stated?   _____   _____

Comments _____

_____

_____

3. Are the objectives specific and measurable?   _____   _____

Comments _____

_____

_____

4. Are objectives correctly classified?   _____   _____

Comments _____

_____

_____

5. Do objectives include higher order thinking?   _____   _____

Comments _____

_____

_____

6. Is the rationale clear and justifiable?   _____   _____

Comments _____

_____

_____

7. Is the plan's content appropriate?   _____   _____

Comments _____

_____

_____

8. Is content likely to contribute to achievement
   of objectives?   _____   _____

Comments _____

_____

_____

9. Given the time frame and other logistical
   considerations, is the plan workable?   _____   _____

Comments _____

_____

_____

10. Will the opening likely engage students?   _____   _____

Comments _____

_____

_____

11. Is there a preassessment strategy?   _____   _____

Comments _____

_____

_____

12. Is there a proper mix of learning activities for
    the time frame of the lesson?   _____   _____

Comments _____

_____

_____

13. Are the activities developmentally appropriate
    for the intended students?   _____   _____

Comments _____

_____

_____

14. Are transitions planned?   _____   _____

Comments _____

_____

_____

15. If relevant, are key questions written
    and key ideas noted in the plan?   _____   _____

Comments _____

_____

_____

16. Does the plan indicate how coached practice
    will be provided for each student?   _____   _____

Comments _____

_____

_____

17. Is adequate closure provided in the plan?   _____   _____

Comments _____

_____

_____

18. Are needed materials and equipment identified and are they appropriate?   _____   _____

Comments _____

_____

_____

19. Is there a planned formative assessment, formal or informal?   _____   _____

Comments _____

_____

_____

20. Is there a planned summative assessment?   _____   _____

Comments _____

_____

_____

21. Is the lesson coordinated in any way with other aspects of the curriculum?   _____   _____

Comments _____

_____

_____

22. Is the lesson likely to provide a sense of meaning for students by helping bridge their learning?   _____   _____

Comments _____

_____

_____

23. Is an adequate amount of time allotted to address the information presented?   _____   _____

Comments _____

_____

_____

24. Is there a thoughtfully prepared and relevant
    student assignment planned?   _____   _____

Comments _____

_____

_____

25. Could a substitute who is knowledgeable
    follow the plan?   _____   _____

Comments _____

_____

_____

NOTES

EXERCISE 5.8

Reflecting on an Interdisciplinary Thematic Unit: Self-Check

Instructions. Now that you have completed this guide, check yourself on this final list. In the appropriate place to the right of each item, write in the numeral

3 *if you have acquired definite readiness or awareness about the item*

2 *if you have a comfortable level of readiness or awareness*

1 *if you are still uncomfortable with the item; need more work and information*

0 *if you have little or no awareness or knowledge about it*

Share the results with your instructor if you are working in a group.

	3 aware	2 somewhat aware	1 needs work	0 not aware

When developing an ITU for an integrated curriculum, I reflected on the following related knowledge and skills:

Introduction to an Interdisciplinary Thematic Unit (Chapter 1)

1. I am aware of the concept of integrated curriculum and can recall terms such as thematic instruction and multidisciplinary teaching.

2. I am aware of some of the learning styles and their relation to integrated curriculum.

3. I am knowledgeable about the spectrum of design for integrated curriculum and where some of my teaching efforts can be located on the spectrum.

4. I am aware of the role of an effective teacher in an integrated curriculum.

5. I am aware of ways to provide diversity and a multiculturalistic perspective in the curriculum.

6. I am aware of features of class management in active inquiry.

7. I am familiar with the role of student input in an ITU.

	3 aware	2 somewhat aware	1 needs work	0 not aware

8. I am aware of the role of the school in curriculum integration.

9. I am aware of the role of curriculum standards.

10. I know of ways to use technology and community resources as instructional resources.

11. I am familiar with the advantages and limitations of an integrated curriculum.

12. I can develop a list of topics related to the theme or topic of an ITU.

13. I can locate and use informational sources about ITUs.

14. I recall information from a teacher interview about an ITU.

Initiating an Interdisciplinary Thematic Unit (Chapter 2)

15. I have gained knowledge about selecting a theme for an ITU.

16. I can identify criteria for selecting a theme.

17. I am familiar with curriculum standards and related resources.

18. I am aware of national professional standards as sources for information.

19. I am aware of ways to select a theme.

20. I can investigate a specific scope and sequence for an ITU.

21. I am familiar with problem-solving inquiry.

22. I am familiar with the experiences in the learning experiences ladder.

23. I know ways to use the community as a resource for people- and place-based learning.

24. I can select a theme, investigate specific questions, and find resources for an ITU.

	3 aware	2 somewhat aware	1 needs work	0 not aware

Developing Objectives (Chapter 3)

25. I feel confident about writing objectives for lessons in an ITU.

26. I am knowledgeable about instructional objectives and their relationship to aligned curriculum and authentic assessment.

27. I can recognize standards-based education.

28. I can recognize performance outcomes that are overt or covert.

29. I am knowledgeable about writing criterion-referenced objectives.

30. I can classify instructional objectives in the cognitive, affective, and psychomotor domains.

31. I am familiar with the use of student logs, portfolios, and journals.

Assessing Student Learning (Chapter 4)

32. I am familiar with several purposes of assessment.

33. I am knowledgeable about several principles that can guide an assessment program.

34. I am familiar with the meaning of authentic assessment.

35. I know the advantages and limitations of authentic assessment.

36. I can record and evaluate student verbal and nonverbal behaviors.

37. I am familiar with the use of student journals, writing folders, peer conferencing, teacher-student conferences, and conference logs in assessing student learning.

38. I am familiar with examples of scoring guides for assessing students.

39. I am aware of the value of using portfolios for assessing students and their work.

	3 aware	2 somewhat aware	1 needs work	0 not aware

40. I feel comfortable using checklists for student assessment.

41. I can maintain records of student achievement.

42. I feel comfortable grading and marking student achievement.

43. I know some guidelines for determining grades for students.

44. I know several purposes for testing and know when and how to use traditional and standardized tests.

45. I can construct a brief test that has assessment items that measure against objectives.

46. I am aware of different types of assessment items.

47. I am familiar with the meaning of the term *content validity.*

48. I can prepare formative and summative assessment items for my ITU.

Completing Your ITU: Finalizing Activities, Lessons, and Units (Chapter 5)

49. I can select an activity to initiate an ITU.

50. I can help students assume roles as a way to introduce them to various disciplines.

51. I am familiar with a question map to initiate an ITU.

52. I can select a culminating activity for the closure of an ITU.

53. I am familiar with initiating activities, developmental ones, and culminating activities.

54. I am aware of suggested components for selecting learning activities.

55. I am familiar with a sample interdisciplinary lesson plan.

56. I am aware of suggested components for writing a lesson plan.

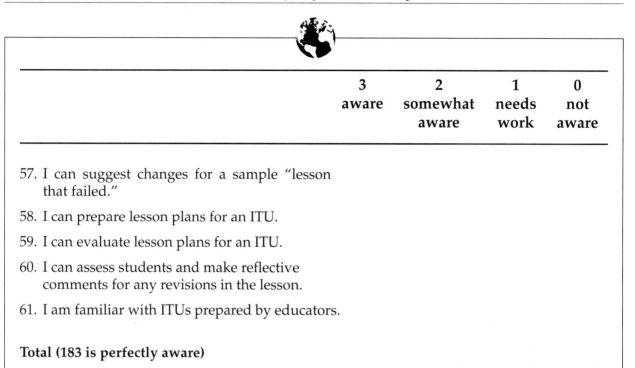

	3 aware	2 somewhat aware	1 needs work	0 not aware
57. I can suggest changes for a sample "lesson that failed."				
58. I can prepare lesson plans for an ITU.				
59. I can evaluate lesson plans for an ITU.				
60. I can assess students and make reflective comments for any revisions in the lesson.				
61. I am familiar with ITUs prepared by educators.				

Total (183 is perfectly aware)

CHAPTER NOTES

1. L. F. Hergert, "Snapshots of Service-Learning: Factors for Its Integration and Sustainability in School Districts," *Educational Horizons*, pp. 195–197. (Summer 2002).

2. See, for example, C. E. Knapp, *Just Beyond the Classroom: Community Adventures for Interdisciplinary Learning* (Charleston, WV: ERIC Clearinghouse on Rural Education and Small Schools, 1996).

3. J. Beane, *Integrated Curriculum in the Middle School* (Urbana, IL: ERIC Clearinghouse on Elementary and Early Childhood Education, 1992).

4. P. L. Roberts, *A Green Dinosaur Day: A Guide for Developing Thematic Units in Literature-Based Instruction, K–6.* (Needham Heights, MA: Allyn & Bacon, 1993).

5. Selected, adapted, and paraphrased from standards by American Association for the Advancement of Science, National Science Teachers Association and the National Research Council's National Committee on Science Education Standards and Assessment, 1995.

6. Courtesy of Kristie Darras of the Elk Grove Unified School District, Elk Grove, CA.

7. More adapted standards by American Association for the Advancement of Science, National Science Teachers Association, and the National Research Council's National Committee on Science Education Standards and Assessment, 1995.

8. This information about the science experiment is from R. J. Ryder and T. Hughes, *Internet for Education* (Upper Saddle River, NJ: Prentice Hall, 1997), p. 98.

9. Think-share pairs (T-S P) is a technique for developing students' metacognition (thinking about their own thinking, using higher level thinking skills, or comprehending expository material) where each student is asked to think about an idea (theme, topic, word, phrase, text selection, concept), share thoughts about it aloud with a partner (or discuss homework assignments, write partner responses to study questions, or summarize a science activity), and then report the pair's thoughts back to the whole group. This information is from R. D. Kellough and P. L. Roberts, *A Resource Guide for Elementary School Teaching: Planning for Competence* (5th Edition), (Upper Saddle River, NJ: Merrill/Prentice Hall, 2002), pp. 84, 118, 269, 270, 312. Other techniques are available for developing metacognition skills (thinking about one's own thinking or using higher level thinking skills or comprehending expository material). For know-what to know-what-learned (KWL) see D. M. Ogle, "K-W-L: A Teaching Model that Develops Active Reading of Expository Text," *Reading Teacher, 39*(6), 564–570 (February 1986); For know-what to know-learned-questions (KWLQ) see P. R. Schmidt, "KWLQ: Inquiry and Literacy Learning in Science," *Reading Teacher 52*(7), 789–792 (April 1999), and K. M. King and L. M. Parent Johnson, "Constructing Meaning via Reciprocal Teaching, *Reading Research and Instruction*," *38*(3), 169–186 (Spring 1999); For preview-question-read-state-test (PQRST), see E. B. Kelly, *Memory Enhancement for Educators* (Bloomington, IN: Fastback 365, Phi Delta Kappa Educational Foundation, 1994), p. 18; For survey-question-read-recite-review (SQ3R), see F. P. Robinson, *Effective Study* (rev. ed.), (New York: Harper & Brothers, 1961); For survey-question-read-recite-record-review (SQ4R), the original source is unknown; but for survey-read-question-recite-review (SRQ2R), see M. L. Walker, "Help for the 'Fourth Grade Slum'—3RQ2R Plus Instruction in Text Structure or Main Idea," *Reading Horizons, 36*(1), 38–58 (1995).

10. If you have input about major high-dollar school or district purchases, consider an electronic whiteboard to assist you as you demonstrate a new procedure, highlight something, annotate a phrase electronically, save selected lessons for absent students or save something for future reviews. To do this, use one whiteboard (SMART Technologies, Suite 600, 1177 11th Avenue SW, Calgary, Alberta, Canada, T2R 1K9) that runs on Windows or Mac, attaches to your computer through the USB port for its power, and has software that transfers what you outline, anecdote, write, or sketch on the whiteboard to your computer's monitor. Additionally, you can project images from your computer screen to the whiteboard where your finger serves as the mouse's pointer. This means that while teaching class you can touch a program icon on the whiteboard and the program opens, touch a file icon and access your files, or touch save and save your file/lesson. Further, you can run computer applications, locate something on the web/Internet, finish a spreadsheet, or use an electronic stylus to underline something in green electronic highlighter or to annotate or marginalize anything projected on the whiteboard. All this is shown on the large board at eye level or higher for the students in your class to see, and if you wish, can connect with each student's computer in a computer room/laboratory.

11. See D. M. Ogle, "K-W-L: A Teaching Model that Develops Active Reading of Expository Text," *Reading Teacher, 39*(6), 564–570 (February, 1986).

FOR FURTHER READING

Barkley, R. (1990). *Attention deficit hyperactivity disorder: A handbook for diagnosis and treatment.* New York: Guilford.

Batesky, J. (2000). Thoughts on the practice of teaching: A professor's experience. *Contemporary Education, 72*(1), 53–57.

Bondy, E. (2000). Warming up to classroom research in a professional development school. *Contemporary Education, 72*(1), 8–13.

Braun, L. W. (2001). *Introducing the Internet to young learners. Ready-to-go activities and lesson plans.* New York: Neal-Schuman.

Cross, C. T., and Rigden, D. W. (2002, April). Improving teacher quality. *American School Board Journal, 189*(4), 24–27.

Garcia, E. (1994). *Understanding and meeting the challenge of student cultural diversity.* Boston: Houghton Mifflin.

Goldhaber, D. D., & Brewer, D. J. (1999). Teacher licensing and student achievement. In M. Kanstoroom and C. E. Finn (eds.). *Better Teachers, Better Schools.* Washington, D.C.: Thomas B. Fordham Foundation.

International Society for Technology in Education. (2000). *National educational technology standards for students: Connecting curriculum and technology.* Eugene, OR: Author.

Kawka, B., & Burgess, B. (2001). *V-trip travel guide-classroom strategies for virtual field trips.* Eugene, OR: International Society for Technology in Education.

King, P. H. (1998, October). Teacher making dramatic difference. *The Sacramento Bee,* A3.

Loewen, J. W. (2001, Fall). The content crisis in K–12 social studies and history courses. *Educational Horizon,* 20–22.

National Association of State Directors of Teacher Education and Certification. (2000). *NASDTEC manual 2000: Manual on the preparation and certification of educational personnel* (5th ed.). (Dubuque, IA: Kendall/Hunt Publishing), Table E-2.

Palardy, T. (2001, Summer). The rank book: Forum on education & academics. *National Forum: Phi Kappa Phi Journal* 3–9.

Schmidt, P. R. (1999, April). KWLQ: Inquiry and literacy learning in science. *Reading Teacher, 52*(7), 789–92.

Sharp, R. M., Sharp, V. F., & Levine, M. G. (2001). *The best web sites for teachers* (4th ed.). Eugene, OR: International Society for Technology in Education.

Thompson, G. L. (2002). Elementary teachers, in *African American teens discuss their schooling experiences.* Needham Heights: Greenwood Publishing Group.

NOTES

APPENDIX

PLANNING MASTER 1.1

Self-Check Exercise: Overview of Teacher Interactions

Instructions. The purpose of this exercise is to gain insight into a teacher's perceptions of an ITU experience and identify the behaviors that other teacher candidates include in their interactions in the classroom. Share your examples with others. Do you agree with all of the examples given? Why or why not?

Teacher Interactions	Your Examples
Centering learning on students	_____
	_____
	_____
	_____
	_____
	_____
	_____
Guiding students	_____
	_____
	_____
	_____
	_____
	_____
	_____
Facilitating unit groups	_____
	_____
	_____
	_____
	_____
	_____
	_____

PLANNING MASTER 1.1
Continued

Teacher Interactions

Your Examples

Demonstrating reading aloud

_____

_____

_____

_____

_____

_____

Assessing and evaluating

_____

_____

_____

_____

_____

_____

Others selected by the group

_____

_____

_____

_____

_____

_____

Notes

PLANNING MASTER 1.2

Self-Check Exercise: Overview of Student Interactions

Instructions: The purpose of this exercise is to identify student behaviors that teachers expect to see in their interactions during an ITU experience. Share your examples with others.

Student Interactions	Your Examples
Choosing, discussing, researching	_____
	_____
	_____
	_____
	_____
	_____
	_____
Learning in groups	_____
	_____
	_____
	_____
	_____
	_____
Reading, responding, reporting	_____
	_____
	_____
	_____
	_____
	_____

PLANNING MASTER 1.2
Continued

Student Interactions   **Your Examples**

Selecting topics   _____

                                 _____

                                 _____

                                 _____

                                 _____

                                 _____

                                 _____

Scripting and bookmaking   _____

                                 _____

                                 _____

                                 _____

                                 _____

                                 _____

Others selected by the group   _____

                                 _____

                                 _____

                                 _____

                                 _____

                                 _____

Notes

PLANNING MASTER 1.3

Interactive Exercise: Student Input in an ITU

Instructions. The purpose of this exercise is to identify student input for an ITU. *Option 1:* For students, make an overhead transparency of this master, project it onto the board, and outline the graphic with chalk/marker. *Step 1:* Engage the students in contributing input/questions for a selected topic or theme for an ITU that supports the curriculum for the grade level. Model thinking aloud to make a decision to place each input under a discipline heading and then write the remarks under the heading. *Step 2:* After modeling, have students suggest where to place further input and choose an appropriate discipline heading. *Step 3:* After discussion about which activities/research process will help them find the answers to the questions, have them record the information on paper or in their study journals. This record can be used as a reference during follow-up discussions during the study. (See graphic, p. 294)

Other options:

Option 2: Your group members can take the roles of students in a selected grade level and identify some input statements/questions/activities/ research process that students might contribute to a selected theme/ topic for an ITU.

Option 3: For students, you can draw a large circle on the board and divide the circle into parts with diameter lines. *Step 1:* Label each part with a discipline heading. *Step 2:* Have students ask questions about what they want to know about the theme and write each question on the circle in the appropriate section. Have students tell what they can do to find the answers to their questions. *Step 3:* If appropriate, ask students to copy the circle and questions for their portfolios and refer to the circle in future discussions.

PLANNING MASTER 1.3
Continued

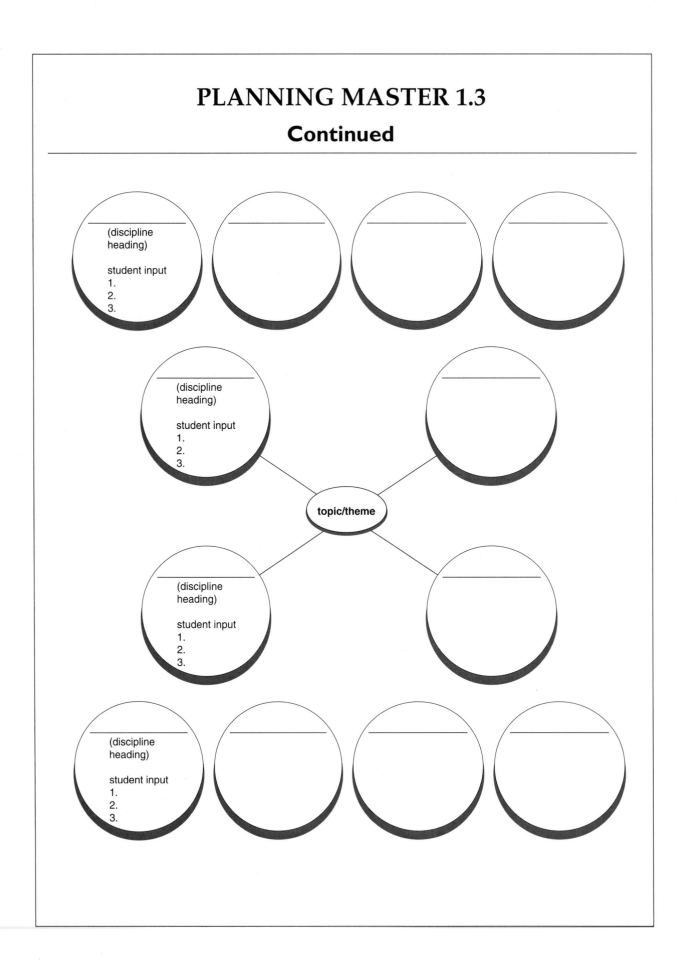

PLANNING MASTER 1.4
Interactive Exercise: Student Input with a Unit Theme-Beam

Instructions. The purpose of this reusable exercise is to provide interactive access for student input into an ITU. For students, make an overhead transparency of the unit theme-beam on this planning master, project it on to the board, and have student volunteers outline the light and beam graphic with chalk/marker. Different students may outline the graphic each time it is used. Additional student volunteers can also include the following:

Designer. The student or students responsible for seeing that the unit theme-beam is drawn on the board. Have the designer highlight the interactive area of the transparency and "turn on" the unit theme-beam by placing a sheet of yellow acetate (which can be trimmed to a smaller size) over the beam area on the transparency.

Facilitator. The student or students responsible for engaging others in asking questions related to the theme (i.e., being group leader, calling on students, asking for clarification, reminding peers to take turns).

Writer. The student or students who write each question within the lines of a beam on the graphic. After each question, writers can also write names of each student contributor and appropriate discipline heading suggested by the group.

Checker. The student or students responsible for seeing that every member contributes to input and every member records the group work in writing.

Reporter. The student or students responsible for discussing what the group learned during a short debriefing session (class meeting) after unit theme-beam work. To draw the group's attention to each question/topic and highlight what is being discussed, have the reporter place a thin strip of a different colored acetate under or over each question on the transparency on the unit theme-beam as each question is discussed.

PLANNING MASTER 1.4

Continued
Sample: Unit Theme-Beam

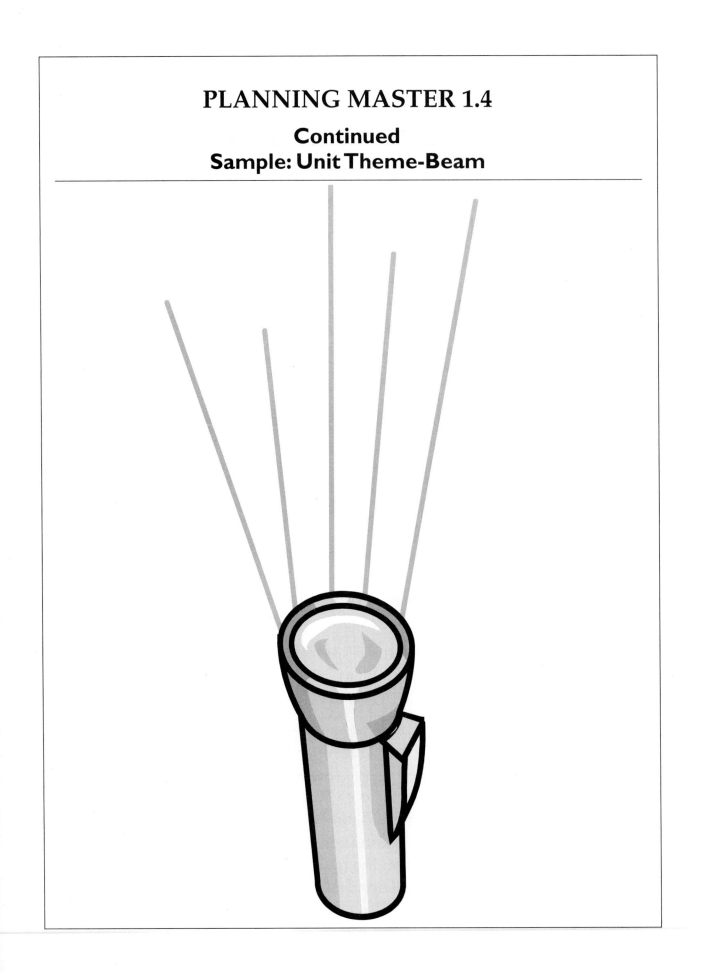

PLANNING MASTER 2.1

Self-Check Exercise: Is This Theme One that Has . . . ?

Instructions. The purpose of this exercise is to provide a guide for your selection of a theme for an ITU. Respond independently to the following features about theme selection and then share your responses with those of your classmates. Add features to the list if you wish. My selected theme is _____. Is this theme one that has:

	Yes	No

1. A connection to documents

Comments:

_____

_____

_____

_____

2. A connection to curriculum standards

Comments:

_____

_____

_____

_____

3. Background from teacher's experience

Comments:

_____

_____

_____

_____

PLANNING MASTER 2.1
Continued

Yes   No

4. Value, worth, and substance

Comments:

_____

_____

_____

_____

5. Proper length; not too short or too long

Comments:

_____

_____

_____

_____

6. Available materials and resources

Comments:

_____

_____

_____

_____

PLANNING MASTER 2.1
Continued

	Yes	No

7. Application to real world

Comments:

_____

_____

_____

_____

8. Active learning, interest, and motivation

Comments:

_____

_____

_____

_____

NOTES

PLANNING MASTER 2.2
Self-Check Exercise: Planning Real-Place Education

Instructions. The purpose of this exercise is to provide a guide for planning an event related to real-place, place-based (field trip) education with a student group. Independently read the following features about scheduling a site for real-place education and decide which features you would/would not discuss with the students in your classroom. Which features would you add? Delete? Share your list and reasons for adding or deleting features with others in your group.

	Discuss	**Do Not Discuss**

Student-teacher decisions

Pre-learning prior to trip (do research, create questions, read stories, write own stories, discussions, comparative activities)

What do we want to find out? (student-generated questions)

Conduct during traveling to site (safety rules, permissions, emergency information, information sheets to parents, introducing parent volunteers, providing name tags, maps of site)

Alternate plan for bad weather

PLANNING MASTER 2.2

Continued

	Discuss	Do Not Discuss
Features of place-based education		
Where we'll go		
Name of contact person		
Travel plans		
Time to arrive/depart		
What will be needed (lunch, money, water)		
Permission needed		
Adults going		
Provision for first aid		
Restroom location		
Teacher's pre-trip visit		

Features I want to add:

PLANNING MASTER 3.1

Self-Check Exercise: Classifying Cognitive Objectives

Instructions. The purpose of this exercise is to assess your ability to classify cognitive objectives. For each of the following, identify by the appropriate letter the highest level of operation involved: K (knowledge), C (comprehension), AP (application), AN (analysis), S (synthesis), and E (evaluation). Check your answers and then discuss the results with your peers. Your understanding of the concept involved is more important than whether your score is 100%.

_____ 1. Given a picture of examples of styles in classical Greek architecture, the student will recognize the style of a column as being Ionic, Doric, or Corinthian.

_____ 2. Given an information retrieval chart, the student will recognize the roles of Greek citizens.

_____ 3. After reading detailed instructions, the student will participate and make a hand puppet.

_____ 4. The student will create a verse using a four-line stanza.

_____ 5. The student will explain his or her critical appraisal of an essay on a selected topic or theme.

_____ 6. Given a selection of colors, the student will correctly identify by name the ones shown.

_____ 7. The student will be able to recognize faulty logic in campaign advertising.

_____ 8. Given the political and economic facts, the student will identify a reasonable hypothesis concerning the causes of a recent altercation, riot, gang battle, or belligerence between groups.

_____ 9. The student will devise a method to prove that a ray bisects an angle.

_____ 10. Given an Internet website, the student will locate information related to the theme or topic of an ITU.

Answer key

1. C	6. K
2. K	7. E
3. AP	8. AN
4. S	9. S
5. E	10. K

PLANNING MASTER 3.2

Self-Check Exercise: Classifying Psychomotor Objectives

Instructions. The purpose of this exercise is to assess your ability to classify psychomotor objectives. For each of the following, identify by the appropriate letter the level ranging from simple gross locomotor control to the most creative and complex level that requires fine locomotor control and originality: MO (moving), MA (manipulating), CO (communicating), and CR (creating). Check your answers and then discuss the results with your peers.

_____ 1. Given a jump rope, the student will successfully jump the rope five times without missing.

_____ 2. Given appropriate materials, the student will plan and successfully grow flower seeds.

_____ 3. Listening to a teacher-read story, the student will demonstrate active listening skills, including asking questions and giving responses.

_____ 4. The student will write a brief musical jingle.

_____ 5. Given a microscope (magnifying glass), the student will correctly grasp and carry the scope (glass) to his or her desk.

_____ 6. Given a musical instrument of choice, the student will play the C scale.

_____ 7. The student will be able to describe his or her feelings about the extinction of animals in the rain forest areas.

_____ 8. Given appropriate art materials, the student will replicate an environment for a favorite animal that is endangered or faces extinction.

_____ 9. The student will correctly grasp a baseball bat when batting.

_____ 10. Given an item to observe, the student will accurately draw/sketch what is observed through the microscope/magnifying glass.

Answer key

1. MO	6. MA
2. MA	7. CO
3. CO	8. CR
4. CR	9. MO
5. MO	10. CO

NOTES

PLANNING MASTER 3.3
Self-Check Exercise: Classifying Affective Objectives

Instructions. The purpose of this exercise is to assess your ability to classify affective objectives. For each of the following, identify by the appropriate letter the major level involved from least internalized to most internalized: REC (receiving), RES (responding), VAL (valuing), ORG (organizing), and INT (internalizing). Check your answers and then discuss the results with your peers. Your understanding of the concept involved, and the idea that some overlap occurs from one level to another, is more important than whether your score is 100%

_____ 1. Given directions, the student will recall the ones for enrichment activities in the classroom.

_____ 2. Given a selection of books related to a topic or theme, the student will read at least one for enrichment.

_____ 3. The student will support actions against race, sex, or gender discrimination.

_____ 4. The student will form judgments about proper behavior/actions in the classroom.

_____ 5. Regarding assignments, the student will practice independently.

_____ 6. Given a group discussion, the student will listen and describe the ideas of others.

_____ 7. The student will protest against discrimination.

_____ 8. The student will adhere to a personal work ethic.

_____ 9. The student will act according to a defined code of behavior.

_____ 10. Given an Internet website, the student will read information for enrichment.

Answer key

1. REC	6. REC
2. RES	7. VAL
3. VAL	8. ORG
4. ORG	9. INT
5. INT	10. RES

NOTES

PLANNING MASTER 4.1

Self-Check Exercise: Learning Assessment Checklist

Instructions. The purpose of this exercise is to provide a guide for your development of a learning assessment checklist for your students. Independently read the following items and decide if you would include each in a checklist that you would develop for your students who are studying in an ITU in your class. Which ones did you decide to include and why? What deletions, if any, did you make? Share your responses with others in your group.

STUDENT _____ **DATE** _____

TEACHER _____ **CLASS** _____

	Yes	No
1. Can identify theme, topic, main idea of ITU	_____	_____
2. Can identify contributions of others to theme	_____	_____
3. Can identify problems related to ITU study	_____	_____
4. Has developed skills in:	_____	_____

_____ Applying knowledge _____ Locating information

_____ Assuming responsibility _____ Ordering

_____ Classifying _____ Reporting to others

_____ Decision making _____ Self-assessing

_____ Discussing _____ Sharing

_____ Gathering resources _____ Studying

_____ Inquiry _____ Thinking

_____ Justifying choices _____ Using resources

PLANNING MASTER 4.1

Continued

_____ Listening to others   _____ Reading maps/globes

_____ Organizing   _____ Reading text

_____ Others   _____ Reasoning

_____ Problem identification   _____ Working singly

_____ Problem solving   _____ Working with others

Additional features added:

Additional teacher and student comments:

GLOSSARY

accomplished practices another term for state-published standards.

accountability reference to the concept that an individual is responsible for his/her behaviors and should be able to demonstrate publicly the worth of the activities carried out.

achievement accomplishments that often involve praise and exertions.

activities actions or physical engagements that start a unit in motion are called *initiating* activities; those that make up the day-to-day momentum of the unit are the ongoing *developmental* activities, and those that bring the unit to a natural close are referred to as *culminating* activities.

advance organizer preinstructional cues that encourage a mental set; used to enhance retention of materials to be studied.

affective domain the area of learning related to the learner's attitudes, feelings, interests, personal adjustment, and values; can include the way a learner receives and responds to or values stimulus, demonstrates a system of consistent beliefs and behavior, or organizes a system of values.

aims general educational objectives.

aligned curriculum refers to the matching of standards, objectives, instruction, and assessment to stated goals.

alternative assessment assessment of learning in ways that are different from traditional paper-and-pencil objective testing, such as a portfolio, project, or self-assessment. *See also* authentic assessment.

AmeriCorps NCCC an intensive 10-month public service program for people ages 18 to 24 who are often called the "A" people by students when they see the "A" insignia shoulder patch on the clothing of volunteers who visit their schools and engage in one-on-one classroom assistance. These volunteer opportunities were created by the U.S. Congress in 1993 along with the Corporation for National and Community Service that administers a network of public service programs. Some programs include AmeriCorps VISTA (Volunteers in Service to America), a program for people 18 and older who work with community groups throughout the United States. Learn and Serve America encourages students of all ages to increase their learning potential while providing community service in neighborhoods where they live. The National Senior Service Corps uses the experiences and skills of America's seniors as volunteers.

analytical learner a student who perceives information abstractly and processes it reflectively. The analytic learner prefers sequential thinking, needs details, and values what experts have to offer. Analytic learners do well in traditional classrooms.

anticipated measurable performance refers to the student performance that indicates that the objective has been achieved.

anticipatory set *see* advance organizer.

assessment the process of finding out what students have learned as a result of instruction. Some educators consider it a relatively neutral process that can include collecting objective data from measurement sources and information from anecdotal records, using teacher observations, and making value judgments. *See also* evaluation.

assignment(s) a component in a lesson plan that identifies what students are instructed to do as a follow-up to the lesson; can be homework or in-class work that gives students an opportunity to practice and enhance what is being learned.

auditory modality   learning through instruction from others (mainly through talk).

authentic assessment   the use of evaluation procedures (usually portfolios and projects) that are highly compatible with the instructional objectives; this condition is where the assessment procedure connects with the instructional objectives. Authentic assessment is also referred to as *accurate, active, aligned, alternative, direct,* or *performance assessment.*

behavioral objective   a statement of expectation describing what the learner should be able to do upon completion of the instruction. *See also* curriculum standards.

behaviorism   a learning theory that focuses on a student's changes in behavior as an indication of learning; equates learning with changes in observable behavior.

block scheduling   a procedure that gives a teacher and students large blocks of time (e.g., 2 hours) in the school program. It facilitates individualized instruction and grouping of students to meet needs and abilities. Individual teachers or teacher teams can organize and arrange groupings of students for varied periods of time, thereby more effectively individualizing the instruction for students with various needs and abilities.

brainstorming   a strategy of instruction used to create a flow of ideas that facilitates the students' responses without peer judgment/criticism.

career portfolio   a collection of samples of students' work that will document their abilities to move forward to another grade level, to a work environment from a school environment, or to postsecondary education. Sometimes called a showcase portfolio when it contains a student's best work in the ITU or subject. *See also* portfolio.

CD-ROM   compact disc with read-only memory; contains encoded information on a compact disc.

character education   relates to instruction regarding development of values such as honesty, kindness, respect, and responsibility (i.e., transmitting moral values that is seen by some as a responsibility of today's educators).

classroom management   a teacher's system of establishing a climate for learning including techniques for preventing and handling student misbehavior.

closure   an educational practice for bringing a lesson to an end (a close that gives students a sense of completeness, of accomplishment and comprehension); a closure can help students to synthesize the information learned from the lesson. *See also* lesson conclusion.

cloze type procedure   an instructional strategy where the student is asked to supply every nth word that has been left out of a passage of reading—often text from the student's reading material. This strategy asks the student to put meanings together during the process of reading and can be varied according to a teacher's preference, (i.e., deleting only nouns, deleting only one word in every sentence, or deleting every tenth or twentieth word).

coaching   a procedure that details ways that the teacher intends for students to interact in the classroom; also referred to as the follow-up. It includes individual practice, dyad practice, small group work, and conferences or mini-lessons during which students receive guidance and coached practice from the teacher and/or their peers. *See also* mentoring.

cognition   the process of thinking.

cognitive domain   the area of learning related to the student's intellectual skills; this can include assimilation of knowledge, retention, comprehension, application, analysis, synthesis, and evaluation.

cognitive-experimentalism   the theory postulating that learning is interaction with the environment through discovery and inquiry; the learner constructs new perceptions that lead to performance changes.

cognitivism   a theory that holds that learning entails the construction or reshaping of mental schemata. Also known as *constructivism.*

common planning time   a regularly scheduled time during the school day when teachers who teach the same students meet for joint planning, parent conferences, materials preparation, and student evaluation.

common sense learner   a student who perceives information abstractly and processes it actively, is pragmatic, and enjoys hands-on learning; sometimes finds school frustrating unless the student can see immediate use to what is being learned; can be a learner who is at risk of not completing school or dropping out.

compact disc (CD)   a disc on which a laser has enscribed information digitally.

competency-based education   refers to students performing the competencies called for by stated objectives. *See also* performance-based, results-driven, and terminal objectives, and outcome-based education.

conceptual knowledge   type of learning that refers to meaningful, higher levels of thinking.

constructivism   a theory postulating that mental processes mediate learning; includes cooperative learning type of instructional strategies that involve small groups of learners working together and assisting one another in the educational tasks; emphasizes support for one another rather than competition. *See also* cognitivism.

cooperative learning   a genre of instructional strategies that use small groups of learners working together and helping each other on learning tasks; stresses support for one another rather than competition.

cooperative teacher-student log   entries written daily by the students before leaving their class, period, or school about what was learned that day. In some classes, the teacher responds to the entries.

covert behavior   the behavior of the learner that is not observable outwardly.

criterion   a standard (model, example) used to judge performance.

criterion-referenced assessment   assessment in which standards are established and behaviors are judged against preset guidelines, rather than against the behaviors of others; refers to determining the progress of a student toward reaching the guidelines.

criterion-referenced grading   refers to determining student grades on the basis of preset standards.

criterion-referenced objective   identifies standards and/or guidelines for learning behaviors through the components of audience, behavior, conditions, and performance level. When students perform the competencies called for by stated objectives, their education is considered successful. Also known as competency-based, performance-based, results-driven, or outcome-based education.

criterion-referenced testing   refers to student tests that are designed to check a student's knowledge of/or skills in a specific area of subject matter represented on the test.

critical thinking   refers to a student's ability to recognize and identify problems and discrepancies, to propose and test resolutions, and to arrive at tentative conclusions based on the collected data.

cross-age tutoring   a student from another grade gives special educational help or lessons to a particular student or students.

curriculum   originally derived from a Latin term referring to a race course for the chariots, the term still has no widely accepted definition. As used in this text, curriculum is that which is planned and encouraged for teaching and learning. This includes both school and nonschool environments; formal (overt) and informal (covert, hidden) curriculums; and broad as well as narrow notions of content—its development, acquisition, and consequences.

curriculum standards   statements of the essential knowledge, skills, and attitudes to be learned.

decision making   a conclusion made after consideration that includes a planning or preactive phase; a teaching or interactive phase, an analyzing or reflective phase, and an application or projective phase.

diagnostic assessment   *see* preassessment.

didactic teaching   *see* direct instruction.

direct instruction   the teacher controls student attention and behaviors usually of the entire class, as opposed to permitting students to have greater control over their own learning and behaviors.

discovery learning   involves learning in which the students identify a problem, develop hypotheses, test the hypotheses, and arrive at a conclusion. *See also* critical thinking.

divergent thinking   thinking that expands beyond original thought.

diversity   a state of differences and similarities, or likenesses and unlikenesses; can mean a variety or can mean a combining form such as *many* as is meant in prefix *multi* in *multicultural*.

DVD (digital versatile disc)   like a CD-ROM but with a much greater storage capacity.

dynamic learner   a student who perceives information concretely and processes it actively. This learner prefers hands-on learning and is excited by anything new. Dynamic learners are risk takers and are frustrated by learning if they see it as being tedious and sequential. In a traditional classroom the dynamic learner could likely be an at-risk student.

effective school   a school where students master basic skills, seek academic excellence in all subjects, demonstrate achievement, and display good behavior and attendance. Known also as an *exemplary school.*

effective teaching   engaging students in high rates of academic learning through hands-on and minds-on meaningful instruction, cooperative and collaborative interactions, clear communication, monitoring progress, and a thematic curriculum in which students participate; behaviors of effective teachers include communicating warmth and content enthusiastically, holding students accountable, giving students time to learn, having realistic expectations for students, including routines as part of class management, and selecting meaningful educational tasks for students.

empowerment   involves students' learning to think better of themselves and their own individual capabilities.

evaluation   like assessment, but includes making sense out of the assessment results; often a process that considers the results of a student's assessment based on standards, criteria, or a scoring guide (rubric). Evaluation is more subjective than is assessment.

exemplary school   *see* effective school.

expository learning   the traditional classroom instructional approach that proceeds as follows: presentation of information to the learners, reference to particular examples, and application of the information to the learner's experiences.

facilitating behavior   teacher behavior that makes it possible for students to learn.

facilitating teaching   *see* indirect teaching.

feedback   information sent from the receiver to the originator that provides disclosure about the reception of the intended message.

formal curriculum   the plans for teaching and learning in school and nonschool environments in an overt, open format that supports the development and acquisition of selected content.

formative assessment   evaluation of learning in progress.

formative evaluation   refers to evaluating a student's ongoing learning during a study.

goal, course   a broad generalized statement about the expected outcomes of a course/unit/ITU.

goal, educational   a desired instructional outcome that can be broad in scope.

goal, teacher   a desired instructional outcome that a teacher hopes to accomplish.

goals   the objectives of schools, curricula, and courses.

graphic map   a visual representation of concepts and their relationships. For example, questions about what students want to know related to a selected theme for an interdisciplinary thematic unit are written in groups under headings of disciplines. *See also* visual map.

halo effect   a positive or negative effect related to grading students' papers that reflects knowledge of whose paper the teacher/reader is reading. Relates to grading papers where the

students have put their names (rather than numbers) on the front (instead of the back) of their papers.

hands-on learning   active student learning, and learning by doing.

hidden curriculum   unwritten rules of behavior, attitudes, and values that students often have to accept to succeed.

high-stakes assessment   an assessment whose results carry serious consequences, for example a student's grade promotion rests on the student's performance on one test; or the student's graduation from high school rests on the student's performance on a single test.

holistic learning   learning that incorporates emotions with thinking.

homogeneous grouping   a grouping pattern that usually separates students into groups based on their intelligence, school achievement, or physical characteristics.

imaginative learner   a student who perceives information concretely and processes it reflectively, and who learns well by listening and sharing with others and integrating others' ideas into his or her own experiences.

inclusion   the commitment to the education of each special-needs learner, to the maximum extent appropriate, in the school and classroom he or she would otherwise attend.

independent inquiry   an instructional strategy that permits students to self-select topics for study, set goals, and work alone to attain them.

indirect teaching   student-centered teaching using discovery and inquiry instructional strategies.

individualized instruction   *see* individualized learning.

individualized learning   the self-paced process whereby individual students assume responsibility for learning through study, practice, feedback, and reinforcement with appropriately designed instructional packages or modules.

inductive learning   learning that proceeds from the specific to the general. *See also* discovery learning.

informal curriculum   can be referred to as covert/hidden curriculum that is not outwardly observable.

inquiry   involves learning during which the student designs the processes to resolve the problem. *See also* discovery.

inquiry learning   like discovery learning, except here the learner designs the processes to be used in resolving the problem; requires higher levels of cognition.

instruction   planned arrangement of experiences to help a learner develop understanding and to achieve a desirable change in behavior.

instructional module   any freestanding instructional unit that includes these components: rationale, objectives, pretest, learning activities, comprehension checks with instructive feedback, and posttest.

instructional objectives   statements of learning expectations that identify what the learner should be able to do after instruction. Each can contain four components that reflect the learner, the overt behavior, the conditions, and the level of performance. *See also* performance-based objectives and terminal objectives.

integrated (interdisciplinary) curriculum   an organization of the curriculum that combines discipline/subject matter that historically has been taught separately. Similar terms include integrated studies, thematic instruction, holistic education, multidisciplinary teaching, interdisciplinary curriculum, and interdisciplinary thematic instruction.

integrated curriculum, a spectrum of design   an organization of the teacher's efforts from the least integrated instruction to the most integrated level that is affected by the factors of student input, decision making, and blending of disciplines.

interdisciplinary teaching team   a collaboration of two or more teachers who represent different disciplines or subject areas and who teach the same students in a way that combines subject matter formerly taught separately.

interdisciplinary thematic unit (ITU)   a study with a basic theme (e.g., migrations) that crosses boundaries of two or more disciplines.

internalization   the extent to which an attitude or value becomes a part of the learner. That is, without having to think about it, the learner's behavior reflects the attitude or value.

intervention   a teacher's interruption to redirect a student's behavior, either by direct intervention (e.g., by a verbal command) or by indirect intervention (e.g., by eye contact or physical proximity).

introduction   a feature in a lesson plan that is used to prepare students mentally for the lesson; can be initial instructions or actions. Also brings the beginning of the lesson into play, into use, or into practice, or brings the lesson to the students' notice; can also be referred to as the *set* or *initiating activity* or the *stimulus*. The introduction can include an incentive of some kind or something that rouses the student's mind/spirit or his or her interest in a lesson activity.

intuition   instinctive knowledge; knowing without conscious reasoning.

journal   usually a notebook that contains a student's writing and entries about what is being learned in the ITU and personal writing about the student's interests and experiences. *See also* life-writing journal, thinkbook, or learning log.

junior high school   includes students in grades 7 through 9 or 7 and 8 who keep a schedule and study a curriculum similar to a high school schedule and curriculum.

kinesthetic modality   learning by doing and being physically involved.

K-W-L   a teaching method for determining prior knowledge, developing higher level thinking skills, and comprehending expository material. Students recall what they already *know* (K), determine what they *want* to learn (W), and later assess what they *learned* (L).

learning   experiences that lead to the development of understandings and changes in behavior. For different interpretations of learning, see *behaviorism* and *cognitivism*.

learning center   an instructional strategy that uses activities and materials located in a special area in the classroom; designed for students who work independently at his or her own pace to learn one area of content. *See also* learning station.

learning log   a student's journal or notebook that contains a student's writing. *See also* journal.

learning modality   the way a student receives information. Four modalities are recognized: visual, auditory, tactile (touch), and kinesthetic (movement). The modalities refer to the sensory portal, or input channel, by which a student prefers to receive sensory reception (modality preference), or the actual way a student learns best (modality adeptness).

learning resource center   the central location in the school where instructional materials and media are stored, organized, and accessed by students and staff.

learning station   like a learning center except that, whereas each center is distinct and unrelated to others, learning stations are sequenced or in some way linked to one another.

learning style   the manner in which a student learns best in a given situation.

learning targets   competencies that students are expected to achieve and that are derived from the district and state curriculum standards. Performance objectives, or parts or subdivisions of learning targets sometimes referred to as goal indicators. Instruction is designed to teach toward those objectives.

lesson conclusion   a lesson plan feature that brings the lesson to a close (an end). It provides students with a sense of completeness and—with effective teaching—accomplishment and comprehension because it helps students to synthesize the information learned from the lesson. *See also* closure.

lesson development   a lesson plan section that details the activities that occur between the beginning and the end of the lesson and the transitions that connect the activities.

lesson extender   a lesson plan feature that identifies a plan for what to do if the students finish the lesson and time remains. This means that along with the work that relates to the objective(s), a teacher can plan some enrichment for a student who has achieved the objective or plan some supportive (remedial) work for a student who is struggling and needs a related activity in a rearranged manner so he or she can be successful.

life-writing journal   a student's notebook that includes personal writing about the student's interests and experiences. *See also* journal.

longitudinal portfolio   a collection often kept by a teacher for each student with anecdotal notes and records and parent correspondence; sometimes called the record-keeping portfolio.

looping   an arrangement in which the cohort of students and teachers remain together as a group for two or more years at a particular school; also referred to as *multiyear grouping, multiyear instruction, multiyear placement,* and *teacher-student progression.*

magnet school   a school that specializes in a particular academic area, such as the arts, international relations, science, or mathematics and technology.

mastery learning   the concept that a student should master the content of one lesson before moving on to the content of the next; has the expectation of students to achieve one set of competencies before moving on to the next set.

meaningful learning   refers to a student who achieves one set of competencies and then moves on to the next set after assessment.

measurement   a descriptive and objective process that includes the collection of quantifiable data about specific behaviors (including tests and statistical procedures) and interpreting data.

mentoring   one-on-one coaching, tutoring, or guidance to facilitate learning; a procedure that can include follow-up and individual practice, dyad practice, small group work, and conferences or mini-lessons during which students receive guidance and coached practice from the teacher and/or their peers. *See also* coaching.

metacognition   a student's understanding of his or her own thinking; includes ability to plan, monitor, and evaluate one's own thinking.

middle grades   grades 5 through 8.

middle level education   any school unit between elementary and high school; some organization plans include a campus and buildings for students in grades 5 through 8, other plans serve grades 6 through 8 or grades 7 and 8.

minds-on learning   refers to learning in which the student is thinking about what is being learned (i.e., intellectually active).

modality preference   primary modality preference or strength can be determined by observing a student. The preference/strength can also be mixed and can change as the result of experience and intellectual maturity. A student can integrate modalities (i.e., engage more than one sensory input channel and use several modalities at once or stagger their use), which has been found to contribute to better achievement in student learning.

modeling   the teacher's direct and indirect demonstration, by actions and by words, of the behaviors expected of students.

multicultural education   a focused attempt to help students understand facts, generalizations, attitudes, and behaviors derived from their own ethnic roots as well as others; a part of the curriculum designed to help students unlearn racism and biases, and recognize and appreciate contributions made by all members of society.

multilevel teaching   the use of several learning levels in the same group or classroom as learners work on different tasks leading to the same objective or to different objectives. Also referred to as *multitasking.*

multimedia   the combined use of sound, video, and graphics for instruction.

multiple intelligences   refers to a theory of different intelligences as opposed to just one general intelligence; other intelligences that have been described are bodily/kinesthetic, interpersonal/intrapersonal, logical/mathematical, musical, naturalist, verbal/linguistic, and visual/spatial.

multipurpose board   a writing board with a smooth plastic surface used with special marking pens rather than chalk. Sometimes called a visual aid panel, the board may have a steel backing and then can be used as a magnetic board as well as a screen for projecting visuals.

multitasking a strategy for using several learning levels in the same class where students attend to different tasks that lead to the same objective or to different objectives. Also referred to as *multilevel instruction.*

multitext reading refers to the use of several reading sources reflecting various reading levels for different students; students can read different books leading to the same objective or can work on different objectives.

non-standardized grading an approach designed by a teacher or a teaching team for their own unique group of students. It can include selecting a percentage standard for the criteria for letter grades, a point system, preset standards, and the communication of educational progress to the learner's parents/guardians.

non-standardized tests tests that are designed by a teacher or by a teaching team for their own unique group of students.

norm-referenced individual performance is judged relative to overall performance of the group (e.g., grading on a curve), as opposed to being criterion-referenced.

objectives the learning expectations of units and lessons are called *instructional objectives.* Also called *performance* and *terminal* objectives.

orientation set *see* advance organizer.

outcome-based education refers to statements of learning expectations that identify what the learner should be able to do after instruction. When the students perform the competencies called for by stated objectives, their education is considered successful. *See also* competency-based education and performance-based, results-driven, and terminal objectives.

overlapping a behavior in which a teacher is able to attend to more than one matter at once.

overt behavior outwardly observable behavior of a student.

peer tutoring an instructional strategy during which one peer, as a tutor, helps another peer to learn.

performance assessment a specific type of student response that is assessed and that lends itself to assessment that is authentic.

performance-based instruction instruction designed around the instruction and assessment of student achievement against specified and predetermined objectives.

performance-based objectives statements of learning expectations that identify what the

learner should be able to do after instruction. The written objectives can include four components that reflect the learner, his or her behavior, the conditions, and the level of performance. *See also* competency-based, and outcome-based education, and performance-based, or terminal objectives.

portfolio a collection of samples of student work related to an ITU, progression to another grade level, the requirements of a study, or the teacher's objectives. *See also* career portfolio.

portfolio assessment an alternative approach to evaluation that assembles representative samples of a student's work over time as a basis for assessment. Samples of student work can be related to an ITU, a chosen profession, preparing for another grade level, the requirements of a study, or the teacher's objectives. *See also* selected work portfolio, longitudinal portfolio, or career portfolio.

preassessment refers to a diagnostic judgment of what students know or think they know prior to the instruction.

problem-centered inquiry an arrangement of learning experiences related to a problem, in part or as a whole, to be solved; can relate to an interdisciplinary thematic unit.

procedural knowledge type of learning that refers to the accumulation of pieces of information.

procedures a statement, perhaps listed in steps, that tells the learner how to accomplish a task.

project-centered learning a teaching strategy that can provide for multilevel instruction through projects that engage the learners. Students can do different projects simultaneously to accomplish similar or different objectives.

psychomotor domain the area of learning where the student develops and becomes proficient in locomotor behaviors/skills of moving, manipulating, communicating, and creating.

reciprocal teaching a form of collaborative teaching where the teacher and the students share the teaching responsibility and all are involved in asking questions, clarifying, predicting, and summarizing.

reflection the conscious process of mentally replaying an experience.

reflective abstraction *see* metacognition.

reliability in measurement, the consistency with which an item or instrument is measured over time.

results-driven objectives identifies standards and/or guidelines for learning behaviors through the components of audience, behavior, conditions, and performance level. When students perform the competencies called for by stated objectives, their education is considered successful. *See also* competency-based and outcome-based and performance-based education.

retrieval chart   a chart where information is placed/recorded/stored and can be reviewed by the student as needed.

romanticism-maturationism   theory postulating that learning entails adding new ideas to a subconscious store of old ones in the learner's mind.

rubric   a scoring guide or outline of the criteria used to guide the assessment of a student's work. *See also* scoring guide.

schemata   (singular, schema) the mental constructs through which students organize their perceptions of knowledge and situations; perceptions can be organized as concepts and connected relationships.

school restructuring   a collection of activities that change basic assumptions, practices, and relationships in the organization, thus leading to improved learning.

school-within-a-school   sometimes referred to as a cluster, family, house, pod, or village; it is a teaching arrangement where one team of teachers is assigned to work with the same group of about 125 students for a common block of time, for the entire school day or, in some instances, for all the years those students are at that school.

scoring guide   a prescribed/established form or method or educational outline of the criteria used to assess performance of students; also called a *rubric*.

secondary school   usually a campus and buildings to serve students for any arrangement of grades 7 through 12.

selected work portfolio   a collection of samples of student work as required or recommended by the teacher, sometimes called the working portfolio that holds all of a student's work related to an ITU or a subject. *See also* portfolio.

self-contained classroom   commonly used in the primary grades; it is a grouping pattern where one teacher teaches all or most all subjects to one group of children.

self-paced learning   *see* individualized learning.

sequencing   arranging ideas in logical order.

service learning   a teaching and learning approach that teaches civic responsibility and enriches learning when it integrates academics with community service.

simulation   an abstraction or simplification of a real-life situation.

spectrum of design of integrated curriculum   depiction of a range of teaching experiences that reflect levels from least integrated instruction to most integrated instruction.

standardized tests   tests that have been constructed and published by commercial testing companies and are used by districts/states to determine student achievement mainly in reading, science, social science, and math.

standards   that which is established as a model or example of quality or what something should be; a criterion. *See also* curriculum standards.

standards-based education   lessons when the objectives are aligned with specific curriculum standards.

summative assessment   the assessment of learning of students after instruction is completed.

tactile modality   learning by touching objects.

teacher portfolio   a collection of assignments given to the class, data on performances of students, and reflective notes about each assignment.

teaching   *see* instruction.

teaching style   the way teachers deliver instruction; their distinctive mannerisms complemented by their choices of teaching behaviors and strategies.

teaching team   refers to two or more teachers who work together to provide instruction to the same group of learners. They can teach together simultaneously or alternate instruction.

team teaching   two or more teachers working together to provide instruction to a group of students.

terminal objectives   educational statements of aims, actions, and points to be reached that specify what the student should be able to do after instruction; terminal objectives in writing can include information about the learner, the anticipated overt behavior, the conditions, and the level of performance. *See also* performance objectives.

thematic unit   refers to the instruction of a study built on a central theme or concept.

theme   refers to the message, the point, or the main idea represented by a word, phrase, or sentence that underlies a study through an interdisciplinary unit. The theme also can incorporate a concept such as *changes*, *migrations*, or *civilizations*.

thinkbook   a student's notebook that includes personal reactions to material related to the study. *See also* journal.

think-share pairs   a technique for developing students' metacognition in which each student is asked to think about an idea (theme, topic, word, phrase, text selection, concept), share thoughts about it aloud with a partner (take notes if needed), and then report the pair's thoughts back to the whole group.

think time   *see* wait time.

topic   subject matter relating to a theme under study.

traditional teaching   teacher-centered direct instruction, typically using discussion, lectures, textbooks, and worksheets.

transition   in a lesson, the planned procedures that move student thinking from one idea to the next or that moves their actions from one activity to the next.

validity   in measurement, the degree to which a measuring instrument or item actually measures what it is intended to measure.

visual map   a graphic representation of concepts and their relationships. For example, words related to a key word are written on the board (transparency, chart, on paper) in groups (or categories) around the key word and the groups are labeled (generalizing).

visual modality   refers to learning mainly by seeing/viewing/use of vision.

wait time   in the use of questioning, the period of silence between the time a question is asked and the inquirer (teacher) does something, such as repeats the question, rephrases the question, or asks another question.

whole language learning   a point of view that focuses on meaning through language production, risk-taking in learning, independence in producing language, and the use of a variety of print materials in reading, writing, and other communicative situations.

withitness   the teacher's timely ability to intervene and redirect a student's inappropriate behavior.

year-round school   a school that operates as is traditional, that is with the state's required number of school days, but with the days arranged over 12 months rather than the more traditional 10. Most common is a 9-weeks-on/3-weeks-off arrangement. Sometimes the term *year-round* is used to refer to a school's/district's plan to extend the school year for 1 or 2 weeks in the spring or fall or for both semesters. This plan still provides a month or more summer break.

CHILDREN'S BOOK INDEX

NAME INDEX

SUBJECT INDEX